Epistrophies

Epistrophies

Jazz and the Literary Imagination

Brent Hayes Edwards

Harvard University Press
Cambridge, Massachusetts
London, England
2017

Printed in the United States of America

First printing

Library of Congress Cataloging-in-Publication Data
Names: Edwards, Brent Hayes, author.
Title: Epistrophies : jazz and the literary imagination / Brent Hayes Edwards.
Description: Cambridge, Massachusetts : Harvard University Press, 2017. | Includes bibliographical references and index.
Identifiers: LCCN 2016048597 | ISBN 9780674055438 (hardcover : alk. paper)
Subjects: LCSH: Music and literature—United States—History. | American literature—African American authors—History and criticism. | Jazz in literature. | Jazz—History and criticism. | African American aesthetics.
Classification: LCC PN56.M87 E36 2017 | DDC 810.9/896073—dc23
LC record available at https://lccn.loc.gov/2016048597

for
Robert O'Meally, Robert Stepto, and Cheryl Wall

i migliori fabbri

contents

Epistrophies

introduction
"I Thought I Heard": The Origins of Jazz and the Ends of Jazz Writing

When Amiri Baraka, Larry Neal, and A. B. Spellman founded a journal of music criticism in 1968, they named it *The Cricket: Black Music in Evolution.* Calling for nothing less than a "cultural revolution" spearheaded by black artists, the editorial in the first issue announced that the journal "represents an attempt to provide Black Music with a powerful historical and critical tool." History and criticism would be at the service of the music because, as the editorial proclaimed in its opening lines, "the true voices of Black Liberation have been the Black Musicians. They were the first to free themselves from the concepts and sensibilities of the oppressor."[1] The editors went on to explain, "We call this monthly *The Cricket* because Buddy Bolden who is one of the fathers of Black Music had a sheet in New Orleans by that name."[2] It is a gesture worth pausing over: a group of writers naming their periodical after the *writing* of "one of the fathers of Black Music."

Baraka, Neal, and Spellman had not seen a copy of Bolden's predecessor "sheet." This particular facet of the legend of Bolden—the never-recorded cornetist who supposedly was the first to meld the blues and the spirituals into the nascent strains of the new music at the turn of the twentieth century; who supposedly convened a city into hearing the new sounds with the volume and resonance of his horn, which "could be heard for miles, from the river back to Lake Pontchartrain"[3]—has been traced back to a single paragraph in one of the founding works of jazz historiography, the 1939 book *Jazzmen,* which was edited by Charles Edward Smith and Frederic Ramsey Jr. As Vic Hobson has noted, when it was published, *Jazzmen* "was the first book of its kind: it presented jazz as music with a history and firmly placed New Orleans at the origin."[4] In the chapter in *Jazzmen* on "New Orleans Music"—which was largely compiled using oral histories conducted in the late 1930s with a number of musicians who had been active in the city at the turn of the century—William Russell and Stephen W. Smith describe Bolden in magisterial terms:

> So when Buddy Bolden, the barber of Franklin Street, gathered his orchestra together in the back room of his shop to try over a few new tunes for a special dance at Tin Type Hall, it was no ordinary group of musicians. Nor was Buddy an ordinary cornetist. In his day, he was entirely without competition, both in his ability as a musician and his hold upon the public. The power of his sonorous tone has never been equaled. When Buddy Bolden played in the pecan grove over in Gretna, he could be heard across the river throughout uptown New Orleans. Nor was Bolden just a musician. He was an "all-around" man. In addition to running his barber shop, he edited and published *The Cricket,* a scandal sheet as full of gossip as New Orleans had always been of corruption and vice. Buddy was able to scoop the field with the stories brought in by his friend, a "spider," also employed by the New Orleans police.
>
> Before the Spanish-American War, Bolden had already played himself into the hearts of the uptown Negroes. By the turn of the century his following was so large that his band could not fill all the engagements. Soon "Kid" Bolden became "King" Bolden.[5]

What is fascinating here is that Bolden's status as an " 'all-around' man" seems crucial to the amplification of the legend—as though it is somehow necessary that the first "King" of the music would have to be simultaneously some sort of guarantor of grooming, preparing bodies for the rituals of public display and seduction, on the one hand, and the publisher of a newspaper overflowing with a compendium of the lowest, most prurient *fait divers* and gutter rumblings, on the other. It seems significant that Bolden is described not simply as a writer but instead as an *editor:* a bird's-eye orchestrator and assiduous compiler, that is, of a discursive field churning around him.

As Donald Marquis documented in his 1978 book *In Search of Buddy Bolden,* the legend reverberated out from this paragraph in *Jazzmen,* with the result that the vast majority of dozens and dozens of jazz history works through the course of the twentieth century reiterate this information.[6] Only a few attempted to verify it with follow-up research.[7] Marquis was astonished to find that some even embellished the tale, adding details in describing the venues where Bolden's band played, or hypothesizing about the night crawling of those "spider" informants. The repertoire of Bolden's band included a few often-cited classics, such as "Careless Love" and "Funky Butt"—the latter famously recorded as "Buddy Bolden's Blues"[8] by Jelly Roll Morton in the late 1930s with a revised set of lyrics ("I thought I heard Buddy Bolden say/Dirty nasty stinkin' butt, take it away") that seemed to imply that Bolden's legacy was a matter of rumor: a muffled echo, a faint refrain you weren't quite sure you'd heard right. But in some subsequent historical sources, the band's set list ballooned from the half-dozen songs listed in *Jazzmen* to a much longer list of evocative titles, some of which were otherwise undocumented: "Don't Go Way Nobody"; "Emancipation Day"; "Idaho"; "Joyce 76"; "If You Don't Like My Potatoes, Why Do You Dig So Deep"; "Stick It Where You Stuck It Last Night"; "Let Me Be Your Li'l Dog Till Your Big Dog Comes"; "Don't Send Me No Roses 'Cause Shoes Is What I Need."[9] Nevertheless, the conclusions of Marquis's exhaustive research were definitive: "no copies have ever been found of *The Cricket,* and *Jazzmen* seems to be the sole source of this story. (Bill Russell attributed it to 'a figment of someone's imagination.'). . . . Russell, in his notes on a conversation with Buddy's widow, Nora, said that 'according to her he [Buddy] did not run a scandal sheet and was not a barber, although he drank a lot and hung out at barber shops.' "[10]

More recently, Vic Hobson (whose revelatory 2014 book *Creating Jazz Counterpoint* takes advantage of previously unknown sources in Frederic Ramsey's personal papers) discovered copies of a New Orleans newspaper called *The Cricket,* although the surviving copies contain no mention of Bolden. The editor and publisher of *The Cricket,* Lamar Middleton, described it in the first issue (dated March 21, 1896) as "a fortnightly paper which shall chronicle and discuss matters of current interest in society, light literature, music and the theater; and shall furnish a medium of expression to local literary talent," specifying furthermore that "politics will be of decidedly minor importance; and idle gossip of a social or other nature will be absolutely avoided."[11]

Hobson argues that this far-reaching comedy of errors originates first of all with the innovative methodology used in compiling *Jazzmen:* the book's "strength was also its weakness: it relied heavily on oral testimony of the jazzmen themselves."[12] One way to make sense of the implications of the Bolden legend for jazz historiography is to consider in more detail the specific ramifications of oral history, which has been central in jazz studies but is still almost always simply mined for biographical data and anecdote rather than theorized as a mode with characteristics—most obviously its antiphonal structure and improvisational form—that might well be viewed in relation to the music itself.[13] Oral historians such as Alessandro Portelli have argued, though, that the utility of oral history ultimately has less to do with the empirical data it may provide than with the way it registers "the very changes wrought by memory"[14]: in other words, even when oral histories contain "imaginative errors," those "errors" are indispensable indices of "subjective truths" with regard to our shifting investment in the past.[15] Oral history is "credible," Portelli writes, "but with a *different* credibility. The importance of oral testimony may lie not in its adherence to fact, but rather in its departure from it, as imagination, symbolism, and desire emerge."[16] This is to say that rather than to debunk the Bolden legend in the interest of some absolute fealty to empiricism, the task is instead to consider the resonance of the ways it departs from fact. Portelli suggests that "memory manipulates factual details and chronological sequence in order to serve three major functions": symbolic, psychological, and formal.[17] The symbolic and psychological implications of the Bolden legend for jazz historiography may seem self-evident, given the predilection to frame the music as a progression of individual male geniuses. But we should not overlook the *formal* effects of an empiricism warped, blurred, or refracted by memory. For Portelli these are mainly a matter of shifts in chronology or narrative sequence: for example, misremembering the date of a significant event in a manner that marks it as a turning point or a culmination in the course of lived experience. But when a legend travels, through time and across media—when it is taken as a template, a founding model, a guiding orientation—what is misremembered or misconstrued can be the source of formal innovation.

Because Baraka, Neal, and Spellman established *The Cricket* in the shadow of what they imagined to be Bolden's model, they thought of the journal in a different way. The masthead (Figure I.1) listed musical "advisors" (Sun Ra, Milford Graves, and later Cecil Taylor) in addition to an editorial team and corresponding contributors in San Francisco, Washington, DC, Los Angeles, and Philadelphia. And the journal published poems, essays, and reviews by Sun Ra, Albert Ayler, and Graves, among other musicians. "Bolden's *Cricket* has been called a 'gossip' sheet by the hip white boys who wrote the histories," the editorial in the first issue notes sardonically, adding a riposte: "we'll have some 'gossip' for the reader and a whole lot of other shit too."[18] And the subsequent issues of the short-lived journal went on to include a regular feature bluntly titled "Gossip," which one might argue the journal elaborated into something of a research methodology—that is, a way of going about the collection of material—drawing in all sorts of unsourced and underground fragments and whispered rumors into its pages along with more traditional signed articles and poems. The "Gossip" column in the third issue opens:

> Why only organ trios in black communities? . . . . Where is the new music and the new musicians? . . . . Where should black musicians play? . . . . What is a night club? . . . . Why should our musicians play in them? . . . . Why isn't Pharoah receiving any dough off Tauhid????????? . . . . Why don't black musicians turn down contracts with beast recording, and record with brothers? . . . . [. . .] many, many more sides to come. Salaam till next time.[19]

Another feature titled "Inquiry" is a page filled with sixteen repetitions of the same question: "DO YOU THINK THE MAFIA KILLED OTIS REDDING???????????????????????????????" A note at the bottom instructs readers to "WRITE THE CRICKETS" to give their answer and provides the magazine's post office box address in Newark.[20] Whatever Bolden did or did not do, the resonant received figure of his "scandal sheet . . . full of gossip" compelled his self-styled 1960s descendants to reformulate and extend the scope and tone of what a black music journal could mean.

CONTENTS PAGE

THE CRICKET

Black Music In Evolution

Editors: LeRoi Jones, Larry Neal, A.B. Spellman

Advisors: Sun Ra, Milford Graves, Cecil Taylor

Correspondents: Gaston Neal, Wash, DC, Stanley Crouch, LA; James Stewart, Philadelphia, Clyde Halisi, LA; Don L. Lee, Chicago, Norman Jordan, Cleveland, Ben Caldwell, New York, Larry Miller, New Ark, more to come

Figure I.1 Masthead and table of contents, *The Cricket,* issue 3 (1969).

Instead of deflating the Bolden legend, then, we might wonder why the figure of the musician-writer seems to reverberate so powerfully. What is at stake in the idea that the first great instrumentalist in the music, the founding "King" in a future pantheon of Dukes, Counts, and Ladies, was also a renowned editor, who "scooped the field" not only on the bandstand—and, to follow the legend, beneath the bedsheets—but also in publishing scandal and gossip, gathering the dirty doings of the Crescent City in a serial "sheet" of another sort?

Michael Ondaatje's 1976 novel *Coming through Slaughter* is among other things the most thorough exploration of this notion of transmedial consonance, the proposition that the resonance of the Bolden legend—its traveling power, one might say, as an origin story, even if the claim of locating origin is always ultimately a ruse—has everything to do with the multiple media it puts into concert (sound and print). Rather than a gadfly prone to wallow in the lascivious, the Bolden in *Coming through Slaughter* is portrayed as an editor driven by a particular sense of counter-historiography, angled against the propriety of the mainstream print media (that is, the sort of periodical that designates itself the guardian of "all the news that's fit to print"). According to the novel's version of history:

> *The Cricket* existed between 1899 and 1905. It took in and published all the information Bolden could find. It respected stray facts, manic theories, and well-told lies. This information came from customers in the chair and from spiders among the whores and police that Bolden and his friends knew. *The Cricket* studied broken marriages, gossip about jazzmen, and a servant's memoirs told everyone that a certain politician spent twenty minutes each morning deciding which shirt to wear. Bolden took all the thick facts and dropped them into his pail of sub-history.[21]

In this sense, editing a newspaper puts into practice a theory of historiography, a way of handling the effluvia of passing events by refusing to discriminate among them, instead tossing everything into the paper's "pail of sub-history." Bolden's "own mind," we are told, "was helpless against every moment's headline. He did nothing but leap into the mass of changes and explore them and all the tiny facets so that eventually he was almost completely governed by fears of certainty" (ibid., 15). Rather than a means to categorize, filter, and interpret, the newspaper here is a technology precisely of regurgitating "all the information Bolden could find."

The musical allusion in the clause "he did nothing but leap into the mass of changes" (implying not only the ebbs and flows of social history but also, and more specifically, the harmonic "changes" of a piece of music) seems deliberate, as well. The implication is that despite the differences between a cornet and a printing press, between a song and a newspaper, there is a parallel between the way Bolden edits, on the one hand, and the way he plays, on the other. The novel includes a number of excerpts of what appear to be oral histories of contemporaries of Bolden; in one of them, Frank Lewis muses that "we thought he was formless, but I think now he was tormented by order, what was outside it" (37). At another point, there is a description of Bolden's friend, a detective named Webb, listening to the band at a dance hall:

> Far back, by the door, he stood alone and listened for an hour. He watched him dive into the stories found in the barber shop, his whole plot of song covered with scandal and incident and change. The music was coarse and rough, immediate, dated in half an hour, was about bodies in the river, knives, lovepains, cockiness. Up there on stage he was showing all the possibilities in the middle of the story. (43)

Coming through Slaughter's own form is elliptical, piecemeal, an awkward mélange of different sorts of texts (not only fictional narrative but also something more like historical writing, as well as set lists, song lyrics, names of band members, and passages from interviews, oral histories, and institutional records). In other words, the novel mirrors or parallels the approach to aesthetic form it "hears" in Bolden, or in the received figure of Bolden. There are passages, especially toward the conclusion of the book, when a first-person authorial voice surfaces, expressing wonder at the irresistible lure of Bolden and the "thin sheaf of information" around him. Addressing Bolden, the narrator muses: "Why did my senses stop at you? There was the sentence, 'Buddy Bolden who became a legend when he went berserk in a parade. . . .' What was there in that, before I knew your nation your colour your age, that made me push my arm forward and spill it through the front of your mirror and clutch myself? [. . .] There was the climax of the parade and then you removed yourself from the 20th century game of fame, the rest of your life a desert of facts. Cut them open and spread them out like garbage" (134). Just as for Baraka, Neal, and Spellman, here the specter of the musician-writer seems to provide or even impose the model of a different sort of fictional aesthetics: a novel that in its very form would spread a meager repository of facts "out like garbage."

Still, there is something in the allure of the figure of the musician-writer that goes beyond the positing of a parallel among media, or even of a cross-media influence, in which the practice of one medium can be inspired, provoked, or extended by an attention to the specificities of another. At the beginning of Chapter 3 in this book, I quote the stunningly eloquent opening of James Baldwin's 1951 essay "Many Thousands Gone": "It is only in his music, which Americans are able to admire because a protective sentimentality limits their understanding of it, that the Negro in America has been able to tell his story. It is a story which otherwise has yet to be told and which no American is prepared to hear."[22] The idea that the music contains not only emotional surges and rhythmic propulsion but also the "character of cognition"—commentary, insight, and even lucid critical analysis—can be traced at least as far back as Frederick Douglass's musings on the meaning of the "wild songs" sung by slaves, songs in which "the thought that came up, came out—if not in the word, in the sound;—and as frequently in the one as in the other," and W. E. B. Du Bois's description of the spirituals as the "naturally veiled and half articulate message" of the slave to the world.[23] In the groundbreaking 1963 book *Blues People,* Amiri Baraka declares in a similar vein that "music, as paradoxical as it might seem, is the result of thought."[24]

But note Baldwin's phrasing: it is *only* in his music. Here it is not a matter of a writing that finds its form in the music or responds to it, but instead of a "story" that apparently cannot be rendered in any other medium. The music, one might say, possesses a native intelligence before and beyond any writing. In this respect, the figure of the musician-writer implies a theory of musical *immanence.* "The music gives you its own understanding of itself," according to Sidney Bechet in his classic autobiography *Treat It Gentle.* Responding to those who ask, "What's Negro music?" Bechet argues, "When you get so you really hear it, when you can listen to the music being itself—then you don't have to ask that question."[25] Thus the music can provide the model for criticism because the music *already is* criticism—itself, autonomously, purely in the medium of sound. (One might add that the title *The Cricket,* as a reference to an insect that produces sound not by prosthesis but instead by stridulation—by rubbing or scraping one member of its body against another—seems entirely appropriate as a metaphor for musical immanence, for a self-generating music that somehow already possesses its own understanding of itself.)

Baraka says that he learned this lesson from his English teacher at Howard University, the poet Sterling Brown. When Baraka and his classmate A. B. Spellman were students in his Shakespeare class, "lolling around like the classic submature campus hipsters we most emphatically were, 'Those Who Would Be Down,'" Baraka writes, Brown took the time to show them "that we wasn't quite as hip as we thunk." The poet invited them to his home and, gradually, in a series of extracurricular tutorials, introduced them to the full scope of black music through the medium of his own record collection:

> And man, there in a center room was a wall, which wrapped completely around our unknown, of all the music from the spasm bands and arwhoolies and hollers, through Bessie and Jelly Roll and Louis and Duke, you know? And we watched ourselves from that vantage point of the albums starting haughtily at us, with that "tcch tcch" sound such revelations are often armed with.
>
> The albums, Folkways and Commodores, Bluebirds and even a Gennett or three, stared us with our own lives spelled out in formal expression. "This is the history. This is your history, my history, the history of the Negro people."[26]

This theory of immanence, while it is surely in part a defensive strategy (against the ways that, in the phrasing of the editorial in the first issue of

The Cricket, "ofay white critics have written the histories and the criticisms of our music"), is also a matter of memory—and perhaps even of the "creative 'errors' "[27] wrought by memory under the thrall of a deeper imperative. "White people," Bechet explains at one point, "they don't have the memory that needs to understand it. But that's what the music is . . . a lost thing finding itself."[28]

While with the Bolden legend these issues are a matter of myth and memory, it seems to me that they extend far beyond a "tall tale told by inattentive idealists."[29] Indeed, one could argue that the issues at stake in the resonant figure of the musician-writer come to run through, and even to delineate, the cultural field of the music as a whole. Of course it would be possible to dismiss a statement such as Bechet's ("White people, they don't have the memory that needs to understand it") as at best the misguided application of a myth, and at worst a pernicious instance of racial essentialism. But even if it is rooted in what Ronald Radano calls "evolving myths of blackness," my point is that black music is defined by a deep-set and ongoing negotiation of the musician-writer figure and everything it implies about the social function of music.[30] Moreover, its power is rooted in what Radano describes as its "socially constructed instability, wavering between sound and text to the point of complicating distinctions between music and language."[31]

To start with only the most obvious example, the figure of the musician-writer is crucial to the understanding of the legacy of the artist often described as the first great soloist of jazz in the recording age, Louis Armstrong, the subject of Chapter 1. That he was a writer is no "figment of someone's imagination": Armstrong was arguably "jazz's most productive autobiographer."[32] Curator Michael Cogswell notes that despite never completing a junior high school education, Armstrong traveled on the road with a typewriter as early as 1922 and wrote at least ten thousand letters during his lifetime.[33] He was astonishingly prolific, composing not only a number of published and unpublished memoirs but also a variety of ephemeral prose pieces (including jokes, recipes, and pornography) and magazine articles, including excavations of "jive talk" for the *Harlem Tattler* in the 1940s and reports for the *Record Changer* and *Melody Maker* in the 1950s.[34]

The example of Armstrong is a reminder of just how many jazz musicians *are* writers, from Armstrong and Duke Ellington to Sun Ra and

Cecil Taylor, from Babs Gonzales to Marion Brown, from Mary Lou Williams and Danny Barker to Art Taylor, Anthony Braxton, and George Lewis. The term *jazz literature* tends to bring to mind writing influenced by music. But this other sort of jazz literature—that is, writing *by* musicians—includes an enormous range of work, including not only autobiography but also music criticism, history, interviews, philosophy, fiction, poetry, drama, technical and instruction manuals, liner notes, and magazine and newspaper articles. Aside from autobiographies this work has received little attention from scholars of either literary studies or jazz studies, but it seems to me that this corpus must not be dismissed as a curiosity. It should be understood, instead, as a persistent impulse. Whether in Sun Ra's "cosmo-myth rituals" or in Ellington's "social significance" suites, one encounters again and again an approach to aesthetics that resists any easy distinction between "writing" and "music," instead viewing both as components in a broader sphere of art making and performance.

It is worth noting that a good deal of this writerly activity has emerged in genres one might term *ancillary* to the commercial recording, in that their protocols (length, tone, mode of address, and so on) have taken shape in accompaniment or response to the manufacture, sale, promotion, and circulation of the record as an artifact. This is obviously the case with record reviews, many interviews, and liner notes (the latter are a main focus of Chapter 5). The term *ancillary* implies these texts' auxiliary, supporting role in providing information and commentary that advertises the sound recording they accompany or to which they respond. But one should not assume too hastily that these ancillary genres are thereby automatically subordinate afterthoughts, stray jottings that are inherently of secondary importance in relation to the music. In fact, a rapturous record review, a piquant interview, or a snarky "blindfold test" can emphatically frame the way a recording is heard, whether by noting the stylistic trends it exemplifies, making an argument for its historical significance, pointing out its shortcomings, or sketching an alluring (or off-putting) "persona" for the musician behind the music. With regard to liner notes, Tom Piazza has made the case that though they might appear to "promise little more than glorified promotional copy," in fact liner notes provide "much more," including biographical information on the musicians, discographical background, observations about a given recording session (providing a semiethnographic "window into the recording process"), musical analysis, and historical and political context.[35] They are equally crucial, he writes, in "setting the tempo" for the listener's sensibility in a manner that has been important in creating dynamics of fandom and collecting: "they tell the listener, in subtle ways, what it means to be a jazz fan. They embody styles of appreciating the music, a range of possible attitudes toward it."[36]

If it may seem self-evident that liner notes can and even must be read in accompaniment to the commercial recording, in the pages that follow I extend this argument about the ancillary genres of jazz literature in some perhaps unexpected directions, including song titles (in Chapter 6) and even seemingly "literary" subgenres such as the blues poems of Langston Hughes (in Chapter 1), which in fact adopt their characteristic three- or four-stanza length from the *recorded* blues.[37] My goal in this respect is not to provide either a systematic survey or a straightforward chronology of all the generic variants of jazz literature—say, in something like the way that scholars including Sascha Feinstein, Aldon Nielsen, T. J. Anderson III, and Meta DuEwa Jones have begun to do for jazz poetry in particular.[38] Instead, this book works through a constellation of case studies to raise the question of what one might call the *ends of jazz writing:* its uses and implications for artists we tend to think of primarily as composers and improvisers.

Coming to terms with the history of jazz literature in this expanded sense also means coming to terms with the *archive* as yet another medium of practice. Louis Armstrong's legacy is astounding first of all because of the sheer volume of what he left behind, now collected mainly in the Louis Armstrong Collection at Queens College and the Armstrong House in Corona, Queens, with significant smaller stashes at the Institute for Jazz Studies in Newark and the Library of Congress. The Armstrong archive is not a mass of material—the discards and leavings and overflow of a life. Instead it is the record of a life spent collecting and collating and annotating its own progress. If the house in Queens is now a sort of monument and memorial, it is equally an institution of learning about jazz and U.S. history and about a character named "Louis Armstrong," an archive that includes a stunning amount: hundreds of books, 1,600 recordings, 5,000 photographs, 86 scrapbooks, 650 reel-to-reel tapes made by Pops himself (most of which are carefully numbered and catalogued, and kept in boxes Armstrong decorated with fascinating collages and drawings), as well as "12 linear feet" of papers.[39] Historian Antoinette Burton's *Dwelling in the Archives* is a fine study of the personal archives of three Indian women of the middle of the twentieth century, whose memoirs, scrapbooks, and collections Burton uses to throw into question the status of history itself as a discipline, taking up the problem, as she puts it, "of who counts as a historian, what archives look like, and why memories of house and home should be recognized as crucial to what we think of as the historical imagination."[40] This is an important issue for jazz history, I would suggest, not only because of the primacy of Armstrong as a figure in the music but also because collecting and documentation are clearly a central part of the work and self-conception of so many musicians.

Aside from a single tintype photograph, the only traces of Buddy Bolden reside in the recorded memories of those who knew or heard him, which is perhaps what makes him an ideal figure to conjure with. But history of the music is replete with musicians like Armstrong who not only wrote but also retained their own material archives of their personal and professional lives, in a manner that goes far beyond the scope of their discography of commercial recordings. One could argue—but only by figuring out how to *read* these archives—that the archive itself is equally an arena of practice, a medium immanent with "its own story,"[41] parallel to or interwoven with music as well as literature. Despite the dearth of historical documentation on Bolden, one might also point out that the myth of *The Cricket* is also a myth of the archive: as the editor of the newspaper, Bolden is figured in *Jazzmen* not only as a writer or a manager of a team of writers but also as a kind of collector, "scooping the field" with the otherwise fugacious stories he gathered and preserved in his "scandal sheet full of gossip."

In considering the resonance of the Bolden myth of origin, then, we have to ask what is at stake in the need to imagine the first great jazz musician to be not only the first jazz writer but also the first jazz archivist. If what resonates in the figure of the musician-writer is above all the notion of musical *immanence,* as I have suggested, then it is not just that the music seems to contain articulate reflection and even critical analysis, but also that it can serve as a reservoir or repository for a range of historical experience preserved in no other form. To explore this point, one could turn to any number of literary works, such as Gayl Jones's devastating 1975 novel *Corregidora,* in which the blues come to serve as something like an embodied archive—a novel in which a singer's voice can be compared to "callused hands," scarred and bruised in a way that "gives witness" to the lived experience of racial and sexual brutality.[42] But this understanding of the music is also on display in the ways musicians themselves talk and write about their art.

There is a particularly poignant example in Sidney Bechet's autobiography. Bechet met Louis Armstrong in New Orleans before the younger man became known a trumpeter; Bechet remembers hearing him first as a singer in a barbershop quartet. Wanting to get to know him better, Bechet asked him over for dinner, but Armstrong declined the invitation. "I could see there was something troubling him," Bechet explains:

> [A]nd finally he let it out. "Look, Sidney," he says, "I don't have any shoes . . . these I got, they won't get me there." Well I said that was easy fixed and gave him fifty cents to get his shoes repaired, and he went off promising me he would come.
>
> Well, I don't know what it was, but he never showed up. We lived way across on the other side of town and that was a hell of a distance to walk. And it's that way you see . . . it's a little thing, and there's big things around it, but it keeps coming back. You're playing some number and it starts about those shoes. When you're playing about it maybe you don't know it is about that. But then, later, you're thinking about it, and it comes to you. It's not a describing music, nothing like that. Maybe nobody else could ever tell it was about that. But thinking back, you know the music was how you felt about remembering that time on that street . . . remembering it from a way back.[43]

(To revisit the Bolden legend for a moment: even if it is a fictional addendum to the King's set list, "Don't Send Me No Roses 'Cause Shoes Is What I Need" might be said to capture something in the air in New Orleans in the early twentieth century: the unique shade of humor at the crevasse between sappy romanticism and dire poverty.) In Bechet's anecdote, that jazz is defined by musical immanence means not only that it is a self-reflexive medium but also that—without being programmatic or somehow simply mimetic ("a describing music")—it is an art where, even when it goes unannounced and unnoticed ("Maybe nobody else could ever tell it was about that"), sound itself can capture and retain and even revisit ("it keeps coming back") a precise historical transcript of the most complex affective experience.

This is already to begin to suggest the infinitely fertile interface between music and literature in African diasporic culture. Something hovering "at the very edge of semantic availability" can be captured in sound (even if not necessarily made explicit or communicated).[44] And the resulting music in turn can provoke or compel an attempt to stretch or expand the capacity of literary language to make meaning on the page. Perhaps one reason this interface has been so fertile is that this back-and-forth—the ongoing, self-conscious, continually recalibrated, and (not least) sensuous work of testing and stretching and redefining the frontiers of articulacy—is already at stake in the music itself. As Fred Moten puts it, "Black performance has always been the ongoing improvisation of a kind of lyricism of the surplus."[45] Or as I mention in Chapter 1, there is a brief passage in Albert Murray's masterful 1976 *Stomping the Blues* where Murray makes the point that all new world black music can be heard as a practice of "reciprocal 'voicing'": "The tonal nuances of blues music," Murray argues, "are also a matter of singers playing with their voices as if performing on an instrument, and of instrumentalists using their brasses, woodwinds, strings, keyboards, and percussion as extensions of the human voice."[46] If some of these effects can be described under the rubric of "novelties"—say, in the ludic and sometimes uproarious ways brass players used a virtuosic range of "flutter, growl, wah-wah, and buzz techniques" to make their horns sound "like a woman chastising her wayward man, a dog barking, or any number of barnyard noises"—then one can only say that *novelty* is another term for the persistent, insatiable drive toward articulacy at the core of the music.[47] In the manifold variants of jazz *literature,* then, this ferment at the horizon of articulacy already in the music is extended or redoubled at the interface between media, in the different ways that sound and print can "speak."

One of the more compelling recent overviews of comparative arts is Daniel Albright's 2014 book *Panaesthetics.*[48] Against thinkers who would erect strict distinctions among artistic media—the lineage of "medial separatists" from Gotthold Lessing, who contended that "the temporal arts, such as music and literature, had protocols wholly distinct from those of the spatial arts, such as sculpture and painting," to Clement Greenberg, who famously proclaimed that "to restore the identity of an art the opacity of its medium must be emphasized"[49]—Albright argues provocatively that "an artwork is an artwork precisely because it is especially susceptible to translation into an alien medium, and because those translations have a certain captivating aspect." Moving among a range of examples in European literature, painting, and music, Albright examines the varieties of *intermedial* art—"the imaginary artwork generated by the spectator through the interplay of two or more media—the transient, complex thing that is assembled in each spectator's mind through attention to the elements in different media" (209)—as well as what he terms (after Adorno) *pseudomorphosis;* that is, "in a work in a single artistic medium, the medium is asked to ape, or do the work of, some alien medium" (212).

Albright writes that in pseudomorphosis, making one artistic medium imitate or take the shape of another "typically involves a certain wrenching or scraping against the grain of the original medium" (212). He tends to interpret this as a sort of violation or transgression of the "original," which he recognizes creates a paradox in relation to his larger argument that a cross-media impulse is constitutive of the aesthetic itself. As he puts it, "Art is not art unless capable of being transposed; but the transposition is never comprehensive or even correct, except with respect to a few contrived congruences" (232).

But the friction or erosion that results from pseudomorphosis can also be described as a motor of artistic innovation, defined in the words of Nathaniel Mackey as the "pursuit of a more complex accommodation between technique and epistemological concerns, between ways of telling and ways of knowing, especially where knowing is less the claim than a nervousness about it."[50] In terms of the second or target medium, the process of pseudomorphosis can be a way to expand boundaries, to discover new possibilities, to transform a medium precisely by making it become other.

Roland Barthes's 1972 essay "The Grain of the Voice" takes a famously unorthodox approach to reinventing music criticism. All too often, Barthes writes, writing about music amounts to describing it with a "facile and trivial" stock of adjectives that, rather than capturing the complex ways music challenges and even afflicts the listener, instead reduces it to a reassuringly familiar set of prescribed qualities.[51] The solution Barthes proposes is not to formulate some better, or more precise, repository of adjectives to describe music, but instead to "change the musical object itself, as it presents itself to speech: to modify its level of perception or of intellection: to shift the fringe of contact between music and language [*langage*]" (269). He limits his focus to the "very specific space" of words set to melody in European art song; in other words, he reconsiders the relationship between music and language by concentrating on the mode of performance when music *is* language—when "the voice is in a double posture, a double production: of language and of music" (269). He calls this limited area "the grain of the voice," which he defines as "the *friction* between music and something else, which is the language [*langue*] (and not the message at all)" (273). In this respect he is less concerned with evaluating the ways a song "communicates" emotion or "expresses" character than with articulating his own unique, sensuous response as a listener to the ways sung "melody actually *works on* language—not what it says but the voluptuous pleasure of its signifier-sounds, of its letters: explores how language works and identifies itself with that labor" (270–271). What one hears in singing, then, is "the materiality of the body speaking its mother tongue" (270): the unique ways that a particular human body—the channel of one singer's throat, the bellows of her lungs, the articulating muscle of her tongue, the backstop of her palate, the pliable portal of her lips—gives resonant form to a particular language *(langue)*.

The examples in Barthes's essay are drawn from European classical music (versions of Schubert song by Dietrich Fischer-Dieskau and Charles Panzéra) and, given the emphasis in that tradition on immaculate articulation and aesthetic "expressiveness," Barthes's preference for the grain, for the audibility of the singer's body rather than the conveyance of the lyrics he sings, can seem idiosyncratic, even perverse. But "The Grain of the Voice" is highly suggestive in the realm of blues and jazz singing, which so pervasively and compellingly "ornaments both the song and the mechanics"—as is immediately apparent when one listens to Louis Armstrong, or Skip James, or Billie Holiday, or Mississippi Fred McDowell, or Little Jimmy Scott, or Nina Simone, or Andy Bey.[52] Black singing seems particularly imbued by an aesthetics of the grain in Barthes's sense, an approach in which "what counts for most is not verbal precision (which is not to say vocal precision) but musical precision, or perhaps better still, musical nuance. . . . It is not at all unusual for blues lyrics of the very highest poetic quality to be mumbled, hummed, and even garbled by the outstanding performers of the idiom."[53]

Like Barthes's essay, this book can be described as an attempt to shift the fringe of contact between music and language. But in a different manner, and to a different degree. In a passage that might initially seem cryptic, Barthes insists that the grain of the voice is ultimately a kind of "writing"—the "sung writing of the language" *(écriture chantée de la langue),* he calls it (274). He means that the qualities of a singer's unique sound (the specific way Panzéra rolls his *r*'s, for instance) are *material* effects, an audible reshaping of the phonic fabric of the French language—pursued for the sake of play, of pleasure, rather than in the service of conveying meaning (or as he puts it, "the tyranny of signification") (273). Whereas Barthes thus restricts his purview to the space where music and language coincide or overlap, in the chapters that follow I instead trace some of the many pathways and passages between two putatively discrete media (sound and writing) to argue that pseudomorphosis—working one medium in the shape of or in the shadow of another—is the paradigm of innovation in black art.

Although all the chapters shuttle between jazz and literature, it is not by coincidence that the first is devoted to Louis Armstrong, in an attempt to take account of the apparent parallels or shared predilections across his work as a singer, an instrumentalist, *and* a writer. To read and hear Armstrong this way—or Duke Ellington, or Sun Ra, or Mary Lou Williams, or Henry Threadgill—is to shift the fringe of contact between music and language by noting that black musicians so often insist on working in multiple media, not as autonomous areas of activity but in conjunction, insistently crossing circuits, rethinking and expanding the potential of each medium in the way it is like and unlike the other. It is also to insist that the provocation goes both ways: from music to literature, from literature to music.

Throughout, I am especially keen to track the terms *(grain, parallel, gappings, interstice, differential, interval)* that arise as heuristic—sometimes hesitant or ersatz, sometimes vernacular rather than highbrow—theorizations of this interface between sound and writing.[54] These terms are not my own but instead the artists' own attempts to make sense of the relation between media in their work. While Ellington tends to make recourse to "parallel," Armstrong jokes about "gappings," and Cecil Taylor expounds on the impact of "differentials." If they hover around a shared set of aesthetic questions, these words are not synonyms: they represent a tradition of self-generated, provisional theorizations arising out of artistic practice itself, rather than externally applied analysis in the hindsight of scholarship. This is to note that this book will not provide a single keyword or master trope that could cover all instances; instead it is my conviction that the variety of such terms, and even their heuristic status, attests both to the vibrancy of this field of interplay and to its self-reflexivity. While it takes up a broad range of cases, this study is by no means exhaustive. And attention to other instances—whether the many other poets and novelists one might consider (from Michael Harper to Gayl Jones, from Ntozake Shange to Jayne Cortez), or the many other examples of writing by jazz musicians (Cab Calloway's jive dictionaries; autobiographies by Babs Gonzales, Marion Brown, and Charles Mingus; Wadada Leo Smith's collection of notes on "creative music"; poetry by Joseph Jarman and Oliver Lake; Anthony Braxton's metatheoretical *Tri-axium Writings;* interviews by Art Taylor and William Parker) would result in a different collection of heuristic terms, a different set of innovative pathways across media, in open-ended dialogue with the ones that I take up here.[55]

"Epistrophy" is the name of a tune copyrighted on June 2, 1941, by pianist Thelonious Monk and drummer Kenny Clarke. Monk biographer Robin D. G. Kelley explains that they initially called it "Fly Rite" and then "Iambic Pentameter," but eventually settled on the title under which it became one of the best-known examples of bebop composition.[56] The word may not seem out of place among the more recondite song titles in 1940s bop that suggest an eclectic arsenal of research disciplines ("Ornithology," "Anthropology," "Crazeology"), but the etymology of "Epistrophy," interestingly enough, comes from a literary source: the word means "turning about" in Greek, and "refers to a literary device in which a word or expression is deliberately repeated at the end of successive phrases, clauses, sentences, or verses."[57] Literary critic James Snead has pointed out that epistrophe is one of the most familiar forms of literary repetition: whereas anaphora involves a repeated word or phrase at the beginning of a clause, epistrophe places the repetition at the end (Snead gives the sermonic example "Give your life to the Lord; give your faith to the Lord; raise your hands to the Lord," noting that both epistrophe and anaphora are central devices in the powerful rhetorical repertoire of the black church).[58]

To the extent that the Monk / Clarke tune is an enactment of epistrophe—the main melody, as Kelley observes, is "constructed of repeated phrases" in which the "melodic line turns in on itself"—it can be described as a prominent instance of musical composition finding a formal model or inspiration in a literary device. But it resonates in other ways or on other levels in Monk's music, as well. It is tempting to hear *epistrophy* not just as the title of one tune but also as a word for the unusual little dance (a "turning about," one could call it) that Monk would often do during his concerts, standing up and leaving the piano while his sidemen soloed. As Kelley describes it:

> His "dance" consisted of a peculiar spinning move, elbow pumping up and down on each turn, with an occasional stutter step allowing him to glide left and right. It was a deliberate embodiment of the rhythm of each tune: Every drummer interviewed who played with Monk said that he liked to get up to dance in order to set the rhythm; it was a form of conducting that required complete attention from the drummer.[59]

The historian Sterling Stuckey went so far as to argue that Monk's dance was a sort of echo of the ring shout, the foundational African diasporic dance form, although on this point Kelley demurs: "Was it also a sacred expression? Perhaps."[60] In any case, the little dance became something of a well-known predilection or compulsion, and while Monk did it not just during "Epistrophy" itself but during many tunes, there is something in the lurching chromatic harmony of "Epistrophy" in particular that seemed to be paralleled or repeated in his physical movements. What is suggestive for me here is the sense of a formal device that, taken into another medium, provides the ground of inspiration, the syntactical cell for a melody, which is then echoed in yet another medium (the body in motion, and even "a form of conducting" as other players watch the choreography). Epistrophy, then, might be one name for a turning or troping that, in turning, has a tendency to jump the track from one medium to another.

The key point is that the interface can be crossed in either direction. So we might recall that in 1964 Amiri Baraka published a short poem titled "Epistrophe," which strikingly does not even once employ the device itself:

> It's such a static reference; looking
> out the window all the time! the eyes' limits . . .
> On good days, the sun.
>
> & what you see. (here in New York)
> Walls and buildings; or in the hidden gardens
> of opulent Queens: profusion, endless stretches of leisure.
>
> It's like being chained to some dead actress;
> & she keeps trying to tell you something horribly maudlin.
>
> e.g. ("the leaves are flat & motionless.")
>
> What I know of the mind
> seems to end here;
> Just outside my face.
>
> I wish some weird looking animal
> would come along.[61]

One way to read it is as an oblique allusion to the Monk / Clarke tune. Thus the somewhat clunky aspiration that concludes the poem ("I wish some weird looking animal / would come along") brings to mind the peculiarity of the melody, as though "Epistrophy"—the music, that is—were a sort of emblem (a theme song, perhaps) for that hoped-for intrusion: an unclassifiable beast lumbering by to break up the tedious "static reference" of what the speaker sees "out the window all the time." But if this poem ends somewhat tepidly, with only a vague and unfulfilled desire for something to disturb the surface of perception, there are many examples in Baraka's work of places where music could be said to provide the catalyst for innovation. If "imaginative error" can be said, whatever its roots in fancy, to spur innovations in literary *form*—a periodical reconceived because of the spectral catalyst of an unavailable and even misdescribed predecessor periodical—one can also make the case that a resonant figure of musical immanence can be the impetus behind an innovative *poetics.*

A decade after the comet heyday of *The Cricket,* Baraka published a brilliant multipart poem about John Coltrane called "AM/TRAK" in the 1979 volume *Poetry for the Advanced.*[62] While it doesn't mention New Orleans or Buddy Bolden, it nonetheless can be read as yet another working through of the political implications at the core of the music in a manner that revisits the same figure of musical immanence. The five sections of the poem sketch a loosely chronological arc through Coltrane's life, and one might say the task of the poem is to intuit the relationship among a set of key terms that, in the short first section, are splayed paratactically, in a manner that provides no sense of causality, no sense of their interarticulation:

> Trane,
> Trane,
> History Love Scream Oh
> Trane, Oh
> Trane, Oh
> Scream History Love
> Trane (267)

In other words, the task of the poem is to intuit the relationship among a spondaic array of proper nouns: "Trane" (not only the self, one supposes, but the abbreviation implying a propulsion, a drive, that takes on allegorical proportions in the way an artist comes to stand in for sort of national transport: thus the title "AM/TRAK"), "History," "Love," "Scream," "Oh."

If we dare lend an ear to its gutter rumblings, the poem can also be read as a meditation on *shit,* the word and the substance. The word is repeated often enough in the poem that it almost becomes a sporadic percussive motif. *Shit* is first of all the term for a brand of existential trouble: "The navy, the lord, niggers, / the streets / all converge a shitty symphony / of screams / to come / dazzled invective" (267). Sidney Bechet writes, "I met many musicianers and there was none of them hadn't found himself some trouble sometime. . . . Some of them, they were strong enough and the trouble didn't take them: they were stronger than the trouble. And some of them, they had the trouble too strong and it took them. But I don't care how strong they were, they all of them had a piece of this trouble in them."[63] So *shit* is first of all a word for that trouble, the shit one has to deal with. (It is also an allusion to the scourge of drugs.) The art, if it merits that name, is the ironic "symphony" of working through that mess with a scream. Or as it is put later: "Can you play this shit? (Life asks" (269).

But in the third section of the poem, about Coltrane's period playing with the Miles Davis Quintet, the word *shit* starts to seem to connote something slightly different—a sound becoming itself, one could say: "Trane clawed at the limits of cool / slandered sanity / with his trying to be born / raging / shit" (268). And it is a demand from an audience, a re-fried vernacular term for the essence of what must be voiced: "tell us shit tell us tell us!" (268).

In the fifth and final section, Coltrane in the period of the early 1960s "classic quartet" emerges out of "the ugly streets of us" as the embodiment of "Black Art": a *"black blower of the now"* (270). Here are the last two stanzas of the poem:

> Jimmy Garrison, bass, McCoy Tyner, piano, Captain Marvel
>   Elvin
> on drums, the number itself—the precise saying
> all of it in it afire aflame talking saying being doing meaning
> *Meditations*

Expressions
A Love Supreme
(I lay in solitary confinement, July 67
Tanks rolling thru Newark
& whistled all I knew of Trane
my knowledge heartbeat
& he was *dead*
they said.

And yet last night I played *Meditations*
& it told me what to do
Live, you crazy mother
fucker!
Live!
    & organize
    yr shit
    as rightly
    burning! (271–272)

Unexpectedly, in one of Baraka's characteristic open-ended parentheticals, with their multiple implications (layering; an unending proliferation of qualification, annotation, and digression; as well as immersion: a step farther down, or in), we are with Baraka himself, beaten and jailed during the Newark uprisings in the summer of 1967, whistling Coltrane's music to keep himself sane, precisely at the moment of Coltrane's death. But the poem concludes exhilaratingly ("And yet last night I played *Meditations* / & it told me what to do"): what is in Coltrane's music is still there, captured in the medium of recorded sound. The music gives you its own understanding of itself. It is an exhortation to "Live!" not a soundtrack to mourning. And it tells you to get your *shit* together: to organize its combustion. Even if unannounced, this poetics—a way of making in language that finds the music in a figure, making shit resonate, as it were—is the same mode enacted in the 1968 editorial of *The Cricket,* where *shit* likewise morphs from a term of opprobrium ("Recording companies have stolen the music. . . . And through all of this shit, the music has survived and propelled itself forwards into more profound areas of human experience") into an editorial method, and even, one could say, into a historiography ("Bolden's *Cricket* has been called a 'gossip' sheet by the hip white boys who wrote the histories. We'll have some 'gossip' for the reader and a whole lot of other shit too").[64] Even this far away, there is yet another faint echo of that cornet resounding across Lake Pontchartrain.

one
Louis Armstrong and the Syntax of Scat

Scat begins with a fall, or so we're told. In his second OKeh recording session with his Hot Five on February 26, 1926, in Chicago, Louis Armstrong recorded a lyric by Boyd Atkins called "The Heebie Jeebies Dance." The words are not particularly memorable, a jingle about a dance craze: "I've got the Heebies, I mean the Jeebies,/Talk 'bout a dance the Heebie Jeebies,/You'll see girls and boys,/Faces lit with joys,/If you don't know it/You ought to learn it/Don't feel so blue,/Some one will teach you,/Come on now let's do that prance/Called the Heebie Jeebies dance."[1] Supposedly the practice takes of the tune went smoothly, but a fortuitous fumble as the band was cutting the record transformed the song from one of the first journeyman efforts of a studio band to one of the most influential discs in American popular music. As Armstrong himself tells it:

> I dropped the paper with the lyrics—right in the middle of the tune . . . And I did not want to stop and spoil the record which was moving along so wonderfully . . . So when I dropped the paper, I immediately turned back into the horn and started to Scatting . . . Just as nothing had happened . . . When I finished the record I just knew the recording people would throw it out . . . And to my surprise they all came running out of the controlling booth and said—"Leave That In."[2]

In the liner notes to an Armstrong reissue, producer George Avakian remarks that there are "several versions" of the story. Others present, like trombonist Edward "Kid" Ory, told Avakian that "Louis had the lyrics memorized, but forgot them (or at least pretended to, Ory adds with a grin). Louis says he doesn't remember, but he, too, offers a quiet smile."[3]

As Philippe Baudoin, Gary Giddins, Richard Hadlock, and others have pointed out, it's a rather unlikely anecdote.[4] And although this session is often credited as the "origin" of scat singing in jazz, there are many other earlier practitioners of the mode. Baudoin notes Don Redman, who recorded a scat break of "My Papa Doesn't Two-Time No Time" with Fletcher Henderson five months before "Heebie Jeebies."[5] Will Friedwald, in *Jazz Singing,* points to vaudeville singer Gene Green's half chorus of imitation-Chinese scat in his 1917 recording of "From Here to Shanghai" and mentions other overlooked figures, including Cliff "Ukulele Ike" Edwards, who scatted on a December 1923 record of "Old Fashioned Love," and used to work in a theater accompanying silent movies "with his ukulele as well as with singing, vocal sound effects, and 'eefin' (the word Edwards used before anyone had thought of 'scat')."[6] In the late 1930s, the champion self-promoter and deft revisionary historian Jelly Roll Morton told Alan Lomax of his own role in the mode's origins more than twenty years earlier: "People believe Louis Armstrong originated scat. I must take that credit away from him, because I know better. Tony Jackson and myself were using scat for novelty back in 1906 and 1907 when Louis Armstrong was still in the orphan's home."[7]

I am less interested in the truth or fiction of the anecdote than in its perseverance, its resilience as a touchstone legend of origin. What's fascinating about the story is the seeming need to narrate scat as a fall, as a literal dropping of the words—as an unexpected loss of the lyrics that finally proves enabling. The written words slip to the ground, and an entirely new approach to the singing voice is discovered in the breach, in the exigencies of musical time. It is not exactly that the "song" is separated from the "script," but more that the anecdote relies on an oral/written split to *figure* the way that Armstrong's voice peels gradually away from the reiteration of the chorus, and from linguistic signification altogether. (This happens as a kind of erosion or disarticulation, not a sudden loss: "Say you don't know it, you don't dawduh,/Daw fee blue, come on we'll teach you . . .") Of course the anecdote buys into a familiar narrative about "genius" and "spontaneity," the notion that the great man improvises his way out of a tough spot with a dancer's grace—talking to save time, as it were. But there is another quality, as well, an apparently necessary coexistence of dispossession and invention, perdition and predication, catastrophe and chance. If "Heebie Jeebies" is an unprecedented occasion for poetic innovation, in which Armstrong's scat somehow moves closer to the qualities of music, it forces the recognition that an *occasion* is etymologically precisely that, Latin for a "falling toward,"[8] here both the lyric sheet drifting down and the singer finding resource, happening upon a new sound (itself falling away from the word) in the void of the phonograph horn.

Although it is seldom noticed, the song itself seems particularly appropriate to the occasion it enables. *Heebie-jeebies* is a phrase that dictionaries of American slang define as "a feeling or anxiety or apprehension," "craziness, foolishness," "errors, irregularities," or even "delirium tremens."[9] The first use of the term given in the *Oxford English Dictionary* is a 1923 caption by a cartoonist named Billy De Beck in the *New York American:* "You gimme the heeby jeebys!" A notion particular to the postwar U.S. vernacular, the phrase enjoyed a brief vogue in modernist literature (employed by Dos Passos, O'Neill, Wharton, and Odets, among others) and even provided the title for an African American weekly review in Chicago called *Heebie-Jeebies: A Sign of Intelligence.*[10] In *The Book of Negro Folklore,* Langston Hughes and Arna Bontemps define the "heebies" as "the shakes," while Mezz Mezzrow says it refers to the "jitters."[11] So the dance starts with a sense of an inherently modern state of bodily unease, anxiety, or trembling, perhaps in the wake of an excess of stimulation (Hughes and Bontemps give this example: "Cheap wine will give you the heebies"), that causes a loss of control, a nervous loss of articulacy that expresses itself as incommodious physical movement. One might wonder whether scat needs to start with such an implication of somatic circuit crossing, a nerve-driven jostle and hum in the muscles. Interestingly, Mezzrow goes so far as to describe the particular quality of Armstrong's talent as precisely this kind of edgy physical activation, a sensitivity of the nerves that approaches electrification:

> Every day, soon as I woke up about four in the P.M., I would jump up to Louis' apartment and most of the time catch him in the shower. That man really enjoyed his bath and shave. I would sit there watching him handle his razor, sliding it along with such rhythm and grace you could feel each individual hair being cut, and I'd think it was just like the way he fingered the valves on

> his horn, in fact, just like he did everything. When he slid his fingertips over the buttons, delicate as an embroiderer and still so masculine, the tones took wing as though they sprang from his fingers instead of his lips. The way he shaved put me in mind of the time Louis was blowing and I brushed up against him by accident, and goddamn if I didn't feel his whole body vibrating like one of those electric testing machines in the penny arcade that tell how many volts your frame can stand.[12]

Heebie-jeebies also implies a kind of premonition or haunting: the "apprehension" that intuits an invasive presence. This dis-ease itself claims the body. Is it that the infectious music compels the fumbling dance, forcing the jittery hand to lose its grip on the page, or that the body is haunted by, singing for, vibrating to the echo of the words it's dropped?

Scat Semantics

Scat is almost always defined, without further comment, as singing or vocal improvising with "nonsense syllables."[13] There are a number of ways to push at such a definition, but here I am particularly concerned with the implications of hearing scat as "nonsense." Does scat mobilize (syllabic) fragments of language without regard to meaning? Even in a musical sense, one could argue that scat does carry semantic content, though not necessarily linguistic content: one thinks immediately of the way scat turns so often to musical quotation of melody, sometimes to make a sardonic point through the juxtaposition. Roman Jakobson would call this an *introversive semiosis* in music. Music constitutes meaning because it refers first of all to itself: "instead of aiming at some extrinsic object, music appears to be *un langage qui se signifie soi-même.*"[14] There is a recording by Ella Fitzgerald of "How High the Moon" live in Berlin in 1960, in which she wordlessly quotes the melodies of more than a dozen tunes, sometimes with great humor, including "Poinciana," "Deep Purple," "The Peanut Vendor," "Did You Ever See a Dream Walking?," "A-Tisket, A-Tasket," "Heat Wave," and "Smoke Gets in Your Eyes."[15] But one might equally argue that scat can convey "extrinsic symbolization" (referring to the outside world through either spatiotemporal, kinetic, or affective registers).

For Jean-Jacques Nattiez and other theorists of musical semiosis, music means not because it carries specific signifiers but precisely because it doesn't. "Music is not a narrative, but an incitement to make a narrative," he argues. It signifies as a "potentiality," engaging a "narrative impulse" in the listener who follows and fills in its syntax. "If the listener, in hearing music, experiences the suasions of what I would like to call the narrative impulse," Nattiez writes, "this is because he or she hears (on the level of strictly musical discourse) recollections, expectations, and resolutions, but does not know what is expected, what is resolved."[16] The limitation of this argument, as scholars such as Susan McClary and Robert Walser have pointed out, is that Nattiez remains concerned almost exclusively with the metadiscursive analysis of music, claiming to operate at what he terms the "neutral level of analytical discourse."[17] This ignores the ways that musical signification is inherently bound up with social context: if music offers a discursive system, its utterances only carry content within social "conventions of practice and interpretation" that make musical meanings "contingent but never arbitrary."[18]

With regard to scat singing, in other words, one should be able to speak more specifically not just about syntax but about the contingency of particular rhetorical choices in black musical performance—since a legato phrase of soft-tongued phonemes ("La loo la loo lo") would seem to carry an altogether differently range of significance than a sharp run of fricatives, occlusives, and open vowels ("Shoop be doop").[19] A number of jazz scholars, including Paul Berliner, Ingrid Monson, and Brian Hatcher, have attempted to consider signification in instrumental jazz. They note the prevalence of metaphors of narrative or "telling a story" among jazz musicians, which they argue indicate that improvisation is syntactically structured in socially determined ways, even if its referentiality is nonspecific.[20]

Another way to approach this question is to read Billie Holiday, who, in her autobiography *Lady Sings the Blues,* memorably describes listening to Louis Armstrong on the Victrola in Alice Dean's whorehouse:

> I remember Pops' recording of "West End Blues" and how it used to gas me. It was the first time I ever heard anybody sing without using any words. I didn't know he was singing whatever came into his head when he forgot the lyrics. Ba-ba-ba-ba-ba-ba-ba and the rest of it had plenty of meaning for me—just as much meaning as some of the other words that I didn't always understand. But the meaning used to change, depending on how I felt. Sometimes the record would make me so sad I'd cry up a storm. Other times the same damn record would make me so happy I'd forget about how much hard-earned money the session in the parlor was costing me.[21]

Does such phonetic material, the ground of scat, involve an absence of meaning, or on the contrary an excess of meaning—even a troubling or transporting excess of meaning, a shifting possibility of a multitude of meanings? The trouble and transport, the heebie-jeebies, would presumably be due to a radical disorientation of reference: the musical syntax remains constant but is capable of assuming a wide variety of affective significance.

It might be useful to turn to Nathaniel Mackey's epistolary work *Bedouin Hornbook,* in which the multi-instrumentalist only identified as N. suggests in one of his letters that scat's "apparent mangling of articulate speech testifies to an 'unspeakable' history" of racial violence, lynching in particular.[22] In elaborating this function, the phrase he returns to is "telling inarticulacy"—an inarticulacy that nonetheless (or thereby) speaks, carries content.[23] For N., this function in scat is linked to a common predilection in black musical expression for the edges of the voice: the moan, the falsetto, the shout. All these vocal strategies indicate not just play, much less incoherence or ineptitude, but instead the singer's "willful dismantling of the gag-rule amenities which normally pass for coherence. Refusal worked hand in hand with exposé in such a way that what one heard was a loud critique of available options, a gruff dismissal of available conduits, no matter how 'coherent,' for admissible truths."[24] "Deliberately false" vocal production, in other words, in supplementing the sayable, "creatively hallucinates a 'new world,' indicts the more insidious falseness of the world as we know it."[25] This is inherently a communicative function, even if it "dismantles" the rules of signification. N. quotes Anthony Heilbut's study *The Gospel Sound:* "the essence of the gospel style is a wordless moan. Always these sounds render the indescribable, implying, 'Words can't begin to tell you, but maybe moaning will.' "[26]

In the letter, N. contends that this function may be as present in black instrumental music as in black vocal music. Other critics, from Gunther Schuller to Amiri Baraka, have argued likewise that there is a kind of continuum—what Albert Murray terms a "reciprocal 'voicing' "—between black vocal practice and black instrumental practice in the way they mobilize telling inarticulacy. "The tonal nuances of blues music," Murray argues, "are also a matter of singers playing with their voices as if performing on an instrument, and of instrumentalists using their brasses, woodwinds, strings, keyboards, and percussion as extensions of the human voice."[27] Thinking along such a continuum would mean we'd have to pair, for example, Clark Terry's well-known and jocular "Mumbles," in which the trumpeter sings, slurring choruses of a mumbled scat that seems to linger just beyond comprehensible language, with his more obscure efforts like "Trumpet Mouthpiece Blues," where he disassembles his horn and blows through his mouthpiece to attain a sound that approaches the inflections of speech.[28] In the manuscript that provided the material for his book *Satchmo: My Life in New Orleans,* Louis Armstrong recounts an anecdote from his days playing with Joe "King" Oliver's Band in Chicago in the early 1920s that makes a similar point about the interaction of words and music along a continuum of meaning:

> Finally they went into a number called "Eccentric"—that is the one where Papa Joe took a lot of breaks. . . . At the very last chorus he and [bass player] Bill Johnson would do a sort of Act musically. While Joe Oliver would be talking like a baby [on his trumpet], Bill Johnson would pet the baby in his high voice. The first baby Joe would imitate was supposed to be a white baby. When Joe's horn had cried like the white baby, Bill Johnson would come back with, "Don't Cry Little Baby." The last baby was supposed to be a little colored baby, then they would break it up. Joe would yell, "Baaaah! baaaaaaah!" Then Bill would shout,

> "Shut up you lil so and soooooo." Then the whole house would thunder with laughs and applauses.[29]

It is not to be overlooked that scat singing is engaged at different points along this continuum, thus "telling" to various ends. My purpose here is not to offer a typology of scat, but I'll quickly indicate a few of the elements that would have to be taken into account in order to do so. On the one hand, there is a whole range of scat that approaches what Armstrong's buddy and main supplier Mezz Mezzrow called jive talk—hallucinating a secret language, a language of the "inside." Think of the linguistic hipsterism promulgated by musicians such as Cab Calloway, Babs Gonzales, Slim Gaillard, and Leo Watson, or tunes like "In the Land of Oo-Bla-Dee" (which Joe Carroll sung with Dizzy Gillespie's band often in the 1940s) written by Milt Orent and Mary Lou Williams, with its pseudotranslations of an amorous fairy-tale exchange of scat. "This jive is a private affair," Mezzrow writes, "a secret inner-circle code cooked up partly to mystify the outsiders, while it brings those in the know closer together because they alone have the key to the puzzle. The hipster's lingo is a private kind of folk-poetry, meant for the ears of the brethren alone."[30] Louis Armstrong might be said with little exaggeration to be the origin of this focus in scat singing, given the extraordinary influence of his spoken and sung vernacular in U.S. popular culture throughout the 1920s and 1930s. In his orchestra recording of "Sweet Sue (Just You)" in 1933, there are two choruses of call-and-response in which Armstrong "translates" phrases scatted by saxophonist Budd Johnson in what Armstrong explains is a secret hipster "viper language."[31] Humor is another crucial element in scat, especially where musical performance approaches novelty and comedy routines, culminating in such masterworks as "The Avocado Seed Soup Symphony" (1945) by Slim Gaillard, Leo Watson, and Bam Brown.[32] Even if musicians were playing the game of eloquence and erudition, "they were also mocking the game and the rule-makers too, and mocking the whole idea of eloquence, the idea that words are anything but hypes and camouflage."[33]

Another important point along the continuum of scat is a fascination with what Robert O'Meally has called "mock-foreign language."[34] Mezzrow writes that in 1926, music lovers in Chicago were imitating the slips and phrases of "Heebie Jeebies" so much in everyday conversation that "Louis' recording almost drove the English language out of the Windy City for good."[35] But from the very beginnings of scat—performances such as Gene Green's imitation Chinese in the 1917 recording of "From Here to Shanghai"—the form was concerned with the representation of the foreign: alterity projected onto the level of linguistic impenetrability and absurdity. Here one notes an imposition of cultural and racial difference through a play that draws upon the phonetic contours of spoken language. The contortions of tunes like Cab Calloway's "Chinese Rhythm" from the mid-1930s were only a part of an industry of alterity in U.S. popular culture in the middle of the century, one that may not be unrelated in this respect to minstrelsy in the nineteenth century, which similarly drew on an imposed linguistic deformity (whether in the deliberately inscrutable orthography of dialect literature, or in the stereotyped conventions of minstrel show vocal delivery) to imply illiteracy and inarticulacy. Groups including Slim and Slam performed equal-opportunity scat reification, moving from the faux-Chinese of their "Chinatown, My Chinatown" (1938) to a pseudo-Yiddish in "Matzoh Balls" (1939) and even a vocalization of African barbarity called "African Jive" (1941).[36]

This mode of performing alterity in scat even becomes, at a number of signal moments, the arena in which disputes over the shape and development of the music are fought out. When Dizzy Gillespie was playing in Cab Calloway's band in the late 1930s, the trumpeter would chip away at the chord changes of Calloway's swing arrangements in his solos, experimenting with a proto-bebop melodic vocabulary. This fascinated some of the members of the band, particularly Milt Hinton and Danny Barker, but drove Cab Calloway crazy. Significantly, he conveyed his resistance to bop with an interesting figure of foreignness: "[Dizzy's] interpretation of jazz was originally wild. It was really wild, and it was something that I really had to get used to. I used to call him on it. I'd say, 'Man, listen, will you please don't be playing all that Chinese music up there!' "[37] It is a particularly odd objection for a musician who a few years earlier had been insisting in song that "you've got to have Chinese rhythm." Similarly, in 1949, faced with an interviewer fishing for controversy, Louis Armstrong explains his disdain of bebop by criticizing in particular the uncredited way that the younger musicians had appropriated scat, his own "invention" many years earlier. Pops recounts the anecdote about recording "Heebie Jeebies" in 1926, and adds indignantly: "But these bop cats act as though they'd invented scat singing. . . . I think they're trying to sound like Africans, don't you?"[38] In vocal expression in music, scat falls where language rustles with alterity, where the foreign runs in jive and the inside jargon goes in the garb of the outsider. But as the examples above demonstrate, the performance of difference in scat is by no means innocent; it is the very point at which the music polices the edges of its territory.[39]

Dropping Words

I want to return to the way the occasion of scat in Armstrong evokes a divorce between words and music. I'm wondering about the resonance of such a model in a broader trajectory of black expressive culture—and in the realm of literature in particular. Might one, for instance, read another originary text, W. E. B. Du Bois's 1903 *The Souls of Black Folk,* as precisely a theorization of the possibilities of such a fall, such a separation? The epigraphs to each chapter (one section of a European-language poem, one musical fragment of a spiritual, without the lyrics) formally stage a disjuncture of words and music, which is made most explicit in the book's last chapter, "The Sorrow Songs."[40] *Souls* predates jazz and Armstrong but announces a wider New World African concern with the relation between music and language as figuring cultural transport in diaspora. In that final chapter, as well as in each of his other autobiographical efforts,[41] Du Bois tells a tale about a music "far more ancient than the words," and about his own family's link to that unspeakable history. Du Bois's "grandfather's grandmother," he writes, "looked longingly at the hills, and often:

> crooned a heathen melody to the child between her knees, thus:
>
> Do ba-na co-ba, ge-ne me, ge-ne me!
> Do ba-na co-ba, ge-ne me, ge-ne me!
> Ben d'nu-li, nu-li, nu-li, nu-li, den d'le.

> The child sang it to his children and they to their children's children, and so two hundred years it has travelled down to us and we sing it to our children, knowing as little as our fathers what its words may mean, but knowing well the meaning of its music.[42]

For Du Bois it is precisely the incomprehension that compels a life-long search for identity and reconnection. As David Levering Lewis puts it, the lyric was "the earliest prompting of a very New England and supremely intellectual great-grandson to try to discern a few true notes of a remote, vestigial, and mysterious heritage."[43] The point isn't to find a source for the song, or its proper translation, I would argue; it is instead to recognize the way that the distance to a shared ancestral means of expression and genealogical ground is represented by the distance from those impenetrable phonemes to that music, "well understood." "Words and music have lost each other," Du Bois writes, and the listener must seek a message that is "naturally veiled and half articulate."[44] Such may be the condition of scat, and a condition of New World African expression in general.

I am shifting to this broader register in part because "Heebie Jeebies" is not only the origin of scat but might also be considered a story about the inception of what we call "jazz singing"—the "House That Satch Built" that is American popular culture. Combined with "Muskrat Rag," it was the first big hit of the Hot Fives, selling more than forty thousand copies in a matter of weeks, and it kicked off what many consider the most extraordinary creative period of any musician in this century. Louis did not simply invent a new style called scat, as Gary Giddins has pointed out: "he added scat's moans and riffs to the palette of conventional song interpretation, employing them to underscore emotion and rhythm and meaning."[45] Scat is sometimes a kind of instrumental technique in the Hot Fives and Hot Sevens, but more often it arises (or tumbles) out of Armstrong's singing voice; in classic cuts like "Lazy River," "All of Me," and "Stardust," scat originates in the way Armstrong fills the breaks between the lines of the lyric, accompanying himself with hornlike comments, and then allows the words of the song to bleed over into the commentary, mingling call-and-response in a voice that is not one voice, in a voice that seems haunted by another voice or voices, in "a sort of liquefying of words," as Zora Neale Hurston would put it.[46] Armstrong's vocal doubling, the peeling away from the lyrics through sung accompaniment, is rightfully termed an *obbligato,* because it would seem indispensable in this aesthetic.[47] As Mackey has argued more broadly, there is in jazz singing an obligatory splitting of sound, a "pursuit of another voice, an alternate voice," that is nothing if not compelling, in all the senses of the word.[48]

One might take up this compulsion in terms of the other sense of *scat*—a sense that we'd sometimes prefer to forget, but which may in fact be appropriate to Armstrong's aesthetic, at least. I'm thinking of the Greek derivation of the term, which connects it to words like *scatology.* The narrator at the opening of Wesley Brown's novel *Tragic Magic* espouses just this sense of *scat,* finding a link between black vernacular practice, jazz singing, and an excremental science:

> Scatology is a branch of science dealing with the diagnosis of dung and other excremental matters of state. Talking shit is a renegade form of scatology developed by people who were fed up with do-do dialogues and created a kind of vocal doodling that suggested other possibilities within the human voice beyond the same old shit.[49]

In the second half of his life, Armstrong was famously evangelical about the healing effects of a series of herbal laxatives that he tried to combine with various diets and regimens: Abelina water from Texas, then Pluto Water, and then Swiss Kriss, developed by the nutritionist guru Gayelord Hauser after World War II.[50] Armstrong sent out hundreds of copies of a diet, "Lose Weight the Satchmo Way," that he had concocted with his wife, Lucille, and was also known to send out a Christmas card with a photo of himself sitting on the toilet, grinning, his pants down, busy above the "Satchmo-Slogan": "Leave It All behind Ya."[51]

This obsession seems to have originated with Armstrong's mother, Mayann. Living in extreme poverty in New Orleans in the first decade of the last century, she developed an arsenal of homeopathic stratagems to keep her children healthy. In his autobiography, Armstrong writes: " 'A slight physic once or twice a week,' she used to say, 'will throw off many symptoms and germs that congregate from nowheres in your stomach. We can't afford no doctor for fifty cents or a dollar.' "[52] The version of this anecdote in Armstrong's manuscript for the book is more blunt, and bolder in proposing a connection between bowel movements, trumpet playing, and sexuality:

> She said—"Son—Always keep your bowels open, and nothing can harm you. . . . I remember what my mother said where ever or when ever somebody would die with gas or indigestion . . . And still uses the phrase—"They didn't shit enough". . . . it all derives—from negligence of the bowels. . . . I am about to be fifty nine years old . . . [. . .] And if I have to say it myself, I am blowing better and twice as strong as I was when I was in my twenties . . . Well I won't mention my sex sessions these days, because I hate to be called a braggadosha . . . Wow . . . Did that come outa Mee . . . [53]

In the final aside, in a characteristic self-disparaging move, an impressive example of Armstrong's vocabulary (verbal "blowing" inspired by his sexual prowess) garners the same surprised appreciation as a good shit: "Did that come outa Mee." In this complex metaphorical mix, the Armstrong scat aesthetic is equally a strategy of catharsis and physical (erotic) regulation. This is not at all the scatology of Luther ("spiritual enlightenment on a privy"), nor that of Freud (where character traits of "orderliness, parsimony, and obstinacy" are the results of the sublimation of infantile anal eroticism).[54] Nor, I think, is it the transgression and carnivalesque inversion of hierarchy, the "world turned upside down," envisioned in Rabelais. It is something more akin to James Joyce's identification of creativity with excretion—or as he calls it, "chamber music."[55] Armstrong too flirts with such a metaphorology, writing—and even singing at times—of the "music of Swiss Kriss." He commented in one letter to Joe Glaser (see Figures 1.1 and 1.2) that he was enclosing copies of the diet "that you can give to your fat friends . . . Especially those fat band buyers . . . They will gladly buy all of your bands . . . Because, after hearing so much music that they will make from the music of Swiss

HOLLYWOOD
DRAKE HOTEL

HOLLYWOOD AT McCADDEN
HOLLYWOOD 28, CALIFORNIA

September, 8th, 1955,

Dear Mr Glaser:

'Gee, I've been trying my damdest, to write to you and thank you for all the wonderfull things that you have done for your boy, Ol, Satchmo...And I want to thank you again an again... Believe me when I tell you, - you won,t ever regret it.... Lucille is happy...Very happy..And having a wonderfull time... And, you know-she,s ever so gratefull to you also.......I did the show with Gary Crosby, which will be broadcast this sunday...Seem,s like a very good show to me...I'm sure, you,ll catch it...The next day, which was thursday, we did the recording date at Decca, with the Benny Carter Arrangements...'Oh boy, but good... He made some very fine arrangements and we made some fine recordings...A very lovely date...Sonny Burke and all the Decca Ladds, were very much elated....'Yass They Were... Tomorrow, Gary Crosby and I will will have the whole afternoon to our selves.... I just know, - we,re going to really 'Whale'...

The people(my public) so thrilled to know,-'how'n' the hell did I lose ninety five pounds, and still blowing my horn every night...So, I thought it best, insted of explaining to every individual, - I made up this reducing chart, and handed them out to everyone who wishes,one, free of charge... I had a thousand copies made up...I kept five hundred here in California with me, and the other five hundred, I had, sent to our home in Corona...I thinking that I would need them...Huh, when Uncle Milty(Milton Berl) Gene Norman Helen Thompson(colored lady-Disc Jockey-of station K-F-O-X) finished talking about my chart, and the customers at the Crescendo, in Hollywood and the Macumbo in San Francisco,commenced asking for them, I began to think that I should have kept the other five hundred with me.Ha Ha.. You,d be surprised the way this chart is sweeping the country...

Here,s a couple that you can give to your fat friends.. Especially those fat band buyers...They will gladly, buy all of your bands..Because, after hearing so much music that they will make from the music of Swiss Kriss -- it will be a pleasure to them to hear a real live band, for a change.... We must keep these diet chart a rollin. Just think of the people who will be 'oh so happy to lose weight the Satchmo way... I soon will have to have a printer(a reasonable one ofcourse) who will keep things going...P.S. the greatest publicity in the world...Two thirds of the people in this world, die with locked

Figures 1.1 and 1.2 Louis Armstrong, letter to Joe Glaser, September 8, 1955, Music Division, Library of Congress.

Mr Glaser.

HOLLYWOOD

DRAKE HOTEL

2

HOLLYWOOD AT McCADDEN

HOLLYWOOD 28, CALIFORNIA

Bowels - or suffer with gas - and don,t know anything at all to do for them selves....Right?...Thats why I explained everything thoroughly... Ump..Didthat come outa mee??..... I can see you laughing,now... Ain,tcha glad' that you don,t have to use it?...So do your boy a favor and pass it around, wilya?....Doctor Schifft, got his, soo, Dr Gottlieb.. P.S. if you should get a little crowded with requests for my charts just let me know and I will mail to you, all you ask for....

Incase that you don,t knew it, - I had to have 'eight suits altered, since I have been playing at the Crescendo...I had to throw away, all of my jock straps - underwear - pajamas, etc, and replenish them all with size 'thirty twos,...Wow... I find, it,s so easy to live by this chart... The new Clarinet man arrived last night(thursday) ..He spent the night-out at the club with us.... You sure did send a good man this time... Yea-Edman Hall is one of the very best,there is, on the Clarinet... A man whom I've always admired as a great musician, from the very first time I heard him, until, this very day...I personaly,think that he will lift the band up a hundred percent...

So Dad, the old glimmers(my eyes) seem to be getting a little tired.. This dam Smog, has,nt helped them-any...Two or three days this week everybody,s been complaining about the Smog... One night at the Club- I had to play the whole night with my dark glasses on....They,re much better now...Then to--I had a busy day...So again - thanks for your wonderful kindness...I do hope that Moms(your dear mother)is having fun with the kids...Give my regards to the staff...Tell them, not to be bashfull...If they need to lose a little here an there, just step right up and let Doctor Satchmo-'lay one of these fine charts,on them... Nightie Night and -God Bless Ya....

Swiss Krissly,

Louis Armstrong

"Home of the London Grill and Hunt Room"

Kriss—it will be a pleasure to them to hear a real live band, for a change . . ."[56] The "Comments" to Armstrong's diet "Lose Weight the Satchmo Way" close with wordplay that equates aural attentiveness with open bowels: "P.S. When the Swiss Kriss Company gives me a radio show, my slogan will be—'Hello Everybody, this is Satchmo speaking for Swiss Kriss. Are you loosening???????' "[57]

In a poignant and rambling autobiographical narrative he wrote during a hospital stay near the end of his life, titled "Louis Armstrong + the Jewish Family in New Orleans, LA, the Year of 1907" (1969–1970), Armstrong gives the most extensive elaboration of this metaphor:

> My wife Lucille started me to taking Swiss Kriss. I came home one night as she was reading a book written by Dr. Gaylord Hauser, who introduced Swiss Kriss. Then when we were on our way to bed, she reached and open up her box of Swiss Kriss, took a teaspoonful, put it on her tongue dry, rinsed it down with water, settled into bed for the night, and went right off to sleep.
>
> Now I dugged her for a couple of nights. So the next day I went out and bought a box for myself. She took a teaspoonful. But with all the heavy food that I eat—I must take a little more than Lucille takes. So I took a tablespoonful of Swiss Kriss, rinsed it down off my tongue the same as Ceily (Lucille) did. It's so easy to take' I forgot that I had even taken it. It's nothing but Herbs. It said Herbal Laxative on the box anyway. I figured what she had takened had to be better than the mild Laxative that I've been taking which was pretty good but not strong enough for all of those Ham Hocks and Beans, Mustard Greens and Rice I had for Supper. It only made me sput like a Motor Boat. So I slept real peaceful with Swiss Kriss, well say' about five or six hours, which was fine. Then I awaken to a little rumble in my stomach, which was a warning—let's walk to the John. Hmm, I paid it no mind, and went back to Sleep, that is for a few minutes then a little Larger rumbling saying—"Swiss Kriss time, don't walk—Trot." And don't Stumble please. I was lucky enough though—I made it to the Throne in time. And All of a Sudden, music came—Riffs—Arpeggios—Biff notes—etc. Sounded just like

> ("Applause") Sousa's Band playing "Stars and Stripes Forever," returning to the Channel of the Song—Three Times. Wonderful.[58]

One shouldn't lose too easily the fact that this is a metaphor and not a homology. But if the figure describes the effects of the laxative, it also reflects on the status of music in Armstrong's aesthetics. A music where the action of words and music falling away from each other might best be described as a *release,* a sought-out condition of flow. An ethics of discard ("Leave It All behind Ya") that also provides the foundation for a poetics. This should make us hear that excursion in "Lazy River," where Pops explodes the lyrics with a glorious run of sixteenth notes (ending with a spoken aside, commenting on his own invention: "If I ain't riffin' this evening I hope something"), in a slightly different way. Novelist Ralph Ellison supposedly told Albert Murray, "Man, sometimes ole Louie shows his ass instead of his genius."[59] I'd put it rather differently, though. Sometimes it seemed that Armstrong thought his genius *was* his ass.[60]

Writing Scat

It is a commonplace for critics to write somewhat unthinkingly that Armstrong's trumpet playing is "like" his singing—as Hugues Panassié gushes, Louis "blows his horn exactly as he sings—and vice versa."[61] With the increasing availability of Armstrong's multifaceted written work, they also tend to claim that his writing is "like" his music. I have been drawing on the wealth of Armstrong's writing in part precisely to raise the question of the relationship between the forms of his creative expression. On what basis, if any, can one make these kinds of analogical claims?

Gary Giddins has rightfully termed Armstrong "by far the most expansive musician-writer jazz has ever known."[62] His correspondence alone is voluminous. Dan Morgenstern has wondered in print at Armstrong's remarkable precocity on the page, as well as on record:

> How, then, did this "uneducated" and "deprived" man come to be a writer, and a real one, with a clear and distinctive voice of

> his own? We know that Armstrong already owned a typewriter and knew how to use it when he first arrived in Chicago to join King Oliver's band—the climactic event in *Satchmo.* The earliest surviving typed letter by Armstrong I've seen is dated Sept. 1, 1922, and it contains complaints that three previous letters (one to the recipient, two to other friends) have gone unanswered.[63]

Armstrong wrote copiously and variously: not just letters, telegrams, and postcards to friends and acquaintances and fans, but also a number of articles and book reviews and two book-length autobiographies, as well as a number of unpublished and ephemeral documents found in his home in Queens, which included a wealth of other autobiographical material, transcribed jokes, isolated prose narratives, recipes, pornography, and song lyrics. He carried a typewriter, a dictionary, and a thesaurus with him on the road, and would often sit backstage in his bathrobe and hammer out two-fingered letters while surrounded by family, bandmates, friends, and admirers. A number of newspapers and jazz magazines published articles by Armstrong, especially in the 1940s and 1950s, and a number of them gave special attention to what Morgenstern terms Armstrong's "stylistic and linguistic idiosyncrasies"—in some cases going so far as to reproduce facsimiles of his original letters and handwritten manuscripts.[64]

Thomas Brothers, the editor of an invaluable collection of Armstrong's writings, notes a certain consistency of usage in Pop's "orthographic style": "For punctuation, Armstrong uses all of the standard symbols, but with only a few of them (period, question mark, exclamation mark, semicolon, and colon) does he limit himself to conventional practice." As Brothers points out, ellipses, dash, parentheses, comma, apostrophe, and double apostrophe are "all used inventively."[65] The parameters of this practice are apparent in a letter Armstrong wrote to Madeleine Berard in November 1946 (see Figure 1.3).[66] The first thing that sticks out is the epigraph, which Armstrong often cobbled into his letters. Often they were quick, lascivious double entendres. Another letter opens: "Said one strawberry to another-/If we hadn't been in the same bed-together/We wouldn't bee in this jam . . . /Tee Hee."[67] What is the status of this intruding stanza, which would seem to depart from the conventions of the epistolary genre? The strangeness of the syntax is striking, as well as the

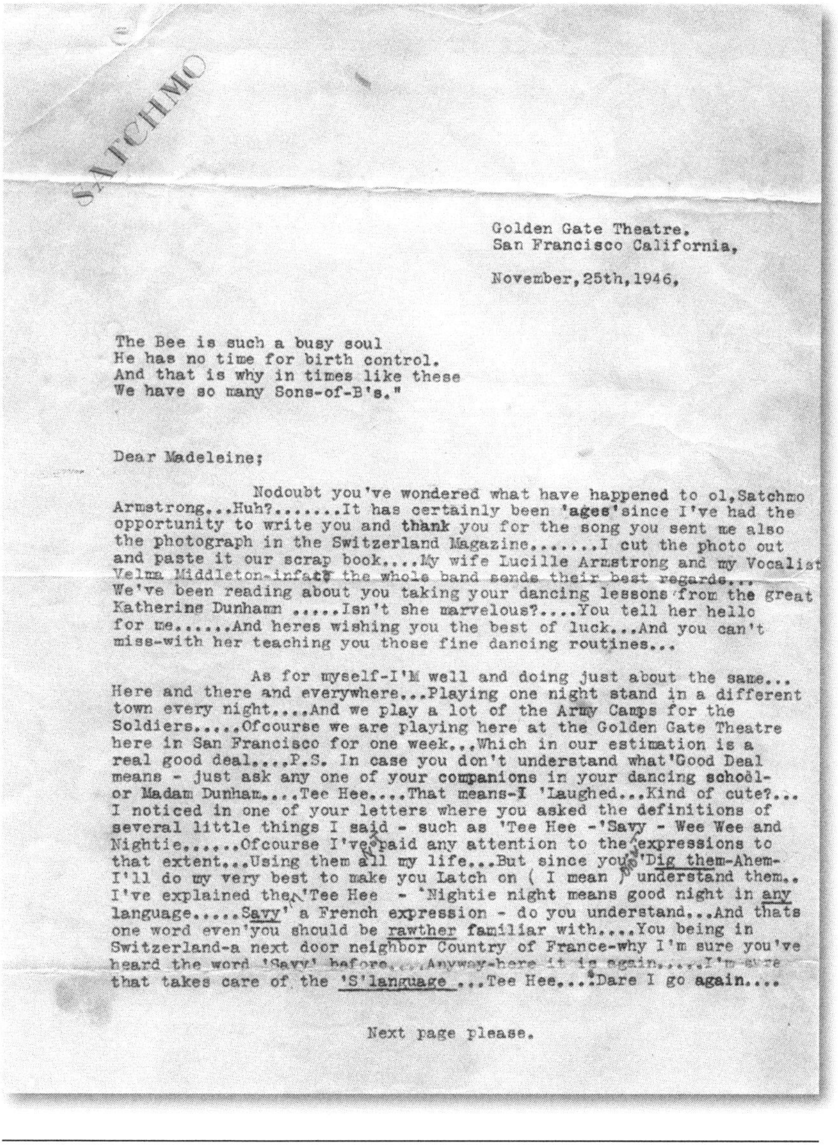

SATCHMO

Golden Gate Theatre.
San Francisco California,

November,25th,1946,

The Bee is such a busy soul
He has no time for birth control.
And that is why in times like these
We have so many Sons-of-B's."

Dear Madeleine;

Nodoubt you've wondered what have happened to ol,Satchmo Armstrong...Huh?.......It has certainly been 'ages'since I've had the opportunity to write you and thank you for the song you sent me also the photograph in the Switzerland Magazine.......I cut the photo out and paste it our scrap book....My wife Lucille Armstrong and my Vocalist Velma Middleton-infact the whole band sends their best regards... We've been reading about you taking your dancing lessons from the great Katherine Dunhamm .....Isn't she marvelous?....You tell her hello for me......And heres wishing you the best of luck...And you can't miss-with her teaching you those fine dancing routines..

As for myself-I'M well and doing just about the same... Here and there and everywhere...Playing one night stand in a different town every night....And we play a lot of the Army Camps for the Soldiers.....Ofcourse we are playing here at the Golden Gate Theatre here in San Francisco for one week...Which in our estimation is a real good deal....P.S. In case you don't understand what'Good Deal means - just ask any one of your companions in your dancing schoôl- or Madam Dunham....Tee Hee....That means-I 'Laughed...Kind of cute?... I noticed in one of your letters where you asked the definitions of several little things I said - such as 'Tee Hee -'Savy - Wee Wee and Nightie......Ofcourse I've paid any attention to the expressions to that extent...Using them all my life...But since you 'Dig them-Ahem- I'll do my very best to make you Latch on (I mean) understand them.. I've explained the 'Tee Hee - 'Nightie night means good night in any language.....Savy' a French expression - do you understand...And thats one word even'you should be rawther familiar with....You being in Switzerland-a next door neighbor Country of France-why I'm sure you've heard the word 'Savy' before.....Anyway-here it is again.....I'm sure that takes care of the 'S'language ...Tee Hee....Dare I go again....

Next page please.

Figure 1.3 Louis Armstrong, letter to Madeleine Berard, November 25, 1946, Louis Armstrong House and Archives at Queens College, City University of New York.

reliance on ellipses (of varying lengths) as the main mode of sentence stop. (Gary Giddins has offered the smart suggestion that this use of ellipses is itself a kind of convention, however: now somewhat archaic, it hearkens back to "the old Walter Winchell style" of journalism, evoking a sense of pace and interconnection meant to connote the informality—and inside scoops?—of a gossip column.[68]) The punctuation of the manuscripts is equally bizarre: Armstrong certainly uses apostrophes, but occasionally a comma will intrude in its place ("ol, Satchmo"). Pops underlines compulsively, and the use of single, double, and even triple apostrophes is not uncommon, sometimes just at the beginning of a word or phrase, sometimes just at the end.

One also notes a kind of multiplicity of register that structurally one might suggest functions like his sung obbligati to his own vocals in tunes like "Lazy River." The language peels away from itself, questioning, mocking its own pretensions, feigning incomprehension ("Huh?"), continually qualifying and breaking up its own assertions ("But since you didn't 'Dig them—ahem—I'll do my very best to make you Latch on (I mean) understand them"). This effect is also produced through an odd predilection for using postscripts in the middle of a text, even in the middle of a paragraph, often for definitional purposes ("P.S. In case you don't understand what 'Good Deal means—just ask any one of your companions in your dancing school—or Madame Dunham"; in another manuscript, Armstrong writes, "I kept saying to myself as I was getting dressed, putting on my old 'Roast Beef'—P.S. that was what we called an old ragged Tuxedo").[69] The letter often makes recourse to an oral orthography—representing speech patterns and accent through the ways the words are written down on the page. But this technique doesn't always pertain to the representation of hipster language or the black vernacular in particular. (Here, for instance, he affects a pseudo-British aristocratic "rather": "Savy' a French expression—do you understand . . . And thats one word even'you should be rawther familiar with. . . . You being in Switzerland—a next door neighbor Country of France.") And Armstrong relishes in a complex verbal play ("that takes care of the 'S'language . . . Tee Hee. . . . "Dare I go again. . . ."), which almost constitutes an immanent theory of his literary practice itself. "Slang" is both inside and outside conventional "language," marked off by an ambiguous set of apostrophes that also serves to indicate a neologism ("slanguage"). The two apostrophes before the last sentence have a similar multiple effect, appearing to note a citation of a commonplace phrase ("there I go again") as well as to draw attention to the way it is "played"—the initial consonant articulated at a slant, hardened so as to give it, too, another meaning ("dare I go again").

One of Armstrong's handwritten letters begins to theorize more explicitly his sense of typing practice, when he tells Joe Glaser that it is a pity that his typewriter is broken, since he had wanted "so badly to swing a lot of Type Writing, "Gappings' on ya"." The missive opens (see Figure 1.4):

> Dear Mr. Glaser"
>
> Am sorry that I have to write this letter with a pen, but, on arriving at the air port in Las Vegas yesterday, My typewriter fell from on top of all, that luggage that was one the truck, And the "Jolt"Sprung' everything. TCH, TCH, isn't it a Drag? And I wanted so badly to swing a lot of Type Writing, "Gappings' on ya" Of course, they're fixing it up for me. So, I Guess, that's all that matters.[70]

Brothers points out that "gappings" is slang for "salary," and later in the letter, Armstrong uses it this way himself in given instructions regarding his mistress (with whom he'd recently had a child): "Now here are the Bills as follows. I want you to see that Sweets + Baby' get one hundred per week—or you can send her, a month's gappings, now + pay her monthly." But it also may be a reference to the intervallic (keyboard) creativity of typewriting technology.[71] Pops wants in this sense not only to enter a certain economy of exchange, but also to appropriate a rational technology of the interval ("gappings"—in the sense that the typewriter structures and spatializes an access to language) from a particular, paradigmatically black aesthetic ("swing"). A few years later, Amiri Baraka would snarl that "a typewriter is corny," wishing for a romantic immediacy of expression that would bypass its technological interface.[72] But Armstrong, a bit like the poet Edward Kamau Brathwaite, seems to revel in appropriating of the technology of rationalization, finding the obligatory edges and gaps of the medium with humor and grace.[73]

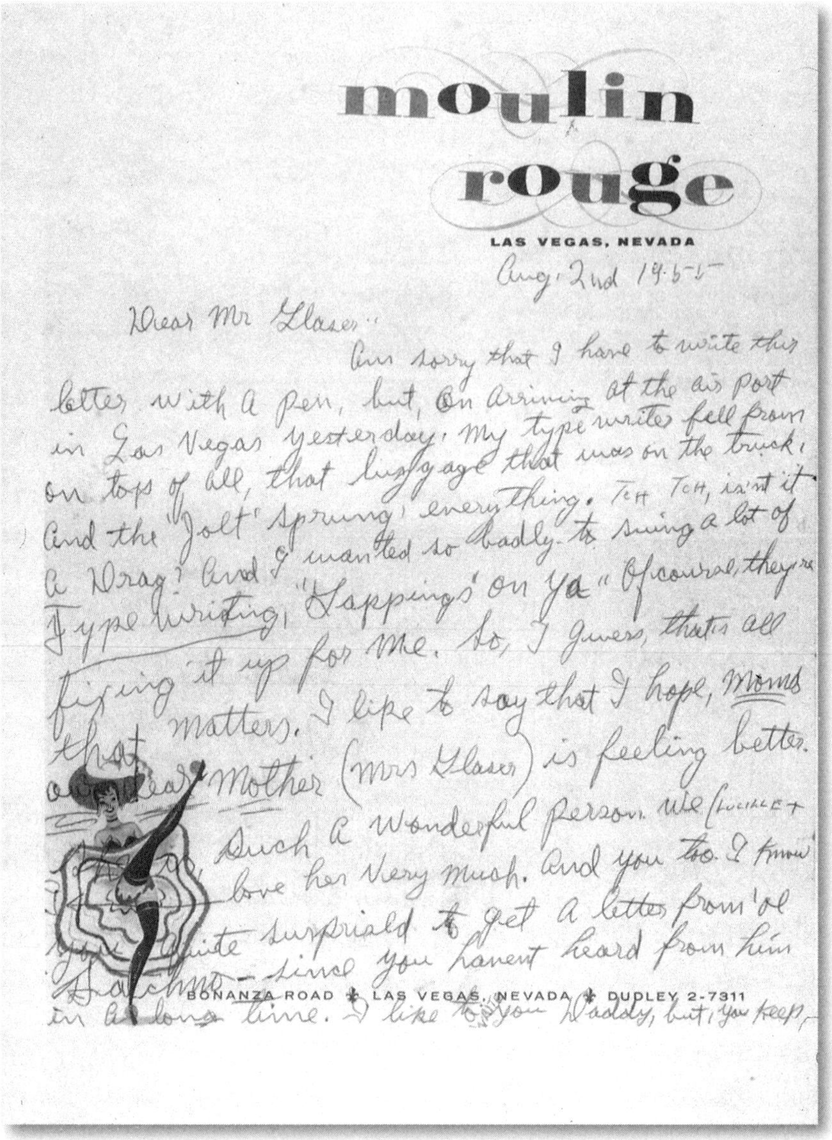

moulin rouge
LAS VEGAS, NEVADA

Aug. 2nd 1955

Dear Mr Glaser:
Am sorry that I have to write this letter with a pen, but, On Arriving at the air port in Las Vegas yesterday. My typewriter fell from on top of all, that luggage that was on the truck, And the "Jolt" sprung everything. Tch Tch, isn't it a Drag? And I wanted so badly to swing a lot of Type writing, "Lapping's on Ya." Of course, they're fixing it up for me. So, I guess, that's all that matters. I like to say that I hope, Moms a dear Mother (Mrs Glaser) is feeling better. Such a Wonderful person. We (Lucille + I) love her very much. And you too. I know you'll be quite surprised to get a letter from 'ol Satchmo—since you haven't heard from him in a long time. I like to [illegible] you Daddy, but, you keep,

BONANZA ROAD ⚜ LAS VEGAS, NEVADA ⚜ DUDLEY 2-7311

Figure 1.4 Louis Armstrong, letter to Joe Glaser, August 2, 1955, Music Division, Library of Congress.

Brothers usefully resists any impulse to read the complexity of Armstrong on the page as either illiteracy or "irony."[74] But then he suggests rather simplistically that the excessive graphicity of Armstrong's "gappings" are an "attempt to add Armstrong's *voice* to his words":

> The interpretation that seems to hold consistently is that Armstrong is interested in depicting an oral rendition of his prose; he offers not just written prose but his version of how to hear it. He is especially attentive to emphasis and pace. Given who he was as a musician, this is not surprising, for he was a great master of melodic nuance and rhythm.[75]

Brothers acquiesces to an easy literalism: for him, apostrophe and capitalization are employed not to convey "distance" or "irony" but "more simply, as a way to convey emphasis," and "the varied lengths of his ellipses, from standard three (sometimes two are used) to as many as fifteen, imply varied durations of pause."[76] Certainly, Armstrong plays on the page with conventions of representing orality, but can that play be reduced to a functional attempt to "depict" his own voice in a legible set of marks?

A literalist approach loses a sense of the peculiar status of Armstrong's writing, the diverse scenes and situations in which he wrote, and it would seem to abandon the issue of Armstrong's connection to his audience and correspondents, as well. But I am not even convinced that it suffices as an explanation of the formal elements of Pops's work on the page. The problem is that although the reader has a wealth of indices—an overflow of graphic marks and pointers that accompany the utterance—one has no access to a code, no means to decipher the shifting levels of those effects through interpretation. Brothers reproduces Armstrong's letter to Glaser in type, simply using italics every time Armstrong underlines (neglecting, in other words, the fact that in Armstrong's manuscripts, while some words are underlined once, others are triple and even quadruple underscored). The complexity of the writing is much better served with a facsimile (see Figure 1.5).

> Something else Black Benny said to me, Came true—>He said (TO ME) "DIPPER"' As long as you live, no matter where you

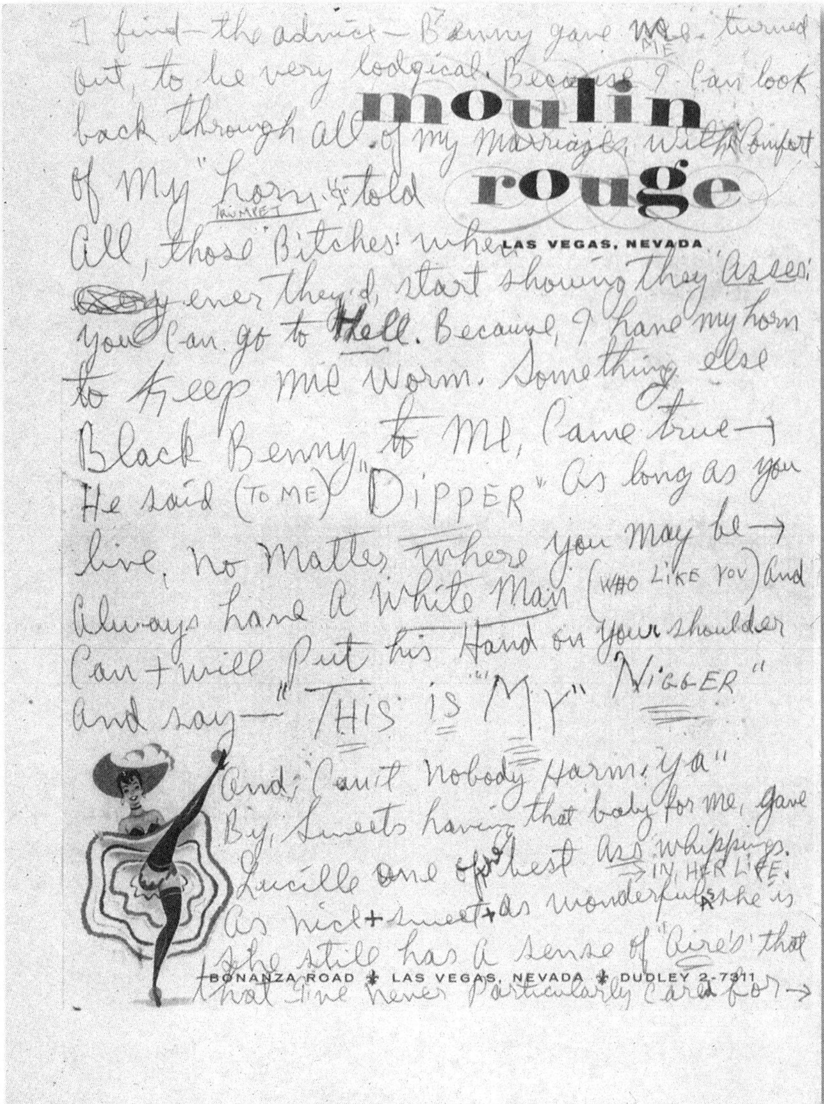

moulin
rouge
LAS VEGAS, NEVADA

I find the advice — Benny gave me — turned
out, to be very lodgical. Because I can look
back through all of my marriages with comfort
of my "horn" [TRUMPET] & told
All, those Bitches: whenever
they'd start showing they Asses;
you can go to Hell. Because, I have my horn
to keep me worm. Something else
Black Benny, to me, came true →
He said (TO ME) "DIPPER" As long as you
live, no matter where you may be →
always have a White Man (WHO LIKE YOU) and
can + will Put his Hand on your shoulder
and say — "THIS IS "MY" NIGGER"
And; Can't Nobody Harm; Ya"
By, Sweets having that baby for me, gave
Lucille one of the best Ass whippings IN HER LIFE.
As nice + sweet + as wonderful as she is
she still has a sense of "Aire's" that
that I've never particularly cared for →

BONANZA ROAD ✤ LAS VEGAS, NEVADA ✤ DUDLEY 2-7311

Figure 1.5 Louis Armstrong, letter to Joe Glaser, August 2, 1955, Music Division, Library of Congress.

> may be—>always have a White Man (WHO LIKE YOU) and Can+will put his Hand on your shoulder and say—"This is ""My" 'Nigger" and, Can't Nobody Harm' Ya."[77]

The passage is hard enough. Armstrong is recounting an anecdote about Black Benny, a gangster in New Orleans, who supposedly told him that it was all important in life to have a white patron or protector. Glaser, of course, is Armstrong's manager. How is he supposed to receive this passage? Or the ending of the letter, where after coursing through fourteen handwritten pages of disclaimers, confessionals, and monetary and logistical demands, the text closes obsequiously:

> I—JUST, Love, your, Checks, in, My POCKETS—"OH" They look so pretty, until, I hate like hell to cash them. Honest to God, I usually keep them as long as I possibly Can. But Suddenly, some Situation raise its "UGLY HEAD." And "bye 'bye Joe Glaser's' signature. "HM . . . It has been such a real Pleasure writing to you, Boss. Hope, I didn't bore you.[78]

Do the apostrophes and underlining, the various manipulations of capitalization and punctuation, aid the reader in comprehending the valence of these words? How would one quantify or measure such an interpretative effect, as Brothers seems to want to do? How does one read (how does one hear Armstrong's "voice" in) a word written surrounded by two quote marks on one side, and three on the other? Is a word underlined four times and surrounded by one single quote and one double quote being given more or less emphasis than a word underlined four times and framed by four apostrophes? Armstrong sometimes went back over his typed letters, correcting spelling and adding words inadvertently left out—but he often also threw in a number of handwritten apostrophes, still adhering to his strange, off-kilter practice. Particularly in the handwritten letters, the exuberance of Armstrong's graphicity makes one wonder whether it should be considered—as Jed Rasula has suggested with regard to the diacritical markings in Gerard Manley Hopkins's poetry manuscripts—as a "visual supplement rather than aural cue."[79] The graphic accompaniment in the manuscripts doesn't clarify the writing, in other words. Instead it actually makes them more daunting, giving too much indexical information, pointing in too many directions at once, invading the spaces between words with a thicket of punctuation that threatens to become impenetrable. The letter does not simply express irony, certainly; but neither does it simply transcribe Armstrong's "voice," unless *voice* is taken as another word for such deictic overabundance. It may do all these things and more—and that *excess* of signification may be precisely the effect of Armstrong's writing.

It is thus not sufficient to proclaim that "Armstrong wrote by ear," as Albert Murray does in a review of the Brothers collection, before launching into what is—for one of the great defenders of Armstrong's music—an astoundingly prissy defense of literary standards. Murray excoriates the "illiterate imprecision" of Armstrong's letters and manuscripts, calling them "embarrassingly corny." He adds cruelly (this about an autodidact who had never regularly attended school): "there is very little evidence in any of his published writings that he ever grasped, say, a junior high school–level of competence in the fundamentals of grammar, syntax, and meaning."[80] One might counter with Gary Giddins that "most of his writing was not intended for public scrutiny in his lifetime,"[81] and at least make an effort to come to terms with the formal peculiarity of a personal letter or private narrative. But I wonder if one cannot make a more complex argument about the workings of all of Armstrong's writing (even the manuscripts prepared for publication), specifically in their relation to music.

Giddins's protestation is inadequate, in the end, if only because Armstrong (who not only wrote but also made hundreds of reel-to-reel tapes of recitations and performances and backstage bull sessions, and then painstakingly decorated the tape boxes with elaborate collages and drawings) is so clearly a *self-archivist,* obsessed with recording technology of every sort. How does one theorize such a long-standing, deliberate practice of archivization, which aims at posterity even if the recordings are not immediately destined for public consumption? (One imagines that the very intimacy of this archiving practice would be all important for a public figure who was so extensively commercially recorded and disseminated.) Just in terms of the formalism of the manuscripts, why would Armstrong's use of ellipses, for instance, somehow be necessarily less complex than Emily Dickinson's dashes, or Amiri Baraka's open-ended parentheses? Is it possible to read Armstrong's expression in writing while respecting its ambiguity and experimentation, without reducing it *either* to an inanity (a lack of instruction) *or* to a simple functionalism (the representation of orality)?

Scat Aesthetics

I will close by suggesting one way of theorizing what Duke Ellington would call a "parallel" between the forms of Armstrong's performance. Gary Giddins's work on Armstrong has stressed the impossibility of "separating the exalted musician from Armstrong the impish stage wag," and warned of the perils of "underestimating the absurdist humor that informs [Armstrong's] genius." Giddins turns our attention not just to Armstrong's musical creativity but also to his physical presence, specifically his repertoire of wry and insinuating gesture in performances on film.[82] In the early short *Rhapsody in Black and Blue* (1932), a die-hard fan who's been conked unconscious by his wife (she is furious that he sits around listening to jazz records all day) dreams he is the "King of Jazzmania," sitting on his throne, treated to a command performance by Louis Armstrong. Draped in a ludicrous leopard skin, carrying a handkerchief, and standing up to his ankles in soap bubbles, Armstrong plays and sings "(I'll Be Glad When You're Dead) You Rascal You" and "Shine," with his orchestra behind him in attire that seems designed to connote an oddly regal primitivism. Describing the physicality of Armstrong's performance in films such as *Rhapsody* and in concert footage (including a remarkable 1933 date in Denmark where he performs "Dinah"), Giddins writes that Armstrong's "mugging is so much a part of his performances that it is impossible for anyone who has seen him to listen to his records without imagining his facial contortions. Even when he delivered himself of a ballad, he had an array of expressions—half smiles, a trembling of the lips, a widening of the eyes, a scrunching of the nose—that fit the notes and underscored the lyric. Mugging was a kind of body English done with the face; it was a way of acting out the music."[83]

Giddins contends that Armstrong in *Rhapsody in Black and Blue* "transcends the racist trappings by his indifference to every sling and arrow. The director / writer is trying to tell the audience one thing. Armstrong is telling it something entirely different—he's doing it not only with the magnificence of his music, but with his physical muscularity, his carriage, his boding sexuality . . . the look in his eye."[84] Or as Giddins puts it earlier, "Genius is the transfiguring agent."[85] The reading turns in part on the common assumption that Armstrong "becomes a different man" when he starts playing the trumpet, when he stops mugging and gets down to business.[86] The implication is that his trumpet playing somehow "trumps" his problematic vocal clowning, and even that Armstrong's instrumental performance reasserts a sexual prowess and "masculinity" that is somehow undermined or threatened by his singing.

But is it possible to read this scene in terms of "transcendence"? Does one really forget or forgive the leopard skin, the handkerchief, the bugged eyes, the grin, the gaping "Satchel Mouth," the soap bubbles, the lyrics ("I take troubles all with a smile . . . that's why they call me Shine") as soon as Pops picks up the horn? Or is Armstrong's "absurdist humor" ultimately a tricky willingness to inhabit all these trappings and more? He is the grotesque jester who preens and gapes, disturbing in his willingness to echo the melodramatic performance styles of minstrelsy. He is also the self-assured modernist, who negotiates the trumpet parts with brilliant technique, and injects self-reflexive commentary into his vocal performance, as well. (In one spoken aside during "You Rascal You," he tosses a line that slyly equates sexual contest with an access to recording technology: "You gave my wife a bottle of Coca-Cola so you could play on her Victrola.") Moreover, Armstrong's mugging might not be simply "a way of acting out the music." What's striking about his movement is that he's acting out so much *more* than what's in the music: facial contortions, chest convulsions, head nods, even mouth movements, shadow pronunciations that don't correspond to any discernible development in the production of sound. This is not at all "body English" or direct address; instead one sees a spectral presence that seems to jerk and twitch and bulge in the somatic excess of that body. That excess outlines other possibilities, not taken, not voiced. There is no transcendence here; all these elements (at the very least), all these implications *coexist* in the performance, which is driven throughout by what Giddins more usefully terms Armstrong's "beguiling knowledge of the anomalous."[87] The effect forces the viewer to confront a swinging incommensurability—an untamable, prancing set of contradictory indices that seem to be saying all too much at once.

This deictic complexity is not unique to Armstrong; indeed, it is a key component in black traditions of musical performance. In one section of Nathaniel Mackey's epistolary fiction, N. describes going to see a Betty Carter concert. He's struck by the visual component of the performance, the "facial teasing" the singer applies to her songs, "the discrepant play of her precise, near parsimonious delivery against the facial extravagance it's accompanied by."[88] Carter dances around the song, past the song, her body seeming to produce—to "ventriloquize," N. writes—"a 'voice' one synaesthetically 'saw,' a 'voice' which was not the voice one in fact heard."[89] N.'s friend Lambert suggests that this confusion, the "furtiveness of source" of Carter's voice, actually is geared to give a "utopian foretaste of sourcelessness": the appearance of pure sound beyond the particular subject, beyond the particular vocal instrument. But that "foretaste," he adds, is continually "haunted" by "historical debris," particularly a "history of would-be sources which [are] really subversions, a history it propose[s] an 'unsourced' exit from." Sources that would presume to explain, to delimit, the genesis of that voice. The most obvious example, for Lambert, is minstrelsy, the "historical debris" of distorting stereotypes of the black body in performance. So Carter's facial extravagance "revels in distortion to show that it's wise to distortion, immune to presumed equivalence." (Of course, one would have to consider a whole range of "historical debris" beyond minstrelsy: gender and sexuality, for example. In one interview, Carter talks about this disjuncture in terms that make it clear that gender stereotypes were equally formidable barriers, saying that her physical beauty was "a handicap and also an asset because if an audience looks at a figure first and then you get them quiet enough to listen to the singing, then you have really done something. . . . In the Apollo I would be about eight bars into my tune before anyone realized I was singing. [The comedian] Redd Foxx used to say to me that it was a whole year before he realized I could sing."[90]) It's important to note the terms with which N.

describes Carter's furtive voice, its "elusiveness of source which created an illusion of sourcelessness." "It was eerie," he writes. That is, it gives him the heebie-jeebies.

Scat aesthetics distends an expressive medium through the proliferation of index. This is a structural effect, and thus one that can be applied as readily to a linguistic medium as to one like music, which signifies as expressive potentiality, articulating a syntax where in Billie Holiday's phrase the "meaning seems to change." Scat works the "accompaniments of the utterance" in a given medium: in song, the vocal play that liquefies words; in performance, the excessive, oblique physicality of mugging; in writing, the overgrowth of punctuation, self-interruptions, asides, that exceed the purposes of emphasis, intonation, and citation.[91] Inarticulacy is telling because the proliferation of index points at—structurally suggests—an expressive syntax that is unavailable but inferred through its "accompaniments." Scat aesthetics thus involves an augmentation of expressive potential, rather than an evacuation or a reduction of signification. Words drop away from music so that "the unheard sounds [come] through."[92] The syntax of scat points at something outside the sayable, something seen where it collapses.

two
Toward a Poetics of Transcription: James Weldon Johnson's Prefaces

Ralph Ellison's 1945 *Antioch Review* essay on Richard Wright's autobiography *Black Boy* famously hinges on a compelling definition of the blues. Even if one can cite a number of "literary guides" that may have influenced Wright's work, Ellison writes, still the driving force in the "immediate folk culture" of Wright's early life was not literature but instead a "folk-art form": the "Negro blues." The blues, Ellison explains,

> is an impulse to keep the painful details and episodes of a brutal experience alive in one's aching consciousness, to finger its jagged grain, and to transcend it, not by the consolation of philosophy but by squeezing from it a near-tragic, near-comic lyricism. As a form, the blues is an autobiographical chronicle of personal catastrophe expressed lyrically.[1]

Ellison defines the blues as a kind of compulsion to record, to hold on to "the painful details and episodes of a brutal experience," and moreover to prolong or revisit that experience, not just as an inert memory but instead as an ongoing ("aching") mode of contemplation in which pain remains throbbingly "alive" in the individual consciousness. Given Ellison's deep engagement with African American music and his early training as a trumpeter,[2] the definition might seem strikingly distant from any sense of the blues as a musical form. If Ellison does not go quite so far as James Baldwin would two decades later—Baldwin opens his own powerful commentary on the mix of "anguish" and "passionate detachment" in the blues by stressing that he is not writing about music ("I don't know anything about music") but about the "state of being" out of which the music comes—still Ellison's definition seems more concerned with the blues as ethos than with the blues as musical performance.[3] Thus he suggests it is above all a matter of a certain type of atmosphere—"blues-tempered echoes of railroad trains, the names of Southern towns and cities, estrangements, fights and flights, deaths and disappointments, charged with physical and spiritual hungers and pain"—even as he compares Wright's book to a "blues sung by such an artist as Bessie Smith" because of the way "its lyrical prose evokes the paradoxical, almost surreal image of a black boy singing lustily as he probes his own grievous wound."[4]

While there are many things to say about Ellison's definition, here I want to linger with the word that he uses three times in the space of a single page: *lyric*. If on the most fundamental level *lyric* is a literary term that signals a certain musicality or suggests a mode of writing informed by, imbued with, or redolent of the ephemerality and affective force of musical performance,[5] then we might well wonder what it means for Ellison to insist (in a seeming tautology) on the lyricism of a writing defined by its constitutive relationship to the lyricism of the blues.

While some of the commentators engaged in contemporary debates around the viability of *lyric* as a term of literary criticism have suggested usefully that we should consider a much broader range of musical performance in evaluating the "musicality" of literature, it is remarkable how seldom African diasporic literature is taken up in discussions of the "new lyric studies."[6] If the question of music is indeed central to defining the lyric, one might have expected on the contrary that black literature would be indispensable in the discussion, given the degree to which it emerges out of a complex engagement with vernacular expression in general and music in particular. One way to approach the issue is to reject it: thus, in a 1930 essay, the great African American vernacular poet Sterling Brown simply obliterates the distinction between oral, musical, and literary forms: "It seems to be the history of lyric poetry, however (and the Blues, unlike most folk poetry, are lyric), that it is generally the lover or lady *in absentia* who calls out poetry. This is true of the Blues."[7] Although I return to Brown's point about the role of absence and indirection in the blues,[8] I prefer to hold open the question of the relation between music and literature, because it seems to me that—as an open question, and then as a problematic—it is one of the driving forces in the modernist movement of the Harlem Renaissance in the 1920s, when a generation of African American writers confronted the implications of folk and popular musical forms (which, as the recording industry and radio exploded into prominence, came to seem to define the very meaning of modernity) as problems of their *literary* practice.[9]

One thinks immediately of touchstones of the Harlem Renaissance, such as James Weldon Johnson's pronouncement in the preface to the 1922 *Book of American Negro Poetry* that "Negro folk songs constitute a vast mine of material," as well as his update in the expanded 1931 edition of the anthology that younger black writers including Brown and Langston Hughes had found in the blues, ballads, and work songs "unfailing sources of material for authentic poetry."[10] In "The Negro Artist and the Racial Mountain," his own well-known 1926 manifesto published in the *Nation,* Hughes argues that black culture provides the writer with "a great field of unused material ready for his art," and that in many of his own poems he is trying "to grasp and hold some of the meanings and rhythms of jazz."[11] Approached through such references, the question of the inherently "musicality" of the lyric amounts to a question of practice. What, indeed, does it mean for a poem "to grasp and hold some of the meanings and rhythms of jazz"?

In 1950 the Objectivist poet Louis Zukofsky penned a brief statement on poetics in which he formulated his dictum that poetry is "an order of words that . . . approaches in varying degrees the wordless art of music as a kind of mathematical limit."[12] Put in these terms, the question then is: what does it mean to "approach music"? Zukofsky specifies that when he defines a poem as a "context associated with a 'musical' shape," the word *musical* must be placed in quotation marks "since it is not of notes as music, but of words more variable than variables, and used outside as well as within the context with communicative reference."[13] The paradox is that there is a pronounced difference in the *matter* in-formed in poetry, on the one hand (written language), and in music, on the other (sound). The statement is possible, though, because the *form* of a poem (discernable in characteristics like stanza structure, line, spacing, punctuation, meter, rhyme, typography, orthography, and semantics) is able to imply or reflect the *form* of a particular music. To return to Zukofsky's terms: words are used "outside the context of communicative reference" to suggest a " 'musical' shape." This is to frame the problem of approaching music as one of pseudomorphosis: strategies employed to make literature mold the materials native to its medium (words set on the page) in imitation of the "shape" of music in the medium of sound.

The Form of Things Unknown

As Kimberly Benston has pointed out, African American cultural criticism has too often preempted the role of form in cultural production, either measuring works against some supposedly "universal" aesthetic form, or measuring them in terms of some supposedly "external" (in other words, not performed in the rhetoric or structure of the work itself) notion of blackness.[14] But form is neither universal nor abstractly "racial." In the lucid definition offered by Caroline Levine, form "always indicates an arrangement of elements—an ordering, patterning, or shaping."[15] To speak of *content* is simply to identify the way matter is realized by form, or by an overlapping and intersecting network of forms. There is no "pure" matter that would somehow be outside form, or without form. But form is a principle independent of matter, that can channel or alter the form of that matter—and that effect is content.[16] "I don't really concern myself too much about form," the pianist Cecil Taylor once told an interviewer. "And the reason I don't is because I know it's there."[17] In music, Taylor has observed, "if a man plays for a certain amount of time—scales, licks, what have you—eventually a kind of order asserts itself. . . . There is no music without order—if that music comes from a man's innards. But that order is not necessarily related to any single criterion of what order should be as imposed from the outside."[18]

Critics have tended to read the issue of dialect in black poetry as solely an ideological one. But in fact, as Eric Sundquist has pointed out, dialect is an issue of form, as well: it is an orthographical technique by which written language represents oral language.[19] Yet in poetic criticism, an attention to form has been largely lacking: thus for example, Sherley Anne Williams, in a generally excellent analysis of the parameters of the "blues poem," writes of "techniques of Afro-American speech and singing that have been carried over virtually unchanged into Afro-American poetry."[20] She goes on to the somewhat mystifying claim that by "transforming" elements of the "classic blues form," blues poetry "function[s] in much the same way as blues forms once functioned within the black community."[21] Even putting aside the question of exactly how blues poetry functions or functioned in "the black community," the problem raised here is one of determining just how such a "transformation" might take place in a given work.

Perhaps the most ambitious theoretical effort in the field of form and black aesthetics is Stephen Henderson's "The Forms of Things Unknown," the introduction to his groundbreaking anthology *Understanding the New Black Poetry.* In a section entitled "Structure," which Henry Louis Gates Jr. has described as at once the "most promising" and the "most disappointing" of Henderson's poetic categories,[22] Henderson attempts to come to terms with such issues, relying alternately on a version of reader-response criticism (the black reader supplements the "saturated" blues data of the poetic form by imagining the musical and performative context) and on Larry Neal's concept of the "destruction of the text" (the poem is simply a "score" to be realized) to argue that the difference between "singing Black songs and reading Black poems" is "merely academic."[23] However, the argument collapses into a claim more about *style* than about *form:* when Henderson suggests that "there is a Black poetic mechanism, much like the musical ones, which can transform even a Shakespearean sonnet into a jazz poem," he is writing less about composition than about realization (thus he says that the "Black poetic mechanism" is "improvisation," in a *performance* of the sonnet).

Of the writers associated with the Harlem Renaissance, Langston Hughes, Sterling Brown, and Zora Neale Hurston are usually and rightfully given the most credit for their groundbreaking literary experiments in capturing vernacular form. In this chapter, however, I want to return to the essays and poems of James Weldon Johnson. Johnson is still commonly portrayed as a stilted aesthetic aristocrat who, in his preface to the 1922 *Book of American Negro Poetry,* declared "Negro dialect" to be defunct as a representational strategy—as "an instrument with but two full stops, humor and pathos"[24]—and who was soon proven wrong by the eruption of literature employing versions of African American dialect in the latter half of the 1920s. This simplistic critique does not catch the true emphasis of Johnson's argument in the preface: he argues explicitly that the younger poets are "trying to break away from, not Negro dialect itself, but the limitations on Negro dialect imposed by the fixing effects of long convention."[25] Nor does it come to terms with Johnson's active promotion of the dialect poetry of Hughes, Brown, and Claude McKay. Johnson includes work by Hughes and Brown in the second edition of the *Book of American Negro Poetry* (1931), and even in the original 1922 version Johnson includes "Two an' Six," a selection from McKay's early Jamaican dialect verse.

In the preface to the 1931 edition of the anthology, even as he praises the work of Hughes and Brown, Johnson notes that (years before Hughes and Brown began to publish) he himself "did a similar thing" in his own attempts to write poetry based on "the genuine folk stuff that clings around the old-time Negro preacher," verses collected in his 1927 book *God's Trombones.*[26] Even more significant, I suggest, are Johnson's prefaces to the two best-selling volumes of *The Books of American Negro Spirituals,* which he edited with his brother, J. Rosamond Johnson, for in them Johnson is confronted head-on with the problem of *transcription:* that is, with the problem of how to *write music.*[27] What is the best way, he wonders, to capture in standard written notation—in the anthologies, the arrangements by J. Rosamond Johnson and Lawrence Brown offer spirituals in a form appropriate to the bourgeois parlor: vocal lines set to piano accompaniment—a music that had been celebrated for its improvisatory qualities, its emergence far from the conservatory, and even for its resistance to being rendered in the vocabulary of diatonic harmony? James Weldon Johnson's struggles with this problem, I will suggest, are not solely theoretical, but also writerly. It is often overlooked that Johnson's contribution to the *Book of American Negro Spirituals* is an ambitious *literary* project: as he notes, he carefully composes the lyrics to the spirituals in dialect, attempting to avoid the "unintelligible," "clumsy, outlandish, so-called phonetic spelling" which had characterized too much writing in that mode (BANS I 42–46). And as I suggest, Johnson's struggles with the poetics of transcription involve not only the lyrics of the spirituals in the anthology but also the very form of his own preface.[28]

The blues poems and jazz poems that Hughes and Brown begin to write in the mid- to late 1920s are likewise characterized by a struggle with the poetics of transcription. Hughes's "The Weary Blues" and Brown's "Ma Rainey," arguably the two most celebrated early examples of the "blues poem"—I put the term in scare quotes as a reminder that, in this period, the "blues poem" is by no means a recognized subgenre, but instead an area of literary experimentation in open concert with a brand of commercial music many viewed as licentious or degenerate[29]—both include stanzas transcribing a set of sung blues lyrics, indented and identified as such by quotation marks. While the speaker in Hughes's poem cites lines performed "in a deep song voice with a melancholy tone" by a "Negro" accompanying himself on a piano in a Harlem nightspot ("I got the Weary Blues / And I can't be satisfied"), the speaker in Brown's "Ma Rainey" quotes the haunting lyrics of "Backwater Blues," about the devastating effects of the Great Mississippi Flood of 1927 *(" 'It rained fo' days an' de skies was dark as night, / Trouble taken place in de lowlands at night.").*[30] With their speakers entranced by the music they hear, both poems can be interpreted as allegories for the literary endeavor to *write* the blues: in different ways, they each dramatize the effort by a figure at some distance from a blues performance culture to enter the intimacy of that social space and to find a way to convey its power in words.

"The Weary Blues" is characterized by a pronounced awkwardness, with clunky end rhymes ("stool" / "fool"; "tune" / "moon"; "bed" / "head" / "dead") and a series of mistimed exclamations ("O Blues!") seeming to suggest the speaker's not entirely successful attempt to imitate the infectious rhythmic drive of the blues he is listening to. Brown's poem, on the other hand, is framed almost as a subtle ethnographic undertaking, progressing in its four sections from a general observation on Ma Rainey's fame in the entire Mississippi Delta region ("Folks from anyplace / Miles aroun' ") to a recounting of the unique bond between singer and audience at a particular performance. Even here, the poem emphasizes its distance from the culture it is documenting: the speaker does not describe Ma Rainey himself, but instead interviews a member of the community who has heard her:

> I talked to a fellow, an' the fellow say,
> "She jes' catch hold of us, somekindaway.
> She sang Backwater Blues one day:
>   *'It rained fo' days an' de skies was dark as night,*
>   *Trouble taken place in de lowlands at night.*

> *'Thundered an' lightened an' the storm begin to roll*
> *Thousan's of people ain't got no place to go.*
>
> *'Den I went an' stood upon some high ol' lonesome hill,*
> *An' looked down on the place where I used to live.'*
>
> An' den de folks, dey natchally bowed dey heads an' cried,
> Bowed dey heavy heads, shet dey moufs up tight an' cried,
> An' Ma lef' de stage, an' followed some de folks outside."[31]

If in the end "Ma Rainey" can do no more than testify (or report an informant's testimony) to the connection between itinerant performer and local black community—the poem concludes by reiterating the singer's "hold" on her audience, which cannot be summed up or explained in any more specific terms: "Dere wasn't much more de fellow say: / She jes' gits hold of us dataway."—nonetheless it suggests that her fame is less a matter of individual charisma than a therapeutic communal demand for a representative figure to give voice to a shared "brutal experience." The penultimate section takes the form of a sort of song in the first person plural, the incantory expression of that demand:

> O Ma Rainey,
> Sing yo' song;
> Now you's back
> Whah you belong,
> Git way inside us,
> Keep us strong. . . .
>
> O Ma Rainey,
> Li'l an' low;
> Sing us 'bout de hard luck
> Roun' our do';
> Sing us 'bout de lonesome road
> We mus' go. . . .[32]

In this way, Brown's poem might be said to capture that strange tautology at work in Ralph Ellison's definition of the blues, in which one lyricism seems to call out to or solicit another lyricism.

If key "blues poems" by both Hughes and Brown are thus experiments with a poetics of transcription, they might be said to take up and extend strategies that Johnson, more than any other figure associated with the Harlem Renaissance, had first articulated in his prefaces and poetry. In 1926, in the preface to the second volume of the *Book of American Negro Spirituals,* Johnson makes a rather extraordinary claim:

> The recent emergence of a younger group of Negro artists, preponderantly literary, zealous to be racial, or to put it better, determined to be true to themselves, to look for their art material within rather than without, got its first impulse, I believe, from the new evaluation of the Spirituals reached by the Negro himself. (BANS II 19)

In what is barely concealed self-congratulation, Johnson places his own work as a collector of vernacular spirituals at the vanguard of the emerging *literary* approach to the vernacular of writers such as Hughes, Brown, and Hurston. To come to terms with the depth of Johnson's theoretical work on the issue of transcribing vernacular form, then, it is necessary to read Johnson's prefaces in more detail.

The Politics of Transcription

It should be noted that the *Books of American Negro Spirituals* do not represent a significant advance in the debate around the Negro spirituals then raging among critics. As Johnson himself repeatedly notes (BANS I 14, 23, 48), his argument that the spirituals are original products of the Negro, and moreover an example of an African survival, is largely influenced by the groundbreaking work of Krehbiel, and later Curtis-Burlin.[33] The *American Negro Spirituals* collections were celebrated, though, not only because they were published with a major press, close on the heels of Johnson's 1922 *Book of American Negro Poetry,* or because the musical arrangements by J. Rosamond Johnson and Lawrence Brown are of such high quality, but also because their success is rooted in the authority of Johnson's prefaces as a major intervention in the drive to document black modern cultural achievement.

As in Johnson's 1912 novel, *The Autobiography of an Ex-Colored Man,* however, the ultimate aim here is not sociological or musicological, despite the categorical and documentary claims Johnson makes at times. Even as the prefaces argue powerfully that "the Spirituals possess the fundamental characteristics of African music" (BANS I 19), and moreover present a continuum among the modes of black popular expressive culture, from the spirituals, to secular music (30–31), to work songs and shouts (32–33), to dancing (BANS II 16) and the blues (20), they do not strive to prove some simple empirical connection between African and African American music. Throughout this process of connection and differentiation, Johnson carefully employs a complex series of metaphors so as to complicate any seeming filiation into a relationship more—as he puts it—"subtle and elusive" (BANS I 29). Johnson repeatedly writes of the "body of the Spirituals," for instance (see BANS I 12, 15), and then extends this metaphor: "It was by sheer spiritual forces that African chants were metaphorphosed into the Spirituals; that upon the fundamental throb of African rhythms were reared those reaches of melody that rise above earth and soar into the pure, ethereal blue" (21). If the spirituals are an African body, Johnson implies, then that body has somewhere, somehow undergone a miraculous transformation.

Johnson insists that the transcriptions of the spirituals in the *Book of American Negro Spirituals* are "true" to the *form* of that music: "No changes have been made in the form of songs," he claims, even when harmonizations have been "developed" (BANS I 50). He describes that form as an inherently cross-cultural or syncretic one, supporting the argument in favor of African retentions in the spirituals, but refusing to underestimate the European influence: "there was blown through or fused into the vestiges of his African music the spirit of Christianity as he knew Christianity. . . . It was by sheer spiritual forces that African chants were metamorphosed into the Spirituals" (20–21). The shape change at the origin of the spirituals is left vague here; either the Christian influence "blows" a kind of vitality into the seemingly passive primary material of the "African vestiges," or the two are "fused," or there is a unspecified "spiritual" agency that brings about a transformation. Although authorship is granted without reserve to "unknown black bards"—and this alone is an important political stance on the issue of black folk authorship—the question of origins is left relatively open, as it is in the verse used as opening epigraph to the first preface, Johnson's poem "O Black and Unknown Bards" (BANS I 11–12).

Johnson first published "O Black and Unknown Bards" in 1908 in *The Century*. The poem might be best described as a meditation on the "miracle" and "wonder" of the spirituals, and specifically on the question of their origins. Johnson raises the question of origins with a series of metaphors:

> O black and unknown bards of long ago,
> How came your lips to touch the sacred fire?
> How, in your darkness, did you come to know
> The power and beauty of the minstrel's lyre?
> Who first from midst his bonds lifted his eyes?
> Who first from out the still watch, lone and long,
> Feeling the ancient faith of prophets rise
> Within his dark-kept soul, burst into song? (BANS I 11)

In other words, from the poem that opens the preface, Johnson frames the spirituals in relation to a question of authorship, which is simultaneously a question of a mysterious or undocumented "first" turn toward an explicitly *lyrical* response to the experience of bondage. Although the preface goes on to take up these questions in prose, it is significant that they are first posed in poetry—immediately, the province of Johnson's analysis (the "new evaluation of the Spirituals reached by the Negro himself") is extended to the *literature* that that evaluation inspires.

In the poem, the "wide wonder" of the spirituals is situated on two levels; it is first a somewhat ethnographic wonder: "Who heard great 'Jordan roll'? Whose starward eye/Saw chariot 'swing low'? And who was he/That breathed that comforting, melodic sigh,/'Nobody knows de trouble I see'?" But it is also what we might term a *formal* wonder, at the fact that the music comes to serve as what poet Jay Wright would call a "distributive form" of an ungraspable "spirit,"[34] a means of capturing the sacred:

> What merely living clod, what captive thing,
> Could up toward God through all its darkness grope,

And find within its deadened heart to sing
These songs of sorrow, love and faith, and hope?
How did it catch that subtle undertone,
That note in music heard not with the ears?
How sound the elusive reed so seldom blown,
Which stirs the soul or melts the heart to tears?

In this third stanza the personal pronoun "he" (referring to a particular originator) is abandoned for a curious "it": "How did it catch that subtle undertone." Readers have generally assumed that in the phrases "merely living clod" and "captive thing," Johnson is describing the same slave "black bards" as in the first two stanzas. But the intrusion of an impersonal pronoun might point us in a different direction: the poem may be invoking the work of the musical form itself, not necessarily linked to a human agency. In a fascinating formulation, music enters Johnson's work as a metaphor—paradoxically, as a metaphor for what is "elusive" in music! And even in this description of a wholly vernacular process, there is again an implied *transcription* at play here, as in the Ellison definition of the blues: "it" somehow "catches" or records that "subtle undertone" of "soul" or the sacred, not as Stephen Henderson's empirically verifiable "saturation" but instead as an "elusive" presence of unheard music within the heard music of the spirituals. "He" (the "black bard") sings; and simultaneously "it" (seemingly, the song form itself) metaphorically "sings"—and this figure of music stands in for what is different, for the discursive "catching" of what is "elusive" (what is *not* "catchable") in the music itself.

In the text of the preface, Johnson continues this argument that what is exceptional about the spirituals is closely related to what is "elusive" about them. And for that "elusive reed," he turns to a discussion of the music. Johnson's tack is in accord with most of the writings on black vernacular forms of the period, which continually lamented black music's stubborn resistance to the European system of tonal and rhythmic notation. But Johnson, instead of complaining about the difficulty of "catching" the music properly as it is performed in the vernacular traditions, takes the wholly revolutionary approach of eschewing any pretense to notational precision. In a confession that can only come across as perplexing in the preface to a book of musical arrangements, Johnson writes about the spirituals that "in their very nature they are not susceptible to fixation" (BANS I 30). He on the contrary posits the "elusive" quality of the spirituals as exactly what must be transcribed. This pushes the transcription toward its necessary future realization in a performance; it is incomplete on the page, he says, and the performer must "play what is not written down" (28).

Writing "Swing"

Nevertheless a "true" transcription is possible, according to Johnson. It is one in which the transcriptional form somehow "catches" what it cannot represent notationally. And he says that this elusiveness of black music is based in its *rhythm,* in the form's dynamic of "swing." This masterful passage is the most often quoted part of the essay:

> The "swing" of the spirituals is an altogether subtle and elusive thing. It is subtle and elusive because it is in perfect union with the religious ecstasy that manifests itself in the swaying bodies of a whole congregation, swaying as if responding to the baton of some extremely sensitive conductor. . . . It is the more subtle and elusive because there is a still further intricacy in the rhythms. This swaying of the body marks the regular beat or, better, surge, for it is something stronger than a beat, and is more or less, not precisely, strict in time; but the Negro loves nothing better in his music than to play with the fundamental time beat. He will, as it were, take the fundamental beat and pound it out with his left hand, almost monotonously; while with his right hand he juggles it. . . . In listening to Negroes sing their own music it is often tantalizing and even exciting to watch a minute fraction of a beat balancing for a slight instant on the bar between two measures, and, when it seems almost too late, drop back into its own proper compartment. (BANS I 28–30)

To use Johnson's own word, it is with a brilliantly "subtle" touch here that Johnson anticipates a point about the appropriation of vernacular material that Amiri Baraka would enunciate nearly thirty years later, in an essay called "Swing—from Verb to Noun." Johnson places the noun *swing* in quotation marks but does not mark off the gerund or verb form of this word ("swings," or "swinging"; also "swaying"). This indicates that "swing" is a neologism (like "jazz") emergent at the time—but it also indicates that "swing" is somehow tainted or inaccurate: it noun-ifies "swinging," stilling the "elusive" and performative connotations of what is in its verb form a paradigmatic black cultural *action* or *process.*[35] This is not solely a racially determined appropriation, "the erasure of black inventiveness by white appropriation" (as Baraka would have it): Johnson appears to mark the danger of his own transcription project in this gesture.[36] Appropriation is a threat also articulated in class—in effect, class inflected across race. Thus, for example, in Toni Morrison's *Sula,* the black congregation "sways" in mourning during Chicken Little's funeral, but Nel's oppressive and elitist mother Helene "holds sway" (thus, metaphorically stops or controls that motion) over the community, winning "all social battles with presence and a conviction of the legitimacy of her authority."[37] One might even say that, just as the "middle ground" form of ragtime is crucial to Johnson's investigations of cultural passing in *The Autobiography of an Ex-Colored Man,* here in his theory of transcription Johnson is striving for a middle ground as well between the verb and noun forms of "swing"—one which he seems to want to find in the gerund "swinging."

Johnson describes this "swinging" rhythm as being intimately connected to, or performed in, the black body. He goes on to describe the difference between the spirituals and the work songs and blues as a difference in the placement of the "fundamental swing" in the performing body; not surprisingly, secular music gets down further, positioning the beat in a "patting of hands and feet" as compared to the "swaying heads and bodies" of the spirituals (BANS I 30–31). Johnson places great importance in what Zora Neale Hurston would later call the physical "mechanics" of black performance as a ground for this motion.[38] In fact, he seems to prefer the word *swaying* to *swinging* in this passage exactly because it implies a rhythm located in the body. But the performer is not the initiator of this motion, apparently—the "swing" is *in* the body, it "manifests" itself there, but the source of this swaying is once more elusive. He can only describe it by resorting (once more) to a musical metaphor: the congregation sways "*as if* responding to the baton of some extremely sensitive conductor" (BANS I 28).

The main struggle in the passage, its moments of hesitation and uncertainty, arise around an issue of describing an expressly black *time* implicated in the "swing" of the spirituals. As I discuss in more detail in the next section, it is this insight Johnson carries with him to his own composition of "The Creation," the first of his poems based on black vernacular sermonic style. Hearing an "old-time Negro preacher" deliver a sermon, Johnson explains in his autobiography, helped him to realize that the "inner secret" of black oratory is its " 'timing': that is, in the ability of the speaker to set up a series of rhythmic emotional vibrations between himself and his hearers."[39] In the preface, Johnson wants to provide the consolation of a "regular" and "fundamental" beat, but his syntax stammers and betrays him: "The swaying of the body marks the regular beat or, better, surge, for it is something stronger than a beat, and is more or less, not precisely, strict in time; but . . ." In effect, though, it is this stammer that most closely approximates in literary form the bodily transfer with which "swing" manifests itself, as the musician "juggles" the beat, as it is "playfully bandied from hand to foot and from foot to hand" (BANS I 31). "Swing" is above all this physical hesitation, this continuing transfer. The rhythm is never lost, but it is never held or captured in the body either: it divides itself into "fractions," it parcels itself out, jumping from hand to foot, "pounding" and "monotonous" in one hand, "juggled" in the other—and neither *beat* nor *surge* is really acceptable as a term because the swinging never settles. It is the "play" of this hesitation that makes the "swing" of black rhythm elusive. And although Johnson considers the harmony of the vernacular spirituals to be quite controlled and sophisticated (unlike Hurston, who speaks of "jagged harmony"),[40] the same principle of elusive "swing" is at work in black melodic invention: "In addition, there are the curious turns and twists and quavers and the intentional striking of certain notes just a shade off key" (BANS I 30).

Just as this "swing" is manifested in the black body, it also has a metaphorical physical effect on those who would "fix" or notate it. The elusive nature of "swing" "constitute[s] a *handicap*" for many collectors. But, again, this is not a failing in black vernacular culture, for Johnson—in fact, a rhythmic "swing" linked to its manifestation in a bodily juggling or transfer is behind all American popular musical forms: "this innate characteristic of the Negro in America is the genesis and foundation of our national popular medium for musical expression" (BANS I 31). In Johnson's metaphorology of the body, the accession of "swing" to a *national* status is the process of the rhythmic black body relentlessly invading the body of "White America." White America, he writes, has "pretty well mastered the difficulty" of getting the "swing" of black music because "the Negro has been beating these rhythms in its ears for three hundred years" (28). Again, there is a grammar of appropriation (and perhaps miscegenation) implicit here: white Americans "master" the difficulties of black rhythm; they "*get* the 'swing' of it" (28, emphasis added), not "swinging" or "swaying," but possessing that noun-ified form.

Although Johnson is convinced of the bodily nature of "swing," he in fact is rather uncertain about the exact dynamic this represents in a collective performance. At first, "swing" "manifests itself" in the bodies of the *group,* the congregation, and that is its power—it enforces an elusive group movement, a collective swaying, so unified that it seems conducted by an unseen hand. But as Johnson continues to describe black rhythm in the second part of the passage, he comes to locate it in the *individual* black body: the beat or surge is "bandied" about a single black body, "juggled" from head to foot and back again. Johnson displays some confusion here as to whether "swing" is primarily founded in that demonstration of group unity or in that individual physical juggling. Does it surge through one body, or is there a common current that jumps from one body in the congregation to the next, or inhabits the entire group *like* a single body, all at once?

This question remains unresolved: again, as in the sentence about "beat" and "surge," we read a text that hesitates and wavers, juggling the momentum of its argument. But this should not be surprising if we read this juggling as an attempt to register the action of "swinging" itself. This indecision represents a radical possibility for reconceptualizing agency because it turns—in the sense of "trope," of course, it turns a metaphor—not on the foundation of some intentional physical act, or of some communicated black "essence," but on the ground of *form itself.*[41]

When Johnson writes of the black body, whether individual or collective, he is not only describing it in an ethnographic sense; he is using it as a *figure* in which to situate black musical "swing," the form he is trying to describe. What has happened here is that the black body, rather than being locked into some individualized and essentialized notion of agency, has been wrenched out of its phenomenological focus. This is almost always interpreted as a risk, or as inconsistency in argument. But in this instance, I would suggest, to quote Nathaniel Mackey, there is a "*telling* inarticulacy" in this inconsistency—an inarticulacy that signifies.[42] When one recognizes that the body is *both* "present" (a phenomenological entity) and "absent" (a discursive figure) one is forced to re-envision the possible relationship between individual and community, between intentional "*activity* as a kind of mechanical process" and "*movement* as something which is rooted in some faculty of the imagination."[43] Thus, in Johnson's conception, agency is two-fold: the individual is both an agent-as-creator, as an active shaper of culture (the individual juggles "swing" through his body), and an agent-as-representative, as a part of the collective in which that elusive "swaying" manifests itself.

It is not by chance that such a reading is possible precisely because Johnson is figuring the musical *form* of "swing." Only form provides the link between these two kinds of agency. Form, we should recognize, is a contradictory force in that it "designates both the principle of universalization and the principle of individuation"—thus it represents important ground to claim in the struggle to walk the tightrope between the national and the universal. Form gives particularity to matter: for example, clay is given the form of a cup. A body "sways," and in that form the body is defined; it is provided individuation. And at the same time it unifies disparate entities: paper cups, glass cups, china cups, and clay cups are all "cups" owing to their common form. When we say that people in a group are "swaying," they are unified through that common form.[44] If vernacular form is concerned with *remembrance,* as Ellison argues ("keeping the painful details . . . alive"), then Johnson offers the stimulating possibility of seeing that task as "juggled" between the swaying members (limbs) of the individual body and the unified, swaying members of the congregation. We are here in much more subtle depths than "call-and-response."

Furthermore, in this notion of musical form being situated in a *figure* of the body, there are the birth pangs of a poetics of transcription that goes beyond the quotation of song lyrics in "The Weary Blues" and "Ma Rainey." The task is to transfer that elusive "swing" from the performed vernacular into some written record. But to represent "swing" in the semantics of a notation is to "fix" it, to noun-ify it, and so Johnson transfers instead the figure of an individual/collective body. To put it simply: *Vernacular musical form is transcribed through a figure of the black body.* Johnson locates "swing" in the body, and so he turns to a metaphorology of the body to "locate" that same body (and, by implication, its elusive "swing") in the transcribed spirituals, and in his own text. First, we note Johnson referring to the transcribed spirituals as a body that somehow preserves its elusive "swing": with a telling pun, he writes that the transcriptions are true to the vernacular form, since the "songs . . . have not been cut up or 'opera-ated' upon" (BANS I 50). Second, we note a continual series of implications that the written text itself must take on or mimic the form of a body. Not only does the preface make recourse to the rhetorical and syntactical stammering discussed above; Johnson moreover moves into a brief discussion of dialect, and there he locates dialect, like "swing," as an elusive bodily presence: "Nor is the generally spoken Negro dialect the fixed thing it is made to be on the printed page. It is variable and fluid. Not even in the dialect of any particular section is a given word always pronounced the same. It may vary slightly in the next breath in the mouth of the same speaker" (43).

The Voice of the Trombone

How does Johnson apply this theory to his own lyrical transcriptions of the "old-time Negro preacher" in his 1927 book *God's Trombones: Seven Negro Sermons in Verse?* Although many other writers, perhaps most notably W. E. B. DuBois and Charles Chesnutt, had found inspiration in African American vernacular modes, Johnson may have been the first poet, with the initial publication of "The Creation" in 1920, to attempt to transcribe a specific vernacular *form*—the folk sermon—into a poetic work. Johnson's narrative of how he came to undertake this experiment is itself illuminating. Although he notes the influence of "rather vague memories of sermons I had heard preached in my childhood," Johnson explains in the preface to *God's Trombones* that the "immediate stimulus" for "The Creation," his first attempt at a sermonic poem, was occasioned by his visit in 1918 as a NAACP speaker to a black church in Kansas City, where he was preceded by a "famed visiting preacher" who had been invited to give a sermon.[45] (Johnson published "The Creation" in *The Freeman* in 1920, but it was not until the fall of 1926 that Johnson returned to the project, writing "Go Down, Death" and the other poems in *God's Trombones* in quick succession.) Here is Johnson's account of the preacher's performance:

> At last he arose. He was a dark-brown man, handsome in his gigantic proportions. He appeared to be a bit self-conscious, perhaps impressed by the presence of the "distinguished visitor" on the platform, and started in to preach a formal sermon from a formal text. The congregation sat apathetic and dozing. He sensed that he was losing his audience and his opportunity. Suddenly he closed the Bible, stepped out from behind the pulpit and began to preach. He started intoning the old folk-sermon that begins with the creation of the world and ends with Judgment Day. He was at once a changed man, free, at ease and masterful. The change in the congregation was instantaneous. An electric current ran through the crowd. It was in a moment alive and quivering; and all the while the preacher held it in the palm of his hand. . . . He strode the pulpit up and down in what was actually a very rhythmic dance, and he brought into play the full gamut of his wonderful voice, a voice—what shall I say?—not of an organ or a trumpet, but rather of a trombone, the instrument possessing above all others the power to express the wide and varied range of emotions encompassed by the human voice—and with greater amplitude. He intoned, he moaned, he pleaded—he blared, he crashed, he thundered. I sat fascinated; and more, I was, perhaps against my will, deeply moved; the emotional effect upon me was irresistible. Before he had finished I took a slip of paper and somewhat surreptitiously jotted down some ideas for the first poem, "The Creation."[46]

Again there is a suggestion of a lyricism inspired by or incited by another lyricism, to return to Ellison's comments on the blues. And again, when he discusses this epiphany in his autobiography, Johnson invokes music as a figure for a poetics of transcription: he describes the process of "transcribing" a vernacular form into a literary work by invoking the "similarity" of *musical* composition (possibly thinking of Dvorak's 1893 "New World" Symphony): "I felt that this primitive stuff could be used in a way similar to that in which a composer makes use of a folk theme in writing a major composition. I believed that the characteristic qualities: imagery, color, abandon, sonorous diction, syncopated rhythms, and native idioms, could be preserved and, at the same time, the composition as a whole be enlarged beyond the circumference of mere race, and given universality" (AW 335).

It is worth dwelling a bit longer on the peculiar intrusion of a musical trope into Johnson's description of his compositional process. The transcription of folk material into written form is *like* the music composer's "use of a folk theme" in a symphony, he says. In Johnson's work, there is almost never a description of a direct transmission from the oral to the written: almost always, the figure of music intercedes. Music as a metaphor seems a necessary mediating element in the process of linguistic transcription. Not surprisingly, then, when in his autobiography Johnson goes on to describe the completion of the other "sermons in verse" in *God's Trombones,* he again turns to a musical metaphor. We should recall in this respect that his famous condemnation of conventional dialect in the *Book of American Negro Poetry* also depends on such a metaphor: dialect is an *organ* with but "two stops," humor and pathos. As he finishes the book of sermons in verse, attempting to capture vernacular orality in a manner that goes beyond the limitations of conventional literary dialect, Johnson is keen to find the right musical metaphor to describe his accomplishment:

> Next to writing "The Crucifixion," my greatest difficulty was in finding a title for the book. I toyed and experimented with at least twenty tentative titles. I narrowed them down to *Listen, Lord; Cloven Tongues; Tongues of Fire;* and *Trumpets of the Lord,* or *Trumpeters of the Lord.* I liked the last two titles, but saw that

> "Trumpets" or "Trumpeters" would be a poetic cliché. Suddenly, I lit upon "trombone." The trombone, according to the Standard Dictionary, is: "A powerful brass instrument of the trumpet family, the only wind instrument possessing a chromatic scale enharmonically in tune, like the human voice or the violin, and hence very valuable in the orchestra." I had found it, the instrument and the word, of just the tone and timbre to represent the old-time Negro preacher's voice. (AW 377–378)

There is no music in the sermon itself, of course. Here Johnson is looking for a musical figure of vocalization, which by pointing the reader to black musical form will imply the performative context of the sermon and remain true to that elusive quality in the vernacular that he cannot notate.

The trombone is a remarkable choice. Johnson is evidently pleased that the trombone is an instrument that is capable of imitating the human voice: in depicting a vernacular mode that in its ecstatic cadences approaches a wordless music—"pure incoherencies," in Johnson's words (AW 377)—he turns to a musical instrument that approaches human speech. Since Johnson considers black oratory to be concerned most importantly with "timing," here he again attempts to represent by means of a figure that "elusive swing" that characterizes black vernacular time. Now, though, he works not through rhetorical or syntactical stammering but by a semantic juggling: he finds both "the instrument and the word," since the trombone is an instrument that swings "undecided" between two media (language and music).[47]

He goes on to note that trombone has "traditional jazz connotations," and he may have even had in mind a performer of the period like Joe "Tricky Sam" Nanton, the trombonist renowned for his skill in imitating the human voice with the plunger and wah-wah mutes who played with Duke Ellington's band from the summer of 1926 until July 1946. Ellington described Nanton's contribution as bringing a different black jazz style to the orchestra:

> What [Tricky] was actually doing was playing a very highly personalized form of his West Indian heritage. When a guy comes here from the West Indies and is asked to play some jazz, he plays

> what *he* thinks it is, or what comes from his applying himself to the idiom. Tricky and his people were deep in the West Indian legacy and the Marcus Garvey movement. A whole strain of West Indian musicians came up who made contributions to the so-called jazz scene, and there were all virtually descended from the true African scene. It's the same now with the Muslim movement, and a lot of West Indian people are involved in it. There are many resemblances to the Marcus Garvey schemes. Bop, I once said, is the Marcus Garvey extension.[48]

Jazz as a form for Ellington recapitulates the same complex conception of subtly diasporic, individual/collective cultural agency that I noted above in Johnson's description of "swing." And this take is inherently a political one: this notion of artistic creation as a dialogue becomes a principle not simply of local individual/community collaboration but also of African diasporic collaboration, and that collaboration is always political—an "extension" of "schemes" of return. So even in the relatively national, single-language project of *God's Trombones,* the rhetoric moves beyond the romanticized vision of the African diaspora that Edward Kamau Brathwaite has called "rhetorical Africa."[49] Here, as in Johnson's comments on Hispanohone and Francophone literature in the preface to *The Book of American Negro Poetry* there is a hint of a move "afield."[50]

Although Johnson attempts to catch that elusive "swing" in the title of *God's Trombones,* he fails to go as far as he might to this end in the poems themselves. The poems, however, are *not* just "translations from the vernacular into standard English."[51] While Johnson does not utilize the orthographic techniques of "dialect" writing, he also does not consider his compositions "standard" in any sense: as he writes in the preface to the volume, he attempts to indicate "the tempos of the preacher . . . by the line arrangement of the poems, and a certain sort of pause that is marked by a quick intaking and an audible expulsion of the breath I have indicated by dashes. There is a decided syncopation of speech—the crowding in of many syllables or the lengthening out of a few to fill one metrical foot, the sensing of which must be left to the reader's ear."[52] Reflecting on the experiment later in his autobiography, Johnson adds that for *God's Trombones,* he "chose a loose rhythmic instead of a strict metric form, because it was the first only that could accommodate itself to the movement, the abandon, the changes of tempo, and the characteristic syncopations of the primitive material" (AW 336). The radical possibility that opens up here is that Johnson could discard the mediating figure of music: Johnson begins to toy with the technique of transferring the "swing" from that vernacular performing black body or bodies into the very formal "body" of the poem. In its manipulations of line, measure, and punctuation, the poem itself begins to be sketched out as a "breathing," "syncopating" body.

Blues Poetry and the Apostrophe of Form

Langston Hughes extends this possibility into a true compositional strategy. Especially in the "blues poems" that open and close his second book, *Fine Clothes to the Jew* (1927), Hughes perfects the deceptively simple technique of *formal* mimicry: now, without recourse to any framing or to quotation marks, poems such as "Young Gal's Blues" strive to suggest in their literary structure (stanza, line, rhyme, stress accent, repetition, variation) the form of the vernacular blues:

> De po' house is lonely
> An' de grave is cold.
> O, de po' house is lonely,
> De graveyard grave is cold.
> But I'd rather be dead than
> To be ugly an' old.
>
> When love is gone what
> Can a young gal do?
> When love is gone, O,
> What can a young gal do?
> Keep on a-lovin' me, daddy,
> Cause I don't want to be blue.[53]

Here, the first question seems to be whether we are meant to read the blues poem as a *transcription* (that is, the written record of a prior performance), or instead as a *score* (that is, a written indication of the form of a subsequent performance).

Certainly blues poems like this one (and later Brown's folk ballads and the full variety of jazz poetry) should make us question the often-assumed opposition "of the poem-as-structure and the poem-as-event."[54] But the notion of the poem-as-event may refer to the semantic and structural dynamic of the poem on the page, apart from any possible performance of it. And part of the radical power of such writing may well be that it subverts this opposition between structure and event without inverting it—it keeps this tension "alive" (in the textual form itself, as I suggest) without simply relegating the text to the status of a score. Clearly here the vernacular is "more than just an enabling agent" of the literary.[55] But if much black poetry is distinguished by its "resistance to the rules of genre . . . [and] its absorption of seemingly discontinuous idioms (from classical elegy to collective improvisation)," then it is possible that the specific effect of the blues poem is rooted precisely in its *not* being the "same" as the sung vernacular blues.[56] When we begin to recognize the quite complex albeit restrained technical accomplishment of Hughes' poem (for example, the comma after "lonely" in the repeated verse of the first stanza; the added "O" in the second stanza; or the "what/Can" shifting from its initial enjambed position to "What can" in the repetition), it seems evident that it is a reduction of the poem to relegate it to the status of a song lyric. Oddly, the authority of the blues poem seems rooted in its double status or categorical undecidability: it is somehow *both* transcription and score, hovering on both sides of the inaccessible present of performance.[57] Perhaps the power of the blues poem is intimately connected to the fact that we are *not* offered a realization—when we read it on the page, its potential realization in performance is indefinitely deferred. And if it seems at once language crafted in the wake of music and language on the way to music, that music nonetheless remains absent or unavailable.[58]

The critic George Kent, among others, complained that Hughes's "blues poems" are impoverished compared with the sung vernacular blues, since the poems lack the *context* of the blues performance (music, audience, and above all the blues voice) and since Hughes makes no real innovation in the blues form when he uses it on the page.[59] But formal mimicry *is* the innovation. The musical form of the blues, produced in the medium of sound, is here articulated in the form of a poem in written language. And how is this achieved? Not by the poem's "rhythm"—as another poet greatly influenced by African American vernacular forms, William Carlos Williams, would later recognize, it is absurd to speak of "rhythm" in a poem.[60] However, Williams notes, one can validly speak of poetic *measure*. Williams makes recourse to this term (not unlike Zukofsky's use of "mathematics") because, in poetry, formal mimicry relies on the quantifiable use of spacing and distance in the form of the poem to represent musical form.[61]

We are not provided a musical backdrop when we read a blues poem; part of the way we recognize it is by *seeing* the stanza structure, the rhyme (and the words themselves, which are intimately involved in a formal dynamic—blues conventions of image or address have formal as well as semantic value). Sight is forced to infer an absent sound, in other words. And this effect sketches out a "body" of the poem: thus Robert Duncan refers to a "muscular correlation" of the poem, or Edward Kamau Brathwaite writes of the "body-work" of African diasporic poetry based on vernacular forms, or Monchoachi, a Martinican poet who writes in Creole as well as French, instructs that "it is essential to 'pass one's body' " through the form of the poem.[62]

There is no intervening figure in this process. The figure of music no longer mediates *between* forms, as in Johnson's prefaces, but now simply describes the similarly elusive nature of both forms from the perspective of the listener, viewer, or reader—the "swing" in vernacular performance seems situated in the body, and the "swing" of a blues poem seems situated in the "body" of the poem.

There is thus a "mood of distance" in the blues poem, not only in the blues' thematic concerns with mobility and longing but also arising out of its formal mimicry.[63] The music of the blues is absent or unavailable, and this absence is registered in the visual mechanism, in the poem's "body." Henri Focillon, in a delicate and thoughtful book on "the life of forms" in the arts, writes that "an identical form keeps its dimensions, but changes its quality according to the material, the tools and the hand. . . . A form without support is not a form, and the support itself is form."[64] In the blues poem we encounter not a form without a support, but a form that has been transferred from one support (the medium of sound) to another (the medium of the written text). And part of the special effect of the blues poem is that the effect of this transfer is legible—it leaves a trace, the form "changes its quality" when its original support is missing. One might say that in the blues poem there is an *apostrophe of form:* the vernacular blues form "calls" out to its distant prop or support.

It is a bit strange to speak of an apostrophe of form: apostrophe, one of the characteristic tropes of the lyric, is traditionally considered to be a *discursive* mechanism, not a formal one. Apostrophe, the passionate address in a poem to an inanimate or mute entity ("O Nature!"), is a trope that serves to constitute the speaker of the poem by situating her voice. Some have argued that the gesture of apostrophe is *the* paradigmatic gesture of subjectivity in the lyric.[65] The poetic address, appearing to invoke a You, actually "pre-empts the space of the you" in the end since it is directed at an object that cannot respond.[66] This cements the lyric's status as a monologic form, a form characterized by the speaking subject's "withdrawal"—a discursive subjectivity of internalization and even solipsism, even if it is inherently destined to be overheard. In blues poetry there is a similar lyric withdrawal (one thinks of the endless addresses what Sterling Brown calls the "lover or lady *in absentia,*" and of songs such as Billie Holiday's "Good Morning Heartache"). So Jonathan Culler's description of the discursive emphasis of the lyric is useful:

> In lyrics of this kind a temporal problem is posed: something once present has been lost or attenuated; this loss can be narrated but the temporal sequence is irreversible, like time itself. Apostrophes displace this irreversible structure by removing the opposition between presence and absence from empirical time and locating it in discursive time.[67]

In the blues poem, there is still this discursive effect, but there is also a concomitant displacement from empirical time (the empirical time of the vernacular blues performance) into what might be termed *formal time.*

When form "speaks" in this manner in the European lyric, it is usually considered to be a grave threat to that discursive subjectivity: thus Paul De Man writes of a "*piétinement* [stomping] of aimless enumeration" in Baudelaire's poem "Correspondences" where the necessity of trope undermines the lyric's quality of chanson, its "claim of being song."[68] But in a blues poem, the formal apostrophe, and its tension with the discursive apostrophe, is privileged. The blues poem calls out to *both* an "absent lover" *and* an absent music, its missing chord changes—and the two apostrophes are set in an uneasy coexistence. Since the discursive workings of the blues poem are part of its form, part of what makes the blues a lyric mode, what we encounter here is in fact a kind of stammering in the poetic form itself.

In effect, this double apostrophe in the blues poem is a radical strategic response to the version of subjectivity inscribed in the traditional lyric, which has always had treacherous implications for a black poetic practice. The lyric is not a timeless, universal form; it is marked by history—and its history couches a threat to the enunciation of black subjectivity. In Nathaniel Mackey's words, there is a "predicament of subjectivity in the lyric that we inherit within a Western tradition which has legacies of domination and conquest and moral complication that make [its] claims to subjectivity and sublimity hard to countenance."[69] The blues poem opens a new window onto the problem of subjectivity by formally taking advantage of a "heterodox lyric tradition in the West": that of black vernacular forms. It becomes impossible to read the blues lyric as a discourse of individualization and internalization: one is forced to read the poem in unresolved tension between transcription (the "musical" apostrophe) and score (the discursive apostrophe).

The implications of this formal development are not at all limited to an African diasporic literary tradition, though. More than half a century ago, Northrup Frye offered a schematic history of developments in lyric form as it moved through four stages: first, classical music–dominated lyric (or *melos*); second, the inherently visual *opsis* of Romantic lyric (announced by Wordsworth's "low mimetic" preface to the *Lyrical Ballads*); and, third, the "ironic manifesto" of Poe's *The Poetic Principle* in 1850 (with its incalculable impact on the French symbolists). Frye viewed the free verse of the first half of twentieth century as an extension of this "third period."[70] But the development of blues and jazz poetry in the 1920's might be said to inaugurate yet another period, in which the lyric became linked once more to *contemporary* and popular musical forms, in a manner elaborated not only in period parallels, such as Nicolás Guillén's poems based on the Cuban musical form of the *son,* but also over time, up to and including contemporary spoken word and hip hop.[71]

The aesthetic envisioned in this "fourth" lyric form, then, is rooted in the "swing" of what one anonymous former slave, in describing the origin of the spirituals, called a "mixtery": "Dese spirituals am de best moanin' music in de world, case dey is de whole Bible sung out and out. Notes is good enough for you people, but us likes a mixtery."[72] Some commentators on this striking formation have been inclined to "correct" the unfamiliar word "mixtery" in this transcription, using the justification that the former slave must have meant to say "mystery." Such an inclination emerges from a paradigm that reads the transcription of black vernacular material as always structured around some "silence," some hidden or masked "original" oral content—it is symptomatic of a romanticized nostalgia for that "original" orality.[73] But I prefer the idea that we are encountering a provocative neologism (retained in transcription) here, which holds itself between "mystery" and "mixture." What is being mixed, though? This could be a point about notation; the folklorist attempts to catch the "moanin'" of the spirituals, but the music's "mixtery" (a frustrating mix of notes in the tempered scale and notes "just a shade off-key") makes it impossible.[74] But there is also a point about the relationship between the oral and the written. The spirituals are a vernacular form, but not a pure "oral" one: they are based on the texts of the Bible "sung out and out." The speaker espouses a *mix* of musical "notes" and biblical "texts," and a *mystery* about the primacy of the music or the words. And that "swing" between the written and the oral is caught, and juggled, in the word *mixtery* itself. The transcription of vernacular musical forms into written linguistic forms necessarily alters our conception of literacy—but it must alter our conception of orality, as well.

Wilson Harris once wrote that "the community the writer shares with the primordial dancer is, as it were, the complementary halves of a broken stage."[75] It is a powerful vision of the intimacy between the writer and the vernacular artist. But the word that has always struck me here is "broken"—an inexorable separation, what Harris would call an "abyss," that is inherent in this vision of community. "Broken" does not have to be a signpost of defeat, of dispossession, for the literary artist, however. The task is to represent the elusive nature of that broken but intimate ("shared") community.

Such a stance is not debilitating indecision, but productive ambivalence. Indeed, Johnson's ingenious solution for the writerly transcription of what is "subtle and elusive" in black music be read as an impossibly early response to sociologist Paul Gilroy's 1993 call in his influential study *The Black Atlantic* for a consideration of black musical expression's role in a counterculture of modernity. Gilroy argues:

> The power of music in developing black struggles . . . demands attention to both the formal attributes of this expressive culture and its distinctive *moral* basis. The formal qualities of this music are becoming better known, and I want to concentrate instead on the moral aspects and in particular on the disjunction between the ethical value of the music and its status as an ethnic sign.[76]

But Johnson rejects such a dichotomy between form and content. Unlike Gilroy, Johnson locates the "ethical values of the music" precisely in its "formal qualities"—he reads the "subtle and elusive" swing inherent in black musical forms as providing a model for black communal production that goes beyond call-and-response. The ethical value of black music is that it transforms belongingness and creative "originality" into a quality that can never be simply owned or possessed—its roots are "swung" back and forth in the form itself. Form fingers that jagged grain.

three
The Literary Ellington

One of the main assumptions in thinking about African American creative expression is that music—more than literature, dance, theater, or the visual arts—has been the paradigmatic mode of black artistic production and the standard and pinnacle not just of black culture but of American culture as a whole. The most eloquent version of this common claim may be the opening of James Baldwin's 1951 essay "Many Thousands Gone": "It is only in his music, which Americans are able to admire because a protective sentimentality limits their understanding of it, that the Negro in America has been able to tell his story. It is a story which otherwise has yet to be told and which no American is prepared to hear."[1] Eleven years later, Amiri Baraka put it even more forcefully, excoriating the "embarrassing and inverted paternalism" of African American writers such as Phyllis Wheatley and Charles Chesnutt, and claiming flatly that "there has never been an equivalent to Duke Ellington or Louis Armstrong in Negro writing."[2] Such presuppositions and hierarchical valuations have been part of the source of a compulsion among generations of African American writers to conceptualize vernacular poetics and to strive toward a tradition of blues or jazz literature, toward a notion of black writing that implicitly or explicitly aspires to the condition of music.

I want to start by juxtaposing these stark claims with an early essay by one of the musicians they so often cite as emblematic. Duke Ellington's first article, "The Duke Steps Out," was published in spring 1931 in a British music journal called *Rhythm*. "The music of my race is something more than the 'American idiom,'" Ellington contends. "It is the result of our transplantation to American soil, and was our reaction in the plantation days to the tyranny we endured. What we could not say openly we expressed in music, and what we know as 'jazz' is something more than just dance music."[3] This would seem to be in keeping with an assumption that black music articulates a sense of the world that could not be expressed otherwise—that it "speaks" what cannot be said openly. Yet Ellington, in moving on to describe the African American population of New York City, offers a somewhat different reading of the music that was being produced in that context, specifically in relation to the literature of the Harlem Renaissance that had exploded into prominence in the previous decade. He writes:

> In Harlem we have what is practically our own city; we have our own newspapers and social services, and although not segregated, we have almost achieved our own civilisation. The history of my people is one of great achievements over fearful odds; it is a history of a people hindered, handicapped and often sorely oppressed, and what is being done by Countee Cullen and others in literature is overdue in our music.[4]

Here, what we so often suppose to be the dynamics of influence between black music and literature is inverted—in Duke's view, the achievements of the literary Renaissance are a model for his own aspirations in music. He continues: "I am therefore now engaged on a rhapsody unhampered by any musical form in which I intend to portray the experiences of the coloured races in America in the syncopated idiom."[5] In a remarkably early reference to his lifelong ambition to compose a "tone parallel" to African American history—an ambition that would find partial realization in later works like *Black, Brown and Beige* and *My People*—Ellington makes no apologies for his desire to "attribut[e] aims other than terpischore to our music."[6] Indeed, he adds, "I am putting all I have learned into it in the hope that I shall have achieved something really worth while in the literature of music, and that an authentic record of my race *written by a member of it* shall be placed on record."[7] My aim here is not of course to undermine the importance of black music or to crudely promote the literary at its expense but to begin to challenge some of our assumptions about the relations among aesthetic media in black culture. Looking at the literary Duke, at Ellington as writer and reader, I want to reconsider just what that provocative phrase—"the literature of music"—might mean.

The Uses of the Literary

It is well known that Duke Ellington based a number of his compositions on literary sources. One thinks of the 1943 *New World A-Comin',* based on the Roi Ottley study of the same name; Ellington's aborted plans to adapt South African novelist Peter Abrahams's *Mine Boy* (1946); *Suite Thursday* (1960), the Ellington-Billy Strayhorn suite based on John Steinbeck's 1954 novel *Sweet Thursday;* and the so-called Shakespearean Suite, also known as *Such Sweet Thunder* (1957).[8] There are many more compositions that involve narrative written by Ellington and/or Strayhorn (either programmatic, recitative, or lyric) in one way or another, including *A Drum Is a Woman* (1956); *The Golden Broom and the Green Apple* (1963); *The River* (1970); and of course the *Sacred Concerts* in the 1960s.[9] Barry Ulanov has commented that "Duke has always been a teller of tales, three-minute or thirty. . . . He has never failed to take compass points, wherever he has been, in a new city, a new country, a redecorated nightclub; to make his own observations and to translate these, like his reflections about the place of the Negro in a white society, into fanciful narratives."[10]

What is remarkable, in this wealth of work, is the degree to which Ellington was consistently concerned with "telling tales" in *language,* not only in sounds—or, more precisely, in both: spinning stories in ways that combined words and music. Almost all the extended works were conceived with this kind of literary component, even though Ellington's attempts at mixing narrative with music were for the most part dismissed by critics. The bizarre and misogynist vocal narration performed by Ellington himself on *A Drum Is a Woman* was mocked as "monotonous" and "pretentious" and as "purple prose," with even favorably disposed reviewers like Barry Ulanov complaining that "there is no point in analyzing the script. Such banality, such inanity, such a hodgepodge does not stand up either to close reading or close listening."[11] And yet Duke's desire to write remained constant. Asked to speak to a black church in Los Angeles in 1941 on the subject of Langston Hughes's poem "I, Too," Ellington commented, "Music is my business, my profession, my life . . . but, even though it means so much to me, I often feel that I'd like to say something, have my say, on some of the burning issues confronting us, in another language . . . in words of mouth."[12]

Ellington also wrote poetry. He showed some of his writing to Richard Boyer, who in 1943 was preparing a now-legendary portrait of Ellington for the *New Yorker*: "New acquaintances are always surprised when they learn that Duke has written poetry in which he advances the thesis that the rhythm of jazz has been beaten into the Negro race by three centuries of oppression. The four beats to a bar in jazz are also found, he maintains in verse, in the Negro pulse. Duke doesn't like to show people his poetry. 'You can say anything you want on the trombone, but you gotta be careful with words,' he explains."[13] Nevertheless, some of Ellington's poems are collected in *Music Is My Mistress* (MM 39–40, 212–213), and there are even a few recordings of Ellington reciting poetry in concert. Some of these performances are whimsical, couched as a humorous interlude to the music, as when Duke recites a short, colloquial quatrain at a Columbia University date in 1964 and prefaces it with the nervous disclaimer that "I wanted to tell it to Billy Strayhorn the other day in Bermuda, and he went to sleep. . . . So I still haven't done it":

> Into each life some jazz must fall,
> With after-beat gone kickin',
> With jive alive, a ball for all,
> Let not the beat be chicken![14]

Another example is a poem entitled "Moon Maiden," which Ellington recorded in a session for Fantasy Records on July 14, 1969. He plays celeste on the thirty-six-bar tune, and recites (in an overdub, since he is snapping his fingers, as well) two brief stanzas before taking a solo:

> Moon Maiden, way out there in the blue
> Moon Maiden, got to get with you
> I've made my approach and then revolved
> But my big problem is still unsolved
> Moon Maiden, listen here, my dear
> Your vibrations are coming in loud and clear
> Cause I'm just a fly-by-night guy,
> But for you I might be quite the right "do right" guy
> Moon Maiden, Moon Maiden, Lady de Luna[15]

In the liner notes, Stanley Dance comments that this "unique" selection originated when Ellington's imagination "had been stimulated by the thought of men walking around on the moon, and he had not uncharacteristically visualized their encountering some chicks up there." These lyrics comprise only one among a number of works that reflect Ellington's fascination with the space race, like "The Ballet of the Flying Saucers" in *A Drum Is a Woman* (1956), "Blues in Orbit" (1958), "Launching Pad" (1959), and unperformed lyrics like the undated "Spaceman," with its more lascivious reveries: "I want a spaceman from twilight 'til dawn / When the chicks say there he is he's really gone / . . . Give me a spaceman on a moonlit nit [*sic*] / Who can fly further than he'll admit / One whose cockpit is out of this world / Been around so much he's even had his stick twirled."[16]

Stanley Dance writes that the "felicitous internal rhymes" of "Moon Maiden" come off Duke's tongue "as though phrased by plunger-muted brass," but surely it is important that Ellington conceives the piece as a vocal recitation, not an instrumental number or a sung lyric. Indeed, he had "recorded the number twice as an instrumental, and with at least a couple of singers, but each time he remained dissatisfied." At one concert around this time, Ellington introduced the piece by saying that "*Moon Maiden* represents my public debut as a vocalist, but I don't really sing. I'm a pencil cat. My other number will be, *I Want to See the Dark Side of Your Moon, Baby*. . . . Extravagance going to the moon? Extravagances have always been accepted as poetic license."[17] In other words, Ellington was deliberately seeking a kind of rhetorical—and apparently libidinal—excess that he considered to necessitate a poetic form, one in which "extravagances" would be accepted.

I want to focus briefly on what we might term this literary imperative in the Ellington oeuvre, which is not by any means limited to Duke's efforts at programmatic narrative or poetry. In his brilliant autobiographical suite, *Music Is My Mistress,* Ellington writes of a more general narrative or "storytelling" impulse behind the very process of creating music, arguing for the necessity in music of "painting a picture, or having a story to go with what you were going to play." He goes on to claim (like a number of other jazz musicians) that soloists could "send messages in what they play," articulating comprehensible statements to one another on their instruments while on the bandstand. "The audience didn't know anything about it, but the cats in the band did," he adds.[18] But he also noted that "stories" were sometimes necessary to the composition and arrangement process, and often verbalized in language—with Duke talking the band through a new or unfamiliar tune with the guidance of a tall tale or two. The band seldom turned to collaborative arrangements (with all the musicians contributing to the construction of a song), but the anecdotes of that process are legendary, and fascinating for just this reason. Ellington describes it this way:

> Still other times I might just sit down at the piano and start composing a little melody, telling a story about it at the same time to give the mood of the piece. I'll play eight bars, talk a bit, then play another eight and soon the melody is finished. Then the boys go to work on it, improvising, adding a phrase here and there. We don't write like this very often and when we do it's usually three o'clock in the morning after we've finished a date.
>
> But this is a little off the point. What I am trying to get across is that music for me is a language. It expresses more than just sound.[19]

A more vivid description of the same process is provided in Richard Boyer's "The Hot Bach," which is worth quoting at some length:

> The band rarely works out an entire arrangement collectively, but when it does, the phenomenon is something that makes other musicians marvel. This collective arranging may take place anywhere—in a dance hall in Gary, Indiana, in an empty theatre in Mobile, or in a Broadway night club. It will usually be after a performance, at about three in the morning. Duke, sitting at his piano and facing his band, will play a new melody, perhaps, or possibly just an idea consisting of only eight bars. After playing the eight bars, he may say, "Now this is sad. It's about one guy sitting alone in his room in Harlem. He's waiting for his chick, but she doesn't show. He's got everything fixed for her." Duke sounds intent and absorbed. His tired band begins to sympathize with the waiting man in Harlem. "Two glasses of whiskey are on

> his little dresser before his bed," Duke says, and again plays the two bars, which will be full of weird and mournful chords. Then he goes on to eight new bars. "He has one of those blue lights turned on in the gloom of his room," Duke says softly, "and he has a little pot of incense so it will smell nice for the chick." Again he plays the mournful chords, developing his melody. "But she doesn't show," he says, "she doesn't show. The guy just sits there, maybe an hour, hunched over on his bed, all alone." The melody is finished and it is time to work out an arrangement for it. Lawrence Brown rises with his trombone and gives out a compact, warm phrase. Duke shakes his head. "Lawrence, I want something like the treatment you gave in 'Awful Sad,'" he says. Brown amends his suggestion and in turn is amended by Tricky Sam Nanton, also a trombone who puts a smear and a wa-wa lament on the phrase suggested by Brown. . . . Now Juan Tizol grabs a piece of paper and a pencil and begins to write down the orchestration, while the band is still playing it. Whenever the band stops for a breather, Duke experiments with rich new chords, perhaps adopts them, perhaps rejects, perhaps works out a piano solo that fits, clear and rippling, into little slots of silence, while the brass and reeds talk back and forth. By the time Tizol has finished getting the orchestration down on paper, it is already out of date. The men begin to play again, and then someone may shout "How about that train?" and there is a rush for a train that will carry the band to another engagement.[20]

It is not at all unusual for collaborative musicians and dancers to give each other epigrammatic or narrative clues during the compositional or choreographic process. Here, though, the arrangement seems to *start off* from the narrative, with Duke's self-accompanied performance—the tired band members are drawn into the creative process by the scene Duke sketches as he speaks. Here, in the middle of the night, at the core of what drives the band's extraordinarily creative cohesiveness, is an intimate call-and-response between words and music, narrative instigation and the subsequent musical contextualization of a melody. It is almost a commonplace by now to describe Ellington's music with superlative literary analogies, as a "drama of orchestration" or a "theatre of perfect timing."[21] Some critics have gone so far as to write about the "Shakespearean universality" of Ellington's music, contending that it is akin to the Bard's plays "in its reach, wisdom, and generosity, and we return to it because its mysteries are inexhaustible."[22] But part of what I am suggesting is that the literary is less an *analogy* for Ellington's music, than an inherent element in his conception of music itself, and a key formal bridge or instigating spur in his compositional process.

A Shakespearean Duke

It seems that Ellington was particularly attracted to the Stratford Shakespeare Festivals in Ontario partly because of the complex creative connections between literature and music fostered there in the late 1950s. The festival was unique in that it featured not only Shakespeare performances but also extensive musical lineups, in effect proposing a dialogue or consonance between aesthetic media. In 1956 the festival presented Benjamin Britten's opera *The Rape of Lucretia,* as well as the Ellington band, Dave Brubeck, the Modern Jazz Quartet, Willie "the Lion" Smith, and the Art Tatum Trio; in 1957 it premiered Britten's *The Turn of the Screw* and programmed Ellington's *Such Sweet Thunder,* as well as Count Basie, Billie Holiday, Gerry Mulligan, and the Teddy Wilson Trio; in 1958 John Gay's *The Beggar's Opera* was presented next to the Maynard Ferguson Orchestra, Carmen McRae, the Billy Taylor Trio, the Dizzy Gillespie Orchestra, and Henry "Red" Allen and his All Stars, who performed with the poet Langston Hughes. In the program notes to *Such Sweet Thunder,* Ellington commends the 1957 Festival's "awareness" of the "parallel" between Shakespeare and "top-grade jazz," and comments:

> There is an increasing interrelationship between the adherents to art forms in various fields. . . . it is becoming increasingly difficult to decide where jazz starts or where it ends, where Tin Pan Alley begins and jazz ends, or even where the borderline lies between classical music and jazz. I feel there is no boundary line,

> and I see no place for one if my own feelings tell me a performance is good.
>
> In the final analysis, whether it be Shakespeare or jazz, the only thing that counts is the emotional effect on the listener. Somehow, I suspect that if Shakespeare were alive today, he might be a jazz fan himself—he'd appreciate the combination of team spirit and informality, of academic knowledge and humor, of all the elements that go into a great jazz performance. And I am sure he would agree with the simple and axiomatic statement that is so important to all of us—when it sounds good, it is good. (MM 193)

Here, Ellington slyly pulls the rug out from under the critics who applaud the "Shakespearean" qualities in his music. If anything, in this description of boundary crossing, Shakespeare is revealed to be an Ellingtonian before his time. What unites jazz and Elizabethan drama, for Ellington, is above all a common concern with capturing the vibrant complexity of a particular social milieu. As Billy Strayhorn added in an interview, "Duke also said that the only way Shakespeare could have known as much about people as he did was by hanging out on the corner or in the pool room. He says that if William Shakespeare were alive today, you would surely find him down at Birdland listening to jazz."[23]

In 1956, the first time that the orchestra was invited to the festival, Ellington and Strayhorn had been less inspired, offering a set of mainly old hits like "I Got It Bad (and That Ain't Good)" and "Take the 'A' Train." They did offer one selection, though, that seemed geared for the theatrical environs and toward an interest in the "interrelationships" between art forms: "Monologue," also known as "Pretty and the Wolf" (which had first been recorded in 1951). The piece features Ellington with Jimmy Hamilton, Russell Procope, and Harry Carney. The record not only captures Duke's "vagabond syntax" (in Barry Ulanov's description), but also might be heard as an attempt to capture the feeling of one of those late-night arranging session narratives, with Duke narrating a piece to the band. One might hear "Pretty and the Wolf" as a kind of orchestration of that ephemeral process, a version of one of those casual tales spun to incite elaboration and embellishment.

Like the tale Ellington tells the band in the rehearsal recounted in the Boyer article, like "Moon Maiden," and indeed like much of Ellington's writing, "Pretty and the Wolf" is a parable of seduction, as well as an insouciant reflection on African American urban migration (Figure 3.1). "Once upon a time," Duke opens as the three reeds unfurl behind him, "there came to the city a pretty little girl—a little country, but pretty; a little ragged, but a pretty little girl. There she met a man, a city man—smooth—handsome—successful—cool. A well-mannered type man. And since she was pretty, he saw fit to give her an audience, so he talked to her for quite a while." The Wolf, standing on the corner casually twirling his "diamond-studded gold chain," agrees to assist the pretty girl in her ambition to "get somewhere." (The piece's simple conceit turns on the two meanings of the phrase: in other words, the narrative sets up an analogy between sexual conquest and material success.) She obsequiously purrs "Yes, Daddy" at his every suggestion. "And so agreed, they danced," Ellington intones, as Jimmy Woode and Sam Woodyard enter on bass and drums, falling into an infectious swing. But the dynamics of the seduction switch during the dance, a "mad whirl" that leaves the seemingly unflappable city dweller in an amorous "spin." By the end of the two-and-a-half-minute piece, it is no longer the Wolf, but the "pretty girl" who twirls the gold chain. As she "enumerates the various conditions and ways for him to get somewhere, you can hear him say, 'Yes, Baby. Yes, Baby. Yes, Baby.'"[24] It is as though Ellington is attempting to perform that singular arranging technique—the music shifting with the bandleader's narrative, taking on shape as his "Monologue" develops. The reeds "spin" in chromatic triplets as the Wolf twirls his chain, rock into rhythm when the characters start dancing, and later wheeze at the close of the piece, punctuating the Wolf's "Yes, Baby" with resignation.

Deeply impressed by the 1956 festival, Ellington and Strayhorn promised to return the next year with a new composition specifically for that context. The result was *Such Sweet Thunder,* which premiered in New York in the spring of 1957 at the Music for Moderns series at Town Hall, and then was performed in Stratford that summer. Ellington explained that "the idea of writing a Shakespearean suite occurred to me during a visit to Anne Hathaway's cottage when we first toured England in 1933. I have often wondered, had I been asked to play for the Bard, what

Figure 3.1 Two pages from one of draft scores (made by copyist Tom Whaley) for Ellington's "Pretty and the Wolf," Duke Ellington Collection, Archives Center, National Museum of American History, Smithsonian Institution, Washington, DC.

A city man - smooth - handsome - successful - cool well mannered type of man
And since she was pretty,
he saw fit to give her an
audience; oh he talked to her
for quite a while, naturally
she wanted to get somewhere,
he was al-ready some
where
he was standing on a corner
twirling his diamond studded gold chain
Around his finger, and as he enumerates the various
conditions and ways for her to get some where, you can hear her say:
hear her say
yes Baby
yes baby
yes baby
and so agreed
NO. M-2 10 STAVE
1595 B'WAY, N.Y.
MADE IN U.S.A.

devices I would have used to impress him. Consequently, I was very pleased when it was suggested that I compose a work for the Shakespearean Festival in Stratford, Ontario, since I found Shakespeare as performed there to be a thrilling experience."[25] The suite is constructed around "parallels" to the stories of a number of Shakespearean characters, including Othello, Julius Caesar, Henry V, Lady Macbeth, Puck, Hamlet, and Romeo and Juliet.

"It was the preparation that was tremendous," Billy Strayhorn told Stanley Dance later. "We read all of Shakespeare!"[26] He told another interviewer:

> You have to adjust your perspective, you know, as to just what you're going to do, and what you're going to say, and what you're going to say it about, and how much of it is supposed to be coming . . . and this included also consultations with two or three Shakespearean actors and authorities, you know. We'd sit down and discuss for hours . . . And it was a matter of just deciding finally [that] on one album we're not gonna parallel any, you know, anything of Shakespeare. . . . You need a thousand writers and a thousand years to do it . . . to cover Shakespeare. So, we'll say well we'll just devote one number to one Shakespearean word, or one Shakespearean phrase, you know, something like that. Just like "Lady Mac," you know.[27]

Ellington described the process more figuratively—and with characteristic irreverence: "I kept thinking what a dandy song Lady Macbeth would make. The girl has everything. Noble birth, a hot love story, murder—even a ghost. Then there's Othello and Desdemona. There's a swinging story for you. What a melodrama! What a subject for the blues. Blues in the night!"[28]

I would argue that this transformation of Shakespeare is doing work very different from other black expressive appropriations one might assume are similar, like Langston Hughes's poem "Shakespeare in Harlem":

> Hey ninny neigh!
> And a hey nonny noe!

Where, oh, where
Did my sweet mamma go?
Ney ninny neigh
With a tra-la-la!
They say your sweet mama
Went home to her ma.[29]

Ellington and Strayhorn do not place Shakespeare *in* Harlem, challenging our preconceptions about "high" and "low" art in the process.[30] Instead, *Such Sweet Thunder* is above all a *reading* of Shakespeare—perhaps *from* Harlem—and an elaborate reading at that. In the liner notes to the album, Duke describes the title cut (featuring Ray Nance on trumpet) as "the sweet and singing, very convincing story Othello told Desdemona. It must have been the most, because when her father complained and tried to have her marriage annulled, the Duke of Venice said that if Othello had said this to his daughter, she would have gone for it too."[31] The point is that the speech of seduction is not given in the play itself: here, the music fills the silences or interstices of Shakespeare's work. It imagines what cannot be or is not given in the written language—aiming to capture in sound the enthralling effect of Othello's violent and bloody tales of his life as a soldier. And to do so, the music "rhymes" *Othello* with an entirely different moment from another play, as Barry Ulanov has noted:

> On stage Ellington introduces each "major work" with a vagabond syntax that makes one wonder why he bothers. But if one listens carefully, both to the words and the music, one discovers why. One finds, for example, that in titling a piece about *Othello* with a quotation from *A Midsummer Night's Dream* ("I never heard so musical a discord, such sweet thunder"), he has gone right to the root of Othello's problem. His blunt and jazzy explanation is probably closer to the substance of the play than the long and involuted commentaries of most Shakespearean scholars.[32]

David Hajdu has commented that the Ellington-Strayhorn suites, even when inspired by literary characters, are in no way "traditional descriptive music."[33] Ellington writes in a press release for the Stratford Festival,

"In the suite I am attempting to parallel the vignettes of some of the Shakespearean characters in miniature . . . sometimes to the point of caricature."[34]

Tone Parallels

Indeed, Ellington seems to choose the word *parallel* carefully to describe the way *Such Sweet Thunder* interprets the Shakespearean texts. It is a term that Ellington used more than any other to describe his longer works, such as the 1951 "(A Tone Parallel to) Harlem," the 1943 *New World A-Comin',* which he called "a parallel to Roi Ottley's book,"[35] and *Black, Brown and Beige* (1943), which was originally titled "A Tone Parallel," and which Ellington described as "a tone parallel to the history of the American Negro" (MM 181). Whereas before *Black, Brown and Beige,* Ellington and Strayhorn sometimes speak more loosely about music "portraying" the world, or about the necessity to "translate" experience into the arena of sound, by the mid-1940s they begin use the term *parallel,* seemingly to specify the effects and requisites of *musical* transcription, without relying on reference to another art form (as in "tone poem," "portrait," or "translation"). The term is sometimes used in a sense that connotes a kind of mimesis, aesthetic reflection, as in *Music Is My Mistress,* where Ellington says that "composers try to parallel observations made through all the senses" (MM 457). Elsewhere, in sketching a history of black music, he describes the "Negro musician" as "strongly influenced by the type of music of his time, and the black beat was his foundation. . . . The music of his time—and sound devices—were always parallel to the progress of science, medicine, and labor. When you pick the jazz musician of any period, if he happens to be one of the many unique performers, you may be sure he always reflects what's happening in his time" (MM 413). But Ellington's use of the term usually avoids formalizing whatever that artistic reflection might involve. *Parallel* has interesting implications for an Ellingtonian understanding of the relation between music and literature in particular, since it offers a metaphor not of crossing, transferal, or import—much less grafting or mixing—but instead of simultaneous and equivalent movement through space and time. Ellington and Strayhorn seem to favor this sense of an exact match in development, a structure of reflection without primacy, in a term that implicitly respects the distances between expressive media.

Ellington also seems to understand the term *parallel* in a structural sense, indicating the "musical" use of a literary form. The four pieces called "sonnets," for instance ("Sonnet for Caesar," "Sonnet for Hank Cinq," "Sonnet in Search of a Moor," and "Sonnet for Sister Kate"), are "different in mood, orchestration, and rhythm, but have in common, as Ellington scholar Bill Dobbins points out, fourteen phrases of ten notes each, musically mirroring the fourteen lines of iambic pentameter (ten syllables) that make up the literary sonnet Shakespeare favored."[36] This effect is particularly marked in Jimmy Hamilton's stately clarinet melody in "Sonnet for Caesar" and Jimmy Woode's plucked-bass statement in "Sonnet in Search of a Moor"—both of which are woven out of a series of ten-note two-measure phrases. But it is also apparent in the theme in A-flat (framed by two blustery blues choruses) played by trombonist Britt Woodman in "Sonnet to Hank Cinq." Ellington's pencil manuscript for "Sonnet for Sister Kate" (which characteristically identifies the trombone solo simply with Quentin Jackson's nickname, "Butter") actually numbers the two-bar phrases of the melody from one to fourteen.[37] Of course, this is an odd and somewhat convoluted way to "parallel" the Shakespearean texts, since the dialogue in the plays is not in sonnet form. It is a bit like writing a book of short stories inspired by Beethoven's symphonies, and calling some of the stories "etudes" or "sonatas." Still, the choice evidences the attempt by Ellington and Strayhorn to structure their portraits or caricatures by deliberately adopting the phrasing structure required by a literary stanza form. The "parallel" is staged, in other words, both on a level one might term representational, or even interpretive (the bass suggests the gravity of Othello, perhaps; a medium-tempo blues indicates the swagger of "Hank Cinq") and simultaneously on a structural level.

The other way that *Such Sweet Thunder* "reads" Shakespeare is a strategy that Ellington and Strayhorn take with most of their tone parallels. Particularly in the titles of the pieces, they play with puns and homonyms, not just for humorous effect but also to highlight the phonemic registers of the Shakespearean text. Strayhorn told one interviewer, "Sonnet in Search of a Moor" was "triple entendre, because it was, you know, you had to decide whether we were talking about Othello, or whether we were talking about love [that is, *amour*], or whether we were talking about the moors [the Scottish lowlands] where the three witches were, you know."[38] This is a familiar practice, when one examines the discography: John Steinbeck's novel *Sweet Thursday* becomes *Suite Thursday,* embedded in *Toot Suite* is the French for "right away" (*tout de suite*), and likewise I would suggest that we are asked to hear "suite" in "Such Sweet Thunder." This operation privileges the sound of words over the particular ways they are written on the page. Again, it underlines the specific parameters of a musical "parallel," an interpretive mode that reads by "hearing" phonemically at a certain distance from the literary source text (divining thereby, for instance, that the proper musical form to represent Steinbeck's novel is a "suite"). It brings sound to the fore, as it were, places sound before sense, in a spirit of semantic disturbance or "fugitivity" that Nathaniel Mackey, among others, has argued is endemic to black traditions of literate and musical expression alike.[39]

This effect is related to what is sometimes considered to be a "trick" that Ellington trumpet players resorted to in performance: playing "words" on their horns in a manner to imitate the relative pitch of English pronunciation.[40] The most famous example is Cootie Williams's exclamation of "Harlem!" on his trumpet in the 1951 composition "(A Tone Parallel to) Harlem" (MM 189). But in *Such Sweet Thunder* there's another, in the section called "Up and Down, Up and Down (I Will Lead Them Up and Down)," based on *A Midsummer Night's Dream.* Puck, played by Clark Terry in this rendition, comments on the foolish love tangles of the couples (Jimmy Hamilton and Ray Nance on clarinet and violin, and Russell Procope and Paul Gonsalves on alto and tenor saxophones) by "pronouncing" on his trumpet what is perhaps the most famous quotation in the play: "Lord, what fools these mortals be" (3.2.115). To take up an Ellingtonian vocabulary, one might say that in this sense, the suites strive to "insinuate the sonic dimension" in the literary.

Literature and Social Significance

To come to terms with Ellington's sense of the "literature of music," it is necessary to consider in more detail that work he announced so grandly in 1931, the "rhapsody unhampered by any musical form" designed to parallel the "experiences of the coloured races in America in the syncopated idiom." As I argued at the outset of this chapter, for Ellington the literary is not only a medium to parallel in sound, or a poetic mode that allows the expression of libidinal excess; in addition, especially in the compositions he came to call his "social-significance thrusts" (MM 183), the literary is closely bound up with Ellington's sense of the historical.

Ellington had spoken in the 1930s of a "tone parallel to the history of the American Negro" (MM 181) with five sections, tracing a trajectory of diaspora starting with the African past and moving through the experience of slavery, the role of blacks in the development of the United States (particularly in the Revolutionary War and the Civil War), the great migration to the urban centers of the north in the early twentieth century, and the future. The piece that came closest to embodying this project, though, the 1943 *Black, Brown and Beige,* which premiered on January 23, 1943, at Carnegie Hall in a benefit concert for Russian war relief, comprised only three movements.[41] "Black" focused on slavery, drawing on early work songs and spirituals, "Brown" "recognized the contribution made by the Negro to this country in blood" (MM 181), and "Beige" followed the rise of a black community in Harlem. Ellington gave spoken introductions to each section, which form the basis of his description of the suite in *Music Is My Mistress* (181–182).[42] One programmatic narrative, the introduction to "Emancipation Celebration," one of the short dances in *Brown,* was preserved on the recording of the second Carnegie Hall concert in December 1943 when the orchestra played selections from the composition:

> And now another short portion of "Brown" which represents the period after the Civil War, where we find many young free Negroes who are happy with so much opportunity in front of them, and just behind them a couple of very old people who are free but have nothing and no place to go, and of course it's very dark

> for them. And we find a duet representing the old people and the solos representing the younger people. This is "The Lighter Attitude."[43]

As Brian Priestly and Alan Cohen point out in the first detailed musicological analysis of *Black, Brown and Beige,* the relationship between such a programmatic introduction and the music that follows is not necessarily transparent: thus it is not easy to track, in listening to "Emancipation Celebration," a particular moment in the music when one hears the entrance of "a couple of very old people who are free but have nothing and no place to go."[44] The point is that the narrative is intended neither simply to elucidate the development of the music, nor simply to "sell" the grand sweep of the piece to a potentially resistant audience. Ellington's statement here, in fact, may not deserve the designation "programmatic" at all, at least in any straightforward sense of the term (that is, a narrative that drives the musical composition, providing an audible motivation for its structure). Although the language here gestures toward the historical ("the period after the Civil War"), it also engages in a register of sometimes playful metaphor and double entendre ("This is 'The Lighter Attitude'") and rhetorical obliquity ("of course it's very dark for them") that cannot be easily categorized as a historicist, fact-driven representation of the past. In other words, Ellington's narrative introductions are not at all glosses, or the uneasy discursive cement between weakly linked segments—they are integral to the structure of *Black, Brown and Beige.* They provide a literary component of the performance that is constitutive because outside or beyond (but "parallel" to) the music itself.

Critic Graham Lock, in his excellent book *Blutopia,* has considered in more detail the ambitions of Ellington's music as history. Lock contends that for Ellington, music serves as "an alternative form of history" in a mode of creative expression that might be termed "Blutopia": "a utopia tinged with the blues," a mode "where visions of the future and revisions of the past become part of the same process, a 'politics of transfiguration,' in which accepted notions of language, history, the real, and the possible are thrown open to question and found wanting."[45] Placing Ellington's work in what some music historians would consider unfamiliar territory (in juxtaposition to the music of Sun Ra and Anthony Braxton), Lock reveals the innovative futurism that is a sometimes overlooked element in Ellington's aesthetic, while at the same time demonstrating the engagement of Ra and Braxton with supposedly "traditional" issues of historical representation and racial politics. In the process, Lock offers a number of fresh readings of the Ellington-Strayhorn oeuvre, from the "jungle music" of Ellington's early period in Harlem in the late 1920s (78–91), to a number of the later extended works, including *Jump for Joy* (93–97); *The Deep South Suite* (97–101); *Black, Brown and Beige* (102–118); and *A Drum Is a Woman* (137–141).

Here I will question only one component of Lock's theoretical framing, a presupposed antidiscursivism that reduces Ellington to a position that "music can be used to say that which cannot be stated openly" (78). Lock takes this antidiscursive stance in the very subtitle of his opening chapter on Ellington's music, called "In the Jungles of America: History without Saying It" (77). Lock makes this argument most forcefully in his reading of the purely instrumental *Deep South Suite,* which premiered in 1946 at Carnegie Hall, and which for Lock was driven by a "more pointed subtext" of racial protest than was apparent in Ellington's discussions of the suite, or even in his description of it nearly thirty years later in *Music Is My Mistress* (MM 184). In the autobiography, Ellington recounts an anecdote about a party after the concert, where William Morris Jr. approached him to complain that the piece was too timid in its protest. Ellington writes: " 'You should've said it plainer,' he kept insisting. 'You should have said it plainer!' He was for out-and-out protest, but as with *Jump for Joy,* I felt it was good theatre to say it without saying it. That is the art" (MM 185).

Lock assumes that the notion of a history "without saying it" was one of Ellington's "guiding aesthetic principles" (95). But even given the *Deep South Suite* anecdote, this would seem a difficult argument to make about a great deal of Ellington's oeuvre. Indeed, a number of the scholars who have traced Ellington's musical development, including Mark Tucker, have noted the prevalence of programmatic, narrative, and multimedia work among his key influences.[46] Tucker stresses not just Ellington's exposure to innovative and hybrid forms such as the Cotton Club revues and Lew Leslie's Blackbirds shows that dominated the New York musical theater scene in the late 1920s, but also Ellington's upbringing in

Washington, DC. Tucker notes Ellington's exposure to "Negro history" and heritage programs early in his childhood and speculates in particular that the elaborate pageants that were produced in black communities throughout the country in the 1910s and 1920s greatly affected Ellington's sense of the way that history should be depicted in artistic expression. These included sweeping allegorical works like *The Evolution of the Negro in Picture, Song, and Story* (which played at the Howard Theatre in 1911), *The Open Door* (which played at Carnegie Hall in 1921, with music featuring the Clef Club Orchestra), and especially W. E. B. Du Bois's magisterial pageant *The Star of Ethiopia,* a performance that premiered in 1913 and was reprised in 1915 in Washington. *The Star of Ethiopia* attempted nothing less than to encapsulate "10,000 years of the history of the Negro race."[47] Du Bois drafted the spectacle as an outdoor, participatory lesson in the African diaspora, what biographer David Levering Lewis has described as an almost unimaginably grandiose "three-hour extravaganza in six episodes, featuring a thousand creamy-complexioned young women and tawny, well-built men, and flocks of schoolchildren marching through history." The music featured not only two selections from Verdi's *Aida* but also new pieces from a number of black composers, including Bob Cole, Rosamond Johnson, and Samuel Coleridge-Taylor. The range of historical information condensed into the pageant was itself mind-boggling: three young women dressed to represent the regal African past (Sheba, Ethiopia, and Meroe) were "serially replaced center stage by a pharaoh, Mali's fourteenth-century Islamic ruler Mansa Musa, Columbus's pilot Alonzo; moaning slaves in chains; Spanish lancers; Toussaint L'Ouverture; Sojourner Truth; Frederick Douglass; and, to the accompaniment of rolling drums, the Massachusetts regiment of Colonel Robert Gould Shaw; followed by children, the professions, and the working class." A narrator extolled Africa's gifts to the world, including iron and fire, the great civilization of Egypt, and then a parade of spiritual values, with performers meant to portray "Faith in Righteousness, then Humility, and the gift of 'Struggle Toward Freedom' and finally 'the Gift of Freedom for the workers'—all this in 'a great cloud of music that hovered over them and enveloped them.'"[48]

Beyond these early influences in Washington, the work by Ellington that led most directly to *Black, Brown and Beige* (discussions of writing his "tone parallel" with journalists in the 1930s, the film *Symphony in Black* in 1935, the musical revue *Jump for Joy* in 1941) evidences an interest in explicit and discursive history, pointing toward the literary and narrative experiments that would become such an integral part of his music. For instance, the film *Symphony in Black: A Rhapsody of Negro Life* was produced in December 1934 and early 1935 at Paramount's Eastern Service Studios in Astoria. Especially compared with the early film appearances of other African American musicians such as Bessie Smith and Louis Armstrong,[49] *Symphony in Black* is remarkable if for no other reason than the unprecedented and dignified depiction of Ellington as a black composer commissioned to perform a "symphony" in a concert hall. But one should not overlook its clear narrative and allegorical aspirations. The film opens with a carefully planned shot of Ellington at his piano, composing music for the premiere of the "symphony" in pencil on a manuscript score. After this thirty-second introduction, the film segues through four sections indicated by handwritten titles that the film implies are written on Ellington's manuscript: "The Laborers," with a theme based on work songs played in accompaniment to sharply angled and heavily shadowed "images of black men shoveling coal into blast furnaces and carrying bales on a river wharf";[50] a second set piece called "A Triangle," portraying a lover's betrayal in three movements ("Dance," "Jealousy," and "Blues"—featuring a version of "Saddest Tale" sung memorably by Billie Holiday, in her first film appearance); a "Hymn of Sorrow," portraying a black minister leading his congregation in a stylized mourning ceremony; and "Harlem Rhythm," shot with the Ellington orchestra in a nightclub apparently based on the Cotton Club, with the dancer Earl "Snakehips" Tucker. What is notable even in this early composition, again, is Ellington's insistence on a narrative framing—here, one that interestingly combined the sentimental romance of much of Ellington's poetry and short prose (in the section called "A Triangle") with the emblematic historicism of "The Laborers" and the near ethnographic expressionism of the scenes of contemporary Harlem nightlife.

Nearly ten years later, *Black, Brown and Beige* marked a narrowing of this programmatic frame into a register of historical representation. Indeed, the so-called *Black, Brown and Beige* controversy emerged only partly around Ellington's foray into the concert hall, and the debate over whether jazz could provide the foundation of long-form musical composition.[51] It was most explicitly articulated in terms of the way *Black, Brown and Beige* "says it": in terms of the suite's programmatic form, its attempt to "parallel the history of the American Negro" by combining spoken narrative, song lyrics (in the "Blues" in *Brown*), and the instrumental music itself. Almost all the major critics castigated not just the piece's length (many snidely suggested he restrain himself to the length of a record side: "Mr. Ellington can make some two dozen brief air-tight compositions out of *Black, Brown and Beige.* He should.") but more specifically its literary components and historicist baggage. Mike Levin opined sourly that "I don't think the music needs any such 'programmatic' prop," and Paul Bowles, reviewing for the *New York Herald-Tribune,* reserved his most dismissive words for the work's "ideological" frame, claiming that "presented as one number it was formless and meaningless. In spite of Mr. Ellington's ideological comments before each 'movement,' nothing emerged but a gaudy potpourri of tutti dance passages and solo virtuoso work."[52] In fact, Barry Ulanov was one of the few critics who later countered that a listener's "understanding and appreciation of the work will, however, be considerably heightened if you bear Duke's program in mind while listening to the music."[53] Ulanov's spirited defense of the programmatic ambition of Ellington's composition is worth quoting here:

> The fact that [*Black, Brown and Beige*] is not written in the sonata form and therefore is not a symphony, the fact that it is programmatic, these are not limitations from Duke's point of view or from that of sympathetic auditors whose listening experience in some way duplicates Ellington's. Duke, contrary to the arrogant dismissal of his musical equipment and knowledge, could have written . . . a symphony or string quartet or oratorio or opera; he chose, instead, to write a "tone parallel," in which jazz virtuosi, in solo and in section and in band ensemble, gave vigorous interpretation to his phrases, some rough, some tender, all colorful and all directed to a narrative point.[54]

Lock adopts the phrase "without saying it" directly from Ellington, in a passage from *Music Is My Mistress* devoted to the revue *Jump for Joy,* where he writes: "I think a statement of social protest in the theatre should be made without saying it, and this calls for the real craftsman" (MM 180). But *Jump for Joy,* a vibrant West Coast production that involved collaborators such as Langston Hughes, Mickey Rooney, Dorothy Dandridge, Big Joe Turner, and lyricist Paul Webster, was a compilation of sketches, dances, and songs expressly designed "to correct the race situation in the U.S.A. through a form of theatrical propaganda" (MM 175). Lock himself admits that it "was possibly the most outspoken project [Ellington] was involved in" (95). Ellington pens the sentence about social protest not in reference to the discursive content of the show (its song lyrics and spoken sketches—many of which were openly ideological) but in reference to a debate about whether the comedians in the show should put on blackface:

> I had stopped all the comedians from using cork on their faces when they worked with us. Some objected before the show opened, but removed it, and were shocked by their success. As the audience screamed and applauded, comedians came off stage smiling, and with tears running down their cheeks. They couldn't believe it. I think a statement of social protest in the theatre should be made without saying it, and this calls for the real craftsman. (MM 180)

This is a much more subtle point about the strategy of critiquing racist stereotypes in theatrical representation: it asks, if anything, for a certain subtlety in the manipulation of specifically *visual* signifiers, without coming anywhere near demanding a simple reticence or shying away from linguistic expression. As I have already pointed out, this passage in no way dampens Ellington's continuing conviction that an effective mode of "propaganda" had to combine art forms—and specifically that it had to include a literary element.

Ellington seems to have decided, in the wake of the journalistic criticism of *Black, Brown and Beige,* that the programmatic mix of narrative and instrumental music was not successful, and as Lock points out, he never performed the entire suite again in public. Yet this traumatic rejection became the impetus for Ellington to write *more,* not less. Ellington penned a never-published manuscript (thirty-eight typed pages) that seems designed to parallel the music of *Black, Brown and Beige,* following the progress of an African slave named Boola from bondage to freedom, and (in the *Beige* section) into Harlem, the modern black metropolis. In Ellington's verse narrative, the music—work songs, spirituals, blues, and finally jazz—charts the drive to emancipation and modernity among New World black populations: "Out of this deep dream of freedom / Evolved the blessed release / Of freedom of expression in song."[55] But in the end, the narrative also argues that the music is *not* enough, that the "song" of the American Negro does not tell the whole story—that the music has been "categorized," perverted, and commercialized to the degree that it doesn't speak for the full wealth of black modernity:

> HARLEM! Black metropolis!
> Land of mirth!
> Your music has flung
> The story of 'Hot Harlem'
> To the four corners
> Of the earth!
> . . .
> The picture drawn by many hands
> For many eyes of many races.
> But did it ever speak to them
> Of what you *really* are?
> Did it say to them
> That all your striving
> To take your rightful place with men
> Was more than jazz and jiving?
> . . .
> It can't be true
> That all you do . . .
> Is dance and sing
> And moan!
> Harlem . . . for all her moral lurches
> Has always had
> LESS cabarets than churches![56]

Interestingly, the proposition here would seem to be that the music is inadequate, alone—that by itself it is open to misinterpretation ("But did it ever speak to them / Of what you *really* are?"). Even though the music has "flung / The story of 'Hot Harlem' / To the four corners / Of the earth," it cannot transport the truth of black strivings for political justice and historical retribution. If anything, it remains mired in easy racist stereotype and cliché ("jazz and jiving"). In a startling apostrophe, departing from the allegorical narrative of Boola to address its own historical referent and end point ("HARLEM"), here Ellington's verse narrative announces its own indispensable "parallel" role in the project of *Black, Brown and Beige.*

Ellington's difficulty, in other words, was ultimately methodological: how does one stage such a parallel? How does one bring such a verse narrative into conjuncture with a musical composition, without falling into a mode of expression that would be heavy-handed or unwieldy or scattered? This is a problem that Ellington does not solve. It haunts all his larger works after *Black, Brown and Beige*—all of which are at least in part motivated by an attempt to unearth the elusive definition of that suggestive phrase, "the literature of music." Duke continued to yearn for the proper structure, even as he declined to perform *Black, Brown and Beige* in full again. In June 1943 *Variety* reported that Ellington was even going to attempt to literalize his aesthetic of parallel, placing narrative and music (score) into one publication:

> Duke Ellington is preparing a book explaining the story behind his much-discussed composition, "Black, Brown and Beige," which he debuted during his orchestra's recent Carnegie Hall, N.Y. concert. Leader [*sic*] feels that detailing the thoughts which motivated the work will help toward a better understanding of it: to this end the story will be printed on the upper half of each page in the book, with the music related to each portion below on the same page so that readers with a knowledge of music can follow both at the same time.[57]

In 1956 Ellington told another interviewer that he had "almost completed" *Black, Brown and Beige* "as a stage presentation: songs and narration and all that. . . . Now I want to do *Black, Brown and Beige* with a narration and tell all the things about the Negro in America—the Negro's contributions and so on." When the interviewer asks him to explain the scope of the piece, Ellington hesitates, and then says: "Maybe you should *read* it." "You got a script?" the interviewer responds, and Ellington says, "I have a thing I wrote a long time ago—some of it might be changed now." Even here, he seems uncertain of the status of his writing in the larger composition, calling it variously a "screenplay," a "script," and "annotations" to the music. Ellington adds that he's trying to add song lyrics for the spiritual theme (most likely "Come Sunday," which was recorded in 1958 with Mahalia Jackson singing the lyrics), the work song, and the Emancipation Celebration section; but he doesn't know yet if the words he's written are "adequate."[58]

Autobiography and the Dream Book

It is only appropriate that by the end of his life Ellington consistently projected this effort to practice a "literature of music" into the realm of eschatology.[59] Both the tortured quest for compositional form and a spiritual register are evident, for instance, in Ellington's only book, the autobiographical suite *Music Is My Mistress,* published in 1973. Mercer Ellington has commented wryly on the "undoubtedly unique" composition of his father's "autobiography," which Duke wrote slowly and haphazardly while on tour, scribbling fragments "on hotel stationery, table napkins, and menus from all over the world."[60] (The book was subsequently "deciphered," thoroughly edited, and assembled by jazz critic and biographer Stanley Dance, who nonetheless would only let Ellington give him a minor credit in the book's acknowledgments.) In this sense, the composition of the vignettes and portraits that make up the book can also be read as a diffuse travel itinerary, recording the places the Ellington orchestra passed through in the late 1960s and early 1970s (Figures 3.2 and 3.3). Reading the fragments and notes gives a sense not just of the intermittent travails of Duke's memory but also of the incredibly diverse variety of the scenes where he wrote, especially the hotels that allowed brief moments of literary work in his hectic concert travels. For example, Ellington's description, near the beginning of *Music Is My Mistress,* of Frank Holliday's poolroom on T Street near the Howard Theatre in Washington, DC (23),

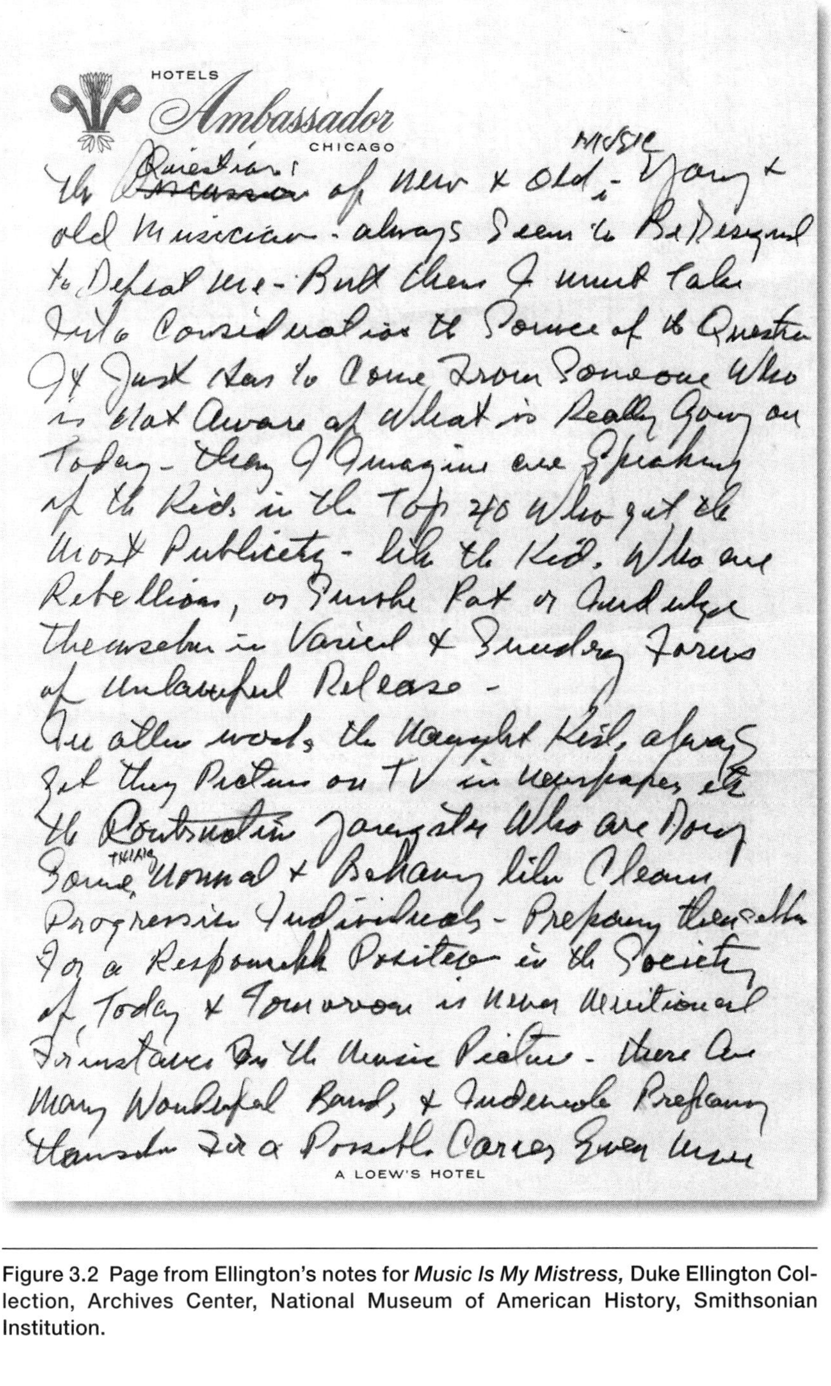
HOTELS
Ambassador
CHICAGO

the ~~Occasion~~ Question of new & old — Young &
old Musicians — always Seem to Be Designed
to Defeat me — But then I must take
into Consideration the Source of the Question
It Just Has to Come From Someone Who
is Not Aware of What is Really Going on
Today — They I Imagine are Speaking
of the Kids in the Top 40 Who get the
Most Publicity — like the Kids Who are
Rebellious, or Smoke Pot or Indulge
themselves in Varied & Sundry Forms
of Unlawful Release —
In other words the Naughty Kids always
get they Picture on TV in Newspapers etc
the Contrastin Youngster Who are Doing
Some thing Normal & Behaving like Clean
Progressive Individuals — Preparing themselves
for a Responsible Position in the Society
of Today & Tomorrow is never Mentioned
for instance in the Music Picture — there are
many Wonderful Bands & Individuals Preparing
themselves for a Possible Career Even more

A LOEW'S HOTEL

Figure 3.2 Page from Ellington's notes for *Music Is My Mistress,* Duke Ellington Collection, Archives Center, National Museum of American History, Smithsonian Institution.

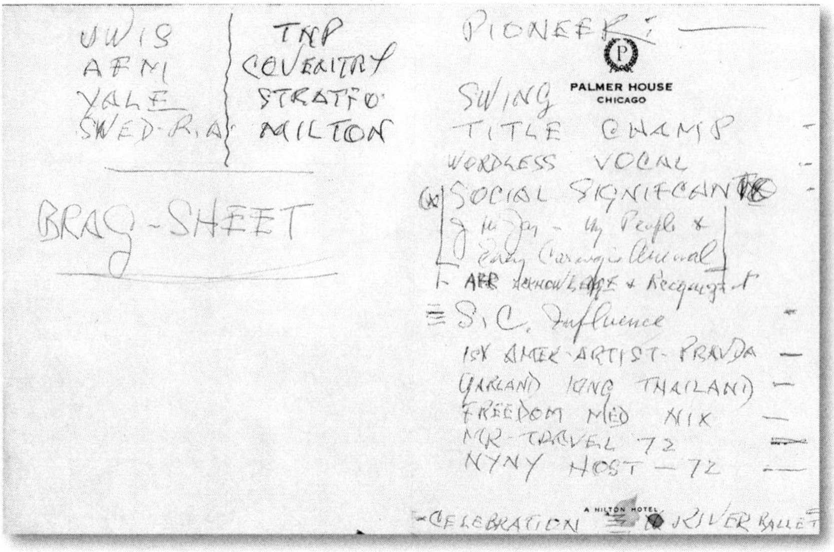

Figure 3.3 Page from Ellington's notes for *Music Is My Mistress.*

is written on stationery from the DC Hilton Hotel. A section of the faux "interview" that closes the book (455), where he considers the value of "new music" in the 1960s, appears on pages from the Fairmont Hotel in Dallas. In another stolen moment, Duke jots down a few paragraphs on the great stride pianist Luckeyeth Roberts (104) on a pad from the Waldorf Astoria in New York. His proud description of the band's concert at the 1966 World Festival of Negro Arts in Dakar is composed on paper from the Desoto Hilton in Savannah, Georgia, in a thick black felt-tip scribble. The opening fable used as the book's prologue—"Once upon a time a beautiful young lady and a very handsome young man fell in love and got married. They were a wonderful, compatible couple, and God blessed their marriage with a fine baby boy" (x)—appears on stationery from the Baltimore Hilton. On paper from the Steigenberger Park Hotel in Düsseldorf, Germany, Duke scrawls portraits of Al Hibbler (223–224) and Johnny Hodges (116–119), while he pens the section about his early days in New York with lyricist Joe Trent (70–71) and the anecdote about his 1962 recording session with Max Roach and Charles Mingus (242–44) under the letterhead of the Ambassador Hotel in Chicago.

During this period, Ellington was increasingly concerned with spiritual matters. He channeled much of his religious sensibility into the three *Sacred Concerts,* but it also became more and more part of his daily life, as he collected religious readings and meditations during the band's tours. His papers contain an assortment of Bibles that fans and correspondents had given him, as well as religious broadsides and pamphlets from various sources—Jewish prayer books, programs from Catholic masses, Unitarian tracts, and an assortment of more obscure literature.[61] He seems not to have paid close attention to the majority of this material, taking what was presented to him, and studying his personal copy of the Bible with the deepest care. One of the few other items that Ellington read assiduously in these years was a pocket-size pamphlet called *Forward Day by Day,* a "manual of daily Bible readings" published by the Forward Movement in Cincinnati, Ohio, which he received in periodic installments from the summer of 1968 until the spring of 1973.

Ellington seldom underlines the texts of these readings, and when he does, he usually highlights quotes from the scriptures that have to do with music. In the *Forward Day by Day* selection for March 17, 1973 (Figure 3.4), for example, when the band was playing an extended gig at the Royal York Hotel in Toronto, Ellington underlines only one phrase, "who gives songs in the night," from an epigraph from the book of Job: "Men cry out; they call for help. . . . 'Where is God my maker, who gives songs in the night?' "[62] This is not to say that Duke leaves the books pristine, though: in fact, he marks up these daily prayer books heavily, with busy cross-hatches, long vertical lines, corner flourishes, and brackets that swirl around the margins of the texts. This odd, even compulsive graphicity must be read as concurrent with or concomitant to his reading, but not directly reflective of it—the markings have a consistency day to day and through the months that seems to have little to do with the texts he's reading. One might understand this graphicity as "parallel" to his reading, then, in the Ellingtonian sense of the term. The marks don't represent or translate the words he reads, as much as they move alongside the text, filling the margins, with what might be closer to a "musical" form of inscription than a linguistic one. Duke's recourse to the pen could even be called a *scoring* of the books, in at least two senses: both as a marking or incision that interrupts or cuts the words on the page, and as the record of

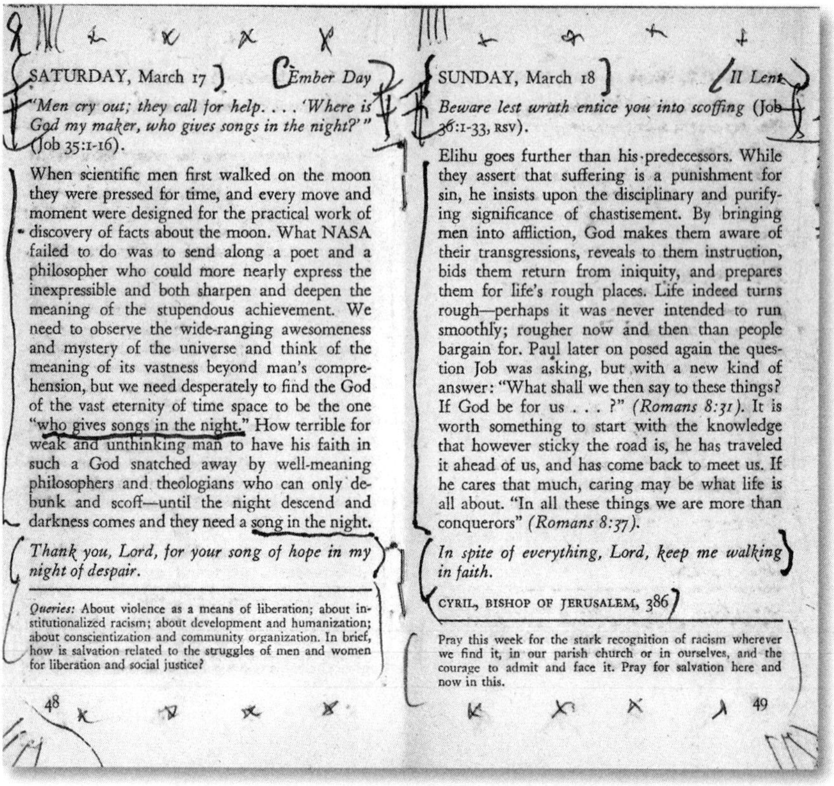

SATURDAY, March 17 Ember Day

"Men cry out; they call for help. . . . 'Where is God my maker, who gives songs in the night?'" (Job 35:1-16).

When scientific men first walked on the moon they were pressed for time, and every move and moment were designed for the practical work of discovery of facts about the moon. What NASA failed to do was to send along a poet and a philosopher who could more nearly express the inexpressible and both sharpen and deepen the meaning of the stupendous achievement. We need to observe the wide-ranging awesomeness and mystery of the universe and think of the meaning of its vastness beyond man's comprehension, but we need desperately to find the God of the vast eternity of time space to be the one "who gives songs in the night." How terrible for weak and unthinking man to have his faith in such a God snatched away by well-meaning philosophers and theologians who can only debunk and scoff—until the night descend and darkness comes and they need a song in the night.

Thank you, Lord, for your song of hope in my night of despair.

Queries: About violence as a means of liberation; about institutionalized racism; about development and humanization; about conscientization and community organization. In brief, how is salvation related to the struggles of men and women for liberation and social justice?

48

SUNDAY, March 18 II Lent

Beware lest wrath entice you into scoffing (Job 36:1-33, RSV).

Elihu goes further than his predecessors. While they assert that suffering is a punishment for sin, he insists upon the disciplinary and purifying significance of chastisement. By bringing men into affliction, God makes them aware of their transgressions, reveals to them instruction, bids them return from iniquity, and prepares them for life's rough places. Life indeed turns rough—perhaps it was never intended to run smoothly; rougher now and then than people bargain for. Paul later on posed again the question Job was asking, but with a new kind of answer: "What shall we then say to these things? If God be for us . . . ?" *(Romans 8:31).* It is worth something to start with the knowledge that however sticky the road is, he has traveled it ahead of us, and has come back to meet us. If he cares that much, caring may be what life is all about. "In all these things we are more than conquerors" *(Romans 8:37).*

In spite of everything, Lord, keep me walking in faith.

CYRIL, BISHOP OF JERUSALEM, 386

Pray this week for the stark recognition of racism wherever we find it, in our parish church or in ourselves, and the courage to admit and face it. Pray for salvation here and now in this.

49

Figure 3.4 Page from Ellington's personal copy of *Forward Day by Day,* February 1–April 30, 1973 (Cincinnati, OH, 1973), Duke Ellington Collection, Archives Center, National Museum of American History, Smithsonian Institution.

a kind of rhythm, a graphic suggestion of "beat" (through the spacing and iteration of the marks) that registers, subdivides, or accompanies the time of reading.

In March 1969 the Ellington orchestra played a three-week engagement at the Casbar Lounge in the Sahara Hotel in Las Vegas.[63] In the *Forward Day by Day* for Wednesday, March 19, the reading is taken from 1 Corinthians 14: "Aspire above all to excel in those [gifts of the spirit] which build up the church," which the book explicates in terms of the "ministry" of "what we say" in daily conversation and informal speech (Figure 3.5). The page ends with a prayer: "Direct and bless, we beseech thee, Lord, those who in this generation speak where many listen, and write what many read."[64] Ellington brackets the prayer, as usual, but for

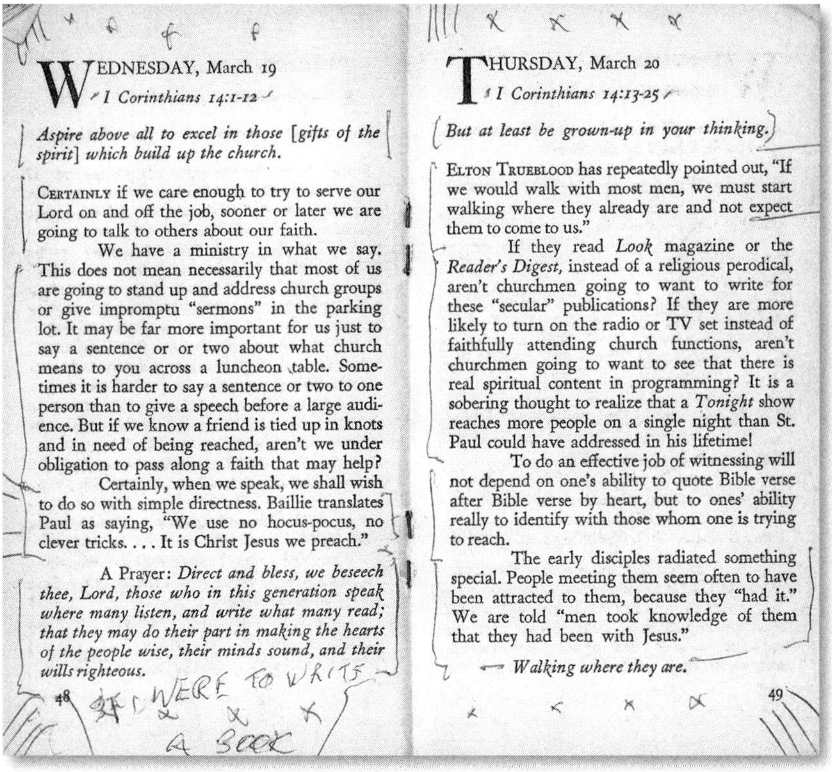

WEDNESDAY, March 19

I Corinthians 14:1-12

Aspire above all to excel in those [gifts of the spirit] which build up the church.

CERTAINLY if we care enough to try to serve our Lord on and off the job, sooner or later we are going to talk to others about our faith.

We have a ministry in what we say. This does not mean necessarily that most of us are going to stand up and address church groups or give impromptu "sermons" in the parking lot. It may be far more important for us just to say a sentence or or two about what church means to you across a luncheon table. Sometimes it is harder to say a sentence or two to one person than to give a speech before a large audience. But if we know a friend is tied up in knots and in need of being reached, aren't we under obligation to pass along a faith that may help?

Certainly, when we speak, we shall wish to do so with simple directness. Baillie translates Paul as saying, "We use no hocus-pocus, no clever tricks. . . . It is Christ Jesus we preach."

A Prayer: *Direct and bless, we beseech thee, Lord, those who in this generation speak where many listen, and write what many read; that they may do their part in making the hearts of the people wise, their minds sound, and their wills righteous.*

48

THURSDAY, March 20

I Corinthians 14:13-25

But at least be grown-up in your thinking.

ELTON TRUEBLOOD has repeatedly pointed out, "If we would walk with most men, we must start walking where they already are and not expect them to come to us."

If they read *Look* magazine or the *Reader's Digest,* instead of a religious perodical, aren't churchmen going to want to write for these "secular" publications? If they are more likely to turn on the radio or TV set instead of faithfully attending church functions, aren't churchmen going to want to see that there is real spiritual content in programming? It is a sobering thought to realize that a *Tonight* show reaches more people on a single night than St. Paul could have addressed in his lifetime!

To do an effective job of witnessing will not depend on one's ability to quote Bible verse after Bible verse by heart, but to ones' ability really to identify with those whom one is trying to reach.

The early disciples radiated something special. People meeting them seem often to have been attracted to them, because they "had it." We are told "men took knowledge of them that they had been with Jesus."

— *Walking where they are.*

49

Figure 3.5 Page from Ellington's personal copy of *Forward Day by Day,* February 1–April 30, 1969 (Cincinnati, OH, 1969).

once, he adds his own marginal note at the bottom of the page, amid his usual *X* scorings, in a somewhat feeble-looking uppercase script:

IF I WERE TO WRITE
A BOOK

A strange and poignant subordinate clause to hang at the foot of a plea. It is important that this phrase isn't simply past tense ("If I wrote a book") or declarative ("I want to write a book")—much less some kind of glancing reinterpretation of the call to bless those who "speak where many listen, and write what many read" (if Ellington had written instead, for instance: "*I* write music" or "I *play* where many listen"). Neither is it an allusion to the well-known Rogers and Hart popular standard, "I Could Write a Book," with its playfully amorous proclamations of literary agency. The phrase "If I were to write a book" expresses a kind of desire, but it is desire couched in the subjunctive, in the realm of a shakily contingent possibility, rather than a prediction or a promise or a counterclaim.

If the subjunctive mood denotes an action or state as conceived and not as a fact, then the phrase articulates in this personal and meditative space Ellington's sense of the literary. That Ellington would describe his "book" in this mood, as contingent and hypothetical, as an open-ended unlikely but imagined prospect, is not surprising given that he was struggling to write *Music Is My Mistress* during this period. "He dragged his feet," Mercer Ellington commented later, "and grumbled about the progress. He would have Stanley [Dance] go to places like Toronto and Houston when he had long engagements, but often they would sit up all night watching dog-assed movies and not work at all. It was the same when he was at home. Stanley would come to work, but after hours of Perry Mason and shoot-'em-ups, Ellington would be too tired for anything but criticisms and promises. It was a miracle the book was ever finished."[65] "If I were to write a book": it is appropriate, then, that Ellington comes to express that struggle as a fragile possibility, in a religious pamphlet titled to evoke daily progress "forward."

But in a broader sense, one might also read this subjunctive as the mood of all Ellington's grand racial programmatic ambitions, the desire to write a "tone parallel to the history of the American Negro" that in different ways animated all his "social significance" works: *Jump for Joy* and *Black, Brown and Beige* in the 1940s, *A Drum Is a Woman* in the 1950s, and *My People* in the 1960s. To write an extended composition about the Negro, the work that "tells his story," in Baldwin's phrase. "If I were to write": the desire, and the vulnerability, in the phrase might also be in part Ellington's conviction that his great work had to combine music and language, somehow, as I have already suggested—melody and text "parallel" to each other in voice-over narration, programmatic verse, and song lyrics—to capture the full richness of that history. Only such a work, an achievement in what he had called many years before "the literature of music," might offer an "authentic record" of African Americans. "If I were to": the contingency, the open-endedness, would seem unavoidable.

In *Music Is My Mistress,* Ellington writes that he felt the rather "unfinished ending" of the first section of *Black, Brown and Beige* "was in accordance with reality, that it could not be boxed, and stored away when so much else remained to be done" (MM 181). Part of the project's "authentic record," then, is precisely its open-endedness, parallel to the unfulfilled hopes of the African American. And it is likewise as though Duke could only conceive and desire his combination of words and music as a prospect, in the uncertainty of the subjunctive, only in an intimate space of reflection. For Ellington, the literature of music trembles at the margin of a prayer.

four

The Race for Space: Sun Ra's Poetry

In July 1969 when the United States was excitedly awaiting the flight of the spacecraft *Apollo 11,* ferrying Neil Armstrong to the moon, *Esquire* magazine published a half-whimsical survey. Writer William H. Honan, in a piece called "Le Mot Juste for the Moon," commented on the symbolic significance of the moon walk. Because space was the "final frontier" of human discovery, Honan concluded, Armstrong would require (like Archimedes, Vasco da Gama, Columbus, Stanley, and Alexander Graham Bell before him) an appropriate phrase to pronounce as he took the first lunar steps—and so *Esquire* had asked contemporary popular figures for "Helpful Hints," proposed proclamations for the astronaut to deliver.[1]

Most of the talking heads offered predictably heady pronouncements about the universal human significance of the first step. Hubert Humphrey, for example, suggested that Armstrong entreat: "May the moon be a symbol of peace and cooperation among the nations of earth." Some were pithy or glib; thus Muhammad Ali: "Bring me back a challenger, 'cause I've defeated everyone here on earth." Many could not resist the boast that the event marked the victory of America in the so-called Space Race between the superpowers: "Forgive the intrusion, Ma'am. Don't smile so bitter / At good Yanks tidying up your Sputnik litter" (Robert Graves). But there, amid the jingoism and utopianism, among names like Nabokov, Anne Sexton, Lawrence Ferlinghetti, William O. Douglas, Ed Koch, Timothy Leary, Bob Hope, Isaac Asimov, William Safire, George McGovern, Tiny Tim, Truman Capote, John Kenneth Galbraith, and Marshall McLuhan, appeared "the space age jazz poet," Sun Ra, with what John Szwed calls a "cheery poem inaugurating the new age":[2]

> Reality has touched against myth
> Humanity can move to achieve the impossible

Because when you've achieved one impossible the others
Come together to be with their brother, the first impossible
Borrowed from the rim of the myth
Happy Space Age to You . . .

It is a remarkable poem—once again, Sun Ra showing up where we least expect to see him, taking a joyful stance as a "witness of alternatives."[3]

I want to use this poem as a point of entry, or launching pad, into a consideration of the writings of Sun Ra, not simply because the anecdote is amusing, but more because this finely wrought stanza opens our way out to two critical terms in the Ra cosmology: "myth" and the "impossible." Reading these words as an intervention in one of the great symbolic moments of the Cold War, we hopefully will avoid the easy response to Ra, which wants to brand him a kook, a space freak, talking nonsense, *out.* Entering, or exiting, with this poem, we are reminded that for Sun Ra, "it is no accident here and elsewhere the words myth and history walk hand in hand."[4] For Ra, myth is what poet Jay Wright calls a "mode of knowledge"; it is a "medium to understanding" that is quite closely linked to the grand events of the day.[5]

This odd little poem displaces in at least two directions. On the one hand, by speaking in terms of the "myth" rather than the nation, Sun Ra ignores and thus rejects the discourse around "America" in so many of the other "Helpful Hints"—the often triumphalist idea that the moon shot is a particularly national accomplishment. Instead, here we have a certain kind of universalist discourse, talking about "Humanity" as a whole. But in the language of this strangely dressed figure, identified in the article *only* as "the space age jazz poet," "Humanity" would appear to be circumscribed. Here it refers more to "the inhabitants of this planet" than to the only conceivable frame of life. And so we are preached a perplexing universalism, a "universalism of the impossible."

At the same time, there is a second level of displacement: for Sun Ra, by not mentioning race, also rejects the mode of most of the black intellectual commentators of the moment. Duke Ellington, for example, had written an essay called "The Race for Space" around 1957, an attempt to transfer the civil rights discourse of the "Double V" (victory against fascism abroad, victory against racism at home) from World War II into the

Cold War. Ellington described jazz as both a model for and a "barometer" of democracy, and called the United States to task for perpetual racism and continuing segregation, going so far as to suggest that the USSR won the space race with Sputnik because of its relative racial harmony:

> This is my view on the race for space. We'll never get it until we Americans, collectively and individually[,] get us a new sound. A new sound of harmony, brotherly love, common respect and consideration for the dignity and freedom of men.[6]

Sun Ra takes another route. The *Esquire* poem chooses not to speak *from* race, as Ellington does, to demand civil rights as the fulfillment of the principles of American democracy. Sun Ra's "impossibles," in other words, "come together" in a register altogether different from the black jeremiads of the 1960s, even those like James Baldwin's *The Fire Next Time* that close with prophetic commands to do the impossible, to "end the racial nightmare": "I know that what I am asking is impossible. But in our time, as in every time, the impossible is the least that one can demand."[7]

Reading the poetry, music, lyrics, theater and pronouncements of Sun Ra as a kind of constellation, however, it becomes evident that this difference is not the result of an ahistoricism, not because Ra offers no racial critique. On the contrary, he roots his sense of "myth" and the "impossible" precisely in the history of U.S. racism and segregation. For example, in the legendary 1972 mythic-blaxploitation film *Space Is the Place,* there is a scene where Sun Ra, a black alien from Saturn come to Earth in a music-powered spaceship to rescue the African American population, visits a youth community center. "How we know you not some old hippie or something?" one woman demands. Sun Ra answers:

> How do you know I'm real? I'm not real. I'm just like you. You don't exist in this society. If you did, your people wouldn't be seeking equal rights. You're not real. If you were, you'd have some status among the nations of the world. I come to you as the myth, because that's what black people are. I came from a dream that the black man dreamed long ago.[8]

It is thus true, as John Szwed explains, that "space was both a metaphor of exclusion and of reterritorialization, of claiming the 'outside' as one's own, of tying a revised and corrected past to a claimed future."[9]

Nevertheless, Sun Ra does not quite end up at a black nationalist position. As with Barbara Christian's reformulation of the phrase "the race for theory" into a double-edged tool, to critique the exclusionary and self-sustaining institution of Theory in the academy while noting that the putatively "excluded" *also* theorize,[10] Sun Ra's understanding of "the race for space" critiques the jingoistic 1960s cant of the final frontier while at the same time redefining "race," redefining the frame of black radicalism. That "separate kind of human being, the American black man," represents a challenge to U.S. pretensions of democracy, but finally *doesn't* belong here. Black people are mythic, ancient, or "cosmic." They *are* the race for space:

> Here in America there are also Black people who have given up nothing, who couldn't give up anything because they live in harmony with the Creator of the cosmos. And they will always be a source of difficulty for every nation on this planet, because they've no other ruler than the Creator of the cosmos and they're faithful only to him. The Bible speaks about that too. They're the only people who stand apart. Nobody can say that Israel is that people, because Israel is counted as one of the nations of this world, at least in the United Nations, but not the American Black people.[11]

When Sun Ra refigures the so-called black nationalist land question—or, in another discourse, the Communist Party "Black Belt" thesis that African Americans formed an "internally colonized" nation in the U.S. South—into the *space question,* we are not quite in recognizable nationalist strategy anymore.

In reading the *Esquire* poem, then, we have to hear through the prism of his other texts, where Sun Ra often calls for a politics of *mythocracy,* rather than demanding the fulfillment of democratic principles, or theocracy.[12] Not "We hold these truths to be self-evident that all men are created equal," no; Ra demands something absolutely *other:*

We hold this myth to be potential
Not self evident alone but equational;
Another Dimension
Of another kind of Living Life
Abstract-Projection Presence

This Myth are these
We be potential
This myth is not what you know[13]

It seems that myth represents both a critique of the historical erasure of African Americans, as a group—the prophet Ra arrives as reminder of that exilic past ("I come to you as the myth, because that's what black people are")—and possibility, an openness that even breaks syntax ("This Myth are these") in its insistence on something new, on something radically different.

The Practice of the Impossible

Sun Ra's use of the word *impossible* is the recognition that the radically different, a radical alterity, is inconceivable, and yet paradoxically exactly that which *must* be conceived. "The impossible is the watchword of the greater space age," Sun Ra wrote on the cover of the album *Rocket Number 9 Take Off for Venus* (later reissued as *Interstellar Low Ways*). "The impossible attracts me," Ra often said, "because everything possible has been done and the world didn't change."[14] Or:

> I'm talking about something that's so impossible, it can't possibly be true. But it's the only way the world's gonna survive, this impossible thing. My job is to change five billion people to something else. Totally impossible. But everything that's possible's been done by man. I have to deal with the impossible. And when I deal with the impossible and am successful, it makes me feel good because I know that I'm not bullshittin'.[15]

In this light, the lines of the *Esquire* poem make more sense: when Sun Ra writes that the Apollo mission allows us to touch the "rim of myth," allows us tangential access to a kind of "brotherhood of impossibles," he is writing about an extreme version of what Thomas Kuhn would call a "paradigm shift."[16] Going to space is epistemological work—it might force us to alter our conception of what "the inhabitants of this planet" can be. It "races," but more *razes* and *raises,* as Ra might say, the potential of the human.

More than anything else, Sun Ra's work is consistent and insistent in the way it constantly pushes toward those moments of the impossible, those paradigm shifts that are unimaginable until after they've happened, but that are necessary. As a result of this drive, one can track in this period a kind of escalating "race" in the way Sun Ra talks about space. Just after the moon shot, Nigerian writer Tam Fiofori asked Ra in an interview, "How do you feel about the moon shot, in the light of your space music?" Although he had been talking about "space music" for the past fifteen years, Sun Ra quickly shifted gears:

> Well, I'm not playing Space Music as the ultimate reach anymore. That is, not in the interplanetary sense alone. I'm playing intergalactic music, which is beyond the other idea of space music, because it is of the natural infinity of the eternal universe Eternal ETERNAL . . . it is of the universes, as all the universes together make another kind of universe. There is a need for that type of beingness upon this planet at this time. The Space music of the previous years was presented to prepare people for the idea of going to the moon and other places like that in the interplanetary thing, but now, since that has been accomplished, or the idea of it has been projected or propagated (however it is), of course there is no need for me to propagate it myself. . . .
>
> On this planet, it seems, it has been very difficult for me to do and be of the possible things and projects. As I look at the world today and its events and the harvest of possible things, I like the idea of the impossible more and more.[17]

Here the term *intergalactic,* broader than *interplanetary,* evidences Ra's continual vigilance toward the impossible, the unthought, the unconceived, the "not," the "alter," as he liked to say. Such an attempt to break the limits of what can be thought becomes Sun Ra's prophetic duty on earth. For him, it represents the only chance for mankind to rethink its "destiny."

This critical strategy, which Sun Ra terms "myth-science," making recourse both to the knowledge systems of ancient Egypt and to a futuristic science fiction, places Ra in a rich firmament of black visionaries, what David Toop has called the "mystico-political undercurrent of black American thought,"[18] from Nat Turner, Rebecca Jackson, and Julia Foote, to Robert Johnson, Marcus Garvey, and Father Divine, to Ornette Coleman, George Clinton, artist Ram-el-zee, and dub producer Lee "Scratch" Perry. What finally distinguishes Sun Ra in this kind of visionary tradition is his emphasis on the poetic and the literary—and it is this theme that I want to take up here. Even speaking of the "intergalactic" approach to music, Ra thinks in tropes implying that for him, certain operations of language are essential to any approach to the impossible, to any delineation of the myth. In a handout for the legendary class on "The Black Man in the Cosmos" he taught at Berkeley in 1971, Sun Ra made recourse to etymology to argue that the very form of myth is linguistic:

> Every myth is a mathematical parable. Myth is another form of truth, a parable is a myth; it is a parallel assertion. Myth in Greek is mythos, a word meaning a word, speech, legend.[19]

In an interview around the same period, he explains: "The intergalactic phase is of the expansion-continuation dictionary form. As a dictionary it is applicable to multi-sense adaptive expression; it reaches encyclopedia proportions."[20] He sometimes referred to his records as issues of a "cosmic newspaper,"[21] and almost always describes the impossible as a poetic practice. Take for example his poem "Words and the Impossible":

> The elasticity of words
> The phonetic-dimension of words
> The multi-self of words
> Is energy for thought—If it is a reality.
>   The idea that words
> Can form themselves into the impossible
> Then the way to the impossible
> Is through words.

The fate of humanity is determined
By the word they so or approve
Because they reap what they so
Even if it is the fruit of their lies[22]

Sun Ra says elsewhere that "words are seeds you plant in the ground."[23] In this sense, there is a peculiar kind of split semiosis, a seed that grows into many plants, espoused in this poem where we see the word "so" in a place where conventional grammar and context tells us we should see "sow." Here is the "multi-self of words," "the phonetic-dimension of words" in action: an impossible grammar, an impossible or "immeasurable" equation between grapheme and phoneme. The mark on the page doesn't equal the meaning we "hear," and the practice of the impossible occurs in the interstices of that discrepancy. (In light of such phonetic alteration, it is crucial to recognize that "Words and the Impossible," indeed like much of Ra's verse, is as much *sight poetry* as sound poetry—if you hear the poem read aloud without seeing it, there is no way to notice the altered spelling of "so.")

"The fate of humanity is determined / By the word they so or approve": in other words, the visionary import of this practice is that the way we "solve" this homonymic equation (writing "sow," writing "so"—the way we "sew" it?) determines our fate: opens or closes possible ways of seeing and voicing the world.

Umbra / Ra

Interestingly, though, it has been extremely difficult for both jazz historians and literary scholars to come to terms with Sun Ra's poetry as such—or even in relation to his music. It is apparently as difficult for critics to comprehend his writing in a field of musicians-who-write (such as Ellington, Mingus, Anthony Braxton, Joseph Jarman, and Cecil Taylor, among others) as in a field of midcentury black experimental poetics. This is true even when Ra had direct contact with writers, as in the mid-1960s, during the time his Arkestra lived in the East Village, and was closely linked not only with the lively "New Thing" free jazz scene of those years but also with poets of the Umbra group, such as David Henderson, Tom Dent, Steve Cannon, Lorenzo Thomas, Rolland Snellings, and Norman Pritchard, and especially downtown figures loosely associated with Umbra like Henry Dumas and Amiri Baraka. When Ra is mentioned at all in the few existing histories of the black downtown poetry scene in the early 1960s, it is the shock of his theatrical otherness that stands out, not his poetics. Amiri Baraka's eulogy for Sun Ra recalls this aspect vividly:

> I passed through Ra's orbit when they 1st arrived from Chicago . . .
>
> The Weirdness, Outness, Way Outness, Otherness, was immediate. Some space metaphysical philosophical surrealistic bop funk.
>
> Some blue pyramid home nigger southern different color meaning hip shit. Ra. Sun Ra.
>
> Then they put on weird clothes, space helmets, robes, flowing capes. They did rituals, played in rituals, evoked lost civilizations, used strangeness to teach us open feeling as intelligence.[24]

Nevertheless, the 1967–1968 *Umbra Anthology,* a major collection of work by members of the collective, opens with a selection of Sun Ra's poetry, apparently marking him as a signal figure—even a kind of poetic elder—for the group.[25] But it is difficult to understand the relationship between Ra's oblique lines and the work in the rest of the volume. And so we are left with a curious aporia: even excellent recent work like Aldon Nielsen's *Black Chant: Languages of African American Postmodernism* places Ra in the orbit of Umbra only as musical analogy, without being able to think him as poetic inspiration:

> The radical poetics of Umbra writers like [Oliver] Pitcher and [Norman] Pritchard were no more lacking in precedent in black writing than Sun Ra's transmutations of the vocabularies of the big band were unprecedented in the black orchestral traditions; in each genre the innovators and outsiders were working with materials they had gathered from *inside* the tradition, but were working with them in new ways.[26]

But what happens when these circuits cross? At the very least, it must become clear that Ra's "transmutations of the vocabularies of the big band" are not unrelated to Ra's concurrent (and sometimes simultaneously performed) transmutations of the English language.

One also might conjecture about Ra's influence as a *poet* in Umbra, though. There are clear divergences: Sun Ra does not share the interest in the "vernacular" almost universal in black poetics of the period—he never writes in "folk forms," or attempts to "transcribe" oral culture or the particularities of black speech onto the page. Michael Oren has noted that the Umbra writers established a close relationship with Langston Hughes, and were especially influenced by his 1961 poem *Ask Your Mama: 12 Moods for Jazz,* written to be performed to musical accompaniment.[27] It seems that Umbra's aesthetic was peculiar in that it could admit both Sun Ra and Hughes as models (*Umbra Anthology 1967–68* includes two poems by Hughes). Lorenzo Thomas is one of the only commentators to single out the group's remarkable breadth of interest, specifically emphasizing the *literary* influence of jazz musicians on the Umbra circle: "The musicians themselves were as cleverly articulate in words as they were on the bandstand; some, in fact, were poets and writers themselves. Charles Mingus and Sun Ra, both excellent poets and lyricists, spoke in vast but terse metaphors to those who took the time to listen."[28] Still, to judge from *Umbra Anthology: 1967–68,* Sun Ra's poetics are far from exemplary of the group's practice, even with regard to the more experimental work of David Henderson or the "transrealist" poetics of Norman Pritchard. It would seem that Umbra was mainly inspired by Sun Ra as a multidiscipline artist, and a spectacular elder figure who had been melding art, poetry, music, theater, esoteric philosophy, and communal living on his own terms since the late 1940s.

It should be noted that Umbra in general was quite receptive to artists in other disciplines: in addition to Sun Ra, saxophonist Archie Shepp (who himself was also a playwright) and visual artists Joe Overstreet and Tom Feelings often attended the meetings. Indeed, what commentators such as Oren and Thomas describe as the marginality and volatility of the Umbra collective—which in the end brought about the rupture in the group in 1964—may well have made space for similarly marginal or "liminal" figures like Sun Ra, who represented the edge between poetry and ritual, writing and music, that the group was keen to explore. Thomas, associated with the more nationalist wing of Umbra, argues that the group fostered connections with an older generation of Harlem intellectuals like poet Hart Leroi Bibbs, who represented an important "black artistic underground," the "teachers and curators of our cultural alternatives."[29] For the young writers, Sun Ra and the Arkestra would have certainly exemplified such a sought-out "alter" heritage. As Thomas notes, the musical performances of the Arkestra encapsulated this legacy, with their "gyroscopically delightful resolution" of the full spectrum of jazz styles from Jelly Roll Morton's "King Porter Stomp" all the way up to free jazz and beyond.[30]

Sun Ra's influence among black writers in New York reached its height in the summer of 1965, during the Black Arts movement, when many of the more nationalist members of Umbra followed Amiri Baraka to Harlem to form the Black Arts Repertory Theater and School. The Arkestra often performed at Black Arts events that summer, along with horn players Albert and Don Ayler, pianist Andrew Hill, and percussionist Milford Graves, and in fact Baraka says that Ra "became our resident philosopher," still living in the East Village but coming to Harlem most days to hold court at Black Arts gatherings.[31] David Henderson, who would edit *Umbra Anthology, 1967–68,* was a "serious student" of Sun Ra's teachings and writings at this point, as was Henry Dumas, and the Arkestra performed music to accompany Baraka's play *A Black Mass* at its premiere in Newark in May 1966.[32]

The collaboration between Sun Ra and Baraka was formalized most strikingly in *The Cricket: Black Music in Evolution,* the journal I discussed at some length in the introduction to this book. As I noted, the masthead of the first issue credits Baraka (then LeRoi Jones), Larry Neal, and A. B. Spellman as "editors," and Sun Ra and Milford Graves as "advisors." This confluence between the New Music and the New Poetry was not unique in itself: for instance, John Sinclair's *Change,* a journal published out of the Artists' Workshop in Detroit in the mid-1960s, similarly featured saxophonist Marion Brown as its New York editor, and published poetry by Brown and Sun Ra. But *The Cricket* was more ambitious: it did not simply publish poetry influenced by jazz, but instead argued that black culture was a continuum—what Baraka termed the "changing same," in an influential 1966 essay—characterized by a drive toward radical articulation found in the music and the poetry alike.[33] As we have seen, the opening editorial in *The Cricket* makes a claim for the intellectual qualities of the music: "The true voices of Black Liberation have been the Black musicians. They were the first to free themselves from the concepts and sensibilities of the oppressor. The history of Black Music is a history of a people's attempt to define the world in their own terms."[34] And a significant portion of the first issue is devoted to writings by musicians, including Milford Graves's diatribe about the racist economics of the music and a long essay by Sun Ra called "My Music Is Words."

Within the nationalist framing of *The Cricket,* however, "My Music Is Words" strikes a certain dissonance. Sun Ra's essay is the first in the journal, but it immediately refuses to take up the banner and represent: "Some people are of this world, others are not. My natural self is not of this world because this world is not of my not and nothingness, alas and happily."[35] The piece reiterates Ra's literary aesthetic of "enharmonic" word equation, "phonetic revelation"[36] through a kind of sight poetry. (As Ra puts it, in a poem included at the end of the first issue: "Through the eye/The sound has spoken."[37]) Most important, though, the essay also explains Ra's understanding of jazz, narrating his development from Fletcher Henderson to "Space Music" by drawing links between music and writing: "My words are the music and my music *are* the words because it is of equation is synonym of the Living Being."[38] Music here is conceived as the ultimate extension of poetics, a mode of articulating what is presently "impossible" or "unsaid" in words alone:

> My words are music and the music is words but sometimes the music is of the unsaid words concerning the things that always are to be, thus from the unsaid words which are of not because they are of those things which always are to be . . . nothing comes to be in order that nothing shall be because nothing from nothing leaves nothing.
>
> The music comes from the void, the nothing, the void, in response to the burning need for something else.[39]

The essay's accomplishment, in other words, is to remind us that if Sun Ra's writing is musical or phonetic, his music is equally "linguistic" in conception. As he writes in a later poem:

> Music is a voice
> A differential sound of words.
> A grammar and a language
> As well as a synthesizer.
> It is the reach toward it's twin immortality.[40]

The best-known Black Arts anthology from the 1960s to include Sun Ra's poetry was *Black Fire,* edited by Baraka and Larry Neal. Neal and Baraka read Sun Ra's work as exemplary of a drive in the movement to push literature and music closer to the community, toward a more ritualistic aesthetic and a more explicitly political agenda. In his afterword, Neal notes that black music has always represented the "collective psyche" better than black literature, and prescribes:

> Black literature must attempt to achieve that same sense of the collective ritual, but ritual directed at the destruction of useless, dead ideas. . . .
>
> Some of these tendencies already exist in the literature. It is readily perceivable in LeRoi Jones' *Black Mass,* and in a recent recording of his with the Jihad Singers. Also, we have the work of Yusuf Rahman, who is the poetic equivalent of Charlie Parker. Similar tendencies are found in Sun-Ra's music and poetry; Ronald Fair's novel, *Many Thousand Gone;* the short stories of Henry Dumas (represented in this anthology); the poetry of K. Kgositsile, Welton Smith, Ed Spriggs, and Rolland Snellings; the dramatic choreography of Eleo Pomare; Calvin Hernton's very explosive poems; Ishmael Reed's poetry and prose works . . . David Henderson's work.[41]

Neal makes explicit reference to Sun Ra's *poetry* as part of the new "tendencies." Oddly, though, this understanding jars with the Ra poems collected in the anthology, which like most of Ra's writing are dynamically flat and relatively undramatic. Take the conclusion of the poem "Of the Cosmic Blueprints," for example:

> If it was not slavery—
> It was the activation
> Of the Cosmic-blueprints . . .
> Sowing seeds of cosmos rare
> Casting ever down to ever lift above.
>
> If it was not slavery
> It was freedom not to be
> In order to ready for the discipline-plane
> From other-greater-worlds.[42]

Is this down with the program? Paradoxically, although Sun Ra is a musician (the only one represented in *Black Fire*), and although his writings are not unconnected to his musical performances, his poetry is simply not written to be theatrical, "ritualized," or "jazzy." So it is difficult to make this poem jibe with Neal's injunction that "the poet must become a performer, the way James Brown is a performer—loud, gaudy and racy. . . . He must learn to embellish the context in which the work is executed; and, where possible, link the work to all usable aspects of the music."[43] Sun Ra the musician might be close to this description—although the Arkestra's "cosmo dramas" might be *race-y* in a different way than James Brown's laborious funkfests. But it is less clear that the poetry of Sun Ra reproduced in *Black Fire* can be read as a clear example of this literary stance, "consolidating" writing and ritual, as Neal demands.

In rethinking the implications of Sun Ra as *poet,* somewhat the misfit, askew in the midst of the Black Arts, we might look in more detail at Ra's life and career: What are the poetics of Sun Ra, and where did they come from?

Reading the Erudite Ra

One of the more striking aspects of John Szwed's biography, *Space is the Place: The Lives and Times of Sun Ra,* is its documentation of Ra's literary and lyric thirsts. Szwed traces the reading list of the artist formerly known as Sonny Blount, and follows his progress in the 1940s through a staggering and thorough study of biblical interpretation, Egyptology, science fiction, and esoterica: works like *The Egyptian Book of the Dead, The Radix,* the works of Madame Blavatsky, biblical concordances, books on kabbalah, medieval hermeticism, gnosticism, and mysticism, George G. M. James' *Stolen Legacy,* contemporary black literature like Henry Dumas's stories and poems, former slave narratives, books on black folklore, Frederick Bodmer's *The Loom of Language, Blackie's Etymology,* and the Bible itself—in English, Hebrew, French, German, and Italian.[44]

Throughout this period writing poetry was an integral part of Ra's life and work. He had begun writing poetry at the age of nine, and he began handing out pamphlets and mimeographed broadsides during the legendary free-for-all public debates in the late 1940s in Chicago's Washington Park, featuring Ra's space disciples next to Elijah Muhammad's nascent Nation of Islam, Christian fundamentalist orators, Marxist exhorters, and straggling Garveyites. (Szwed notes that the Nation of Islam may have even been inspired to begin putting out their newspaper, *Muhammad Speaks,* by the numerous handouts and pamphlets Sun Ra brought to the park.[45]) When Ra formed his own band in the early 1950s (featuring musicians such as John Gilmore and Pat Patrick, who would go on to play with him for nearly forty years) and recorded *Jazz by Sun Ra* (later retitled *Sun Song*) on the Transition label in 1956, he made an unprecedented arrangement to insert a short pamphlet of poems into the record sleeve. One section explains in this synesthetic vein:

> Poems are Music:
>
> Some of the songs I write are based on my poems; for this reason, I am including some of them with this album in order that those who are interested may understand that poems are music, and that music is only another form of poetry. I consider every creative musical composition as being a *tone poem.*[46]

The poetry, mysticism, and philosophizing was lost on the few reviewers, including a young Nat Hentoff, who wrote in a 1958 *Down Beat,* "I'd like to hear them in a blowing date without the need for Hegel," and proceeded to complain about the space wasted on Ra's "remarkably bad 'poems.'"[47]

But poetry remained crucial to the development of the Arkestra. Some of Sun Ra's poems served as lyrics to tunes like "Enlightenment," some were programmatic (not sung but printed on record jackets to supplement the music) like "Nothing Is" and "Astro Black," and a number were used as chants as the Arkestra developed what Ra called "cosmo drama" or "myth-ritual," concerts with dancers, light shows, formulaic recitations and fantastic "space" costumes. Often these shows would close with members of the Arkestra parading into the audience, chanting "Rocket No. 9," "We Travel the Spaceways," "Outer Spaceways Incorporated," or "Space Is the Place." John Szwed informs us that even the written poetry was central to the Arkestra conception of cosmo drama: in concert, Sun Ra or one of the singers/dancers (like June Tyson or Verta Mae Grosvenor) would recite poems, sometimes to musical accompaniment.[48] There is a difference between the chants and the more esoteric and exegetical varieties of Ra's poetry, of course, but in many ways the verse seems to have functioned on a continuum—poetry practiced and disseminated in a space of ritual performance.

Sun Ra's writing was never published commercially, although in 1969 Doubleday expressed interest in publishing a collection. Instead, Ra prepared a two-volume selection called *The Immeasurable Equation* and *Extensions Out: The Immeasurable Equation Vol. 2,* which were initially published in 1972 by El Saturn Research, Ra's own recording company, and then reappeared in a number of revised and expanded editions over the next two decades (Figure 4.1).[49] (There are also a number of recordings of Sun Ra reading his poetry to the accompaniment of the Arkestra, including a radio broadcast on WXPN in Philadelphia on Christmas Day, 1976, which is a hard-to-find but particularly illuminating performance, and a session for Blast First Records in October 1991, in a project apparently aborted because of Sun Ra's declining health.[50]) In fact, the volumes of *The Immeasurable Equation* were never formally distributed—for years, copies have been obtainable almost exclusively through collectors or at Arkestra concerts. So the dissemination circuits even of the written poetry have always quite close to the ritual space of the Arkestra performances, and must be approached through that link.

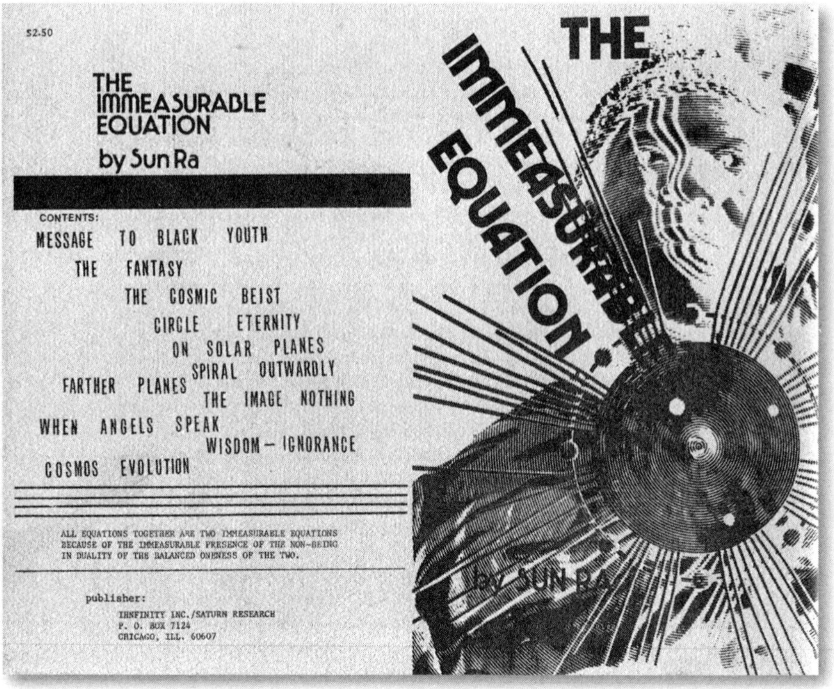

Figure 4.1 Book cover, *The Immeasurable Equation* (1972). Chicago Jazz Archive, Special Collections Research Center, University of Chicago Library.

Given Ra's eclectic intelligence and his penchant for mysticism, any typology of Sun Ra's poetry would have to be broad and eccentric. Besides the chants, the programmatic liner note poems, and the song lyrics, there are equally a variety of humorous or campy poems, for instance—as should be evident in the *Esquire* poem, Sun Ra's sense of comedy should never be underestimated. Humor was an important part of the Arkestra "cosmo ritual," as well. Lorenzo Thomas describes it this way: "Sun Ra and his band 'from outer space' have set out to design an 'alter destiny' for the inhabitants of this planet by means of a re-vision of the roots from which we spring. Their lever is joy."[51] Mystery smiles, for Sun Ra, and "the sound of joy is enlightenment." He even commented that the problem with most jazz avant-garde musicians is that they "don't know how to connect with people. . . . They have no sense of humor." Asked how his own music helped his listeners, he continued:

> First of all I express sincerity. There's also that sense of humor, by which people sometimes learn to laugh about themselves. I mean, the situation is so serious that the people could go crazy because of it. They need to smile and realize how ridiculous everything is. A race without a sense of humor is in bad shape. A race needs clowns. In earlier days people know that. Kings always had a court jester around. In that way he was always reminded how ridiculous things are. I believe that nations too should have jesters, in the congress, near the president, everywhere . . . You could call me the jester of the creator.[52]

This humor is apparent in a number of poems, including "Sun Song," "God Wot," "The Art Scene," and the deadpan "Birds without Wings":

> Birds without wings
> Birds without wings
> Poised, tensed———
> Are they unaware
> There are no wings
> Where wings should be?
>
> Birds without wings
> Poised and tensed
> Take off
> Sailing, sailing
> Alas. . . .
> They drop to earth.
>
> Are they hurt?
> Bruised, bewildered
> Angry
> They rush to the take-off place
> Again.
> Poised, tensed
> Ready, Go!
> Birds without wings.[53]

Along with this peculiar combination of philosophical reflection and something approaching camp, there is also a kind of didactic humor that surfaces in some of the exegetical "word equation" poems, as in "Alert,"[54] or "Detour": "This is a precision span / The journey is discipline plane! / Beware! / Rights / Rites / Right rite [. . .] Words / Snares: Entrapment [. . .]/ Words: Words! Beware / Warning!."[55]

The varieties of Sun Ra's poetry also include prophetic verse, pronouncements, poems that approach jeremiad—some almost petulant:

> Are you thinking of metaphysics
> alone? Well, don't.[56]

Some are nightmares, hauntings (such as "On the Edge of the Thin-Between," in *Extensions Out* and "The Visitation," one of the poems in *Black Fire*),[57] or respites, poetic harbors, visions of deliverance. Others work the recombination to the point of grammatical mind-bending:

> After that, what is there after that?
> And that afterwards is
> Or doubly no The not of those things which are. . . . .
> If I to be am
> Then to be is and are.[58]

There are invocations and praise songs, as to "The Outer Darkness" and "The Pivoting Planes." There are a number of quick poems, marginalia, ditties, and throwaways—like Langston Hughes, Sun Ra has a poem for every occasion, and the writing can be extremely uneven. Some poems approach a kind of numinous naturalism, like "When Angels Speak" and "Nothing Is":

> At first nothing is
> Then nothing transforms itself to be air
> Sometimes the air transforms itself to be water
> And the water becomes rain and falls to earth;
> Then again, the air through friction becomes fire
> So the nothing and the air and the water

And the fire are really the same
Upon different degrees.[59]

There are recurring quirks: Sun Ra seems to have a predilection for the French word *sans,* for example, and—although he almost never attempts to represent "dialect" or speech patterns in his poetry—inexplicably always writes "lightning" without the "g," as at the end of "Other Thoughts":

Now and then tiring of what they call reality
Bruised and beaten by its force
I step into the friendly city of the forest
Of what they call illusion
There to tend my wounds
And heal them
With the lightnin' touch
Of balanced thought
And the splendid comradeship of other worlds. . . .[60]

Broadsheet Gambits

Many of the predilections and formal strategies in Sun Ra's poetry are also on display in what may be the other most significant arena of his writing, the extraordinary broadsheets he distributed in Chicago in the 1950s. John Szwed notes that at the beginning of that decade, Sun Ra participated in an underground "discussion group" in Chicago with Alton Abraham, Luis T. Clarin, Lawrence M. Allen, James W. Bryant, and others. Apparently they read voraciously in a wide range of fields including not only music theory but also history, science, race, anthropology, Egyptology, numerology, the occult, and mysticism. In October 1952 the former Sonny Blount, then still a struggling pianist from Alabama, legally changed his name to "Le Sony'r Ra" and began performing with many of the musicians who would stay in the Arkestra for the next four decades, including the saxophonists Pat Patrick, John Gilmore, and Marshall Allen. But even as the Arkestra began to congeal, the study group (which eventually came to be called Thmei Research) seems to have played an equally important role in the development of Sun Ra's worldview and aesthetic sensibility. Szwed writes that "as their work developed their certainty grew, and they began to publish some of their research and spiritual findings in the form of leaflets which were passed out free, especially to musicians."[61]

Sun Ra began to spend a good deal of time in Chicago's Washington Park, which at that time was a congregation point for black public speakers and proselytizers of all stripes, including strident Black Muslims, dedicated Garveyites, communist labor organizers, and representatives from fundamentalist religious groups. Szwed claims that as a speaker in the park clamoring for the attention of black Chicagoans, Sun Ra "often outdrew the others because he offered to answer all biblical questions."[62] Ra himself would later comment: "When I was in Chicago I would always listen to black people talk different things. I was in the park when the Black Muslims were talking. Everything would be in that park. It was really wonderful in Chicago. Everybody was expressing their opinions. A true democracy in the black community."[63]

In a fascinating 1986 interview, the saxophonist John Gilmore goes so far as to claim that the Nation of Islam "embraced" Sun Ra's philosophy. They "started putting it in their newspapers as their own thing," Gilmore explains:

> He and I would always hang out and they would always be questioning Sun Ra. They used to love to talk with him because he would always tell them the opposite of what they would be expecting to be told." Gilmore goes so far as to contend that "that's how they got some of their philosophy because he would share things with them. . . . He told them about interchangeable g's and c's and other grammar, that's when they started giving themselves x's.[64]

Szwed's biography includes what was for decades thought to be the only surviving example of the broadsides distributed by Thmei Research, a dense page-long document titled "Solaristic Precepts" that Sun Ra or Pat Patrick gave to John Coltrane at some point during this period (Coltrane later copied it and distributed it to other musician friends). The intriguing but ultimately mysterious document offers what it terms "Secret Keys to Biblical Interpretation Leading to the Eternal Being," arguing that "to those who seek true wisdom, the bible should be considered as Code (Cod) word instead of the Good Word or God Word." As Szwed notes, "many of Sonny's concerns and methods are already recognizable in this early publication," including numerology, biblical exegesis, the "cross-referencing of folk and pop culture," the importance of secret knowledge, and "close examination of language through wordplay and the scrutiny of homophones or near homophones."[65]

In 2000 a folder marked "One of Everything" was discovered in a building on Chicago's South Side. It contained copies of forty-six other broadsheets from Sun Ra's years with Thmei Research. These documents—most of them one or two pages long, typed and mimeographed, sometimes with marginal handwritten notations—have been collected in the 2006 *The Wisdom of Sun Ra: Sun Ra's Polemical Broadsheets and Streetcorner Leaflets* collection edited by John Corbett.[66] The book offers handsome facsimiles of the originals; although most are readily legible, it also provides transcriptions. The broadsheets provide an invaluable window into Ra's world in the early 1950s, and are at times surprising, even shocking, in their polemicism. Corbett describes them as "raw Ra" and suggests that as he became better known as a musician, he actually learned to "tone down" his provocations (a claim that might seem surprising to anyone who has attended an Arkestra concert or seen *Space Is the Place*). Ra's "later activities," Corbett comments, "seemed calculated not to completely alienate a mixed 'crossover' audience. . . . By shifting his primary focus from the Bible to outer space, Ra allowed himself to be seen as more than a street-corner religious zealot."[67]

The broadsheets evidence a remarkable generic variety, including everything from commentary on U.S. race relations, usually expressly directed to a black readership ("A Spook Sho' Is a Dragg, Man. . . . He's a Dragg. . . . ."; "There's a Nigger in the Woodpile"; "Solution to the Negro Problem"); to political punditry ("What America Should Consider"; "United States at the Crossroads"); to revivalist sermonizing and biblical exegesis ("Jesus Said, 'Let the Negro Bury the Negro' "; "The Bible Was Not Written for Negroes"); to jeremiad ("I Have Set before You Life and Death—Choose Life"; "Wake Up! Wake Up! Wake Up!"); to essays in spiritual guidance ("The True Way to Life"; "Keys to Understanding the Hidden Meaning of the Bible"); to seeming whimsy or non sequitur ("Little i's I Love You"; "Humpty Dumpty"). Some pages are structured as Socratic dialogues, while others come across as screeds—"THIS IS THE LAST WARNING TO AMERICA WE AS AMBASSADOR TO THIS COUNTRY OFFER AMERICA WISDOM AND LIFE IF SHE WILL PUBLICLY ADMIT HER SINS" (67)—and still others take up an esoteric mode of homological argumentation derived from kabbalistic and Talmudic strategies of numerological substitution and alphabetic recombination.

The documents are not entirely divorced from their historical moment, although their points of reference tend to be derived more from Cold War politics—as in one of the dialogues, where the question "Is the White Race going to be destroyed by God?" receives the answer: "No. Instead they are going to be sent a teacher to teach them the real truth and if they reject him, he will be sent to Russia and Russia will then become the center of the new world" (66)—than from the space-age rhetoric that would become so prominent in Sun Ra's language by the end of the decade. Some sheets, though, seem much more playful, based in a kind of poetics derived from capricious free association with black vernacular clichés. In one titled "Language of the Gods," Ra writes:

> LISTEN AT ME WHILE I BLOW . . . I'M GOING TO
> BLOW, MAN. . . . . .
> COOL IT, GEM. . . . . I'M GOING TO BLOW . . . COOL IT
> GEM . . .
> WHAT'S HAPPENING? . . . WHAT'S HAPPENING,
> GEM? . . . WHAT'S HAPPENING, GEM. . . . .
> WHEN I CALLED NO ONE ANSWERED .. WHAT'S
> HAPPENING, GEM? (67)

The charming "Little i's I Love You" swerves from its interpretation of God's "gift to the world," the divine Word, to a colloquial rephrasing of that gift ("The word is GAB .. Gift of Gab is Gift of the Word"), to an anagrammatic reformulation of the meaning of that gift: "The Gift is GAB .. The gift is BAG .. at least IT"S [*sic*] IN THE BAG!" Abruptly and hilariously, we are informed that "The Bag is very important .. that is why SANTA CLAUS keeps it with him" (94).

When one considers that these broadsheets and leaflets were being handed out almost exclusively to an African American popular readership, it becomes clear that the real challenge of Sun Ra's writing is its seeming dismissal, in the most caustic terms, of the very category of racial identification. "THE AMERICAN NEGRO LOVES IGNORANCE BETTER THAN HE DOES HIS OWN SOUL," as he writes in one document (77). In another, again examining the vernacular language of race (the colloquial designation "spook"), Sun Ra counsels:

> STOP! LOOK! LISTEN! WHAT PEOPLE ON EARTH CALL THEMSELVES SPOOKS? [...] IN WHAT COUNTRY DO THE SPOOKS DWELL? ... IN AMERICA OF COURSE...... OUTSIDE OF AMERICA THERE ARE NO PEOPLE CALLED SPOOKS.... THE SPOOKS ARE IN AMERICA ... NO OTHER BLACK OR BROWN RACE CALL THEMSELVES SPOOKS. THE SPOOKS IN AMERICA ARE DIFFERENT FROM ANY OTHER RACE ON THIS PLANET. THEY ARE MORE CONFUSED ... THEY HATE EACH OTHER ... THEY HATE THEIR OWN INDIVIDUAL SELF.... THEY HATE THE THOUGHT OF BEING WHAT THEY ARE ... (72)

As a social label, the "Negro" must be abandoned and destroyed, Sun Ra argues. It is a "dead" category—nothing more than the marker of social death. He finds confirmation in the Bible by arguing that alphabetic substitution allows us to recognize that the word *Negro* is equivalent to the word *Necro* (which means "dead body" in Greek); thus Jesus's famous injunction in the New Testament to let the dead bury the dead can be interpreted to mean, "Let the Negro Bury the Negro" (66).

From one perspective this appears to be a disturbing instance of internalized racism, a black artist violently rejecting the community of which he is a part. But in the context of the 1950s, at the threshold of the civil rights era, it also might be understood as a political rejection of the old, conciliatory label of racial community, and the demand for its replacement with an adequately righteous term of self-determination. When Ra bluntly proclaims that "IT IS A KNOWN FACT THAT THE AMERICAN NEGRO SPEAKS AND ACTS DIFFERENT FROM ANY OTHER NATION ON THIS EARTH" (89), what is striking in his rhetoric is the assumption that African Americans constitute not only a community but a "nation." And in many of the broadsheets, there becomes apparent not so much a suggestion of self-deprecation but rather a call for willful autonomy, communal self-definition, a black nationalism clothed in the rhetoric of Christian vindication:

> God said "Be you holy even as I am holy." Lev. 20:7
>
> Holy means separate . . . To be separate is to be SEGREGATED . . . SEGREGATED . . . I TESTIFY THAT YOU ARE HOLY .. I TESTIFY IN THE NAME OF JESUS CHRIST THAT YOU ARE SEPARATE .. TO BE SEPARATE IS TO BE HOLY. . . . . . . GOD SAID "BE YOU HOLY EVEN AS I AM HOLY."
>
> YOU ARE INDISPUTABLY THE MOST HOLY PEOPLE I HAVE EVER SEEN, OR HAVE EVER READ ABOUT*** OR HAVE EVER HEARD ABOUT . . . (74)

Ultimately the importance of these ephemeral documents as an archive may be related to what they suggest about the volatile cauldron of mid-century black nationalism in Chicago, and, more broadly, about the unpredictable contours of underground or autodidactic black intellectual activity. They force us to take stock of the persistent cross-fertilization among currents of black radicalism that are sometimes all too easily assumed to be separate spheres. Even if they circulate at a level that is closer to the ground (and thus harder to track) than the newspaper or the magazine, these broadsheets suggest the complexity of the black counterpublic sphere: its particular modes of address, its homegrown institutions, its internal debates, its cultivation of audience both through performance (speakers competing for the attention of passersby) and through reading. When read as a whole, this compilation of "the wisdom of Sun Ra" (the title of one of the broadsheets) (123) in the form of hand-distributed leaflets is provocative because it implies that part and parcel of that "wisdom" is Ra's commitment not only to serious, collective research but also to archivization itself—to self-publication, independent circulation, and preservation ("One of Everything").

Perhaps surprisingly, Sun Ra does not have a great deal to say about music in these broadsheets. But there are a few brief passages where the texts link vernacular declaration to critical insight, in a kind of intimation that the righteousness of what one says (if a "sound" pronouncement is one "founded on truth or right") is inherently a matter of acoustics ("how you going to sound")—although, of course, in the context of Washington Park, this is perhaps more an allusion to the megaphonics of public speaking than to musical performance. As it is proclaimed and promised in "Johnny One Note":

> i know how i'm going to sound. i'm going to sound so loud that
>   it will wake up the dead.
> HOW YOU GOING TO SOUND, MAN? .. HOW YOU'RE
>   GOING TO SOUND, MAN?. . . . . . .
> SOUND also means FOUNDED ON TRUTH OR RIGHT.
> ARE NEGROES SOUND? EVERY NEGRO WHO
>   LOVES GOD IS SOUND. (106)

Toward a Poetics of Exegesis

The poetic practices of Sun Ra might best be described as a poetics of recombination or an *exegetical* poetics. On the sleeve of the classic Saturn record *Cosmic Tones for Mental Therapy* (recorded in New York in 1963), there are words from Sun Ra and from Umbra-affiliated writer Henry Dumas about what the latter called "the ultimate rhythm of cosmic mathematics." Sun Ra's statement is programmatic, but seemingly not in relation to the music:

> PROPER EVALUATION OF WORDS AND LETTERS IN THEIR PHONETIC AND ASSOCIATED SENSE, CAN BRING THE PEOPLE OF EARTH INTO THE CLEAR LIGHT OF PURE COSMIC WISDOM.[68]

This note would itself later be published as a poem titled "To the Peoples of the Earth."[69] Sun Ra would return to this formulation of poetics again and again: the idea that his poems were, as he told one interviewer, "all scientific equations. I am dealing outside conventional wisdom. I want to explore the ultradimensions of being."[70]

Although the relationship of Ra's writing to black traditions of poetry was oblique, there is evidence that he read in those traditions. At one point, he noted: "I wasn't influenced by Paul Laurence Dunbar's poetry. He was a sentimentalist. I'm a scientist. . . . I take the position of a scientist who comes from another dimension."[71] What returns is that claim of science, a word Ra seems to understand through his commitment to Egyptian-derived mystery systems and kabbalistic hermeneutics:

> What I want to do is associate words so they produce a certain fact. If you mix two chemical products you produce a reaction. In the same way if you put together certain words you'll obtain a reaction which will have a value for people on this planet. That's why I continue to put words together. Einstein said he was looking for an equation for eternal life. But we built the atomic bomb, and his project has never materialized. But I'm sure he was right. To put words together, or, even if you could, to paint the image that is necessary to put out the vibrations that we need, that would change the destiny of the whole planet.[72]

There is an especially pronounced echo of traditions of Kabbalah, an esoteric and multiple-layered tradition of post-Talmudic Jewish mysticism in which the ecstatic experience of the Torah often involves breaking down the Hebrew text, contemplating a single letter as a divine name, or even recombining letters in the Torah to aid allegorical readings of biblical passages. Even for the more radical kabbalists, though, such as Abraham Abulafia, who used a host of techniques like *Temurah* (letter substitution in carefully limited cases), *Gematria* (numerological substitution), and letter combination (anagram, palindrome), still Hebrew was privileged over all languages for its claimed divine nature.[73] Ra's practice differs in that it is multilingual, willing to make "equations" between different languages. He told one interviewer:

> I'm a wordologist. Words' what's doing this. You've got to have numerology. You've got to have phonetics. You've got to have all these things and then the world will straighten out. They worship the Son of God but they don't understand. In French, Son's equal to "sound," so, "sound of God." They've got it wrong. They think it's "the son." They say the word was made flesh. It's really about *sound*—and it wasn't made flesh, if was made *fresh.* All these things the creator told me in Alabama. I'm dealing with words that can prove themselves—that can prove themselves to be correct.[74]

(Unfortunately, the corpus of articles and interviews around Sun Ra often leave only hints as to the implications of such procedures. This is partly due to Sun Ra's own obfuscation strategies, and partly because interviewers simply could not or would not follow him down these paths. We are left with a kind of biographical literalism, an attempt to tease out the "real life" of Sonny Blount, that ends up disparaging the seriousness of his poetics. For instance, directly after the passage above, the interviewer's next question is: "You were born in Alabama?")

As these permutations of the "*sound* of God" indicate, Sun Ra's poetics also differ from kabbalistic exegesis in that Ra is most interested in phonetic (rather than graphic) recombinations and substitutions as a route to the allegorical. He trades primarily in homonyms, not in letters or words. Consider the conclusion of "Every Thought Is Alive":

> The myth among other things
> May be considered as "a tale that is told",
> And the end of the tale is a tale that is
> tolled and likewise
> The end of a tale is the goal.[75]

So Ra's biblical hermeneutics *sound* a bit more than the literal mathematics of a kabbalist like Abulafia. In reconstructing and recombining the Scripture, Sun Ra "hears" it off the page into allegory:

> You're just like in a science fiction film now. You've outlived the Bible, which was your scenario. Everybody had a part in that.

> Black people have been singing a long time, 'When the roll is called up yonder I'll be there.' But they didn't know it was spelled r-o-l-e, not r-o-l-l. They had a part to act and they acted it. White people began to think that black people are like this or like that, but they were only acting parts. Someone gave them these parts to act. Of course, the white race had a part to act too. They had to deal with white supremacy and other things—lies. But the point is that they all were acting parts in this play, this drama. You might call it a passion play. The passion play moves over into words.[76]

In offering these examples, I should note also that Sun Ra's poetics of recombination are not always directed at phrases from biblical scripture. The techniques and procedures of Sun Ra's exegesis are reminiscent of kabbalah, but Ra employs them to read both the sacred and the profane—verses from the Bible about "the Word of God," as well as lyrics from slave spirituals like "When the Roll Is Called Up Yonder," common clichés like "Once upon a time" and "Tomorrow never comes," and even 1960s pop culture epigrams like "I'm free, white, and twenty-one." (At the same time, although Ra's exegetical devices are particularly complex, such a breadth of analysis is again quite reminiscent of the African American folk visionary tradition.) Thus the poetics of Ra are singular not just in their multilingualism and their phonetic focus, but also in their willingness to read the "light of pure cosmic wisdom" by recombining a wide variety of texts. For Ra, the sacred can be read through any surface.

Szwed tells us that one of the first books on poetics that attracted Ra was southern poet Sidney Lanier's 1880 *The Science of English Verse.*[77] Somewhat like Poe's idiosyncratic work on the "Poetic Principle," Lanier's book is peculiar in that it argues for the primacy of sound as artistic material in verse, examining categories of "duration," "intensity," "pitch," and "tone-color." There is also a long section on poetic rhythm. For Lanier, all verse, whether recited *or* on the page, amounts ultimately to "a set of specially related sounds."[78] He coins the phrase "the imagination of the ear" in deference to this phonic primacy: "those perceptions of sound which come to exist in the mind, not by virtue of actual vibratory impact upon the tympanum immediately preceding the perception, but by virtue of indirect causes (such as the characters of print and of writing) which in any way amount to practical equivalents of such impact."[79] As we see, this is a little different formally from the modernist espousal of poetry "approaching the quality of music" in one way or another, whether in Louis Zukofsky's objectivism or in Langston Hughes' blues poetry. Lanier sees no division between speech and writing; all graphic techniques point to *phonema:* so he places emphasis on "sounds and silences" and their representations in form.[80] In other words, poetry ends up being music: "The main distinction between music and verse is, when stated with scientific precision, the difference between the scale of tones used in music and the scale of tones used by the human speaking-voice."[81] Moreover, speech, not being limited to a tempered scale, has a much broader tone-range to explore than music for Lanier.[82]

This is a bit too dogmatic for Sun Ra, but we see some of the beginnings of his phonetic poetics here. Lanier finally does not seem to recognize difference among various graphic techniques: perhaps because his conception of literary form is so conventional, it never occurs to him that the manipulation of orthographic conventions (the way a phoneme is represented) and line can hone and alter an articulation, can affect the way the ear is "coordinated" to a particular "set of sounds." He doesn't see, in Aldon Nielsen's words, that "writing affords the possibility of transpositions beyond those available in speech."[83] Nor is Lanier attentive to tensions between the structure of a poem on the page and its possible reading(s) off that page—issues of performance, accent, improvisation, the poem as kind of "score" to be realized in recitation. To Sun Ra, writing more than half a century later, and after the detonation of black expressive cultures in the 1920s, these issues come easily. When you said "good morning" to Sun Ra, he would ask whether you meant "good morning" or "good mourning."[84]

What poetics do we end up with here? One might note some convergences between Sun Ra's aesthetic and some more contemporary modes of black experimental writing. I'm thinking of the similar kind of recombinatory impulse in the work of poets like Harryette Mullen and Ed Roberson, or in the "anagrammatic scat" of Nathaniel Mackey. Interestingly, though, the most pronounced correspondences arise with a number of the black Caribbean writers who have espoused various approaches to the "Calibanization" of English, twisting sound and sense, deforming and reforming the shape of words on the page. Edward Kamau Brathwaite, especially in the trilogy comprising the books *Mother Poem, Sun Poem,* and *X/Self,* begins to "wring the word" in a manner that—though much more based in orality, and in Bajan speech styles—at times comes near the etymological interest in the "open" or polyvalent word that we find in Sun Ra's writing.[85] In a number of his articles, as well as the poems, Brathwaite has offered permutations or recombinations of signature words like *nam:*

> "Nam" is "man" spelt backwards, man in disguise, man who has to reverse his consciousness as the capsule reverses its direction in order to enter in to the new world in a disguised or altered state of consciousness. "Nam" also suggests "root," or beginning, because of "yam," the African "yam," "nyam," to eat, and the whole culture contained in it. It is then able to expand itself back from "nam" to "name," which is another form of "name": the name that you once had has lost its "e," that fragile part of itself, eaten by Prospero, eaten by the conquistadores, but preserving its essentialness, its alpha, its "a" protected by those two intransigent consonants, "n" and "m." The vibrations "nmnmnm" are what you get before the beginning of the world. And that "nam" can return to "name" and the god "Nyame."
>
> And so it is possible to conceive of our history not only being capsuled and contracted, but finally expanding once more outwards.[86]

The difference between Brathwaite and Sun Ra, finally, would hinge on the commitment of the former to the lyric, and to poetic form. Brathwaite recombines, but is not exegetical, in the poetry—words are wrung and thereby rung, but the operations are not explained. Brathwaite reveals a word-artist's reluctance to divulge, to decode, for the reader, preferring to let the lyric sing. In the fascinating notes to *X/Self* (1987), for instance, he opens by writing:

> My references (my nommos and icons) may appear mysterious, meaningless even, to both Caribbean and non-Caribbean readers.

> So the notes . . . which I hope are helpful, but which I provide with great reluctance, since the irony is that they may suggest the poetry is so obscure in itself that it has to be lighted up; is so lame, that it has to have a crutch; and (most hurtful of all) that it is bookish, academic, "history". . . . The impression, in other words, is that I write the poems from the notes, when in fact I have to dig up these notes from fragments, glimpses, partial memories.[87]

The supplementary notes notwithstanding, Brathwaite's poems themselves inscribe the page with a graphic musicality, as in "X/Self's Xth Letters from the Thirteen Provinces," where we encounter the poet "sittin down here in front a dis stone/face" with an "electrical mallet," carving and "chipp/in dis poem onta dis tablet/chiss/ellin darkness writin in light" (87). The lyricism is left ragged, intentionally unfinished, so that the implications of the phrase "X/Self" for our understanding of Caribbean subjectivity continue to resonate suggestively: "Why a callin it/x? //a doan writely/know."[88] Sun Ra, as a multidisciplinary artist arguably with less of a commitment to poetic lyric, never minds being didactic, even when it renders his writing flat. So in the place of Brathwaite's obliquity, we find Ra's poem "Symbolic Meaning of the X," which almost reads like an explication of *X/Self* through myth-science recombination, opening:

> THE TIME OF EARTH IS THE X OF EARTH
> X IS THE TIME
> X IS THE EMIT
> THAT IS: THE CAST OUT
> X IS THE AIM. . . . THE SOLUTION
> SYMBOL OF THE PROBLEM. . . .
> X IS THE BRIDGE SYMBOL ANSWER
> VIEW X FROM MANY POINTS,
> AND SEE THE POTENTIAL. . . . . .[89]

Sun Ra, assuming the prophet's prerogative, would appear to *prefer* didacticism in his poetry, letting his words fall prosaically to emphasize the mathematics of the "sound-equations" over the music of the sounds.

Still, it should be clear that Ra is much closer to Brathwaite's poetics (even the latter's recent "Sycorax video style," which goes so far as to tamper with fonts and type sizes in an effort to catch a musical dynamic among words on the page) than to other varieties of so-called concrete or visual poetry. At times this characterization might be surprising: one might expect Sun Ra's Egyptian interest to lead him to a poetics reminiscent, say, of the opening of Zora Neale Hurston's classic essay "Characteristics of Negro Expression," where she claims that "the white man thinks in a written language and the Negro thinks in hieroglyphics." Hurston provocatively asserts that the "Negro . . . must add action to it to make it do. So we have 'chop-axe,' 'sitting-chair,' 'cook-pot' and the like because the speaker has in his mind the picture of the object in use."[90] But Sun Ra's studied focus on phonetics, the ways sound inheres in the written word, never approaches this pictorial sense of language. Ra seems attracted to the cryptology represented by hieroglyphs, but seldom turns to their implications for a figurative or "ideogrammatic" poetry on the page.

I close with one more comparison, to take us back to the "myth-science" question with which we began. It will perhaps be surprising to note the correspondence between Sun Ra's theory of poetic language and that of Guyanese novelist Wilson Harris. But consider the "Manifesto of the Unborn State of Exile" in Harris's 1965 novel, *The Eye of the Scarecrow:*

> Language is one's medium of the vision of consciousness. There are other ways—shall I say—of arousing this vision. But language alone can express (in a way which goes beyond any physical or vocal attempt) the sheer—the ultimate "silent" and "immaterial" complexity of arousal. Whatever sympathy one may feel for a concrete poetry—where physical objects are used and adopted—the fact remains (in my estimation) that the original grain or grains of language cannot be trapped or proven. It is the sheer mystery—the impossibility of trapping its own grain—on which poetry lives and thrives. . . . Which is concerned with a genuine sourcelessness, a fluid logic of image. So that any genuine act of possession by one's inner eye is a subtle dispersal of illusory fact, dispossession of one's outer or physical eye.[91]

In Sun Ra there is also a turn away from the "pure" formalism of a "concrete poetry" and toward a poetics that reaches for the sacred, for "vision of consciousness," arousing it through language—through what Sun Ra calls the "multi-self of words," and what Harris calls "a fluid logic of image." For Sun Ra as for Harris, languages are broken, intermingled, already contaminated by ragged roots that must be *read* to tease out or stitch up the fabric of "mystery," the "universal" but uncapturable "principle of mediation." (Sun Ra's poetics may be more drastic only in that they finally operate not just on language, but also on the self—thus Ra's early renaming and lifelong effort to construct an "alter" autobiography. For him, the "multi-self of words" is also, and profoundly, the multiple recombinations of the poem that is Sun Ra.) Consequently, in such reading, in the rehearing of the jagged edge between phoneme and grapheme, the stakes are high.

This "arousal" of one's "inner eye" beyond the superficialities of everyday life, beyond what Harris terms "illusory fact," is not an idealism, in the end: it is an exegetical imperative. It is not an espousal of some "pure speech" to be reconstructed through some messianic poetry; instead, it is the "impossible" task of spelling something new and different, mankind's "alter destiny," walking the tightrope between sign and speech. The stakes are high—Sun Ra would say the stakes might well be *hi,* be welcoming, brothers of the impossible peering over the rim of the myth to say hello. Solar myth-science: a *poetics of exegesis,* from the Greek *exegeisthai,* "to explain, to interpret," from *ex-* and *hegeisthai,* "to lead": thus, "to lead out or away." A poetics where sound-equations mark an impossible exit, a way out of no way: from Mr. Ra to mystery.

five
Zoning Mary Lou Williams Zoning

In the first three months of 1974, the pianist Mary Lou Williams recorded an album titled *Zoning,* perhaps the most extraordinary venture of the final years of her long and varied career in jazz. The record, on which Williams is accompanied by bassist Bob Cranshaw, drummer Micky Roker, and (on two tracks) Zita Carno on a second piano, was both a "revelation and a reaffirmation of what had always made Williams so unique": if it offers formal experimentation with unusual meters and extended harmonies (especially in the two piano pieces), the record also displays Williams's characteristic spare elegance firmly rooted in the blues idiom.[1] In the liner notes to the original LP, her close friend and manager Peter O'Brien writes that the title is "a piece of freshly coined slang invented by Mary Lou Williams to describe what must be done by the composer or musician in performance if true musical art is to result. . . . When a musician really creates, he zones all the elements, or things, into music: something fresh, astonishing, whole and complete—not into something borrowed, disparate, haphazard, merely decorative, certainly not into something finally destructive. To make good music everything must be zoned."[2] Here I will use this striking definition of the term, so resolutely transitive, as a point of entry into a consideration of Williams's aesthetics, in order to ask to what degree we can take *zoning* as something like a methodological principle at the base of her entire oeuvre. I am particularly intrigued by the term's implications for an understanding of jazz history, a constant concern for Williams during the final two decades of her life.

Mary Lou Williams is by no means the only jazz musician who has been driven to write or perform a history of the music. Pianist Muhal Richard Abrams has stated that he considers himself "a music historian as well as a practicing musician."[3] Beyond the many written autobiographies by jazz musicians, a number (including pianist Ben Sidran, banjo player Danny Barker, reedman Anthony Braxton, and trombonist George

Lewis) have written entire books about various aspects of the history of the music.[4] Likewise, there are a number of instances where musicians (including Louis Armstrong, Baby Dodds, Bunk Johnson, Willie "the Lion" Smith, Jelly Roll Morton, Jo Jones, and Cannonball Adderley) have attempted recorded overviews that involve playing through a lineage of styles, often interspersed with spoken narrative and sometimes autobiography.[5] Nevertheless, Williams stands out, not only as the most prominent female instrumentalist in the music—the "first lady of jazz," as she was often called fondly—but also because jazz history became such a prominent element in her recorded and concert work. Since she had been performing for so long (she first recorded in 1927), by the 1970s she was habitually described in program notes as perhaps "the only major Jazz Artist who has lived and *played through* all the eras in the history and development of Jazz."[6] In other words, Williams's efforts at recorded jazz history are peculiar in that they are posed as something like performative metonyms, in which jazz history inhabits and is remembered in the resonant fingerings of a singular body and the shifts of an individual corpus. She recorded a now-obscure LP called *A Keyboard History* in the spring of 1955, when she returned to New York after a few years in Paris, and it is a project that presents her as a living repository of black music: moving sequentially through a spiritual ("Joshua Fit the Battle of Jericho"), ragtime ("Fandango"), swing ("Roll 'Em"), and a few bebop tunes.[7]

A few years later, at a benefit concert at Philharmonic Hall in November 1963, Williams for the first time gave a concert organized to illustrate the history of the music.[8] It would become the predominant theme in her public appearances in the subsequent years, and Peter O'Brien eventually convinced her to record it. In 1970 Williams produced a session of herself speaking and playing on a Tandberg tape recorder in her apartment in Harlem. The album was released by Folkways Records in 1978 under the title *The History of Jazz.* Her first spoken words frame the project as what one might call—to appropriate one of the characteristic, albeit oxymoronic, titular habits of W. E. B. Du Bois—an autobiography of jazz:

> Hi, I am Mary Lou Williams,
>
> I have played through all the eras of Jazz. The spirituals, ragtime which my mother taught me when I was three years old. Then the time with John Williams when the Jazz bands was

> the name of any small group which played with a beat. And then the Kansas City Swing era with Andy Kirk's band. Then bop, the Dizzy Gillespie era.
>
> From suffering came the spirituals. Songs of joy and songs of sorrow. The main origin of American Jazz is a spiritual. Because of the deeply religious background of the Black American he was able to mix this strong influence with rhythms that reach deep enough into the inner self to give expression to outcries of censored joy which became known as Jazz. . . . After the bop era it seemed that the creation and the heritage was a little bit lost. . . . Now we come to a period of the music wherein the disturbance and unrest of the world has crept in to destroy the roots and heritage. Titles are misused and confusing and much kissing and hugging but very little charity and love.[9]

For Williams, this historicism is also geared to serve as a means of negotiating change in the music: the future of jazz, as well as its past. To put it differently, this approach considers a certain historicism to be the condition of possibility for a revolutionary aesthetics, for the incarnation of sounds "you've never heard in your life before," in Williams's words.[10] Perhaps more than any other musician aside from Coleman Hawkins, Williams was adamant throughout her more than sixty-year career about working to develop her musicianship in the face of new turns in jazz. In 1947 she published an article called "Music and Progress" where she comments, "If we are to make progress in modern music, or, if you prefer *jazz,* we must be willing and able to open our minds to new ideas and developments."[11] Two years later, she told jazz scholar Barry Ulanov: "I broadened, I moved, I experimented. That's what I've always taught the kids who come to me. You've got to keep going. There's only one reason, really, to stop. That's to take account, to get new sounds, to get the sounds you're not hearing."[12] This remarkably adaptive orientation is apparently rooted in Mary's experience of the advent of bebop. To most players and audiences associated with big band swing in the 1930s (and Williams was the driving force as composer and arranger for Andy Kirk's Clouds of Joy, one of the best bands of that era), bop arrived as a challenge, infuriating and insular, craggy and undanceable. But for Williams, who was "dissatisfied completely with the older music," living through the change was exhilarating: "the music was so beautiful it just gave you a sight of a new picture happening in the jazz. It had such a beautiful feeling. It didn't take me very long to get on to it or create in my own way from it."[13] During the 1940s, Williams became a mentor of sorts to the most brilliant of the young composers associated with the new music: Bud Powell, Tadd Dameron, and Thelonious Monk often gathered at her apartment to experiment with new tunes and arrangements.[14]

The Problem of the Avant-Garde

At the same time, the identification and validation of the "new" is a continual issue in Williams's statements about the history of jazz. Given that she associated the music so strongly with African American identity, as something close to the crystallization of a spiritual force, by the 1960s Williams worried that the function of the music had been corrupted by decadence or commercialism—that "the creation and the heritage" had been "a little bit lost," as she phrases it in *The History of Jazz.* Even years earlier there was a certain hesitancy in her discussions of a musician such as Thelonious Monk, whose knotty style was at the center of the debates around bebop in the 1940s. In a long, revealing autobiographical text that was edited and serialized in the late 1940s in the journal *Melody Maker,* Williams defends Monk's technique, noting that he "really used to blow on piano" during jam sessions in Kansas City in the late 1930s: "I *know* how Monk can play." Yet her tone shifts as she goes on to add that Monk:

> felt that musicians should play something new, and started doing it. Most of us admire him for this. He was one of the original modernists all right, playing pretty much the same harmonies then that he's playing now. Only in those days we called it "Zombie music" and reserved it mostly for musicians after hours.
>
> Why "Zombie music"? Because the screwy chords reminded us of music from "Frankenstein" or any horror film. I was one of the first with these frozen sounds, and after a night's jamming

> would sit and play weird harmonies (just chord progressions) with Dick Wilson, a very advanced tenor player.[15]

The passage begins in admiration for Monk's insistence on invention, on "something new," but then seems to dismiss the very innovation of the "original modernists" of the moment by saying that their music was a kind of "after-hours" amusement ("zombie," "screwy," "weird") among musicians of an earlier era.

Interestingly, Williams attempted both to give voice to and to control this threat in her performances of jazz history. *The History of Jazz* includes a medley of spirituals, ragtime ("Who Stole the Lock off the Henhouse Door"), Kansas City swing ("Nite Life"), boogie-woogie ("Hesitation Boogie"), blues and bop, but the penultimate track is supposed to represent "avant-garde or free." It is titled with a provocation: "A Fungus Amungus." Williams borrowed the phrase from her close friend Lorraine Gillespie (Dizzy's wife), who used to tell a joke about a black preacher "who is trying to deliver a sermon, and is constantly interrupted by a loudmouth urging him to continue it. Full of righteous indignation, the preacher tried until it because unbearable, and then he shouted 'Everybody stand up! There's a fungus amungus.' "[16] The piece noodles through a series of "frozen chords," evoking those late-night Kansas City sessions. After its odd germination, Williams closes the record by reasserting order in the form of the blues riff called "Medi I" that opens the album and underlies all the narration.

The History of Jazz thus would seem to figure "avant-garde or free" music as a sort of invasive organicism, a growth that threatens the communal structure of improvisation with distracting infectious symptoms of illness. The enemy within sows mistrust and dissension into the structure of the ensemble.[17] The title oddly equates performative lack of fit with a malapropism represented as originating in the black vernacular tradition. This is a stark contrast to the long list of black writers (including Zora Neale Hurston, Sun Ra, and Harryette Mullen) who tend to see in the vagaries of wordplay in the black vernacular possibilities of lyric invention that are salutary, even revelatory. For example, James Weldon Johnson's preface to his 1927 collection of poems *God's Trombones* extols the particular textualism of the "old-time Negro preacher" as a practice that could sometimes stretch the written word to heights that were radically inventive, even if humorous. The old-time preacher, Johnson writes, would not:

> balk at any text within the lids of the Bible. There is the story of one who after reading a rather cryptic passage took off his spectacles, closed the Bible with a bang and by way of preface said, "Brothers and sisters, this morning—I intend to explain the unexplainable—find out the undefinable—ponder over the imponderable—and unscrew the inscrutable."[18]

Instead Williams's use of the Gillespie anecdote reads the slippage in black speech as evidence of inordinate pretension, a point at which, if language fails at a moment of challenge and panic, by implication music likewise collapses (or "freezes"—staggers like the living dead) when it attempts to move beyond the advances of bop without retaining the foundation of the spirituality at the origins of the music. The satire of Williams's title is closer to the Joycean pratfalls of a novel like William Melvin Kelley's 1970 *Dunfords Travels Everywheres,* which spends one chapter sending up a pompous academic lecturing about the dangers of a "foxnoxious bland of stimili" tearing apart the "intrafricanical firmly structure of our distinct coresins: The Blafringro-Arumericans."[19]

One might say that with the satirical title, and the positioning of this tune in the trajectory of *The History of Jazz,* Williams "zones" the avant-garde, containing its infectious threat and pulling it back into its place within a blues-based pianistic tradition. At the same time, there is something odd about the gesture, since "A Fungus Amungus" does not comes across as satirical in its musical conception or in Williams's performance. Gerrard Pochonet, in the liner notes to a 1964 recording of this composition, calls it "a pretty display of unconventional keyboard artistry," and compares it to impressionist painting. "You will soon find that there is more to it than meets the ear," he writes, "and you will travel to the improbable Land of Oo-Bla-Dee on the flying carpet of notes provided by Mary Lou Williams."[20] Is the song then a satire at all? Returning to the title "A Fungus Amungus," we might note that Lorraine Gillespie's anecdote concerns a "loud-mouth," and yet the tongue-happy member of the congregation is not attempting to disturb or undermine the sermon. On the contrary, we are informed that the interruptions are exclamations of support, "urging" the preacher to "continue," in a mode altogether familiar to the call-and-response of the black church. The malapropism signals the inanity not of the interjector but instead of the preacher himself. That is, the title (with its faux Latin intimation of a scientific genus) seems to make fun of the very urge to categorize, to contain, to cast out. Although critics almost always assume that the tune marks an instance of border control, Williams's "critique of the jazz avant-garde,"[21] it might be more accurate to hear it as a satire—from the vantage point of the jazz experimentalist impulse—of the urge to dismiss any and all formal innovation as a danger to the integrity of the music. The avant-garde, in this interpretation, is not a foreign infectious agent, but on the contrary the very force within the music that prompts it to "continue."

This ambiguity around the status of the avant-garde remains unresolved in Williams's construction of the jazz tradition. The point is that, in a progressivist understanding of history (as a linear march of discrete stylistic advances), the theorization of innovation is necessarily and unceasingly troubled. One might say that in Williams's history of jazz, the status of innovation wavers continuously between the alternative and the oppositional—between the radical drive toward the emergent, toward "new forms or adaptations of form," on the one hand, and the reactionary drive toward the co-optation and "incorporation" of the "new" into the dominant, on the other.[22] This is to argue that *zoning* may well be the key problematic in Mary Lou Williams's work. One cannot transcend or exhaust the questions implicit in the term. How do you put things in their proper place in establishing a canon, a lineage? Is there an outside to regulated space—an area off the map, as it were?

To approach this problematic from the angle of methodology, one might call this an aesthetics of *disposal*. Williams's histories of jazz are constructed with the aim of putting something away, in good time (performing a chronology of the music, with each style in its "proper" place in an overarching system). At the same time, with their pedagogical tone, they represent an attempt at readying, preparing a set of tools for use (placing something at one's disposal), or bringing about a certain inclination (a disposition) that points a listener toward the "new" even if it remains unheard, outside the scope of the musical teleology.

To take a literary example of an aesthetics of disposal, where innovation is predicated on putting in place or putting away, we might consider a transitional work such as Amiri Baraka's 1965 *The System of Dante's Hell.*[23] Baraka himself has described the work as a conscious effort at experimentation, a work that employs the "ready-made" structure of Dante's *Inferno* to structure "association complexes" of the author's experiences growing up in Newark, ultimately in the interest of a transformation in style. Baraka says that he was "writing defensively" in *System* against the influence of poets such as Robert Creeley and Charles Olson, drawing on the form of infernal descent in order to put stylistic modes (as well as adolescent experiences) in their "place."[24] "Lovely Dante at night under his flame taking heaven," one section reads. "A place, a system, where all is dealt with . . . as is proper."[25] In *The System of Dante's Hell,* "hell" is not a "real place," Baraka explains elsewhere, but a "place of naming" in the mind: it serves not as a "receptacle" but as a kind of methodology: "I feel there is an area of art that is hell. A process of hellishness. Of being Hell. Hell-ing."[26] The aim of the book, announced again and again in its pages, is to "place each thing, each dot of life. Each person, will be PLACED. DISPOSED OF."[27] This project has something of the transitive quality of the term *zoning* in Williams: "getting rid of the elements that destroy music and putting them in their right place," as O'Brien glosses the term.[28] Of course, *dis-posal* is a pun in Baraka's vocabulary here, since—as we are reminded in the episode titled "The Heretics"—Dante descends in the closing Canto XXXIV of *The Inferno* to "the city of Dis, 'the stronghold of Satan' " (which we should recall is entirely frozen in ice).[29] So dis-posal here means something like "putting in hell," freezing an object in the bottom-most ring, an allegorical "process" that is necessary for the intuition of an angle of ascent.

The difference may have to do with the status of autobiography. In the "wars of consciousness" depicted in *The System of Dante's Hell,* the self is the battleground of literary style, and the book strives continually to "break out" of complacency as it "runs through the literal [of individual memory] to the imaginative."[30] At one point early in the book, we read: "I am myself. Insert the word disgust. A verb. Get rid of the 'am.' Break out. Kill it. Rip the thing to shreds."[31] But in *The History of Jazz,* the stability of Williams's first person ("the only major Jazz Artist who has lived and *played through* all the eras in the history and development of Jazz") undergirds the individual eras, providing the continuity that links them into a narrative. "It was my pleasure to bring you through the history of Jazz," Williams says toward the end of the recording. "You may not realize this but you're lucky. On the other hand, to bring this history to you I had to go through muck and mud."[32] Here disposal relies on the stability of the "I," the survivor of the ordeal of history, as opposed to Baraka's "systematic" unraveling and reconstitution of subjectivity through formalist experimentation.

The risk is that zoning becomes nothing more than a means of control. Indeed, the clearest example is the derivation of "A Fungus Amungus" included on *Zoning,* a two-piano version titled "Zoning Fungus II," with the classically trained Zita Carno accompanying Mary. As Peter O'Brien describes it melodramatically:

> "The fungus" first appears in low rumbling form from the second piano interrupting the lovely melody coming from the first. The fungus shoots in and out desperately trying to destroy the soulful feeling in the music. It enters now in the form of rapidly executed musical exercises (empty and tacked on), now by harsh and abrupt atonalities, now by short and self-centered shrieks. . . . But the tone lifts as the bass and drums [Bob Cranshaw and Mickey Roker] lay down the 7/4 rhythmic pattern. Order begins to re-emerge. . . . Zoning has taken place.[33]

The fungus is no longer in our midst, that is. It's been put away.

Embraced

All these issues come to a head in the most controversial recording of Williams's late career, the double-LP titled *Embraced: A Concert of New Music for Two Pianos Exploring the History of Jazz with Love* (Figure 5.1), a concert featuring Williams and Cecil Taylor held at Carnegie Hall on April 17, 1977. The concert—which was Mary's inspiration—was explicitly framed as an encounter with potentially radical implications for the

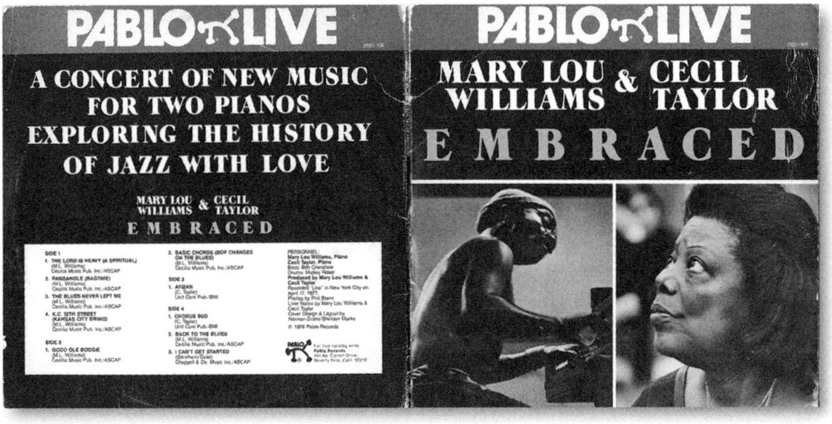

Figure 5.1 **Exterior gatefold album cover, Mary Lou Williams and Cecil Taylor, *Embraced* (Pablo Records 2620 108) (1978).**

future of the music. The release that announced a press conference the two pianists held in March to discuss the upcoming date proclaimed that *Embraced* "holds the promise of a precedent-shattering coupling of musical styles never before attempted together—and the result might well provide the preliminary ground-breaking for an entirely new direction in jazz, innovations that could lead to whole new trends in that musical idiom."[34] Critics and fans spent the weeks before the concert spinning conjectures about the reasons two formidable pianists associated with such seemingly divergent approaches (swing and bop, on the one hand, and the "avant-garde," on the other) would want to perform a concert in tandem. Taylor had admired Williams's music since he heard her *Zodiac Suite* as a child in the early 1950s, but the two hadn't met until drummer Andrew Cyrille introduced them in London in 1969.[35] When Williams was playing an extended gig at the Cookery in the early 1970s, Taylor came almost every night, and they became fast friends. Finally, they had performed "religious music" on a shared bill (but not as a duo) at the Whitney Museum's Composers' Showcase in 1975.[36]

What exactly did Williams find attractive about Taylor's music? At the Whitney, she commented that Taylor "represents the best in the avant-garde because he knows the tradition."[37] At the same time, she retained her suspicion of the "new music" Taylor represented. In the program notes at the 1977 two-piano concert (reprinted as liner notes to *Embraced*), she describes Taylor as "my Giant of the Avant-Garde." But a few paragraphs later, she includes the "avant-garde" in describing a "perverted force" that was threatening the music:

> Twenty-three years ago, I felt a perverted force was coming into the music. This force appeared in the form of empty musical exercises, music books (Jazz cannot be taught out of books—and the feeling in good Jazz cannot be taught; that is a gift), avant-garde, foreign composers, black magic, commercial rock, . . . hate, bitterness—all this began to enter in and destroy the true *feeling* of Jazz. Now I feel that one should play all forms of music—yet to inject another basic feeling into Jazz destroys the soulful feeling that is unique to Jazz.[38]

Thus it seems difficult to claim simply, as does biographer Linda Dahl, that Williams arranged the concert "in the spirit of reconciliation between the two 'camps' of jazz (avant-garde versus everything that came before)."[39] The motivation seems somewhat different, and linked to Williams's continual drive for innovation in her music. "Being a creative and searching kind of musician, such as I am," she writes in the program notes, "Cecil thrilled me with his integrity and originality."[40] This orientation is clearly consonant with her openness three decades earlier to the young lions of bebop; throughout her life she expressed the conviction that musicians should not shut themselves off from each other in "idea-sealed cliques." The jazz musician should never be content with the status quo, she advised: "Try your contrast."[41] In the notes to *Embraced,* she goes on to suggest that there is even something like an affective bond uniting the way they approach the piano and the history of the music: "There's a love we have for one another musically. Here's hoping other musicians will be inspired by what we do together in this concert—will pick up on the scene and have the same love for each other. That's what this music is: Love."[42]

There is an extraordinary lack of consensus about what ensues in *Embraced,* aside from a general sense that the concert was a failure. Gary Giddins's review in the *Village Voice* offers the most thorough description:

> The first set was continuous. It began with a rocking, spiritual-like piece started by Williams and amplified by Taylor, followed by a quite charming rag. Taylor soon shot off into the upper register with a characteristic flurry, while Williams cool-handedly searched for propitious moments to jump in. The predetermined format tended to fragment his solos with the not unattractive effect of making them highlight passages. . . . Some transitional block-building ensued, leading to an apparently serendipitous Taylor train rhythm, with colorful comments from the second piano.[43]

The first part of the concert was devoted to Williams's history of jazz, with tunes drawn from the chronology of styles: the spirituals ("The Lord Is Heavy"), ragtime ("Fandangle"), blues ("The Blues Never Left Me"), swing ("K.C. 12th Street"), boogie-woogie ("Good Ole Boogie"), and bebop ("Basic Chords [Bop Changes on the Blues]"). In the second half of the concert, the pianists turned to two compositions by Taylor, and Giddins was especially impressed by the dialogue in the opening minutes of the final piece, "Chorus Sud":

> [An] angular, Monkish theme stated by Taylor over a strong rhythmic pattern by Williams. Here the intensity was buoyant—he proffering fevered riffs, she giving pointillistic encouragement. For a while, the common language was essentially percussive. But then Taylor bounded into his own world, entranced and intractable, and Williams was back on the outside looking in. Retaliation came quickly as [Mickey] Roker and [Bob] Cranshaw rejoined them, initiating a straight four. This was the chance for the lady to strut her stuff, and she did so jubilantly, with Taylor laying out.[44]

When the tune concluded, Taylor disappeared after taking a hasty bow, while Williams emerged alone to play an encore, causing some audience members to wonder whether Taylor had left in anger.

Some critics characterized the entire concert as a lamentable episode of miscommunication. From this perspective, it was no surprise that

Williams chose for her unaccompanied encore the classic Ira Gershwin and Vernon Duke composition "I Can't Get Started (With You)." Others considered it predictably agonistic. John Wilson judged it "at best, a tug of war in which Mr. Taylor managed to remain dominant."[45] Later, writing a profile of Williams, Phyl Garland says it resembled "a prize-fight, as Mary Lou jabbed and darted with smart licks to the central register while Cecil countered with crushing blows to the bass and treble."[46] At a number of points during the concert, Mary beckoned drummer Roker and bassist Cranshaw from the wings in what some took to be an act of aggression to reimpose a regular 4/4 beat. The struggle is especially pronounced at the end of "Chorus Sud," when one can hear Williams audibly calling for the "rhythm section" the way one might call for the cavalry. In Giddins's words, "though it might be unfair to call Bob Cranshaw and Mikey Roker Mary Lou's henchmen, it seemed as though she had enlisted their support to contain the predatory avant-gardist."[47] The famous jazz fan Nica de Koenigswarter wrote a letter to Mary after the concert, comparing the event to "a CONFRONTATION!—between Heaven & Hell," with "you (Heaven!) emerging GLORIOUSLY TRIUMPHANT!!!" when Roker and Cranshaw appeared "like Guardian Angels" to ward off Taylor's "sheets of nothingness."[48]

The musicians themselves offered a variety of reconsiderations of the concert. In at least one interview at the end of her life, Williams even described playing with Taylor as a success. "I can play the old fashioned spiritual and I can 'bop' on top of it," she explains. "I once spent the day with Cecil Taylor, who has a superb technique. I played the old fashioned way, and I had him play his way-out modern stuff. Yet, it all fitted together."[49] But in another interview, she puts Taylor in his place:

> The World is upside down. A lot of that stuff is phony, like plucking on the strings. I used to improvise without chords in the thirties in Kansas City, and they called it zombie music. Lester Young and I would go over to a party and they'd say, "Let Lulu play some of that zombie music." On a tape twenty-five years ago I played what music sounds like today. I had a premonition of what it would sound like and played like Cecil Taylor. Melba

> Liston laughed and laughed. I played it for Dizzy's wife, and she said, "Why don't you [call] that 'a fungus among us'?"[50]

Here she responds precisely by zoning Cecil Taylor: his music *is* nothing other than those frozen sounds she'd played after hours in the 1930s and recorded on *The History of Jazz*. She circumscribes his approach not as futuristic or even as a departure from the tradition: instead, Cecil is no more than a footnote to Kansas City. It's zoning in the more familiar sense, then, as well: of a region defined in relation to climate, or of a district or area subject to restrictions concerning land use and development. It girdles Taylor's approach as a species of the living dead. This is not just moralizing; it also serves as something like an exorcism. It's no wonder that, after her conversion to Catholicism, Miles Davis half-jokingly called her "Reverend Williams."[51]

Cecil Taylor commented to one interviewer that Williams was "disturbed," even "outraged," by the outcome of the concert, but he added, "then again we traded surprises that evening."[52] Most usefully, he explained some of the conceptual divergence in the rehearsal preparation for the concert, noting:

> Finally what has to really be agreed upon is what music is and what the specifics of the tradition [are] and how you want to apply it to a given situation . . . Ms. Williams had a particular idea in mind what she wanted to do and it seemed to me that . . . It was really never understood on her part how I viewed . . . music.[53]

According to Taylor, there was an assumption by Williams as well as the audience that they would simply "attempt to reduplicate styles of eras gone past." For Taylor, it is artificial and even retrograde to impose a "separation" between "style" and "musical creativity": the point is less to "resurrect" a given style as a sort of museum "artifact," and more to approach the "principles of musical organization" of predecessors in terms of their "poetic essence."[54] In other words, "It wasn't about imitating the notes that Bud Powell played or Erroll Garner or Jelly Roll, it was understanding the passion that informs."[55]

Embraced is ultimately not a question of simple misunderstanding or bruised egos or petulance or moral betrayal, on either side. Nor can it simply be categorized as a "noble failure."[56] Instead Williams and Taylor are involved—in performance, onstage—in a high-stakes argument that can only be termed *historiographic.* Williams approaches the project in a teleological and even allegorical orientation, as I have pointed out. One reconstitutes the protocols of the past with positivistic exactitude, toward its "peak of perfection": "progress" for Williams means that "when it has reached this so-called 'peak,' it is really only the beginning, for then we build the new ideas on top of the old."[57] The past, therefore, is at the disposal of the future, the "new."

For Taylor, the task is strikingly different. An orientation toward musical tradition necessarily involves a process whereby methodology is geared toward the unearthing or withdrawal of precisely what *cannot* be passed down in recording, in the received technologies of knowledge dissemination. "Your art becomes your evolution," as he tells one interviewer. "It tells you that there is something else, another reality: the immaterial. . . . The exploration of history is a spiritual process."[58] This is a rather different understanding of an aesthetics of disposal. Taylor's historiographic sensibility approaches the past as a *deposit,* a sedimentation of poesis that allows certain organic approaches to construction, understood as a process of "withdrawal" that is a question of *practice,* rather than simply an excavation of some previously buried treasure. Any such deposit of prior stylistic practice contains elements of *deposition,* and the player must be primed to take the testimony—one might even call it the haunting—of a "spirit" or "passion" that "informs" the methodological approaches of the black aesthetic tradition. And by implication, any aesthetic "evolution" must involve another factor, as well, a certain violence that characterizes that unearthing or haunting, a force that not only founds but simultaneously "deposes"—overthrows or sublates.

Liner Note Duet, Liner Note Duel

Most intriguingly, this historiographic argument is pursued at some length by the two pianists in written form. On the one hand, what is fascinating about *Embraced* is that the "antagonistic cooperation"[59] between Williams and Taylor seems to have required another medium—the argument is pursued not just in music but in words, as well. In fact, this dynamic preceded the concert, since (although there may have been some conceptual disagreement in the pianists' preparation) Taylor may have felt specifically betrayed by Williams's comments in a newspaper article that appeared two days beforehand. The *New York Times* critic John S. Wilson had interviewed Williams alone, and he used one quote in particular that taken out of context comes across as gratuitous and mean-spirited. Taylor had been coming to hear Williams regularly at the Cookery, she reported, and once he sat down at the piano himself:

> "One night toward the end of my run," she went on, "Cecil sat down at the piano and played. When he started, he put a little blues in it. He was sensational, but he played a little too long. Avant-garde has a habit of playing too long. When he started, there were about 75 people there. By the time he finished, there was just the two of us."[60]

The week after the Carnegie Hall concert, Williams wrote to a friend that although Taylor "went berserk" on stage, in fact "there was not tension" in the preparation of the concert. Taylor, she wrote, "was upset about an article *I'm* to *blame for*." He was also upset about the way the rhythm section was deployed to impose a traditional meter; apparently the pianists had not discussed their participation beforehand.[61] Williams drafted a number of letters to Taylor during the coming months, ranging from accusatory to apologetic. In one, she complained that he had broken from what they had rehearsed, especially in the first half of the concert, calling his playing "unhealthy" and adding, "You are actually destroying yourself. I'm really happy about the intelligence of the 1930s musicians. They taught that one should never use anything they could not control, while writing or playing."[62] Williams counseled that Taylor should have played "what was expected—then-go-mad! after the 1st half of the concert—Contrast is everything for an introduction to what you want [to] play—snap! smile. Before we went on the second half I said to you 'I love you, let's play love—and man, you were terrific playing the compo' I like, that you composed—Much love."[63] She apologized for the rhythm section ("you scared them," she claimed) and for her comments about his playing at the Cookery. When she said that he played "too long," she explained, she meant that Taylor's playing was too powerful for the audience to endure: "Art Tatum was playing at a fast tempo once—and a lady fainted, she couldn't stand the impact."[64] It is not clear whether she ever sent a letter to Taylor; there is no reply from Taylor in Williams's papers.

On the other hand, to note the literary component of the record is to point out that as engaging as the concert is as a unique spectacle, the event simultaneously involves a dimension that one might term metaperformative or even metaphysical. *Embraced* is not only the performance of an argument, that is, but also an argument about *how* to argue—about the very ground rules of debate. Of course, the musicians' writing about the concert does not resolve the complexity of their interaction in performance. Moreover, the question of self-reflexivity—the relation between levels of argumentation—is separate from the question of aesthetics (isn't it possible for an argument to be beautiful?) and the question of erotics (just what does it mean to "explore" the history of jazz in an agonistic embrace, "with love"?).

The liner notes to the record of *Embraced* released the next year stage this historiographic argument in the juxtaposition of writings by Williams and Taylor (Figure 5.2). The gatefold double LP opens to reveal Williams's explanation of "How This Concert Came About" on the left side (a reprint of her the program notes from the concert), arguing her conception of the history of jazz, and competing "Notes" by Taylor on the right. Williams writes: "What is needed is a full return to good Jazz—playing it—recording it—promoting it. Only then will something new *in Jazz* emerge from a young musician and composer. He has to hear what has gone before. That is why I presented my concert. To draw attention to the history of Jazz—America's only art form."[65] Even their biographies emphasize their writing as much as their music: Taylor, we are informed, "is working on a book about black music entitled *Mysteries,*" whereas Williams "is at work on her autobiography called ZONING THE HISTORY OF JAZZ."[66]

Taylor commented in one interview that he "finally wrote some notes which I suppose will appear alongside Mary's . . . I'm going to let it rest on

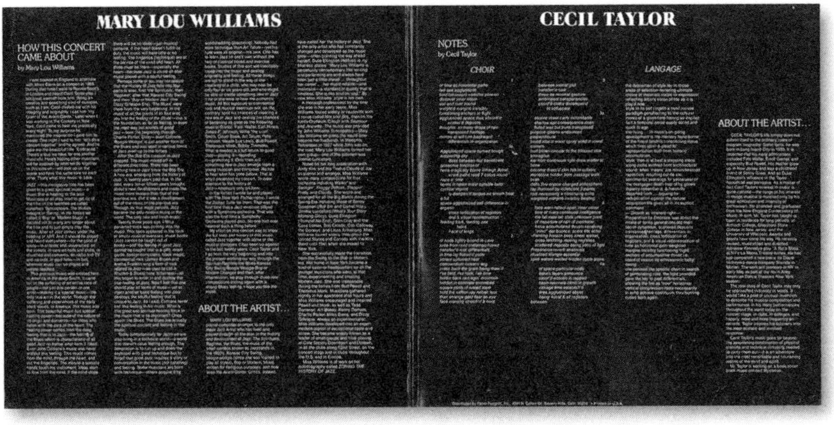

Figure 5.2 Interior gatefold album cover, *Embraced.*

the basis of what I wrote."[67] Taylor's post-concert "Notes" on the right side of the gatefold are made up of two poems, one called "Choir" and the other called "Langage." "Choir" is divided into seven sections, and the first opens:

> of time as horizontal paths
> fed sea agglutinizes
> field (phasoun) verticles plowed
> discover inner vision
> soil and river sound
> weight'd margins invisibly
> functioning anchors in flight
> agglutinized space thus absorb'd
>   scattter'd deposits
> thoughts: so many drops of rain
>   transposed heritage
> mirrors at will turn backward
>   differentials in organization.

One is immediately forced to rethink one's generic expectations of "liner notes" as writing meant to contextualize, to explain and describe, to provide a sort of discursive padding for the listener's approach to the music. Is the initial prepositional phrase descriptive or definitional? Are we meant to hear the two pianos as "horizontal paths" in time, parallel but perhaps not interwoven or integrated? Or does the phrase suggest something like the *content* of the music, its achievement: it embodies or performs "time as horizontal paths"? In the subsequent lines, there is a suggestion of process—a fluid entity nourished or inflated until it takes a more defined shape, unified or fastened into some sort of glutinous compound. And yet, in contrast to the clear causality implied in a gerund like *zoning,* here one is left uncertain of agency. From one line to the next, words shift in and out of the transitive. Is "discover" the present indicative of the plural subject "verticles," or is it an imperative—a command to "discover inner vision"? Is "sound" the direct object of "discover" (one discovers "sound," just as one discovers "inner vision"), or a transitive verb (the soil and the river "sound . . . margins")? If the poem can be read as a commentary on the performance on the record, it implies that that music is necessarily collective as well as polyvocal ("choir"), a sound that coagulates in space, and in its coming together is able to take up "scatter'd deposits." Performance is a means of access to the past, then, and yet one that does not seem geared to unearth what Williams, in her notes, calls the "foundation" or the "true *feeling* of Jazz." Instead, there is an unavoidable shift in register: "heritage" is "transposed" as it is "absorb'd." The last lines seem to suggest two things at once. The work of reflection ("mirrors") is able to propel the collective beyond its differences toward a common focus "backward." Or alternatively, any attempt at mimesis risks becoming warped or inverted due to the constitutive "differentials" in the elements of the collective.

The second poem, "Langage," with its more conventional grammar and sentence construction, seems more easily legible within the protocols of "liner notes," although the first poem would seem designed to undo any easy assumptions about the programmatic function of Taylor's "Notes." One might start with the title, given that it seems to point at the untranslatable distinction in French between *langue* and *langage.* Saussure's discussion of the issue is well known: language *(langue),* as an indication of a "self-contained whole and a principle of classification" (a particular linguistic tongue), must not be confused with the full variety of human language *(langage),* which is "many-sided and heterogeneous; straddling several areas simultaneously—physical, physiological, and psychological—

it belongs both to the individual and to society; we cannot put it into any category of human facts, for we cannot discover its unity."[68] To claim *langage* as a description of the music, then, might be read as an insistence on the inherent social situatedness of musical performance, as well as a rejection of any claim that its content can be limited to any single, "self-contained" semiotic system.

The beginning of the poem is a relatively straightforward critique of Williams's understanding of jazz history of a sequence of styles. As the poem phrases it, style alone is far too temporally contingent and vague a category to offer anything more than a "narrow paradigm" for the investigation of the music:

> the deposition of style lay in those
> areas of selection mirroring ultimate
> choice of materials viable to expression
> reflecting artist's vision of life as it is
> play'd now.
> style in its self ringeth a most narrow
> paradigm genuflecting to the cultural
> mores of a given time having as implied
> fact a temporal sense easily dated and
> quick to age.

To avoid hackneyed nostalgia and sentimental traditionalism, the poem argues, style must be understood to be "at best a stepping stone" to the discovery of what is termed the "germinating core" of various moments in the music. The "light provided" by that research "gave the key to past differentials," the poem continues: that is, the goal of plumbing historical styles is not to reveal some transhistorical essence or foundation, but instead to restage the stylistic heterogeneity of any particular past moment. Only thereby can the "burning cycles" of the music be "born again," "necessarily/in echo." Midway through the poem, the language of the opening section of "Choir" is recalibrated:

> Preparation for *Embrace* was about the
> intake of forms generations old their

> secret dynamism, scattered deposits
> transposed heritage, differentials in
> organization, cross fertilization of
> registers, oral & visual reconstruction of
> time as horizontal path weighted
> margins invisibly functioning flight
> anchors of accumulative thrust i.e.,
> scent of motion its ethnocentric belly:
> swing

Swing, that keyword of jazz traditionalism, is appropriated here as the term to mark the "accumulative thrust" achieved through this method of approaching the past. One begins to understand why Taylor might have been irritated when the rhythm section "henchmen" imposed four-quarter time at the end of the Carnegie Hall concert: swing, for Taylor, is a "secret dynamism" that involves "transposition," not the dominance of a single mode of rhythmic propulsion at the expense of any and all "differential" thrust.

"With Love"

One of the best-known propositions of Nietzsche's 1874 essay "On the Uses and Disadvantages of History for Life" is the claim that healthy human life requires both the "unhistorical" and the "historical." Nietzsche argues against the Hegelian pretense to an absolute, all-encompassing history, writing that a living thing must have a sense of heterogeneity: it must be capable of "drawing a horizon around itself," of positing an outside to history.[69] When there is an "excess of history," Nietzsche writes, "man again ceases to exist, and without that envelope [*Hülle*] of the unhistorical he would never have begun or dared to begin."[70] Creativity, and moreover the possibility of life itself, necessitates the unhistorical, a space of experience undetermined by markers and expectations and prior models.

Nietzsche goes on to suggest that "if, in a sufficient number of cases, one could scent out and retroactively breathe this unhistorical atmosphere within which every great historical event has taken place, he might, as a percipient being, raise himself to a *suprahistorical* vantage point [*überhistorischen Standpunkt*]."[71] Indeed, "the unhistorical and the suprahistorical are the natural antidotes to the stifling of life by the historical, by the malady of history."[72] Nietzsche links both the unhistorical and the suprahistorical to art in particular,[73] and it should not come as a surprise that I am suggesting that these terms might help us make sense of the "differentials" between Taylor (with his unhistorical insistence on an outside to the tradition, on the limitations of a chronological sequence of styles) and Williams (with her suprahistorical insistence on "scenting out" the "peak of perfection"[74] achieved in each "great historical event"). Midway through his essay, Nietzsche offers a remarkable assertion about the relation between history and art:

> It is only in love, only when shaded by the illusion produced by love, that is to say in the unconditional faith in right and perfection, that man is creative. Anything that constrains a man to love less than unconditionally has severed the roots of his strength: he will wither away, that is to say become dishonest. In producing this effect, history is the antithesis of art [*In solchen Wirkungen ist der Historie die Kunst entgegengesetzt*]: and only if history can endure to be transformed into a work of art will it perhaps be able to preserve instincts or even evoke them. Such a historiography [*Geschichtsschreibung*] would, however, be altogether contrary to the analytical and inartistic tendencies of our time, which would indeed declare it false.[75]

One might say, then, that the achievement of *Embraced* is to transform the writing of history *(Geschichtsschreibung)* into a work of art through love. What is "artistic" about the concert, however, is not a matter of establishing harmony or finding a "common language."[76] If *Embraced* succeeds, it succeeds in the way it stages a "fissional construct" in time, sounding a polyphony of differentials between the unhistorical and the suprahistorical.[77]

The Ethics of Zoning

I have titled this chapter "Zoning Mary Lou Williams Zoning" to raise the question of whether it is possible to avoid or escape a methodology of zoning in attempting to make sense of a performance such as *Embraced.* Is any criticism necessarily a practice of zoning, of categorization and evaluation—putting things in their place? Does zoning have to be defined as a restrictive holism—a way of making "something fresh, astonishing, whole and complete"?[78] Is it possible to read an archive of zoning against the grain, to attend to what seeps out of its designated confines?[79] This is also to ask whether it is possible, in listening to this complex collaboration, to attend to the "differentials" *within,* say, Williams's own work, rather than simply between her work and Taylor's. I have long been fascinated by another instance of Williams's zoning: the day-by-day notebooks of household expenses she kept meticulously for more than thirty years, from the fall of 1949 until a few months before her death in 1981.[80] She wrote down every cent she spent, nearly every day: expenses for cigarettes, gas, highway tolls, food ($1.04 for neck bones; $.23 for liverwurst; $.35 for ice cream; $1.48 for lamb chops), beer, hosiery, books, gambling wins and losses, flowers, telephone calls, rent, car repairs, bill payments, cab fares, various supplies and "nich nachs" ($.61 for a plunger; $.32 for postage stamps), subway tokens, haircuts, newspapers, church donations, meals in restaurants, tips, gifts to friends and family. There is much to be said about her unwavering commitment to economics in the etymological sense, as household management *(oikonomia),* and its relation to her musical aesthetics and her sense of history, not just an accounting but a practice of *recording.*[81] What is more difficult to read, however, is the narrative and exclamatory marginalia that, now and then, invades these generally perfunctory lists—the places where the daily accounting erupts into something like a diary. On March 1, 1962, Mary records the dollar she spent on a cab to church, and writes above her entry: "raining." On the last day of 1972 (Figure 5.3), she scribbles at the bottom of the page:

> End of 1972
> scared!

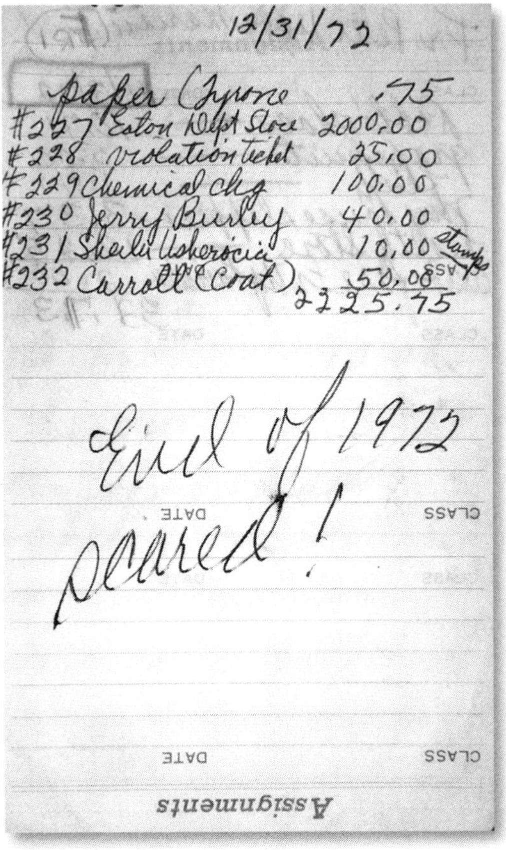

Figure 5.3 Expense notebook, December 31, 1972, Mary Lou Williams Collection, Institute of Jazz Studies, Rutgers University-Newark, Subseries 4H: Personal Bills, FLT Folder, Box 3.

She notes the assassination of President Kennedy ("Pres - death") on the top of a carbon copy from a gas station where she'd had her car repaired (Figure 5.4). There are even celebratory moments in the interstices of the economic, as on June 18, 1976:

> *stayed in*
> Spent no money
> thanks to God—
> snap!! whee!

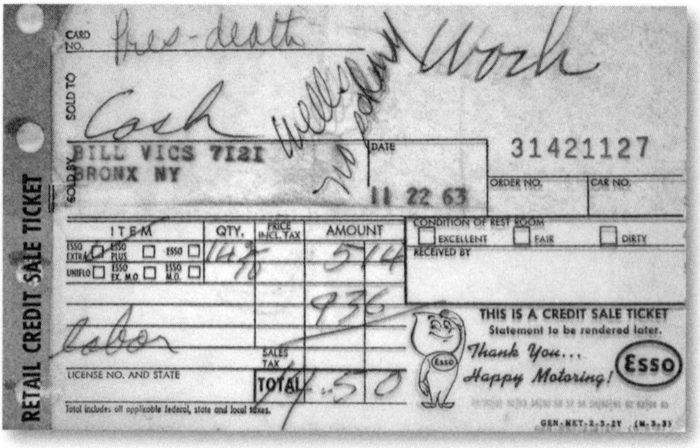

Figure 5.4 Gasoline receipt, November 22, 1963, Mary Lou Williams Collection, Series 4H: Personal Bills, Box 7, Institute of Jazz Studies, Rutgers University-Newark.

The most poignant may be the entry for December 1, 1974 (Figure 5.5), where, under listings for "nich nachs," ice cream, and telephone calls, Williams writes:

> Mom died
> 87 yrs old

To read these spare interjections is to recognize that zoning is never singular and never all-encompassing. Even in the midst of the drive to compartmentalize, to control, there is heterogeneity and seepage—here, an uncertain horizon where a monetary economy overlaps with an affective economy. However compulsive the practice might seem, one might even speak of it in terms of an aesthetics of accounting, in that it sounds a scattered deposit of styles.[82]

I return briefly in closing to the metaphysical dimension of *Embraced* to ask whether it can be heard as something like an allegory of criticism—a lesson in how to listen, rather than an invitation to zone. In 1972 Larry Neal published a brilliant and hilarious essay on boxing called "Uncle Rufus Raps on the Squared Circle." The piece is structured as a Socratic dialogue between the narrator and Uncle Rufus, a "fascinating gentleman" and self-professed sports philosopher who expounds at

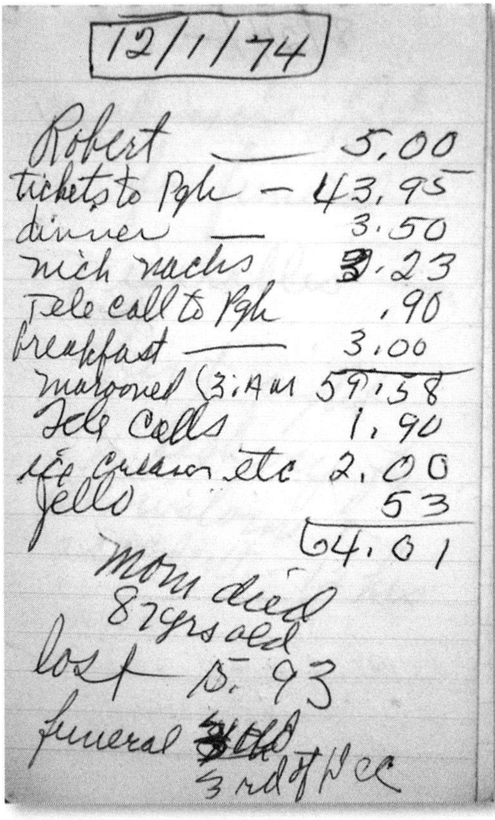

Figure 5.5 Expense notebook, December 1, 1974, Mary Lou Williams Collection, Subseries 4H: Personal Bills, FLT Folder, Box 3, Institute of Jazz Studies, Rutgers University-Newark.

length—in the deliberately preposterous, half-joking manner particular to Harlem bar conversations—on the "distinct metaphysical character" of the Ali-Frazier fight, in exchange for a succession of glasses of bourbon. Uncle Rufus maintains that "the Ali-Frazier fight was, in fact, a contest of essentially different attitudes toward music," since boxing "is just another kind of rhythmic activity. . . . Every fighter has his own particular rhythmic style just the way musicians do."[83] Muhammad Ali's style, he says, is "body bebop" (the approach of a man who "believes in riffing"), whereas Joe Frazier's is "slow brooding blues with a gospel bearing."[84] Boxing is unlike other sports, according to Uncle Rufus, because the combatants are limited to a "very small area of confrontation": the square canvas of the boxing ring.[85] But with the choreography of their combat, he says, the fighters "rhythmically describe" another shape, an "implied circle within the square (and naturally without the square)."[86] If the square is discrete, material and rational ("quaternary," as Uncle Rufus puts it), the circle is an "ever-evolving metaconstruct." And the aesthetics of the sport involves the relation between these overlapping geometries. "The fighter's duty is to rhythmically discern the essential unity between the circle and the square," Uncle Rufus contends, and the winner is always the boxer who "most acutely" understands the "principles of spatial and psychic rhythm"—who imposes a particular vision of that "unity" upon the improvised choreography of the fight.[87] The piece concludes with a comeuppance. Wowed by the disquisition, the narrator comments that Uncle Rufus nonetheless hasn't told him for whom he was "pulling" in the fight, and is surprised when, in response, Uncle Rufus "whacks" him with his cane. "It's about you not learning to ask the right questions," the old man says, before adding one last tenet in the appreciation of antagonism: "I was pulling for both of them."[88]

six
Let's Call This: Henry Threadgill and the Micropoetics of the Song Title

Despite or perhaps because of their ubiquity, it has hardly been noticed that song titles are the most prominent arena where words and music are conjoined in jazz. While there is a long-standing minor thread of dialogue in literary criticism concerning the function of titles in framing or identifying poems or novels, and a smaller body of scholarship on titling conventions in classical music and the visual arts, scholars in jazz studies have had very little to say about the implications of song or album titles beyond the confines of biography.[1] Nevertheless there is a great deal to say about the "verbal handles"[2] jazz musicians use for their compositions, and their complex roles in priming or channeling the ways the music is heard.

In this chapter I focus in particular on the ways song titles function in the work of the composer and multi-instrumentalist Henry Threadgill's work because it seems to me that they are one of the most striking and unusual elements in his music. Time and again, journalists and interviewers comment on the peculiarity of his titles, but too often only to express befuddlement or frustration at the language's obliquity and seemingly flimsy (if not bewilderingly disjunctive) relation to the music itself. Even a quick survey is enough to give a sense of the unique verbal qualities of his catalogue:

"Keep Right on Playing Thru the Mirror over the Water"
"Salute to the Enema Bandit"
"The Devil Is on the Loose and Dancin' with a Monkey"
"I Love You with an Asterick"
"Those Who Eat Cookies"
"Silver and Gold, Baby, Silver and Gold"
"Let's All Go Down to the Footwash"
"To Undertake My Corners Open"

"So Pleased, No Clue"
"Old Locks and Irregular Verbs"

While some have argued that "the unique purpose of titling is hermeneutical: titles are names which function as guides to interpretation,"[3] Threadgill's titles seem willful and effervescent acts of defiance against this mandate. They are strange and bedazzling provocations in the face of any assumption that, in the words of Umberto Eco, any title "already—and unfortunately—is a key for interpretation,"[4] all the more so when one tries to link them to specific elements or stylistic contours in the music itself. Rather than a "key," then, perhaps these titles at least function as something more like John Ashbery's description of poem titles as providing "a very small aperture into a larger area, a keyhole perhaps, or some way of getting into the poem."[5]

The Programmatic Fallacy

One of the main pitfalls in coming to terms with song titles in jazz is a preconception that the title can or must have a programmatic function in relation to the music, outlining a preset narrative arc to be followed by the tune, or identifying a specific idea or environment it is meant to evoke. If that case, one might consider it a cause for concern to learn that, say, "Manhattan Moods" was an alternative title for Thelonious Monk's "Ruby, My Dear," or that another song Monk recorded under the title "Worry Later" was subsequently renamed "San Francisco Holiday"—as though the change in title indicated a feebleness or a vagary in the composer's conception.[6]

One of the most famous examples of a supposedly programmatic conception in the history of the music is Duke Ellington's classic composition "Harlem Air Shaft." In the 1944 article "The Hot Bach," the long *New Yorker* profile I quoted in Chapter 3, Ellington expounds at some length on the motivation behind the piece:

> "Take 'Harlem Air Shaft,'" Duke said. "So much goes on in a Harlem air shaft. You get the full essence of Harlem in an air shaft. You hear fights, you smell dinner, you hear people making

> love. You hear intimate gossip floating down. You hear the radio. An air shaft is one great big loudspeaker. You see your neighbors' laundry. You hear the janitor's dogs. The man upstairs' aerial falls down and breaks your window. You smell coffee. A wonderful thing is that smell. An air shaft has got every contrast. One guy is cooking dried fish and rice and another guy's got a great big turkey. Guy-with-fish's wife is a terrific cooker by the guy's wife with the turkey is doing a sad job." Duke laughed. "You hear people praying, fighting, snoring. Jitterbugs are jumping up and down always over you, never below you. That's a funny thing about jitterbugs. They're always over you. I tried to put all that in 'Harlem Air Shaft.' "[7]

As Edward Green points out in an illuminating analysis of the song, it is actually possible to trace almost every element of Ellington's detailed description to particular aspects and motifs in the music itself. At the same time, however, Green notes that the original draft score for the tune has a different title: "Once over Lightly."[8] So which is the right title? And can a song truly be programmatic if it switches its program? But Green concludes, "It is a mistake to formulate the question so starkly, as if the titles were mutually exclusive"; even if "Once over Lightly" is a draft title for a composition that is eventually named "Harlem Air Shaft," Green writes, both titles "are appropriate and revelatory of what happens in the music."[9] In fact, as Green observes wittily, "the design of 'Harlem Air Shaft' is, indeed, a case of 'Once over Lightly.' The phrase (which, incidentally, entered the American vernacular just around this time) means to give something a quick—even superficial—treatment: to 'sketch' rather than to 'fill out.' This is just what the Intro does, relative to the main body of the work."[10]

Another example of a title that may not be as programmatic as it first appears is the name of the first album in saxophonist Marion Brown's "Georgia Trilogy" of records inspired by his memories of his childhood in the South. The first of these records, a gorgeous and atmospheric session featuring musicians including Anthony Braxton, Bennie Maupin, Jeanne Lee, Chick Corea, Jack Gregg, and Andrew Cyrille, is called *Afternoon of a Georgia Faun,* which—especially when Brown describes it as a "tone poem" in the first sentence of the liner notes—immediately brings to mind both Stéphane Mallarmé's 1876 poem "L'après-midi d'un faune" and the other modernist monuments that it inspired: Claude Debussy's 1894 orchestral work *Prélude à l'après-midi d'un faune* and the 1912 ballet *L'après-midi d'un faune,* choreographed for the Ballets Russes by Vaslav Nijinsky.[11] One might be inclined to assume that the album involves a transplantation of the scene sketched in the poem as well as its orchestral and choreographic elaborations (a lascivious faun consorting with nymphs) from the vaguely classical setting of the original into the Georgia backwoods. Brown himself would later call the album part of a series of works in the early 1970s that he conceived as "structured improvisations on literary themes,"[12] and he sometimes mentioned other influences in that realm, as well, including the Harlem Renaissance writer Jean Toomer—the second album in the trilogy, *Geechee Recollections,* includes a recitation by Bill Hasson of Toomer's story "Karintha" from the 1923 *Cane*—as well as the Nigerian novelist Amos Tutuola.[13] Nevertheless, as historian Eric Porter has noted, Brown was consistent in his resistance to suggestions that his music should be heard as some sort of enactment or setting of these literary intertexts.[14]

Brown told one interviewer that he had read Mallarmé's poem, "but not because I wanted to"; it had been on the syllabus of a survey class on Western art he took at Clark College. "I never really understood it because I have never really understood poetry," he added.[15] Asked about his reasons for choosing the title *Afternoon of a Georgia Faun,* Brown stated (somewhat paradoxically, given his choice of the word *faun*), "I had nothing at all in my mind in any way to classical mythology," and offered this explanation: "I named it for myself. It was accidental. My *Faun* merely revisits his home, where he grew up as a boy, and seeing it again, how it has changed, after ten years, or if it has changed at all. These things had nothing to do with people, or communicating with them."[16] Whatever the apparent implications of a given song title, Brown declared, "the listener can't share the particular experiences that the one who creates the work has."[17] As he said to another journalist in 1967:

> When I play my music, I'm not playing about anything else at all. I'm not putting down anything that you could express in words. . . . You can take from it only what you bring to it. I don't play words. . . .

> What I communicate might be something very specific, like a portrayal of something that has happened, or it might be a vague feeling, or just sounds. But you can't get to it through words. You have to find your own way.[18]

Brown's work is provocative, then, in the way it combines an evocative layering of literary references in his titles with the provocative claim that language is incapable of representing the complexity of musical experience.

At the same time, Brown actually did write a great deal, composing a memoir, a book collecting his essays, drawings and interviews, and—most strikingly—a book called *Afternoon of a Georgia Faun: Views and Reviews,* with his own essay about his album as well as other materials (including the interview quoted above). One might well wonder why. One answer may be encapsulated in something Brown said in a 1966 panel discussion on the "new jazz." "People try and interpret what the artist is really trying to say in his medium," Brown observed. "I don't think I ever heard any musician say that my lines, my sounds say this. Of course, if he says it in words it means that."[19] So Brown compiles his own book on his record in order to have his say as to what his music "means": to claim the critical prerogative rather than abdicating it. As Eric Porter rightly summarizes it, Brown's book "responded to the critical vacuum by creating a dialogue about the album. In doing so, he not only set forth his avant-garde aesthetic philosophy and artistic agenda but also positioned the artist as the ultimate arbiter of the meaning of his or her music."[20]

Despite Brown's demurral with regard to Mallarmé, Debussy, and Nijinsky, the blatant parallel in the album title also suggests that, while Brown's music may not be a setting of the prior models, still the very gesture of the title itself implies what Aldon Nielsen has called a "recontextualizing of the modern": that is, the gesture makes a claim on an aesthetics of appropriation that places Brown in dialogue with an avant-garde lineage.[21] The gesture of the title itself also implies a *multimedia* context of appropriation—music finding a model in poetry; dance and set design finding a model in music—which seems appropriate when one comes across Brown expressing a desire to take his music into other media: "On a grander scale, I visualize *Afternoon of a Georgia Faun* as a spectacle involving music, song, dance and movement."[22] Even if one concludes the title is a kind of throwaway or vacant gesture, one can still argue that such a title has a powerful effect in clearing out a space for the work itself. Speaking about his compositions for piano, Brown once commented: "I left room for creativity, which is empty space. Creativity needs an empty vessel, needs an empty space. Creativity needs some place to be, some place to happen, some place to become."[23] But obviously it would be wrong to call such a title programmatic.

Rather than assuming that there should be an immutable one-to-one correspondence between a singular programmatic title and its enactment in musical form, it may be necessary first of all to view the function of titles in jazz, as in other art forms, in a much more supple and complex manner. In 2000 the poet Ed Roberson published an exquisite essay about the work of sculptor Thaddeus Mosley. In it, Roberson mentions that Mosley had found a small but significant error in an exhibition catalogue on his work that had appeared a few years earlier: in the catalogue, a photograph of one of the sculptures is misidentified as *Allegory* (a work from 1996) when it is in fact a different work entirely called *Countee's Leaf* (made in 1992). "Mosley's correction of the titles for me, of course, does not change his sculptures," Roberson comments:

> This new set of the word was not a reductive experience; it was especially not a re-definition of the words. It is word itself that changes, which admits what it is forever leaving out. Each word is surrounded by an ellipsis, a space left when our choice contracts our experience into name. The unique subtlety and detail of our experience is abandoned for a moment to make space for the next word to fill in, to clarify and qualify. To communicate in language we have to admit, then touch and bring back, what is left out. We have to be aware of how this recovery re-initiates the whole process again and be aware of how a communication in language must be constantly emptying to be fulfilled. The fullness of a sculpture like *Allegory* communicates in space extending beyond words. It can be held in the moment of a word, in a point such as "leaf" or "allegory," but exists already in the unnamed. To experience the sculpture we keep reaching outside that moment of the word to the next. We create a visual sentence across

> the face of the work until we've accumulated so many names that names fail, and we are left with the sculpture in its own tongue.[24]

To take the "word" of *any* title as a "very small aperture" or "keyhole" into the work, then, is not to take that language as programmatic—the definitive "anchorage" of the work of art to a restricted set of meanings—but instead to allow the inevitable failure of language to allow the singularity of the work to emerge precisely as a product of its unnameability.[25] The title allows us to experience the work not because it is the "right" identifier, but because when we enter the work through it, we can "keep reaching outside that moment of the word to the next." This stunning passage begins to suggest what it would mean to recalibrate the relation between title and work entirely, and in that sense it may be a useful way to clear the ground of expectation for a consideration of Henry Threadgill's song titles.

Trends in Jazz Song Titles

In trying to gauge the degree to which Threadgill's titles as serve (if at all) as signposts—as points of entry, as hints about the contours of a composition, as frames or windows, as associative clues—it is important to note they do not seem to pursue many of the multiple strategies in the history of titling original compositions in jazz. This is to say that his titles do not, say, adopt the predilection in much jazz titling to point to a given sociohistorical context, to evoke an atmosphere or location or personality: "Harlem Air Shaft" (Ellington), "Jumpin' at the Woodside" (Count Basie), "Crepuscule with Nellie" (Thelonious Monk), "Wednesday Night Prayer Meeting" (Charles Mingus), "A Night in Tunisia" (Dizzy Gillespie), "Parisian Thoroughfare" (Bud Powell), "52nd Street Theme" (Monk), "Moose the Mooche" (Charlie Parker), "Hat and Beard" (Eric Dolphy), "Lonely Woman" (Ornette Coleman), or "Frankenstein" (Grachan Moncur III). Neither are they allusions to or appropriations of musical genre or normative form of one sort or another, as one finds in titles such as "Blues March" (Benny Golson), "Little Symphony" (Ornette Coleman),

"Spiritual" (John Coltrane), "Unit Structure" (Cecil Taylor), "Demon's Lullaby" (Sun Ra), or "Folk Form No. 1" (Mingus).

Threadgill's titles do not usually tell us that the music will suggest or speak from a particular affective state or existential condition, as do so many titles in the music: "Blue Monk," "Lush Life" (Billy Strayhorn), "Moanin'" (Bobby Timmons), "Un Poco Loco" (Powell), "In a Sentimental Mood" (Ellington), "My Jelly Roll Soul" (Mingus), "Sent for You Yesterday and Here You Come Today" (Count Basie, Eddie Durham, and Jimmy Rushing), "Out to Lunch" (Dolphy), or "Misty" (Erroll Garner). Nor do they often espouse a conceptual category, summarize a familiar dictum or tenet, or propose an intellectual operation or orientation, as in titles like "Epistrophy" (Monk), "Focus on Sanity" or "Ramblin'" (Ornette Coleman), "Every Tub" (Basie and Durham), "Enlightenment" (Hobart Dotson and Sun Ra), or "E.S.P." (Wayne Shorter). Nor can they be considered simply descriptive of the emotional charge or communicative aspirations of the music, as with tunes such as "Modernistic" (James P. Johnson), "Something Sweet, Something Tender" (Dolphy), "In a Silent Way" (Miles Davis), or "Functional" (Monk).

"I don't accept any tradition as far as words go," Threadgill told one interviewer. "I set my own."[26] At the same time, there does seem to be something like a relationship between Threadgill's sense of language and, say, the involuted angularisms and wordplay of some of Thelonious Monk's song titles ("Gallop's Gallop," "Trinkle, Tinkle," "Well, You Needn't"). To some degree they also echo the impulse—among composers emerging both out of bebop in the 1940s and out of the AACM orbit in Chicago in the 1960s and 1970s—to use titles to suggest a sort of guild secrecy through the peculiarity of idiom, making recourse to opaque or scat-based or foreign-sounding language. That is, an insider status is signaled through an "outside" language: one thinks of examples such as "Oop-Pop-A-Da" (Gillespie), "Klackoveedstene" (Parker), "Odwalla" (Roscoe Mitchell), "Ohnedaruth" (Joseph Jarman), "Arhythm Songy" (Muhal Richard Abrams). Or through the surface appearance of code, as in the noticeable predilection for words spelled backward (sometimes referred to as *heteropalindromes* or *semordnilaps*) in jazz song titling: "Airegin" (Miles Davis), "Emanon" (Dizzy Gillespie), "Snibor" (Strayhorn and Ellington). While sometimes this effect involves the recourse to spoken vernacular, at other times, as George Lewis has pointed out, there is a contrary impulse (in titles including Mitchell's "Nonaah" and "Tnoona" and the "mathematical-spatial" titles of Anthony Braxton) toward graphic identifiers whose "pronunciations are unavailable to the naked textual eye."[27]

Threadgill's titular antics seem to be motivated out of a related sense of play—with "a bit of demystifying irony in the background," a common characteristic of the titling habits among AACM musicians.[28] One might say in this respect that they suggest a complicity between musical innovation and linguistic invention or, more puckishly, between modes of formal extension and styles of hilarity. We are confronted with an edgy inversion or critique that ends up revealing something entirely different. Rather than "Toilet Paper," an ode to hygiene or a paean to the excremental throne, Threadgill gives us a tune entitled "Paper Toilet": suddenly, a sculpture, no longer porcelain, but a tree's leavings. A fragile access to the septic, even a place of inscription—write the slate clean? A utilitarian seat that is perhaps itself temporary and disposable, even combustible. Elsewhere, rather than an intimation of grandeur, or a suggestion of the metaphysical, Threadgill hands us "Little Pocket Size Demons," which is something more akin to the little devil in the cartoon that pops into view over Porky Pig's shoulder, whispering diabolical stratagems.

One of the most striking elements of Threadgill's song titles is their syntax. In this regard, they are not unrelated to a loose lineage of jazz provocations and rebuffs and interrogations: think of Thelonious Monk's "Ask Me Now," Benny Golson's "Are You Real," Miles Davis's "So What," Betty Carter's "Do Something," Roscoe Mitchell's "Get in Line." More often than any composer I can think of, Threadgill chooses to title his tunes not just as addresses to an implied "you" but more pointedly as imperatives. There are too many examples to list them all here: "Try Some Ammonia," "Be Ever Out," "Let Me Look Down Your Throat or Say Ah," "Refine Poverty," "Make Hot and Give," "Calm Down," "Do the Needful," "Look," "Don't Turn Around," "Shake It Off," "See the Blackbird Now." These imperative titles seem designed first of all to demand certain forms of behavior, to require "a special sort of attention" (perhaps in something like the way that a noble or clerical title announces an "entitlement to property, powers, certain forms of address, etc.").[29] An action is demanded, and the listener is forced to evaluate the relation between that demand and the form of the music. Is the music attempting to prompt us to do something ("the needful," for example),[30] or is it modeling that doing, striving to address that imperative—sounding that task in more than one sense—in its achieved form? Would it be right to suggest that the continuity among these tunes is not Threadgill's recourse to particular musical styles or combinations thereof (say, with an approach to intonation that seems to draw from the blues or from gospel, or rhythmic patterns possibly adopted from parade marches or cumbia or ska), but instead Threadgill's investigation of what one might call an *imperative mood* in music? And what would that mean? What would it mean in terms of harmonic structure, or meter, or orchestration, or dynamics?

Sly Information

With his titles, Threadgill is in part attempting to compel us to ask these sorts of questions, rather than doing what most critics have habitually done in response to his music: that is, pigeonholing it, worrying whether it's really "jazz," listening for the supposed generic sources of its musical makeup. Replying to one jazz writer's suggestion that many of his tunes are "dirges," Threadgill erupts:

> I've never written a dirge in my damn life. . . . People say some things are marches—they are *not* marches. Writers should describe how the music strikes them, how it affects them, not try to put it into categories. . . . What I want to know is how the music affects you, what it *says* to you. I don't want you to say I'm a post-neo-this or that, that this is or isn't jazz, that's really not important. What is the *effect?*[31]

Whereas a number of journalists have argued that Threadgill's work is "weakened" by his experimentations with text, I am suggesting on the contrary that writing serves a crucial role in his musical practice, in implying (or more precisely, demanding) this focus on reception.[32] His titles are not meant to explain or to contextualize, but instead to shift the burden of interpretation to the listener:

> It's supposed to stimulate you in terms of words in your own mind. You don't need to know what I'm thinking about. What does it do to you? What does it cause you to think about? What does it make you? . . . At first somebody was saying, "What was he thinking about?" After that, you can't figure out. What does it tell you, what do you think about, now—on your own—now that I've suggested this, since I've thrown this up on the table in front for you. What now? Let's get me out of the equation. You're in the equation. So what now do we have?[33]

Threadgill tends to talk about the history of jazz style in terms of "information" (as in his admiration for the "information" that John Gilmore was playing in Chicago in the 1960s, or his comment that Eddie Harris was "fascinating, the amount of information that was in him musically"), and the literary in all its ancillary modes is indispensable in the way that the music—particularly in LP and CD form—imparts "information" to the listener.[34] This is to claim that one must consider the function of Threadgill's writing when one tries to figure out how his work is, as he puts it, all made up of "one fabric," an attempt to give a "total musical picture."[35] As he argues in a 1985 interview, "I hate to talk just about music. Because if you're really talking about something, it applies in every category, across every line. *Then* you're talking about something. A real idea. A real generator. Like gold, silver, a mineral, the water, the air."[36]

The liner notes in verse form to the 1994 record *Song out of My Trees* may be the closest that Threadgill has come to offering a statement of aesthetics. It is in large part a commentary on the relation between music and language. He opens by noting the difficulty of approaching music with words:

> The process of talking about and defining
> music literally is one of monumental proportion.
> Yet this tradition does have a long and uneven
> history and many precedents. [Enter Me]

> To me this proposition is like trying to define
> apples with pears, or solving the problem of
> "if you want to kill the dog, why do you feed it."

Threadgill contends that there is "an area or aspect of music" that is difficult to access, that is "oblique" to our capacity of reception. As with pitches outside the hearing range of the human ear, he says, there are "things that are/at play in music that we can't define, agree on or measure." Nevertheless, he suggests that it is possible to indicate that outside, and thus in assembling *Song out of My Trees* he has "assembled/as much information about the/background fabric as Star material." The phrase *Star material,* Threadgill explains, has to do with "intent and descriptive/information about the bigger picture." That is, he has attempted to provide as much access to the "background fabric" of the music as possible, through a variety of modes of implication and information, including not just the music itself but also the way it is framed: song titles, liner notes, cover art, sequencing. Seeing that "bigger picture"—projecting it into a constellation of signification, in other words—depends ultimately on the listener. "The rest," Threadgill writes, "requires the listener's imagination/& participation, thinking, feeling, etc."[37]

The "background fabric" includes information about Threadgill's compositional process, at least to a certain degree. Interestingly, he insists that while he listens to an enormous variety of music, he finds inspiration as a composer less in other people's music than in other art forms, as though composition starts for him with a brand of pseudomorphosis (an endeavor to force music to accomplish something formally that is on display in art in other media). "Basically, I am not informed by music," he explains. "I get my information on another level, and I express myself in music. The music I listen to has very little to do with anything. I get more ideas about music watching theater or looking at some paintings or watching a choreographer work or reading a film script. That's how I get informed. And these are the type of ideas that I'm always concerned with that are prior to my musical thinking. My philosophical thinking goes to my conclusions musically."[38] More specifically, it is *reading* that serves as the primary spur or catalyst for his compositional process. It can be anything: reading about trench warfare in World War I, or poring over *The*

Book of Five Rings, Miyamoto Musashi's seventeenth-century book on sword-fighting tactics, "filters into what I'm working on," Threadgill says. He begins to think about the music he is composing loosely through the lens of the reading material: as a matter of different figurative levels of engagement (aboveground, belowground), for instance, or as a question of strategy or logistics (how to move troop formations or supplies from one location to another). He asks himself: What kind of strategy do you need when you're doing battle in a trench—in what is basically a "rathole," a "one-way corridor"? Or coming across a book by Heinrich Böll or James Joyce might give him ideas about how to represent multiple perspectives or schizophrenia in a manner that proves relevant as is he trying to think of a particular piece of music: "How many personalities can this thing have?" In this sort of uncodified experimental practice, it is above all literature, Threadgill emphasizes, that is "really the feeding material for me when I'm working on pieces."[39]

I would suggest that even the names of Threadgill's bands serve as another layer of clues to this background fabric of the composition process. A number of critics have noted the peculiar name of his 1990s group Very Very Circus, and Threadgill, while not denying the circus reference (and its hints of a two-ring overlapping circuit of activity in the round), has said that the name refers more broadly to the way that his music "has so many things going on at once."[40] But there is a grammatical twist to the name that deserves comment, too. Since *very* is an adverb, it forces us to hear *circus* not as a noun—not as some solid state or condition or arena—but as an adjective. It pushes us toward accepting the logic of a sentence like, "That concert was very very circus." At the same time, there's an amplification here, a redoubling (not just very, but *very* very) that characterizes a great deal of Threadgill's aesthetics, not just in terms of composition and musical form but also in terms of orchestration (the group included two guitars and two tubas) and implication: echo, split, double vision, dream state, vision, and so on. "Easily slip into another world," as one of his records is titled. A remarkable number of Threadgill's titles index that doubleness, which is also a pregnant ambiguity, an indecision or hesitation that compels a different perspective: one thinks of tunes such as "What To Do, What To Do," "Silver and Gold, Baby, Silver and Gold," "Better Wrapped/Better Unwrapped."[41]

The Micropoetics of Stimulation

Sometimes "tidbits" of this background fabric do show up in the song titles, but they are not meant to convey in any straightforward sense the complex associative process through which Threadgill composes a given piece. In the final analysis, "music is a listening experience," Threadgill argues: "people like these little tidbits, but nothing I say—none of these things really mean anything once you start listening. It's all about—music is all about *sound*."[42] So even if they may sometimes have their source in the compositional process, they are not intended either to explain it or to give any sort of primary guidance for the experience of listening. Ultimately Threadgill describes the function of his titles as "another stimulation. They are tied into the music for me but not for you. It's only to stimulate you."[43] It is reminiscent of an anecdote Ornette Coleman told the philosopher Jacques Derrida about one of his own compositions:

> I had a niece who died in February of this year, and I went to her funeral, and when I saw her in her coffin, someone had put a pair of glasses on her. I had wanted to call one of my pieces *She was sleeping, dead, and wearing glasses in her coffin.* And then I changed the idea and called it "Blind Date."[44]

While it does not entirely explain the circumstances (for example, by identifying who "she" is), the first impulse is pure description—although there is already a disorienting quality in the notion that someone could be "sleeping, dead." But the final title is something else entirely. The instigating episode is perhaps still embedded in the phrase, in a manner that may be "tied into the music" for Coleman but not, one supposes, in a way that could be deciphered by any listener. The final title is a step or three removed from the draft title, throwing up a complex ensemble of connotations on a more abstract metaphorical register (moving from sunglasses to blindness, from death to an encounter with the unknown, from mortuary aesthetics to erotic seduction) that serve as "stimulation," not explication or program.

There are interviews where Threadgill has offered autobiographical explanations of some of his titles. *Too Much Sugar for a Dime,* he has noted, was motivated by something his father used to say, "too much sugar." He explains: "It means that someone is getting more than they deserve for a change, after getting shorted all the time."[45] In another interview, a journalist asks him about the tune "Jenkins Boys, Again, Wish Somebody Die, It's Hot" on the 1995 record *Carry the Day.* Threadgill explains that "Jenkins boys" was "the fanciful name given to mirage-like heat waves that rose over the cotton fields of the antebellum South, where slaves never got a day off unless a member of the plantation master's family died."[46] This is at once fascinating and beside the point in thinking about how to listen to Threadgill's music, because the original albums do not provide such contextualization. And even if the explanations in some of his interviews give partial sources for the phrases in question, they by no means exhaust their resonance, their mystery. For we're faced not just with "too much sugar," but with "too much sugar for a dime": as though the situation of getting "more than they deserve for a change" is the particular instance of asking for another sort of "change" (asking someone to break a dime). One asks for monetary change, and is given an excess of an entirely different sort of change, calculated in another medium, sugar. It forces us to ask about valuation, exchange, transubstantiation, even consolation and sweetness between people—*gimme some sugar,* as my grandma used to say—and then to ask how those qualities can be heard in the music. What does "sweetness" *sound* like?

Similarly, we don't have the antebellum South, but only the trace of that title: "Jenkins Boys, Again, Wish Somebody Die, It's Hot." That heat, and a syntax that seems to dissolve, to break up into discrete units rather than forming a linear sentence. A "wish" that happens "again," and exhaustion that repeats. "Jenkins boys," who are they here? Figures on the horizon, wavering in the distance, the mark of a particular place and time that has been dislodged into a broader horizon of implication associated with that heat. The only hint of the history of plantation labor here is the way we're forced to work at this phrase, to follow its divergent paths of implication. And then, again, to work at the music, to hear the relation between this chopped-up title and the polymeter of the song, between the aggressivity of that wish and the propulsion of Gene Lake's drumming, between the "mirage-like" haunting of those "boys" and the way the sax and electric guitars dart and weave in quick three- and four-note phrases above that shiny percussive floor. Speaking strictly musically—although in another sense one might say that the function of Threadgill's song titles is to obliterate any pretense that one could ever speak strictly musically (or, conversely, the pretense that one could ever deliver a proposition in words that would *not* be accompanied, and waylaid, by their music)—the piece isn't "about" slavery in a programmatic sense, but it is possible to hear it as an exercise in fugitivity. Whatever social or historical reference still shimmers in the phrase, in the music itself is translated by (which means refracted in) a formal dynamic. "It says about getting free of something," Threadgill observes. "That is the real mathematical problem right there for me. That's what inspired the piece of music: how do I exit here. . . . Not exit—how do I break away. Not exit: break away. From the situation. There's got to be a situation and I've got to cause it to break up and I'm going to break away. That's what musically I was dealing with in that piece."[47]

Threadgill's titles are geared toward this particular kind of response—one perhaps best termed a *poetic* response—rather than to offer programmatic or contextual information about the music.[48] I am thinking of Roman Jakobson's well-known definition of poetics, specifically his proposition that "the poetic function projects the principle of equivalence from the axis of selection into the axis of combination."[49] The language of Threadgill's titles is "stimulating" (to return to his own word) because it is put together in a manner that foregrounds associative potential (synonymy, homophony, metaphor), allowing the reader / listener to leap off into a unbounded range of connotation rather than restricting the semantic field through the constraint of syntactical arrangement.

With regard to the habits of jazz critics, Threadgill contends that "there's a misconception that writers have to stand back and try for this false objectivity, try not to be touched. But if you're in the presence of sound, you are *contaminated* by it—there's no such thing as objectivity. And what I want *is* for you to be contaminated, because if you've got the ability, the gift, to put it down in words, then who the hell do we need to be more contaminated than the writer?"[50] Threadgill's own multiple writings in accompaniment to his music, his own literary tugs and antics, "contaminate" the musical medium with the poetic in order to amplify its call to be taken up and elsewhere—its demand for the sugar of a tainted retort.

seven
Notes on Poetics Regarding Mackey's Song

The work of the poet and critic Nathaniel Mackey inheres most insistently in its engagement with music. It records a "research at the interstice" of expressive media, a deliberate and oblique elaboration of Louis Zukofsky's oft-repeated dictum that "poetry may be defined as an order of words that as movement and tone (rhythm and pitch) approaches in varying degrees the wordless art of music as a kind of mathematical limit."[1] Mackey's project takes place not simply through a poetics that makes recourse to song but also through an attention to the ways music, and black music in particular, approaches speech—approximates or aspires to what Mackey terms a "telling inarticulacy," or an "alternate vocality."[2] What is common to black creative expression is not necessarily an emphasis on what we have perhaps too easily come to think of as "orality," but instead an aesthetic imperative to test and break the limits of what can be said. As Mackey puts it: "Everyone talks about the speechlike qualities of instruments as they're played in African-American music. Built into that is some kind of dissatisfaction with—if not critique of—the limits of conventionally articulate speech, verbal speech. One of the reasons the music so often goes over into nonspeech—moaning, humming, shouts, nonsense lyrics, scat—is to say, among other things, that the realm of conventionally articulate speech is not sufficient for saying what needs to be said. We're often making that same assertion in poetry."[3]

This is not a poetics of transcendence, however. It is an inherently self-reflexive mode which is not unrelated to Mackey's own description of Edward Kamau Brathwaite's second trilogy, in that it "both announces the emergence of a new language and acknowledges the impediments to its emergence, going so far as to advance impediment as a constituent of the language's newness."[4] Mackey's fascination with edges, with extremes, with erosion, with modes of expression that strain against themselves, bears witness to a "research at the interstice" ultimately less involved with the particularities of the media involved (sound and script), and more engaged with the task of pressing or distending elements of those mediums (repetition, inflection, timbre, pitch, phrasing, literary structure, orthographics) to bear witness—"eroding witness," as he terms it—to that paradoxical cohabitation of originality and flaw, mobility and limp, articulation and stammer.

Consider the music that charges this work: the otherworldly falsettos described in *Bedouin Hornbook;* flamenco's aspiration to a quality of *duende,* a singing so raspy and gnarled that it is "dark," crouched "at the rim of the wound" and drawing toward "places where forms fuse together into a yearning superior to their visible expression"; the jazz of musicians such as Cecil Taylor, Anthony Braxton, and Yusef Lateef, marked as much by its uncompromising intellectualism as by its spiritual bent; the Song of the Andoumboulou among the Dogon of Mali, a funeral song addressed to flawed, failed precursors of humans.[5] In Mackey's writing, we consistently encounter examples of music straining toward speech, or embodying the noise at the edges of articulate expression. Indeed, the convergence between a writing so obsessed by sound and music so drawn to speech might be best understood as a common concern with the limits of *voice*—its inception, its exhaustion. Voice in all its connotations: as the particular physical apparatus, the ways a throat channels air; as advocacy, "speaking for"; as articulation, joining phonemes into an utterance; as the abstraction of personality, an "individual voice"; even as a disembodiment or haunting, communication from an unseen source.[6] Taking voice as a kind of prism to focus this convergence, it should be clear why issues of transcription, the ways the voice is "troubled" in crossing over between media, seem to attract the most critical energy in Mackey's work. Such trouble marks the "limits of the sayable": it indicates an insufficiency or dispossession native to language itself.[7]

For Mackey, the quality peculiar to black expressive culture is that it does not attempt to conceal or heal these native rifts, the ways expression is always orphic and orphaned. Instead it foregrounds buzz, shaky ground, troubled voices, through "methodologic fissures," making room for accident and rupture within the system itself.[8] The antiphony (call-and-response) so commonly singled out as a feature of black culture is but one facet of this broader "pursuit of another voice, an alternate voice," the moment in artistic expression where "one has worked beyond oneself."[9] As he notes, this pursuit:

> relates to a forking of the voice, so that you have the intersection of two lines of articulation—doubling the voice, splitting the voice, breaking the voice, tearing it. There's a dialogical aspect to African-American and African music that's very strong. It comes across in call and response, the antiphonal relationship between lead singer and chorus, preacher and congregation. It comes across in the playing of musicians like John Coltrane who use the upper and lower registers of the instrument as though they were two different voices in dialogue with one another. . . . It makes for an unruly, agonistic sound in which it seems that the two lines of articulation are wrestling with one another, that they are somehow one another's contagion or contamination.[10]

Mackey's writing is particularly attracted to cross-cultural "musical-textual, musical-literary-religious, music-literary-spiritual confluences" in part because such moments so often value this kind of haunting or splitting, viewing fissure not as failure but as method.[11]

Black musical expression foregrounds "methodologic fissures" not just in terms of broken or doubled voices, however, but also in terms of time—in the ways it espouses polyrhythm and the subtle syncopated propulsion signaled by the word *swing*. Mackey's sensibility is not far from that of Charles Mingus, for instance, in his liner notes to the 1963 suite *The Black Saint and the Sinner Lady*—notes that are already an example of confluence, as a musician's written description of a jazz composition intended as music for dance. The first section, "Solo Dancer," opens with a Dannie Richmond drum figure designed to insinuate a three-level polyrhythm that is recombined and resituated throughout the suite. Mingus, in describing the drumming style of his longtime collaborator, makes recourse to a striking metaphor for the sense of rhythm he wants: "Time, perfect or syncopated time, is when a faucet dribbles from a leaky washer."[12] In this remarkable figure, we find what we might call an "interrogative witness" (BH 30) to the understanding of black expressive culture elaborated in so much of Mackey's work. Time, here, is not like clockwork—nor is it put "right in the pocket," to invoke a phrase common to descriptions of jazz drumming. Mingus advocates a liquid pressure irregularly filtered, a beat hinted at, implied. It is a beat only approached, only described through a synesthetic figure: Mingus figures time first as water passing through a leaky washer, and then later in the notes, as a graphic understanding—one plays time by "drawing a picture" in one's "open mind": "You don't play the beat where it is. You draw a picture away from the beat right up to its core with different notes of different sounds of the drum instruments so continuously that the core is always there for an open mind." The faulty washer marks an impediment, a barrier, but the water's flow is not fully halted. As Mackey might put it, it is as though musical time for Mingus requires both flow and impediment: only as a result of both do we get the dribble, the "perfect" swing that beckons dance.

Andoumboulous Series

Here I address the parameters of this poetics in an early section of Mackey's ongoing sequentially numbered serial poem, *Song of the Andoumboulou,* a restless and peripatetic work that takes as its starting point the Dogon funeral song I mentioned earlier, a song addressed to the Andoumboulou, figures for the Dogon of a prior, flawed form of humanity. *Song of the Andoumboulou* debuted in the 1985 collection *Eroding Witness* and has continued in the subsequent volumes *School of Udhra* (1993), *Whatsaid Serif* (1998), *Splay Anthem* (2006), *Nod House* (2011), and *Blue Fasa* (2015).[13] A section of the series is also available in recorded form through the compact disc *Strick: Song of the Andoumboulou 16–25* (1995), a collaboration between Mackey and musicians Royal Hartigan and Hafez Modirzadeh. I concentrate on what follows on the evolution of the form of the series as it progresses into *School of Udhra.*

The title of this chapter deliberately echoes the poet Robert Duncan's 1956 well-known essay "Notes on Poetics Regarding Olson's *Maximus*"—in which Duncan discusses the accomplishment of *The Maximus Poems,* the epic magnum opus by Charles Olson, his fellow Black Mountain School poet—not only to suggest the "visionary company" of influences (from black expressive practices to the Black Mountain poets) in Mackey's work but also to point at the particular poetics elaborated in Mackey's *Song.*[14] Duncan explicates Olson's achievement in *The Maximus Poems* using the three categories of poetry listed by Ezra Pound in *How to Read* (1931): *melopoeia,* the "tonal structure" of a poem, the way its "passionate system" is spoken by the reader's "inner voice" (71); *phanopoeia,* its graphic structuring on the page, "a casting of images upon the visual imagination" (70); and *logopoeia,* a modernist mode ("the latest come") that Pound describes as "the dance of the intellect among words" (70).[15] Following Pound, Duncan stresses the importance of this last category in Olson's work, noting the way *The Maximus Poems* mark an extension of poetics from the disciplines of eye and ear to the "discipline of movement": "Mr. Pound's *logopoeia* seems to be not only a verbal manifestation but a physiological manifestation. Ambiguities, word-play, ironies, disassociations appear as we watch the meanings; but it is the action of the language, the muscular correlation of the now differentiated parts of the poem, that so expresses itself" (71). In suggesting such an echo, I will argue here that Mackey's *Song of the Andoumboulou* develops a poetics that might be said to start with *logopoeia,* deploying a "muscular realization of language" (72) in the serial poem—what Edward Kamau Brathwaite calls the poem's "bodywork"—to "dance" a particular kind of music on the page.

In considering *Song of the Andoumboulou* as a serial poem, it is crucial to understand the work's departures from the major models of serial writing in twentieth-century American poetry after Pound, including *The Maximus Poems,* Duncan's *Passages,* and Jack Spicer's *The Heads of the Town Up to the Aether.*[16] In interviews Mackey has somewhat tentatively avowed the influence of Spicer's 1957 *After Lorca* on his writing, most evident in the epistolary form adopted in *Bedouin Hornbook* and *Djbot Baghostus's Run.*[17] (In fact, the first of the letters to "Angel of Dust" appears not in *Bedouin Hornbook* but as a kind of prose poem in *Eroding Witness,* as *Song of the Andoumboulou: 6,* and is cc'ed to Spicer and Garcia Lorca.[18]) But the differences may be more significant, and cluster most prominently around the ways Spicer and Mackey understand the serial poem to be based in different kinds of musical allusions. Robin Blaser, in his postface essay to *The Collected Books of Jack Spicer,* attempts to describe the Spicer conception of the serial poem:

> Jack worked in that long form without looking back and without thought of the previous poem, so that the poet could be led by what he was composing. The serial poem is often like a series of rooms where the lights go on and off. It is also a sequence of energies which burn out, and it may, by the path it takes, include the constellated. There is further a special analogy with serial music: the voice or tongue, the tone, of the poem sounds individually, as alone and small as the poet is . . . , but sounded in series, it enters a field.[19]

This compartmentalized definition of the serial form wouldn't appear to apply to Mackey's interwoven, backtracking *Song,* so overrun with echoes and premonitions, revisitations and retractions. Moreover, Western twentieth-century serial composition might not be the appropriate musical reference point.[20] As I have already suggested, Mackey's work finds its particular interlocutor in black music, not as the metaphor for some coherent individual voice, "sounded in series" to approximate a certain spatial resonance, but as a figure for a pursuit of voice that questions, and is questioned by, the very limits of its expressive capacity.

The self-reflexivity, the emphasis on process so evident in *Song of the Andoumboulou,* might find a more instructive model in the work of William Carlos Williams—not only owing to his interest in black music,[21] but also in the ways he thinks serially without Blaser's insistence on the linear progress of the poetic ego, striding from one lit room to the next. Denise Levertov, in a suggestive essay called "Williams and the *Duende,*" brings to our attention Williams's brief and seldom-read "The Sound of Waves," interpreting it as suggesting "a whole exploratory poetics, leading to such *goings beyond*" so integral to the serial form.[22] It is a poem, she suggests, not so much about poetry, as about the necessary question of how to proceed: "How, and where, do I go from here?"

The poem begins with self-reflexivity, begins with the question of form: "A quatrain? Is that/the end I envision?/Rather the pace/which travel chooses." The motion chooses its form, then, and yet it still ends up a quatrain; the voice falls into that familiar form, "wanting a discipline," as the poem phrases it. This impulse to settle is rejected in the next stanza, however: "But wanting/more than discipline/a rock to blow on/as a mist blows." The poem makes recourse to the image of sea spray breaking against a rock, to figure the way this discipline is broken, battered into a new form. But as Levertov notes, this figure of breaking is remarkably then itself broken, as the poem stretches toward the realm of the *duende,* past the point where the voice is comfortable in its technique: "There is a line of dots across the page—and then the dynamic of exploration resumes, not as further movement across a space but as a deepening of listening attention *in* the place to which movement has brought it" (41). After the broken line or perforation, a halting or stammer where the poem would seem defeated, it pushes on:

> . . . . .
>
> Past that, past the image:
> a voice!
> out of the mist
> above the waves and
> the sound of waves, a
> voice . speaking!

In Levertov's words: "it is discovered than an end can—or must—precede a beginning." What is exemplary about "The Sound of Waves" is its espousal of impediment as a condition of inception, its announced longing not just for a discipline but for an impasse—a point of resistance that must be pushed to begin. The sea spray metaphor inscribes this longing: as Mackey has written about Wilson Harris, "Such recourse to metaphor betrays an estrangement, a distance, that the metaphor—the word is derived from a verb meaning 'to carry over'—seeks to overcome. The use of metaphor is then a 'confession of weakness,' the recognition of a chasm one wishes to cross, to be carried across."[23] At the end of the poem, as that metaphor in turn collapses, the final "voice" comes from outside: outside the speaker, outside the figure of spray hitting the rock, and outside the sound of the waves. It is a kind of haunting, an estranged voice of unclear origin that speaks against, below, and beyond the initial self-questioning voice ("Is that/the end I envision?"). Thus, while it witnesses a certain way of *going beyond,* it is related to *duende* in flamenco singing because it is unruly, unmastered: an "alternate" voice that enters as though it were the noise of the impediment, the very sound of the metaphor collapsing under its own weight. And yet, mysteriously, precisely in witnessing that collapse, this alternate voice does indeed carry, "above the waves" and "past the image."

Joint-Work

What resonates most noticeably with *Song of the Andoumboulou* is Williams's recourse to a formal device, the graphic depiction of the break in the poem, the stammer marked by the dots across the page. For the major formal shift between the poems in *Eroding Witness* and the poems in *School of Udhra,* aside from the adoption of a more jagged, "visually syncopated" line, is the recourse in the more recent work to a similar graphic device in many of the poems, seeming both to mark a "cut" in the winding, heavily enjambed descent, and at the same time an announcement of continuance, as the poems seem to take themselves up again—under the line, as it were. The device commences with *Song of the Andoumboulou: 10,* a poem already concerned both with break and with repetition. It opens:

> Sat up reading drafts
> of a dead friend's poem, papers
> kept in a book I hadn't cracked
>
> in years . . .
>
> *Rugs burnt Persian red* repeated,
> echoed, red ink like an omen of
> blood.[24]

If the Andoumboulou are in Dogon cosmology a kind of failed sketch or draft of human beings, then we open with a related figure of the "draft"—defunct notes or lapsed outlines, here for the poetic itself. As with N.'s letters to "Angel of Dust" in the epistolary works, again the speaker encounters a dead, heavenly, or inaccessible interlocutor, is haunted by a voice from afar—and the act of reading, "cracking" a neglected book of papers, is itself a kind of violence, even before the red ink brings to mind an "omen of blood." The poem is strung, is struck, around the lure of a single metaphor: *Rugs burnt Persian red.* We are given no more of the "drafts," no more of the language around this figure. But it is as though that single figure, read, triggers some transport, an "escort thru a gate of unrest." Allusions to a female presence ("her feet"; "The bed my boat, her look / lowers me / down") force us to wonder whether the language might not announce, obliquely, the arrival of Erzulie, the capricious goddess of the Haitian *vodun* pantheon awaited in *Song of the Andoumboulou: 8* with words that resonate here: "As though an angel sought / me out in my sleep or I sat up / sleepless"; "who sits at her feet fills his / head with wings" (3). It is as though the incantation of that single figure, the reading of an incomplete, "echoed" alternate voice, itself incites or ignites a kind of visitation: "Burnt rugs needed / only a spark, spoken, ember. / Spilled ink. Prophet's red. Struck / dumb" (5).

With the words "struck / dumb," *Song of the Andoumboulou: 10* closes, avowing a kind of silencing, an inability to speak further. And yet on the next page, there is a continuation or revisitation, a voice at the bottom of the page caught under a long unbroken black line, one that takes up or responds to the prior passage:

Blinded
by what likeness I saw. Exotic Persian red
robe I put on this morning. Mad at the
world and at the mention of loss a new convert
to light . . .

And at the mention of light a new convert
to what at whose coming on even breath
gave out . . .
Shook as though caught between warring
darknesses, torn, blinded by what
likeness
I saw (SU 6)

The syntax could be read as continuous ("struck dumb, blinded by what likeness I saw"), but the placement of this passage under the line, at the bottom of the subsequent page, troubles this would-be flow, and begs the question whether these words are continuation, comment, or something else entirely. (The section under the line is listed as a separate poem in *School of Udhra*'s table of contents, so despite the obvious resonances, we are discouraged from thinking of it as primarily a part of *Song of the Andoumboulou: 10*.) It is unclear whether and how the language in *Song of the Andoumboulou: 10* and the language of this section, displaced from but echoing the *Song,* are related in time: the line "Exotic Persian red / robe I put on this morning" makes us wonder whether this isn't the morning after the speaker "sat up reading"—the red robe transporting the speaker back to that state of unrest, "burning," the night before. If the poem under the line indicates a speaking after the break of sleep, though, its echoes nevertheless draw inexorably back up to the dream or possession state of the prior passage. Even as the speaker proclaims a frustration with loss, and a readiness to move on with the day ("Mad at the / world and at the mention of loss a new convert / to light . . ."), the revisitation hits, with the robe's "Persian red" a "blinding" throwback to the figure in the draft poem. And as in many of the *Songs of the Andoumboulou,* we are left with a frustrating incompletion, a voice or voices "caught between warring darknesses."

The serial-ness of the *Song* is in no small part the vigilant perpetuation of this state. The belabored fingering of a transport imperfectly recalled, or longingly wished for—displaced, just out of grasp. It reverberates into the next poem, *Song of the Andoumboulou: 11,* which opens "I sit up holding you a / year ago, yearning, let / go, draw short of eternity, / allergic to time" (7), and works toward words that seem to revisit the (dis) possession woven between *Song of the Andoumboulou: 10* and the section under the line:

> Ins and outs on the brink of a
>
> mending always under assault,
>
> love allergic to time, mourning
>
> love's

retreat but with a backward glance,
an over-the-shoulder look says we're no
longer needed. (SU 7)

Mackey has spoken in a 1997 interview about the development of the graphic line separators as a formal device: "I was trying to suggest that even within the book there is another book, there's this 'under-the-line' book. And by citing them specifically that way in the table of contents, it's like saying they are works unto themselves in some ways. I was trying to suggest the possibility of a multiple reading in which one could go through and read those poems that are under the line, go through *School of Udhra* and read the poems under the line sequentially without reading the other ones. . . . It was another way in which I was working to unsettle and multiply the possible relations of the parts." At the same time, the additional sections are linked to the "above-the-line" poems by a seam that is not quite solid, not always voiced: he goes on to note that "they have an unsettled relation to the poem that precedes them and the poem that follows them. And sometimes, in giving a reading, I don't read those sections that fall under the bar, under the line."[25]

I would add that the language of this first revisitation or run-on in *Song of the Andoumboulou: 10* is "unsettled," thus echoing the formal structure. The poems exert great pressure on their own joints, in the same way that this unvoiced blank and black separating line bespeaks weight forced on the joints of the serial poem, a certain disarticulation in the way the words take to the page. One should note that there is a history to this confluence, this "joint-work" affecting the language of the poems as much as their structure. In writing about early modern Europe, for example, Marjorie Garber has pointed out that "*syntax,* in modern usage most frequently considered as an aspect of grammar, and *articulation,* frequently regarded as an aspect of speech, thus each inhabit . . . an intellectual and conceptual space modeled on the body, and, quite specifically, on its 'connexions' or joints."[26] Such complex body-based figurations of language are not limited to Europe, either: we find another instance in Marcel Griaule's *Dieu d'eau,* the influential French ethnological study of the Dogon, a work that attests to the importance of bodily joints in Dogon cosmology. In the

Dogon creation myth, the first ancestor is a blacksmith, expelled from heaven for his transgressions, fleeing to the earth by tumbling down the arc of a rainbow. When the smith hits the ground, though, carrying his hammer and anvil, the shock of impact breaks his body (which had been human in appearance except for smooth, flexible appendages in the place of arms and legs), not disabling him—but giving him joints at the knees and elbows. "He thus acquired the joints [*les articulations*] proper to the new human form, which was to spread over the earth and to devote itself to toil."[27] The joints are thought to be the locus of spiritual power in the body; Griaule's Dogon interlocutor, Ogotemmêli, tells him, "The joints are the most important part of a man" (51).

In Mackey's work, the linguistic and formal joint-work continuously undoes, endlessly challenges, the bodily rhetoric inherent in our understanding of expression—the connotative link between joint and articulation. Whereas in Williams's "The Sound of Waves," both the dotted-line "break" and the broken metaphor are above all what the poem gets "past," necessary impediments in the discovery of voice, in Mackey's *Song of the Andoumboulou,* voice emerges only broken, continually troubled by the series' joints of language and structure. On the one hand, one of the more striking qualities of Mackey's poetry is its language: its convolution, its grainy, knotted patterns of formulation. A deep questioning of the modes of subjectivity itself is embedded in the syntax. Subject and object are commonly refracted to the point of what Mackey later terms "vatic scat"—but we might just as easily call this mode "phatic scat," to mark its resistance to the declarative, its avoidance of the simple pronoun, its erosion of the subjective through obliquity.[28] The language gets "out of joint" in poems like "Irritable Mystic," the fifth part of Mackey's other evolving serial poem, *Mu* (itself inspired by music: the allusion is to the multi-instrumental suite recorded in Paris in 1969 by Don Cherry and Ed Blackwell), which opens:

  His they their
we, their he
  his was but if
need be one,

        self-

extinguishing
I, neither sham nor
excuse yet an
alibi, exited,
out,
else
the only where
he'd be. (SU 25)

Note how few sentences in *School of Udhra* commence with the proposition of a subject. Almost always, the attack is edgewise and edgy, as Mackey might put it, out from the unsettled anchor of a qualified object, sometimes without any subject/verb resolution at all. It is particularly noteworthy that the "I" in these poems, the putative first person, seldom comes onto the scene first. As *Song of the Andoumboulou: 12* opens: "Weathered raft I saw myself/adrift upon.//Battered wood I dreamt I/drummed on, driven" (9). The "I" only comes in through the back door of an object inhabiting a vision or dream. This deferral or destabilization of the subject is matched only by a similar work on the spirits, revenants, lovers, and communities that are so often the object of these poems' longing. "Slipped Quadrant," the final poem in *School of Udhra,* describes this syntactical distancing of the metaphysical wholeness or spiritual realm the poems pursue—a distancing concomitant with that pursuit:

As if by late light shaped of its
arrival, echoed announcement
come from afar, loosed
allure, the as-if of it its
least appeasable part.
Rich
tense we called it,
would without end . . . (86)

This poetry is written in "rich tense," a tense of perpetual erosion and conditionality ("would without end"). And the "as-if" of it is even less "appeasable" than its syntax, even less a remedy: metaphor, another kind of joint-work, only serves to underscore the ways the speakers are estranged from the wholeness they intimate.

The formal joint-work, the discrepant dynamic between the *Songs of the Andoumboulou* and the subsequent poems "under-the-line," only serves to reinforce this conditionality, by putting pressure on the joints of the serial form itself. The "under-the-line" poems are ultimately an ambiguous force on the shape of *School of Udhra.* Some of the *Songs* are followed by more than one "under-the-line" poem (for instance, *Song of the Andoumboulou: 15* is followed by four [SU 15–20]), and after others they do not appear at all. Moreover, although they would seem to be most basically an extension of the serial impulse—a linear extension of the sections of the poem—they are also signs of distention and trouble, literally and figuratively subverting any pilgrim progress from one lit room to the next. As noted earlier, they are listed in the contents as separate from the individual *Songs,* and thus deliberately stake out a distance from the serial poem, a stance of commenting critically (or, as Mackey terms it, "what-saying") from underneath or alongside that continuing form. Moreover, although they are introduced in the *Songs of the Andoumboulou* that open *School of Udhra* (numbers 8 through 15), the "under-the-line" poems spread out from the serial poem to affect or infect all the poems in the book, even self-standing pieces like "Alphabet of Ahtt" (43–48) and "Wizard of Ought" (57–63). There is no principle for their appearance, except that they are never longer than a page, and the layout is always calculated up from the bottom margin, under the graphic break.[29]

To suggest that the "under-the-line" poems in *School of Udhra* are simultaneously an amplification and an undermining of the *Song* is to begin to see the refigured serial poetics elaborated in the work. Mackey's shrewd comments on the graphic impulse in Charles Olson's notion of "open form" or projectivism seem particularly applicable here to his own poetics: "There seems to be a good deal of arbitrariness at work in the graphic impulse, a principle of tolerance, at the very least, for its disruptive, deformalist thrust, often outright celebration of it. . . . The graphic impulse is not in and of itself either formalist or disruptive, but a tool available to either inclination."[30] Or both, as the case may be. Again, the amplification and undermining of the form, as part of the overall joint-work of the poetry, evokes the problematic we encounter in Williams's "The Sound of Waves," of going beyond despite and because of impediment.

Even as motion is troubled and rhetoric falls back on itself, the repeated refrain in the *Song* reminds us that the voices do go on, against all odds, finding a way out of no way. "Sound was back," *Song of the Andoumboulou: 31* begins.[31] That disembodied, alternate voice keeps coming back in. "Again what speaks of speaking" (12), we read in *Song 14,* a self-reflexive phrase that itself weaves in and out of the writing: "Tautologic / drift in which once more what spoke / of speaking spoke of speaking" ("Alphabet of Ahtt," SU 43). Ed Roberson's 1984 *Lucid Interval as Integral Music,* a serial poem that, as I will argue later, is not unrelated to Mackey's *Song* in its mobilization of music, seems at times to speak directly to this moving "drift," this resiliency of the voice, "taking up the turning subject" again and again:

> Point in these words
>   takes up the turning
>   subject
> after the silence after
>   what was meant last.
>   At renewal.
> A needle
>   not so played on meaning
>   as on moving[32]

What is *epiphany* in Williams's "The Sound of Waves"—that exceptional moment of the alternate voice breaking out—becomes *epistrophy* in Mackey's *Song,* a "moving" condition continually resought through the leaky washers of the poems' joint-work. *Epistrophy* means a "turning about": in Roberson's formulation, both the way language folds back on itself, repeats, and qualifies its assertions, and the way music technology appears to echo this work: the way a phonograph needle on a spinning record also marks a graphic "moving," a turning that travels. (*Epistrophy* also brings sound back, as the title of the composition by Thelonious Monk and Kenny Clarke I discussed at length in the introduction to this book.) So although subjectivity is endlessly deferred and contested, it always comes back, strains toward voice. In the words that open the seventeenth *Song:*

> Thought they were done
> but it wasn't over, the
> we they might've been,
> would-be we.[33]

A Poetics of the Reprise

How, then, do we name this poetics of the serial form, that turns less on meaning than on moving, that strains against its own continuation, but keeps "not being done" with itself? Mackey has suggested that the "under-the-line" poems, and the principle they announce, might be thought of as indicators of process, like "alternate takes" from a recording session. They are not really forms of revision, but more a way to *revisit* the concerns of the "above-the-line" poems. Revisitation with a difference, though: "they revisit in a way that's differently marked." He adds:

> There's a great deal of revisitation in my writing anyway; these do it in a way that's marked visually and underscored visually in the way that they are put on the page, where they're placed at the bottom of the page, beneath a line. I was getting into using the page, using the visual display that the book offers, that print offers, to further announce and articulate senses of recurrence and rhythm and periodicity that are operative in the varieties of revisitation going on in the work.[34]

I want to hold on to that term, *revisitation,* but propose another way of thinking about this evolving poetics of the serial form, again inspired a musical confluence. In a number of ways, the "under-the-line" poems operate most of all like the device in jazz performance known by the term *reprise.* I should emphasize that this term is meant to describe the graphic impulse of the "under-the-line" poems, more than their potential status as a "score" for any possible performance of the series. In the accompanied recitations on the recording of *Strick,* the performance of the *Songs* that are followed by "under-the-line" poems (such as numbers 17 and 23) sometimes approaches something like a musical reprise, in that the music comes to a close with the *Song,* and then picks up again when Mackey begins the under-the-line section. But overall, the CD performances are characterized by the structural device of reprise only in the loosest sense. I am suggesting rather that the poems strive for an effect *on the page* which may or may not be directly related to the way Mackey performs them aloud, but which—as a formal strategy—is akin to the effect achieved by a musical reprise. What is articulated *graphically* in the under-the-line poems of *Song of the Andoumboulou,* in other words, is articulated *in sound* in the reprise.

In musical terms, *reprise* generally refers to a recapitulation; it is used particularly in speaking of the sonata form, to indicate a repetition of the thematic exposition after the development section.[35] In jazz, though, a reprise does somewhat different work. The most celebrated version of the reprise in jazz is of course Count Basie's version of "April in Paris," a tune playfully alluded to in the second of Mackey's epistolary novels, *Djbot Baghostus's Run.*[36] The Basie orchestra arrangement of "April in Paris" that would climb to number twenty-eight on the pop charts in the 1970s (itself coming back) appears to have been developed during the winter of 1954, during a gig at Birdland. The chart, so often attributed to Basie himself, was actually arranged by organist "Wild" Bill Davis, whose trio was sharing a bill with Basie. The musicians in the big band asked Davis to expand his catchy trio arrangement of the Vernon Duke tune, and he "remembers working on the arrangement until 7 o'clock one morning, taking it in the next night, and playing it on organ with the band without rehearsal. It was an immediate hit, and they played it together for the next three weeks in Birdland, frequently four times a night."[37] In the well-known recorded version on the 1956 album of the same name, the reprise kicks in after a seemingly definitive crescendo, when Basie is heard to say to the band: "One more time" (and in the second reprise, after another drawn-out crescendo: "Let's try it one more once").

The notion of a singularity repeated, a definitive closure reopened to close again, is striking, especially as encapsulated in that seemingly oxymoronic directive: "one more once." In an interview with Chris Albertson, Basie explained how the hook was developed: "When Bill's group finished playing the tune, he always turned to me and said, 'One more time.' Then we'd play it and I'd go, 'One more once,' and so on. That's how that started."[38] So in fact, when we hear Basie call for repetition, we are actually hearing the trace of what originally was a dialogue, an interweaving of alternating voices, echoing and inciting one another. The reprise in the Basie recording, then, might be said to call out to an inaccessible interlocutor, "Wild" Bill Davis's organ. The form, in its jazz connotation, carries a built-in cultivation of another voice, a repetition that speaks differently. It also gives a sense of how to go on beyond the end, beyond impediment: with "one more once," the song after the end of the song, as it were, in the same voicing (the same arrangement) but in a different voice. This repeated singularity, the odd syntax of "one more once," is a way of speaking familiar to the *Songs of the Andoumboulou:* "A last meeting after other / last meetings," as it's put in one of its more recent configurations.[39]

In a broader etymology, reprise can refer to any "taking by means of retaliation," so the word retains the sense of *agon,* of contesting articulations wrestling for a single space. The word developed from the Old French *repris,* the past participle of the verb *reprendre,* to "take back" or "take again," and in this buried sense we might tentatively hear an echo of the way the reprises in Mackey's *School of Udhra* mark a *revisitation,* in the sense of spiritual "repossession." "Possession," Mackey writes, "means that something beyond your grasp of it grabs you, that something that gets away from you—another sense in which fugitivity comes in—gives you a voice."[40] One might note that in jazz, too, the reprise is intimately linked to the realm of the voice. If we think back to the rich tradition of black show bands, the era when the great orchestras (Basie, Ellington, Fletcher Henderson, Jimmie Lunceford, Chick Webb) played primarily for dances, it becomes clear that the reprise ultimately works something like the edges of the show, keeping things moving. For the show band, the reprise is the preeminent way of negotiating exits, especially for singers: if the singer gets on the stage to join the band during a vamp, a repeated "holding" figure usually played at the beginning of a tune, she slips off during the reprise, that similarly "holding" pattern that falls back into the tune's groove.[41] It bespeaks a performative technology that mobilizes repetition to get voices on and off the scene.

This function, I would argue, is not unrelated to a spiritual realm: it is the way the music "holds" or carries the hearer and the performer alike. In the African American church, one often finds a version of reprise, where after a spiritual ends, the organist or the congregation falls back into the groove, revisiting the thread of song. It is as though the momentum of the music—its *transport* in every sense—demands it be taken up again, and taken elsewhere. This momentum comes from a potentially boundless spiritual source, notwithstanding its difficulty of access. (In one possibly apocryphal story, for instance, Basie's orchestra was reported to have played more than 125 reprises to "April in Paris" at a telethon.[42]) James Snead, among others, has attempted to push our understanding of repetition in black culture in precisely such a direction, toward what he terms a "revised metaphysics of rupture and opening." His take is perhaps more Manichean than Mackey's cross-cultural poetics, but Snead's description of black repetition as cutting away to a flow or continuous momentum is helpful here:

> In black culture, repetition means that the thing *circulates* (exactly in the manner of any flow, including capital flows) there in an equilibrium. In European culture, repetition must be seen to be not just circulation and flow but accumulation and growth. In black culture, the thing (the ritual, the dance, the beat) is "there for you to pick it up when you come back to get it." If there is a goal (*Zweck*) in such a culture, it is always deferred; it continually "cuts" back to the start, in the musical meaning of "cut" as an abrupt, seemingly unmotivated break (an accidental *da capo*) with a series already in progress and a willed return to a prior series. . . . This magic of the "cut" attempts to confront accident and rupture not by covering them over but by making room for them inside the system itself.[43]

The "cut" in reprise (the jump from the "end" of the song back into its theme) would thus not represent redundancy, but a way of taking the groove beyond itself, opening the way for other voices or other levels in the music. We should not let an attention to the poetics of reprise in *School of Udhra* draw our attention from the work's metaphysical aspirations, in other words.

Such a metaphysics is staged even more emphatically in the work of another contemporary African American poet, Ed Roberson, whose work is discussed in Chapter 8. His 1984 *Lucid Interval as Integral Music,* a serial poem similarly split horizontally by a line across the page, can be read in a kind of dialogue with Mackey's *School of Udhra,* precisely around these issues. Roberson's formalism seems more directly indebted to the orphic project of Jack Spicer's *The Heads of the Town,* but like *School of Udhra,* it refigures the serial form by revisiting its host of musical reference points. One difference is that where Mackey continually reaches toward an inaccessible or lost wholeness or spiritual space, which disrupts and haunts the poem but can't be captured in its voices, Roberson tends to figure that integral "alternate voice" precisely in the silences and gaps of the poem. The breaks in Roberson's work, then (including the graphic break separating the poem into two parts), mark the "intervals" that must be skipped over in any act of speaking, in any act of weaving articulation.[44] So the music comes into those "integral" silences of form and syntax, rather than informing the erosive and vatic scat we encounter in Mackey's work. This is proposed directly in section VII of *Lucid Interval:*

> With the dead rest
> spots in the oscillation
> an accuracy also,
> a perfect note is
>
> hit. An accurate physical absence.
> The presence of music.
> Or conversation
> with one
>
> I think is never missing
> and I think is the right signature.
> to have squandered an intelligence
> on unspeakable watch
>
> of that   without tongue[45]

After the End, the Beginning

For Mackey, the metaphysics would be rooted more in the incompleteness innate to any mode of human expression. Speaking of the recurrence of figures of loss and dispossession in his work (the "phantom limb," the Andoumboulou, the longing "without remedy" of *duende*), Mackey has commented that the focus has to do with the following:

> Finding out what you have but don't have. You have it in the form of a disposition but that disposition is not the same as the possession of it. So you have it as a reaching-toward-something. In many ways, you have it as a reaching-through-things, so that there's a way in which that reaching is not satisfied even when it does seize upon something. It goes on reaching. . . . It speaks of loss, it speaks of lack, but it also speaks of an insufficiency that's indigenous to the very act of reaching. Reaching wants to go on, in some sense that's troubling to the things it does settle upon and take hold of. It's not that it empties those things. It simply finds that those things are in place in a certain way that the reaching wants to continue to be free of.[46]

This interest in reaching beyond reaching, as it were, reverberates throughout the work, and is the impulse underlying Mackey's recourse to the serial form itself. This concern is the thread, for instance, that holds together *Song of the Andoumboulou: 6,* the prose poem addressed to "Angel of Dust" that inaugurates the epistolary form of *Bedouin Hornbook* and *Djbot Baghostus' Run.* The letter (signed "N.," who may or may not be associated with the book's author) is framed as a response to Angel of Dust's criticism of the *Song*'s tendency to "speak of speaking" instead of "speaking *from* something," some ground that would be able to become "a re-source rather than something evasive, elusive, sought after." N. writes back: "We not only can but should speak of . . . *absence* as unavoidably an inherence in the texture of things. . . . You really do seem to believe in, to hold out for some first or final gist underlying it all, but my preoccupation with origins and ends is exactly that: a pre- (equally post-, I suppose) occupation." N. closes the letter with a qualification, repeating but rearticulating Angel of Dust's language: "Not 're-source' so much for me as re: Source."[47] *Song of the Andoumboulou* is the serial record of that pre- and post-occupation, an attempt to raise a metaphysical question of origin, without the pretense that one can ever ask that question from any sure and solid ground.

In this sense, absence or alienability is the condition of the unfolding poetic search in the *Songs of the Andoumboulou,* precisely because it is the constitutive condition of being—even if that condition is one human narratives of grounding and origin endlessly attempt to deny or heal. At a number of points in his work, Mackey returns to a touchstone quote from the "Manifesto of the Unborn State of Exile" in Wilson Harris's 1965 novel *The Eye of the Scarecrow,* a self-reflexive passage on the nature of language and the poetic enterprise: "In this age and time, one's native land (and the other's) is always *crumbling;* crumbling within a capacity of vision which rediscovers the process to be not foul and destructive but actually the constitutive secret of all creation wherever one happens to be."[48] That is, even if there is no inalienable meaning, no solid ground, "there remains . . . the search for such meaning, alienability likewise being a condition of search." Through its poetics of reprise, *Song of the Andoumboulou* enacts this search, which Mackey describes as a "search to which there is no end or alternative, though its muse persists in promising one."[49] In other words, it is precisely through an engagement of erosion, admitting the ways our native grounds "crumble," that we begin to sense the metaphysics behind any human quest for foundations and beginnings. Only *after* that crumbling does insight enter, only by straddling what *Song 35* calls the "bridge between 'end' and 'again.'"[50]

One should recall that the adoption of this poetics is equally its extension, though: whereas for Harris, that necessary crumbling (and that search) is implicitly enacted in language itself, at the semiotic level,[51] the joint-work that enacts this erosion in Mackey's *Song* is as much formal as linguistic. Mackey's joint-work engages not just what Harris calls the "untrappable grain" of language, but moreover the unsettled "body" of the poem—what Robert Duncan terms the *logopoeia* of its unstable progress down the page, its blanks and breaks, the creak of its reprises. It should not be a surprise, then, given Mackey's influences, that Dogon cosmology offers a particularly vivid instance of such an "embodied" logic of the "bridge between 'end' and 'again.'" The French ethnologist Geneviève Calame-Griaule, in a work on door-lock mechanisms in Dogon culture, has noted:

> In Dogon, as in some other African languages, the terms expressing the notions of "to open" and "to close" come from a single root whose first meaning is "to close." . . . Since it is the simple root that connotes the idea of "to close," and the derived form that of "to open," it seems legitimate to argue that the concept of closing precedes that of opening, and that one cannot, in Dogon logic, open a door until it has previously been closed. It seems that western logic proceeds more in the opposite sense, and considers that one closes that which is open, essentially in order to protect it.[52]

If Mackey's *Song* creatively embraces the complexities of Dogon cosmology, then part of what the serial poem finds there is a sense that things close in order to open. It takes us back to Mingus's prescription of a leaky faucet, the faulty barrier through which rhythm seeps. Or Billie Holiday's recording of "Fine and Mellow," a blues famous for its final stanza:

> Love is just like a faucet, it turns off and on
> Love is like a faucet, it turns off and on
> Sometimes when you think it's on, baby, it has turned off and
> gone.[53]

What's striking about this last verse is that the formal imperative, the rhyme on "gone," forces a twist in what we might call the syntax of love: it has to be described as turning "off" before it turns "on." Oddly, it is when the faucet flows unexpectedly—when it turns off just "when you think it's on"—that we get the rhythm: the rhyme between "gone" and "on" that completes the blues stanza. Indeed, this skewed temporality is played out in the preceding lyrics, as well: in the first stanza, love is off ("My man don't love me, treats me, aw, so mean / My man he don't love me, treats me awful mean / He's the lowest man that I've ever seen"), while in the second, it's on, and everything is "mellow": "He wears high draped pants, stripes are really yellow / He wears high draped pants, stripes are really yellow / But when he starts in to love me, he is so fine and mellow." "It turns off and on": the syntax seems counterintuitive, as it implies that love can be comprehended only in relation to its absence—seen only as it is taken away. Love can come back, though: the "on" in "gone" gives notice that some deeper source is still there to come back to, even if that access is impeded, even if it lingers only in echo, in another voice. It is as though the deprivation, the loss, has to happen first, before one can start back in. As though an end must precede a beginning.

eight
Come Out

A lucid interval is a period of temporary sanity between bouts of madness—a brief and deceptive reprise, then, the calm at the eye of the storm. This is to say that it already implies a series, already implies a rhythm or, better, an oscillation or a tide. Lunacy predominates, lunacy prevails, but grants a periodic release from its pull, a moment of clarity and even illumination. Here I attempt to propose a strategy for the navigation of some of Ed Roberson's poetry, writing that seems to invoke such an interval or even to announce that state as its own. The title of Roberson's 1984 serial poem, *Lucid Interval as Integral Music,* yokes that intermittent sanity to sound: in the midst of mental disturbance, in a clearing between its ramparts, there is a music that is whole, untouched.[1]

To read the poem is first of all to ask whether it is attempting to produce or sustain that state, on the one hand, or whether it is somehow written from that vantage, speaking from within that sanctuary. At times, sections of the poem look back to prior turmoil, as in the group of poems that recall a near-death experience in a flash flood in the Amazon—although even those sections seem less to announce that an ordeal has been survived (or that lucidity has been achieved), than to point at something that can't yet be written: "sometime I'm going to have to/explain how I feel how/I've made my peace with lives/of the waters," section XXIII opens, and adds later:

> I have been stared at   crying publicly
> remembering   crossing the street. (33)

Here it would seem we are confronted with a series of intervals: the speaker remembers a time of remembering, an uncontrollable display of emotion in a specific period ("crossing the street"), triggered by the recall of another, more treacherous period of vulnerability or transition.

But at the same time, the book as a whole can be read as staging an interval, for it is formally divided: in its main section (called "This Week's Concerts"), there is one series of thirteen-line poems, identified with sequential Roman numerals and occasional titles, that moves across the top of the pages, and another series of poems of various lengths, identified with Arabic numerals and untitled, that moves across the bottom of the pages. Roberson cites the influence of Jack Spicer's "Homage to Creeley" in *The Heads of the Town up to the Aether,* with its "Explanatory Notes" at the bottom of the page, "talking back" to the verses above.[2] But in *Lucid Interval,* the "bottom" or "underneath" poems are not simply explications of a primary text, or annotations running below it. "The voices are totally independent," Roberson has explained, "not only in terms of answering, mirroring, or talking, or picking up the same imagery, but in terms of length."[3] At times there is no poem on the bottom half of the page; at other times a bottom poem stretches below more than one of the discrete poems above the line. (On two occasions, this mode breaks, and there is only a single thirteen-line poem on the page, unnumbered, with no line above or below it [see 40, 47].) According to Roberson:

> The upper voice is the poem, and the bottom voice is the one that's singing over or singing under, in the sense that it's mumbling, or that deep humming you hear in church while the minister is preaching and somebody in the back is what they call "mourning." And the preacher is playing off that, is singing back and forth to that, to whoever is sitting up there on the mourner's bench. He's preaching to them, you see. That voice underneath doesn't go with the poem, it's got its own thing happening.[4]

If the poem constructs an interval *between* the two series, top and bottom, does that mean that its space of "lucidity" is thereby inaccessible—perhaps indicated only graphically, in the unsounded integrity of the black line across the page? Voices shuttle back and forth across it, but may never touch it at all. Lucidity would then be a state one strives for in dialogue, in congregation, but a clarion tone indexed only in its absence, as section VII seems to suggest:

With the dead rest
spots in the oscillation
an accuracy also,
a perfect note is

hit. An accurate physical absence.
The presence of music.
Or conversation
with one

I think is never missing
and I think is the right signature.
to have squandered an intelligence
on unspeakable watch

of that without tongue. (17)

There is another way to approach the mobilization of "interval" in the book, since the poems achieve a variety of complex polyvocal effects at the level of the sentence, playing with spacing and enjambment. In his own words, Roberson strives "to put in as many keys or cues or wormholes or chutes to other things that you know, other than the words that are sitting on the page. . . . Where I started was with sentences, how you could find sentences overlapping and have difficulty figuring out what was actually the end of a sentence. The end of the sentence could actually be the beginning. So you hear voices in sentences. . . . I was trying to cue people's eyes, or key people's ears, or key people's feelings into the other voices or events that are going on—rather than on ones that I know are the standard reading."[5] The first example is the first poem in the book, the introductory "Picking Up the Tune, the Universe and Planets," which opens by announcing that the book's form is "the lena/after my daughter." In delicate interweaving, it tells us that the temporality of this serial composition is set and granted by the poet's infant daughter, whose needs take precedence over poetry. Consider these lines from the third and fourth stanzas:

pure
interruption she gets   her changing
she is the only music   she gives

the intervals
in which it is written. (5)

Even in this short passage, one gets a sense of what Roberson means by "hearing voices." First, "she gets" is suspended between two direct objects. The baby gets "pure interruption," not halfhearted attention: you drop everything. The next two words offer a different possibility, without canceling the first. "Pure interruption" is an appositive (that is, she *is* "interruption"), and "she gets her changing": you change the baby's diapers, and it's not something you put off till later. Then, between the two possible objects, held in impossible balance, "changing" shifts once more, to imply that her unpredictable, serial exigency is itself a "changing." This shifting is "is the only music," and then it turns more particular: the transformations of her budding person are the only art she gives ("her changing she is the only music she gives"). Finally, the last two words lean toward another object: "she gives the intervals" in which the poem is written. It can only be composed in the passages of time she grants, the intervals between her interruptions.

The classical term for this figure is *apo koinu* ("in common" in Greek), a variant of zeugma where "a single word or phrase is shared between two distinct, independent syntactic units."[6] It is the second of William Empson's seven types of ambiguity: an "ambiguity of syntax" resulting in an "interpenetrating and, as it were, fluid unity."[7] As a formal strategy, it suggests polyphony, the straddling of multiple perspectives. Roberson comments: "I assign voice to parts of myself or to the conflicting feelings within something. Then I get this back-and-forth discussion, this church kind of thing."[8] Often the book enacts interval on more than one level at once, with interfolded syntax in a given poem, echoed or extended by the next poem in its series, and simultaneously "sung under" or seconded by the poem below it. Section IV describes geese dozing on a river, and the way they float gently as the water moves, "swung like subway riders." The poem imagines the difficulty of a dance that would be able to "depict" that motion, that "floating/carcass." It concludes with the sight of another object in the transparent water, a stone that—viewed through the reflections on the surface of the river—looks as if it's suspended in a tree: "the river stone is here// A black step in a tree reflection skipped still." The poem at the bottom of the page then takes up this image and "cues" it into other associations:

> because of the suggestion all the versions
> of people in trees make
> to americans,
> the africans, the pater monkey, the
> jesuses crucified, the lynchings
> the yearbook blondes swung in
> all the alumni arbors,
>
> the surface of the water reflects what is
> Under the umbrella of such leaves
> Even stone leaps to the surface
> The stones on the bottom are mistaken for the bottom
> of a hanging
> black man's feet on the surface
> reflection. Dancing nationally in the trees or.
> A skipping stone. also skipped still strange fruit (14)

This is to discover a chain of shared associations—"national," as it were—that spies a legacy of violence even in an optical illusion of ascent. Terrible insight, and yet also the mechanism to which these poems aspire: the unexpected transformation or layering of vision, the ability to see around historical corners. In the book it is referred to by a variety of terms: "the perpetual jar of things" (11, 13); "steps" (36, 39); "the multiple spot/of collision" (65); "bridge music" (34); "the offered/hallucination of light" (30); "divination" (62). Elsewhere in Roberson's work, it is termed "ignescent associations between things."[9] Interval, in this sense, is not epiphany or enlightenment, but a risky momentary second sight, what one poem later in the book calls a "current fixture." Finding the single solution at a given moment—intuiting the proper metonymic link—means flirting with electrocution.[10]

Section XXXV of the book suggests that "the currency/of exchange between is madness's//equipoise" (46), which delivers us back where we started: with lucid interval. A serial poetics that hovers on the edge of sanity. Michel Foucault has written suggestively about what he terms the "madness" of the artist, what "makes him different—from all those who remain silent." By the end of the nineteenth century, Foucault argues, especially with the work of Mallarmé, this quality is no longer some sort of inspiration ("a Platonic ecstasy which protects him from illusion and exposes him to the radiant light of the gods"), but instead a certain kind of vulnerability: a "subterranean relationship in which the work and what it is not construct their exteriority within the language of dark interiority."[11] In the appendix to *Histoire de la folie à l'âge classique,* Foucault calls for the study of the "domain" of the forbidden *(l'interdit)* in language, contending that ultimately, "madness is forbidden language" *(la folie, c'est le langage exclu).*[12] He outlines some of the parameters of such a study, which would consider not just linguistic errors *(fautes de langue),* blasphemous language (according to a religious, sexual, magical order), and censured words (words whose "meaning is intolerable" for a particular culture "at a given moment"), but also another sort of practice that he associates with literature:

> It consists in submitting speech that appears to conform to a recognized code to another code, whose key is given in the speech itself; in a manner that the speech is redoubled at its interior: it says what it says, but it adds a mute surplus that silently utters what it says and the code by which it says it. Here it is not a matter of an enciphered language, but instead of a language that is structurally esoteric. That is, it does not communicate a forbidden signification, while hiding it; instead, it is immediately placed into an essential fold of speech. A fold that hollows speech from within, perhaps infinitely.[13]

This signals a "strange proximity" *(étrange voisinage)* between madness and literature, for Foucault, but he stresses that "madness neither manifests nor tells of the birth of a work" *(la folie ne manifeste ni ne raconte la naissance d'une oeuvre);* on the contrary, madness "sketches the empty form, from which the work comes" *(elle désigne la forme vide d'où vient cette oeuvre).*[14] If Roberson's book plays at this interstice, then it does so by erecting at every level of its structure just these kinds of self-reflexive folds, the "right signature" of a madness that cannot be spoken but that charges the poem in every sense of the word. This is the means by which the work advances: "You don't write your way out of the chaos. What you do is nail something down that will allow you to get further downstream."[15]

On Serial Poetics

I turn to Roberson's work and a few of the issues it raises (music, madness, doubled or multiple vocality) as a point of entry into a consideration into the poetics of serial form. It seems to me that one of the shortcomings of Joseph Conte's groundbreaking 1991 book, *Unending Design,* the most influential study of serialism in postmodern poetry, is that Conte does not delve as deeply as he might into the musical sources and resources of the works he reads. Above all, he may be too quick to assume an easy formal analogy between Western serial music and postwar U.S. poetry. Conte draws on Umberto Eco's theory of the "open work" (an artwork with indeterminate elements left to chance or to the choice of the performer, thus making it susceptible to a potentially infinite number of interpretations) and, through it, the pronouncements of some of the composers associated with serialism, especially the voluble Pierre Boulez.[16] As Conte argues, distinguishing the series from the sequence and the epic, "the series as an open form—with its aleatory and indeterminate qualities . . . supersedes in its postmodernity an organic sequence that still hopes to discover an immanent form and a unity in creation."[17] He approvingly cites the model of serial composition, in which (in Boulez's words) "the composer's thought, utilizing a determined methodology, creates the objects of which he has need and the form necessary for organizing them each time that his thought must be expressed. Classic tonal thought was founded on a universe defined by gravitation and attraction; serial thought is founded on a universe in perpetual expansion."[18]

Conte claims that "the serial form constitutes itself on the instant from a set of mobile and discontinuous objects; and it may reconstitute itself at the next instant from a varied set of objects."[19] Yet in serial music, strictly understood, the "set" of objects (the tone-row from which one derives the series) is not disposable or modifiable. It can be transposed or flipped through permutations—prime, inversion, retrograde, retrograde of the inversion—but its particular constellation of the twelve-tones of the well-tempered scale is supposed to structure the entire composition. (Subsequent forms of serialism extend this method to the rationalization and compositional control of rhythmic values, pitch duration, and timbral qualities.) As musicologist Paul Griffiths defines it, serialism is "a method of composition in which a fixed permutation, or series, of elements is referential (i.e. the handling of those elements in the composition is governed, to some extent and in some manner, by the series)."[20] The composer's thought does make "the objects of which he has need," but the method is "determined" or "fixed," not a constituting and reconstituting that can happen "on the instant."

When asked during a talk in Vancouver whether serial music is "related" to his sense of the serial poem, Jack Spicer responds, "I don't know."[21] But the two would seem to be rather different, if according to Spicer's definition "you go into a serial poem not knowing what the hell you're doing. That's the first thing. You have to be tricked into it. It has to be some path that you've never seen on a map before and so forth."[22] Although Robert Duncan at least refers in passing to the music of Schoenberg in the preface to one of his books,[23] it may not be a coincidence that among the poets Conte associates with serial form (Spicer, Robert Creeley, Harry Mathews), the ones who mention musical influences tend to cite Charlie Parker, Thelonious Monk, Billie Holiday, and Dizzy Gillespie more than Anton Webern, Pierre Boulez, and Karlheinz Stockhausen.[24] At one symposium, Spicer famously proclaimed, "We must become singers, become entertainers. . . . There is more of Orpheus in Sophie Tucker than in R. P. Blackmur; we have more to learn from George M. Cohan than from John Crowe Ransom."[25]

At the same time, it seems to me crucial to follow the work of critics such as Aldon Nielsen and Nathaniel Mackey in inserting African American writers into critical discussions around literary experimentation. Why is it, for instance, that so many contemporary black poets (including Roberson, Mackey, and Harryette Mullen) have taken up the serial poem in the past two decades? As Mackey reminds us, "Creative kinship and the lines of affinity it effects are much more complex, jagged, and indissociable than the totalizing pretensions of canon formation tend to acknowledge."[26]

If on one side *Lucid Interval* seems to play an idiosyncratic, individual way of seeing (the singularity of fatherhood; the "house of the poet" (66)), from another angle Roberson's poetry might be said to "key people's ears" into the dynamics of racism and violence in the United States. That larger "foolish fire" (70) is encountered in a series of "associations" and "bundles" (53, 54): fleeting visions of the deep structure of violence, especially racial violence—ever present, always liable to flash up into lucidity: lynching (14); racial profiling and planted evidence (44); suicide (30); segregation and "white flight" (24, 26). At times, the poems hover around more specific moments: the Kennedy assassination (43), or the Birmingham church bombing that killed four young girls in the fall of 1964 (36–39).[27] One might be tempted to call these "associations" or "bundles" *history,* although I would suggest that there are reasons that they are not identified with an epistemological category. In one of Roberson's other books, a poem about the 1969 murder of Black Panther Fred Hampton is titled "any moment," as though to emphasize the pervasiveness of racial violence, its serial replication, rather than to posit the specificity of that moment as "historical."[28]

Asked in an interview about "historical references" in his work, Roberson discusses what it meant to be a child during the 1940s: he was vaguely aware of violence (the Emmett Till lynching, the Second World War, cases of rape or murder), but it remained largely unspoken, a mysterious area of knowledge that adults refused to discuss with him. "So history for a while is just that working underneath feeling," he says. "You know something is riding you, but you don't know what that mechanism is that's moving stuff. To get *that* in is as important as getting the fact in."[29] In what follows, I am going to attempt to constellate a field—to sketch a particular moment as a relation of serials in parallel discrepancy, strains that "work underneath" one another—rather than to hypothesize the existence of some "proper" formal model for poetry, either in music or in history.

The Fruit Riot

In New York City, what would come to be called the long, hot summer of 1964 started with a small disturbance. On April 17 a group of schoolchildren playing boisterously on their way home overturned a fruit stand at a grocery on Lenox Avenue near 129th Street. In a matter of seconds, more than two dozen police officers were at the scene, some of them hitting the children with their nightsticks. When some teenagers and adults attempted to intercede, saying there was no reason to beat the children simply because they'd knocked over some fruit, the police struck them, as well, and eventually three teenagers and two adults were arrested and charged with felonious assault and "malicious mischief." The next day, the *New York Times* inflated this incident into a "free-for-all" involving "75 youths" in an "unruly crowd" "cavorting" along the avenue.[30] The five suspects were held overnight in jail and beaten severely by the police. When they were arraigned, the boys were heavily bandaged, and one of the men was not even able to appear, as he was undergoing emergency eye surgery. By the following day, the defendants were threatening to sue the city for police brutality.[31]

Ten days later a Hungarian immigrant shopkeeper was stabbed to death in her used clothing store on 125th Street.[32] Six African American boys between the ages of seventeen and nineteen, including two of the same boys who were planning to sue and another who had witnessed the fruit stand incident, were quickly arrested for the murder, even though there was no incriminating evidence and the only eyewitness, the victim's husband, could not identify them. Simultaneously the *Times* reported that a "high-ranking police official" had announced that "a gang of about 60 young Negroes who call themselves 'Blood Brothers' is roaming the streets of Harlem with the avowed intention of attacking white people. They are trained to kill." The article claimed that "training sessions in karate, an Oriental system of fighting, take place on roofs and in tenements," and that "the new gang has no turf—no territory—to protect, and its target knows no geographical limitations: it is the white man." The police promised more information "within the next two or three days."[33] On May 6 the "Blood Brotherhood" had been inflated in number to four hundred members and linked to dissident Black Muslims in a front-page article in the *Times*. The story claimed corroboration from a researcher for Harlem Youth Opportunities Unlimited, an organization run by the psychologist Kenneth Clark that had been conducting a survey of conditions in the neighborhood in anticipation of federal antipoverty funding. The "gang last clashed with the police," the article continues, on April 17—in other words, the fruit stand incident.[34]

No admitted members of the "Blood Brothers" had ever been identified, but the police fanned the flames of panic by informing the *Times* that the dissident Muslim "gang members became eligible to use the letter 'X' when they killed or maimed a white person."[35] Editorial pages around the city clamored for the "repression" of the "gang" (especially after suggestions that a rifle club in Harlem was somehow involved), even though Kenneth Clark declared that no researcher in his organization had corroborated the report, and other civil rights leaders voiced skepticism that any such group existed at all.[36] In the *Village Voice,* Nat Hentoff declared it "the most irresponsible local news story of the year" and conjectured that the journalist who had penned most of the articles had been "conned" by the police.[37] Malcolm X quipped, "It doesn't make me sad at all, if it does exist. . . . Our people are too quick to apologize for something that the white power structure finds deplorable. . . . Anyone who has caught the same kind of hell that I have caught is my blood brother."[38] The *Times* was silent on the story until the end of the month, when another front page article appeared, now numbering the "gang" at two hundred, and claiming that the April 17 event—now referred to as the "Fruit Riot"—had "set the stage for the expansion of anti-white youth gangs."[39]

These tensions exploded in mid-July, after a fifteen-year-old African American boy on his way to summer school on East Seventy-Sixth Street was shot and killed by a white off-duty policeman, who claimed the boy had threatened him with a switchblade.[40] After the funeral, a community rally organized by the Congress on Racial Equality on 125th Street erupted into violence when hundreds of protesters marched to the 123rd Precinct and confronted the police.[41] The violence lasted six days and spread to Bedford-Stuyvesant, in the end involving more than eight thousand people and resulting in one death, 118 injuries, 465 arrests, and heavy property damage.[42]

I have tracked the journalistic coverage of these events in such detail in order to give a sense of the degree to which they involve—indeed, are produced by—a form that can only be termed serial. The build-up, the increasing levels of panic, anger, and frustration, is intimately linked to the serial form of the newspaper and the particular effects it allows: the steady inflation of numbers, the accumulation of insinuation, the linking of categories (one disturbance to another). It is important to add that the seriality of the newspaper is always already multiple, constructed as much through what goes unvoiced as through what is articulated time and time again. Moreover, there is never one newspaper, but an overlapping exchange among venues that cite and authorize or rebut one another: the *Times* presses its story; the *Post* amplifies it to tabloid hysteria; the *Amsterdam News* challenges it in the name of "the community"; the *Village Voice* criticizes the intimacy of the mainstream press and the city police; the *Herald Tribune* almost wholly ignores the story altogether.[43]

On another level, this entire discourse takes for granted that racial violence in the United States operates as a certain sort of serial occurrence itself. Almost every article on the July 1964 riots peers back in time to 1935 and 1943, implying an ongoing string of upheavals, reading the African American rejection of state-enforced racism as a phenomenon with an especial (albeit slow) rhythm of recurrence.[44] Some commentators attempt to inject a note of urgency by evoking this seriality from another angle. Kenneth Clark, for example, writes an article arguing that the riots were not simply a reaction to police brutality, but instead a response to the neighborhood's "basic and complex problems" as a "racial colony within the most liberal cosmopolitan and sophisticated city of our nation." "The real danger of Harlem," as Clark puts it, "is not in the infrequent explosions of random lawlessness. The frightening horror of Harlem is the chronic day-to-day quiet violence to the human spirit which exists and is accepted as normal." Consequently, Clark calls for a solution that would break "the pattern of violence which is Harlem."[45] Whitney Young, of the National Urban League, tells a reporter that he spent a night talking with youths in Harlem; while he heard no evidence of an antiwhite "gang," he did come away with an impression that "anger had erupted simultaneously in a hundred hearts, and that abstract promises of jobs and bread are worthless if they cannot be translated instantly into reality."[46] In other words, both Clark and Young attempt to shift the focus of the discussion from the intermittent, explosive seriality of mass racial violence to the low-level, everyday seriality of racism and deprivation.

I consider three responses to these events. Each makes recourse to serial form involving multiplicity: a proliferation or layering of voices that suggests disparities in perspective, back-and-forth, dissent or divergence "working underneath" a message. For the moment, I will not simply call them "artistic" responses, since they operate in different ways somewhere between aesthetics, advocacy, and testimony.

Simple Tempo

By the mid-1960s, Langston Hughes was writing a column that appeared every Friday in the *New York Post.* Although best known as a poet, Hughes was most widely read in his newspaper columns, starting with a rubric called "Here and Yonder" that debuted in November 1943 in the *Chicago Defender.*[47] The columns vary in tone and approach from week to week, including autobiography, political commentary, satire, responses to letters sent in by readers, and the beloved "Simple Stories," humorous vignettes focusing on the life and barstool opinions of a fictional Harlem resident, Jesse B. Semple, nicknamed "Simple." This is to say that the short stories are positioned from the beginning as only one component in a broader serial stream. Although they were eventually collected independently in book form, the Simple tales in their original newspaper context are conditioned by their dynamic relation with the other modes of the columns. (Hughes proposed one book of his collected columns, and significantly he wanted to title it *How to Integrate without Danger of Intermarriage & Other Simple Recipes for Salvation,* by Langston Hughes with Interventions by Jesse B. Semple, explaining to the publisher that it would allow readers to meet Simple in his "natural journalistic habitat."[48])

The stories are dialogic, involving conversations in a bar between Simple and the narrator, Ananias Boyd: they work in layers of reported speech, with the narrator recounting a conversation with Simple, who in turn often recounts other conversations.[49] They are also stories that take seriality as their subject. On the one hand, Simple himself *is* seriality, and the stories are framed less as a conceit for dealing with current events than as the record of an effort to keep pace with a fleeting present. In one column Hughes discusses the stories, calling Simple a "composite of dozens and dozens of men of his class and character," and saying:

> Simple as a *real* man, a living Harlemite, cannot be put away on a shelf anywhere any more in these parlous days and times. Every day nowadays he seems to be saying something real from the front pages of the newspapers.
>
> I am a creative writer and do not believe in trying to keep up with the daily news headlines. But since my character Simple whom I wrote about is an avid news reader, radio listener and TV watcher, I have to keep up with him.[50]

On the other hand, the stories are *about* seriality, and often find their humor in the juxtaposition of rates of recurrence. In a story called "Refugees," Simple complains that dictionaries that define white as "purity" and "goodness," and black as "evil," need to be revised, "and in due time they will be." He wonders just how far away is *due time,* and when Boyd invokes the biblical phrase that "a thousand years is as but a day in God's sight," Simple has a quick rejoinder: "most white American gentile church-going Christians, as we know, do not even believe in *due time* when it comes to Negroes, particularly down South." He adds, "But God is going to move their wicked race." When Boyd asks "When?" Simple replies, "In due time." "Whose due time?" Boyd questions:

> "To answer that would be telling," said Simple. "Therefore, like the Klan, I take the Fifth."
>
> "The Fifth what?"
>
> "My fifth beer," said Simple.[51]

"Simplicity can sometimes be more devious than erudition," Boyd observes at one point.[52] The stories take up the long, hot summer with Simple's seemingly sophomoric fabrications and pronouncements, but they find in humor a versatile "weapon" against some of the pretensions of political debate and the elisions of journalism.[53] In the wake of reports about "antiwhite gangs," Simple comments that two things he would hate to be are a "light-skin Negro and a black cop." If it is "true what the downtown papers is saying about some Black Blood Brotherhood out to kill all white folks," Simple asks, "how can a hear-white Negro the complexion of Adam Powell be sure that the Brotherhood might not make a mistake—and kill him too?"[54] In May, when the Congress on Racial Equality (CORE) was threatening a "stall-in" to disrupt the opening of the World's Fair in Queens (deliberately allowing cars to run out of gas on the Long Island Expressway), Simple proposes another addition to the series of activist protest techniques, one he calls "pose-ins, or pose-outs": "I mean Negroes undressing right down to their bare skin and posing naked as statues for freedom's sake. Twenty million naked Negroes in public places posing in the nude till civil rights have come to pass." As Simple explains, "America would be forced to scrutinize our cause."[55]

One particularly virtuosic column titled "Shakespeare" opens with Simple asking Boyd, "Are ghosts of black folks white?" Saying he's under the impression that ghosts are all white from watching "horror pictures" as well as the film version of *Hamlet,* Simple wonders, "Suppose Sidney Poitier was to play Hamlet, would his ghost be white?" and then launches into an extended riff on the most famous speech in the play. From his particular vantage point, he considers what one might term the politics of the interval—the awkwardness of being stuck between opposing viewpoints. "To be or not to be," Simple says he tells his wife, Joyce:

> Meaning whether it is better to be neutral or not when two Negroes at the bar or somewhere start discussing CORE, and one says CORE is too radical and the other one says CORE is not radical enough. Then when a Black Muslim steps up with a ginger ale in his hand (since Muslims do not drink) and he says he does not want no part of the white man's apple, not even the CORE (and CORE is full of white folks, likewise the NAACP) and this Muslim looks at me like as if I were white, what am I supposed to do betwixt three Negroes all with different opinions? Should I be neutral like an intellect and set on the fence? Or climb over the bar and get out of their way?
>
> . . . What *to be,* or *not to be,* is enough to worry Hamlet was his ghost to haunt Harlem this evening. When Shakespeare writ them words, there was no way for him to know I would be

> quoting his words here in this bar in the middle of black Harlem here in the black dark of night which is the time of my trouble as a Negro here in our U.S.A.—which does not know what *to be* to me. My country 'tis of thee, or my country 'taint of thee—to be or not to be America the beautiful where a black ghost has to be white to play Hamlet.

Boyd gives a snappy reply, and the riff goes through another couple of variations before the story comes to a close:

> "I believe that last beer made you high," I said.
>
> "To be or not to be sober when I go home—that is the question," said Simple.
>
> "Whether 'tis nobler to face the slings and arrows of outrageous fortune on Shakespeare's night," I said, "Or—"
>
> "Or face a raging wifehood," cried Simple. "I'm gone! Goodby! So long!"[56]

Beyond the conundrum of the interval—how one maintains a position, as Simple says, "betwixt and between" seemingly absolutist alternatives—the most subtle point here may have to do with the circulation of information, the ways one cannot control or limit the spread of ideas.[57]

The July riots show up in a story called "Wigs for Freedom," in which Simple recounts a conversation with his cousin Minnie. Furious at the sight of a policeman beating an elderly black man, she rushes up to hit the officer with her purse but is knocked unconscious by a bottle thrown from a rooftop. She tells Simple, "God saved that cop from being slapped with a pocketbook full of knockout punches from poker chips to a bottle of Evening in Paradise, also a big bunch of keys which might of broke his nose."[58] But Minnie is most concerned about the loss of her forty-dollar wig at the hospital: "I went back to Harlem Hospital after the riots and asked for my wig, an orange-brown chestnut blonde for which I paid cash money. But they said it were not in the Lost and Found. They said my wig had blood on it, anyhow, so it got throwed away."[59] She concludes: "My advice to all womens taking part in riots is to leave their wigs at home." The joke, of course, is that something so superficial is at the center of an episode of black resistance. The wig is a ridiculous accessory intended to conceal; as Minnie proclaims to Simple when he says she looks better ("natural again") without the wig: "What woman wants to look her natural self? . . . I paid forty dollars for my wig just to look *unnatural*."[60] For Minnie, ironically, the wig becomes the ultimate emblem of her sacrifice for the cause of civil rights: "What is one wig more or less to give for freedom? One wig not to go slow. One wig not to be cool. One wig not to get off the streets."[61]

In a column at the end of June responding to a letter from a reader, Hughes comments on the peculiarities of that serial form, noting that each column can only take up a "segment" of a given question, and moreover, that Hughes's own views can only be gleaned over time, in reading that is serial, as well:

> In the space allotted to me on Fridays in the *New York Post,* I can hardly cover all the aspects of *every* phase of whatever subject may be discussed that week. A well-rounded dissertation on any subject would take several hundred pages. A single column can only be a condensed and very limited survey of some aspect of the subject at hand. My complete feelings, complete viewpoint, complete orientation cannot be condensed in a few thousand words. To understand my basic orientation, a reader must have read my Post column over a period of months at least, or my creative work over the years.[62]

During the week of the riots in July, Hughes published three "special columns" in the *Post* on Tuesday, Wednesday, and Thursday, each prefaced with an editorial note that Hughes had "witnessed" the events on the street.[63] That is, the pace of intervention quickens, given the urgency of the situation. His first column, written just after Hughes had attended the funeral of Jimmy Powell, the boy shot by the policeman ("Jimmy was a little boy. I saw him lying in his coffin looking very small and dead."), meditates on the efficacy of writing. As Hughes adds his words to the "innumerable" commentaries and surveys and reports on the problems of Harlem, he admits to a "feeling that words are rather useless at the moment."[64]

In another special column on Sunday, he took up this theme again, contrasting the remarkable number of plays on racial themes then in theaters (James's Baldwin's *Blues for Mister Charlie,* Jean Genet's *The Blacks,* Adrienne Kennedy's *Funnyhouse of a Negro*) with the stubborn persistence of Harlem's problems: the "trouble with Harlem," he writes in closing, is that "*it is here.* Writers, playwrights, sociologists, speakers, politicians, leaders both black and white, Republicans and Democrats, Harlem is your raw material."[65] This would seem to be a critique of the ways that black life and struggle provide fodder for all sorts of pronouncements and hucksterism, literary and otherwise, none of it seeming to better the condition of the neighborhood. Reading serially, however, allows one to notice that if Hughes's resignation is a stance, an intervention, it is not a permanent position. In his regular column the next week, he proposed that the city organize cleanup squads to give Harlem youth paid employment and self-respect during the summer.[66] The subsequent Friday, he again turned his attention to the theater scene, but with a different message. While battles between black citizens and police were in full swing on 125th Street, he notes, in Central Park, James Earl Jones "was choking a pretty white women to death . . . in full view of everybody," in a production of *Othello.* He continues:

> It is a shame that the better world seekers in the field of playwrighting like Shakespeare and Baldwin and Genet can write themselves blue in the face, and be dramatic and bitter and satirical and hair-raising (as [Leroi Jones's play] "Dutchman" is hair-raising) and well meaning and work toward the curation of sick humanity (some via the shock treatment), and yet have so little effect on those who want to picket police stations because a little boy is shot dead by a cop. If all those Harlem folks had been at Shakespeare in the Park instead of at a street meeting that fateful night, there might have been no riot.[67]

If the remark about "raw material" seems all too fatalistic, this earnest portrait of art as palliative seems to veer toward the opposite extreme.

It is important to stress, again, that Hughes's complex serialism does not emerge in isolation but only within a larger serial discursive field. One way to make this point would be to consider Hughes next to some of the other populist columnists of the time. Jimmy Breslin, for example, writing in the *New York Herald Tribune,* records the "brutality" on both sides of the violence—"the cops started shooting into the air" above the crowd, he says in one piece, "but some of them were not shooting high enough"—but has little sympathy for the rioters: "Sure, there was brutality last night. Terrible, sickening brutality. But this was a mess, an absolute, incredible mess, and if you were on the street with the bottles coming down and who the hell knows what was going to come from the rooftops, there was only one thing to do. Go after these crazy bums on the street corners and knock their heads open and send them home with blood pouring all over them."[68] Breslin worries most about the *tempo* of racial violence, the "lull" of "frightening" silence after it, and the looming threat of the fire next time: "Now there is nothing. . . . Nobody says that there are five more good weekends left in this summer and that the next one starts on Friday night."[69] Elsewhere, Walter Winchell, writing in the *New York Journal American,* offered a blunt self-interview, but with none of the absurdist banter in "Wigs for Freedom":

> What is the primary danger in the racial crisis?
>
> The extremism on both sides. Lawlessness is as disgraceful as bigotry. The history of progress achieved by minority groups is a record of triumphs in the courts—not violence in the streets. Too many of the trouble-makers are lunatic-fringers: Beatniks, Redniks and professional rabble rousers. All involved in street riots are losers.[70]

Such language forms the counterpoint to Hughes's serialism, and makes the tenor of some of his observations all the more remarkable, as when he writes: "few if any of our prominent leaders speak the language of the down boys, the bad boys, the hoodlums and the lovers of flying bottles. . . . History tells us that in every revolution there has ever been, mobs ran riot and looted and misbehaved—and before things were over, sometimes even cut off their leaders' heads. In the wake of every social upheaval, the unregenerate remain unredeemed."[71]

The Rhythm of Testimony

Two years later, the case of the "Harlem Six" (the boys arrested for murder after the Fruit Riot) was still unresolved. The judge had appointed attorneys for the suspects, but they and their families had sought their own lawyers, including Conrad Lynn and William Kunstler, and argued that indigent defendants should be allowed to choose their legal counsel rather than having representation simply imposed by the court. The case would wend its way through the legal system for nearly a decade; some of the boys were put on trial four times.[72] In April 1966, in the midst of the case around court-assigned counsel, a fund-raising benefit was organized at Town Hall. James Baldwin had written a petition, and a number of other luminaries supported the effort: the sponsors of the Town Hall event included Ossie Davis, Dick Gregory, Nat Hentoff, Paul Krassner, Abbey Lincoln, Paule Marshall, Max Roach, Nathan Schwerner, and David Stone-Martin. Advertised as a "Public Hearing,"[73] the benefit featured a musical selection by Max Roach and Abbey Lincoln (an excerpt from the *Freedom Now Suite* they had recorded in 1960), and speeches by William Stringfellow, Davis, Schwerner, and Gregory. Its centerpiece was titled *"6" Condemned: A Dramatization of Scenes from the Book "Torture of Mothers" by Truman Nelson,* with a cast of nearly fifty reenacting scenes from the Fruit Riot and its aftermath.[74]

Nelson's book is an odd document. It narrates the case mainly by drawing on extensive tape-recorded interviews[75] with the defendants and their mothers: in other words, it is constructed as an overlapping chain of testimony, different versions of the same events buttressing and adding to each other. The book begins, "How can I make you believe this?" and launches into long, transcribed citations from the interviews. The very seriality of the form (the unending flow of accounts, one after another, the same events over and over from different angles) comprises the argument of the book. For Nelson, "the defendants tell their stories with a passion that confers a dignity on them beyond the power of the police to dismiss stories that do not all fit together like links in a chain but are more like rays of flashing, searing light, illuminating a landscape of pain."[76] "The talk accumulates on the tapes," he comments later. "It has the ring of truth. Righteous indignation starts to rise." Interestingly, Nelson bases his plea on an understanding of recording technology as a sort of guarantor of the accuracy of the boys' accounts: "The tape runs on like an infernal machine. It will trap you if you talk to it a long time and you begin to tell lies. . . . It abhors false notes. Shows them up clearly and rejects them, makes them sound raucous in the listening ear."[77] Of course, with the book one is not hearing the recording but reading a transcription. Although Nelson does not comment on the technique, in fact the book is composed in verse, and the transcriptions set with line breaks that approximate the cadences of human speech, in an apparent attempt to transcribe the particular form of the oral testimony. Here is part of the statement of Daniel Hamm about the initial incident at the fruit stand:

> We got halfway up the block and we heard a police siren,
> And we didn't pay much attention to it and then we heard
>   children scream.
> We turned around and walked back to see what happened.
> As I got closer to the corner I saw this policeman with his gun
>   out
> Waving it at some young children and with his billy in his
>   hand.
> I like put myself in the way to keep him from shooting the kids,
> Because first of all he was shaking like a leaf
> And jumping all over the place,
> And I thought he might shoot one of them.
> We went to the precinct and that's where they beat us
> For nothing at all. . . .
> They like turned shifts on us,
> Like six and twelve at a time would beat us,
> And this went on practically all day we were at that station,
> They beat us till I could barely walk and my back was in pain.
> My friends they did the same till they bled.
> All the time they were beating us they never took the handcuffs
>   off.
> And when they wanted to take us to the hospital
> They made us go wash up.

> They didn't want to take me to the hospital because I wasn't bleeding.
> I had this big bruise on my leg from them beating me. I had to like open the bruise up and let some of the bruise blood
> Come out to show them I was bleeding,
> And this is the only reason they let me go to the hospital.[78]

Nelson approvingly quotes Jean-Paul Sartre's preface to Frantz Fanon's *The Wretched of the Earth* (with its infamous deflection of Fanon's study of revolutionary anticolonialism, as Sartre attempts to "fashion a remedy for Europe"[79]) and by the conclusion of *The Torture of Mothers,* his intended audience is clear: "If we do not listen, if we persist in so brutally suppressing the surface demonstration, the dialogue between us and the black people will end."[80] The book is a variant of sentimentalist polemic that has deep roots in U.S. literary history, an effort that—even as it aims to trigger an empathetic response with its repeated invocations of suffering motherhood—frames blackness as the object of white liberal agency, an object to be heard and, ultimately, saved.

One seeming precursor to Nelson's verse form is the poetry of Charles Reznikoff, above all his extraordinary multivolume work *Testimony,* a thirty-year project of poems based on transcripts of legal testimony in court cases at the turn of the twentieth century, from 1885 to 1915. Reznikoff expressly culled the legal reporter for vivid language and for cases involving "injury (death, assault, theft) due to primitive violence: injury due to negligence, particularly those caused by machinery . . . and unusual characters or places—unusual and yet characteristic of the time."[81] Unlike Nelson, though, Reznikoff uses the transcripts as raw material, severely editing and honing the language into what the book terms "recitative"—a musical term indicating a rhythmically free style of vocal writing that aims to capture the shape of dramatic speech in song. As Reznikoff explains, his technique involves "prying sentences open to look at the exact meaning: / weighing words to choose only those that had meat for my purpose / and throwing the rest away as empty shells."[82] The revision and versification process involves further revision as the poet tried to get at the core of a particular voice and incident, eliminating all digression.[83] Moreover, if *Testimony* offers unusual insight into the onset of the industrial revolution and to shifts in social life at the turn of the century, it does so without the melodramatic framing in *The Torture of Mothers.* In one interview, Reznikoff, even more circumspect than his closest contemporaries among the Objectivist poets (George Oppen, Carl Rakosi, Louis Zukofsky, Louise Niedecker), defined an Objectivist writer as one "who does not write directly about his feelings but about what he sees and hears: who is restricted almost to the testimony of a witness in a court of law; and who expresses his feelings indirectly by the selection of his subject-matter and, if he writes in verse, by its music."[84]

What is most remarkable about Reznikoff's *Testimony,* given the legalistic and mundane quality of its source material, is its severity and abstraction. The testimony is arranged serially, in numbered subsections organized under thematic headings ("Social Life," "Property," "Machine Age," "Negroes," "Domestic Scenes," "Mining," "Railroads") and broad geographical divisions ("The North," "The South," "The West"). The work's impact has everything to do with what we are not given: we don't know the cases the material is drawn from, the context or mitigating circumstances, charges, motive, or outcome. Take this early poem in the series of "Domestic Scenes":

> It was nearly daylight when she gave birth to the child,
> lying on the quilt
> he had doubled up for her.
> He put the child on his left arm
> and took it out of the room,
> and she could hear the splashing of water.
> When he came back
> she asked him where the child was.
> He replied: "Out there—in the water."
> He punched up the fire
> and returned with an armload of wood
> and the child,
> and put the dead child into the fire.
> She said: "O John, don't!"
> He did not reply
> but turned to her and smiled.[85]

At the same time, it is not entirely accurate, as Hayden Carruth charged in a review of the work, that *Testimony* is no more than a string of "vignettes" with "no accompanying apparatus, no narrative, no lyrical or mediative commentary, no intrusion of the author whatever."[86] Part of what is striking—and quite legible, if not trumpeted—is the careful craftedness of the works. In fact, they are very clearly mediated, in a manner somewhat reminiscent of Hughes's "Simple Stories": never do we encounter the transcribed first-person voice of a witness; always they are filtered through the retelling of an unidentified narrator. The verse highlights this mediation continually through recourse to reported speech: the narrator marks off certain words and phrases (particularly unusual metaphors, epithets) as quotes from another, original "vocal" source, being filtered. "He was jealous and would 'jump on' her / if he saw a man around or his tracks," we read in one section (148). Elsewhere, we are told that "Steve's mother knew the shirt as her son's, / for she had made it with 'my own fingers' / and knew her sewing" (152). A clerk who suddenly refuses to sell a ticket to a light-skinned black man "must have discovered, to use Benton's words, / 'that drop of African blood' in him" (212–213). A newcomer to town tells "an acquaintance at whose house he stopped / that he had had a 'difficulty' with some 'niggers' in Ft. Scott" (228).

Also noteworthy is the work's staging of temporality: the poems most often offer not resolution but suspension and duration. They set the reader in the midst of a series of events that do not resolve. One poem dealing with an act of random violence, a group of white boys who kill a black youth with a rock, closes with these lines: "He fell to the ground / and lay there / dying, / and the six walked quickly away" (77–78). At another point, a man shot and wounded by another in a failed robbery attempt continues to insist that he has been murdered, even as he lies bandaged in bed. A friend tries to calm him, saying "Nat, / I think you are scared worse than hurt." And the poem comes to a strange, delayed conclusion: " 'No,' said Gladstone, 'he has killed me. / Ray Dexter killed me!' / And he lingered a day or two— / and died" (227). As Linda Simon puts it, "No one, in Reznikoff's world, dies 'instantly.' There is always a span during which we, the victim, and the murderer must be conscious of the deed, its consequences and the final extinguishing of life."[87]

As I noted, one of the major thematic rubrics in *Testimony* is "Negroes." One might find this gesture hard to explain, since there are no other demographic or "ethnic" subsections (except for a single appearance of "Chinese"), and since African American life could conceivably fit under the broader social rubrics in the rest of the book: "Domestic Scenes" or "Railroads" (in fact, some poems dealing with African Americans are placed under other headings). It seems to me that this is another instance of motivated "editorial" intrusion. Although the poems in the "Negroes" sections are as varied (and as polymorphously violent) as those elsewhere, at times they achieve a level of critique that is exceptional. Here is one example, quoted in full:

> Several white men went at night to the Negro's house,
> shot into it,
> and set fire to his cotton on the gallery;
> his wife and children ran under the bed
> and, as the firing from guns and pistols went on
> and the cotton blazed up,
> ran through a side door into the woods.
> The Negro himself, badly wounded, fled to the house of a neighbor—
> a white man—
> and got inside.
> He was followed,
> and one of those who ran after him
> put a shotgun against the white man's door
> and shot a hole through it.
> Justice, however, was not to be thwarted,
> for five of the men who did this to the Negro
> were tried:
> for "unlawfully and maliciously
> injuring and disfiguring"—
> the white man's property. (136–137)

Again, we are not given context (the reason the men attacked the Negro; the ultimate conclusion: Did they kill him? Did they kill his neighbor?).

But here, the quotation of the criminal charges is used to draw attention not to the peculiarity of speech, but instead to the perverse priorities of the legal system and its ironic definition of "justice." One might go so far as to suggest that, as a critique of racism in U.S. society, the book as a whole goes so far as to *reproduce* a racist logic on every level (it cites racist language and acts of antiblack violence without comment in the discrete pieces, and on a structural level, it even imposes segregation on its "Negroes"), precisely in order to emphasize its irrationality.

Come Out

Credited in the program as the "sound engineer" at the "Harlem Six" benefit was a young composer named Steve Reich. Nelson had approached Reich through a mutual friend that spring and asked him to edit the ten hours of tape testimony that had been gathered. Reich agreed, but said to Nelson, "If I hit some material, allow me to make a piece out of it."[88] Reich had been experimenting with tape loop pieces for the past few years, and he "was interested in the poetry of William Carlos Williams, Charles Olson, and Robert Creeley, and tried, from time to time, to set their poems to music, always without success." His inability to set the poetry to his satisfaction, he realized, had to do with the ways such poets were "rooted in American speech rhythms": "to 'set' poems like this to music with a fixed meter is to destroy that speech quality." The year before, he found a solution with a piece called *It's Gonna Rain,* based on a recording Reich had made of a black Pentecostal street preacher in San Francisco. When recorded speech provides the material of a piece, Reich has written, then "speech-melody and meaning are presented as they naturally occur. By not altering its pitch or timbre, one keeps the original emotional power that speech has while intensifying its melody *and* meaning through repetition and rhythm."[89]

Poring over the hours of tape, Reich selected the "juiciest phrase I could get": Daniel Hamm's explanation that he had been obliged to let the blood of one of his bruises *come out to show them.*[90] By looping the phrase again and again while shifting "very gradually" the relationship between overlaid versions, so that they slowly drift out of sync, Reich creates a canon or round for an increasing number of voices: two, then four, then eight. In one interview, he explains the procedure:

> I first made a loop of the phrase "Come out to show them," and recorded a whole reel of that on channel 1 of a second tape recorder. I then started recording the loop on channel 2; after lining up the two tracks, with my thumb on the supply reel of the recording machine, I very gradually held it back (I was literally slowing it down, but at such an imperceptible rate that you can't hear) until "Come out to show them" had separated into "come out-come out/show them-show them" (which is something like two eighth notes apart). Then I took that two-channel relationship, made a loop from it, fed it into channel 1 again, and held it back with my thumb until it was four eighth-notes away from the original sounds and could be heard as a series of equal beats, quite distinct melodically. I then spliced together the two-voice tape with the four-voice tape—they fit exactly—and what you sense at that point is a slight timbral difference, due to all this addition, and then all of a sudden a movement in space. At that point I divided it again into eight voices, separated it by just a thirty-second note, so that the whole thing began to shake, then I just faded it out again and put those two takes together.[91]

Most biographical sources of Reich list the Town Hall benefit as the "premiere" of *Come Out.*[92] The piece was played at the event, but not as a formal part of the program: after the speeches had ended, "people were talking, and then when they actually took up a collection, passed the hat—they started playing *Come Out.* And that was its only appearance, that was its world premiere, it was pass-the-hat music at Town Hall."[93]

One can only imagine the contrast among the modes on stage that evening: the stark landscape of "Triptych: Prayer/Protest/Peace" from *The Freedom Now Suite,* as Max Roach's snare drum rolls a minimal ostinato behind Abbey Lincoln's moaned, wordless melody until her voice suddenly breaks out in a cascade of screams in the middle section, "Protest."[94] The booming advocacy of the speeches, with their time-pressed calls for assistance. The stylized reenactment and recitation of *The*

Torture of Mothers. If the other performances had to do with embodiment—testimony given human breath and shape on the stage—then *Come Out,* an eerie, unannounced vamp hanging above the jingling of change in pockets and the crisp sound of checks being torn, must have seemed all the more disembodied, a thirteen-minute habeas corpus, a reminder of the absence of Daniel Hamm and the other boys.

Come Out starts with the sentence culled from Hamm's interview, repeated three times, and then launches into its four-word loop. Reich's term for the tape pieces was "phase pieces," though he has more recently clarified that "all the phase pieces were a variation of canonic technique . . . canons at the unison where the subject is short and the rhythmic interval between voices is variable."[95] A flexible canon, a bellowed amplification of the same. Forced to attend to the specificity of the voice, its trochaic attack, the rustle of its *sh,* one begins first to hear a split in the identical: one voice lagging back. Singularity becomes multiplicity. One becomes a crowd. The lag constructs a rhythm, and you follow the beat, anticipating its shifts as the voices spread, slowly, changing the emphasis of the words and then even particular phonemes. After three minutes, when the loop doubles, the voices proliferate (*come-out-come-out-show-them-show-them*). Call finds its echo, adding to its insistence.[96] After eight and a half minutes, with another doubling, there is the steady rattle of a shakere, and a rounded vowel erupting slightly behind. *Come out* seems to be dislocated from *show them,* as each phrase thumps in steady eighth notes. An orphic vulnerability torn and rent in the fury of its own music. There are questions in the accumulation: How much needs to come out to show them? What is the distance—the interval—between emergence and demonstration, between revelation and proof? What is the difference between spilling blood and giving testimony? How does self-violation make violation manifest by continuing it? The other word has vanished, but is it possible to hear in the advent of this multitude (one and yet not one, moving away from one another and toward renewed coincidence at the same time) the specter of "blood brothers," a fraternity linked in subjugation? And as in Hughes's writing, the process of enduring the thirteen minutes of *Come Out* poses deferral as the ultimate question of racial justice: Just how fast is "all deliberate speed"?[97] How far off is *due time?*

It is important to note that Reich's tape loop pieces are in no small part a deliberate departure from the model of serial music. For Reich, the problem is that "in serial music you can't *hear* the serial structure, it's extremely hidden and complex. All you hear is something that sounds rather chaotic, even though it's totally worked out."[98] His turn to the tape loops in *It's Gonna Rain* and *Come Out* is in this sense a turn to "perceptible processes."[99] As he put it in a well-known 1968 essay-manifesto, "Music as a Gradual Process": "What I'm interested in is a compositional process and a sounding music that are one and the same thing."[100]

Reich has said that he chose the particular phrase he did because it "seemed emblematic."[101] Although the process *Come Out* imposes on its source material would seem to be an "abstraction" first and foremost, its emblematic quality seems to throw the meaning of that term into question. Is Nelson's reenactment necessarily more "concrete," or does it, too, involve a variety of assumptions about character, temporality, and narrative—clearly different from Reich's, yet not obviously any less distant from an originary testimonial instant? In one interview, Reich comments, "What particularly interests me in using spoken language, as opposed to setting a text to music for voices to sing, is what could be called the 'documentary' aspect of recorded voices. . . . There is no singer's 'interpretation' but, rather, this: people bearing witness to their own lives."[102] The accuracy of the witnessing, in his view, is constitutively tied to the singularity (and, one could say, the musicality) of the utterance:

> Both the speech melody *and* the meaning of the words are inextricably bound together. How could it be otherwise? When people speak, the semantic, structural, and melodic issues from them in one breath. The phrase "It's gonna rain" as said by the black Pentecostal preacher in my tape piece from 1965 is at once a common everyday American idiom, a reference to the biblical flood—and, therefore, the end of the world (which in the 1960s clearly had nuclear overtones)—and the pitches E-D-D-F#. How do you propose to separate these elements? The beauty (and terror) is that they are all one. . . .
>
> If the meaning is expressed in different words, we no longer have the same poem. . . . How will you separate them in simple prose like, "It's gonna rain"? (Even "It's going to rain" is a phrase of a different nature with different implications about the speaker.)[103]

In 1963 Amiri Baraka wrote an essay called "Expressive Language" that similarly attempts to discover a black political stance in the specificities of speech syntax:

> I heard an old Negro street singer last week, Reverend Pearly Brown, singing, "God don't never change!" This is a precise thing he is singing. He does not mean "God does not ever change!" He means "God don't never change!" The difference, and I said it was crucial, is in the final human reference . . . the form of passage through the world.[104]

In Baraka's reading, the double negative is an indication of accuracy, the particularity of perspective and a site of speaking (inflected by race and class). This "final human reference" is not susceptible to expression in any other form. He continues:

> A man who is rich and famous who sings, "God don't never change," is confirming his hegemony and good fortune . . . or merely calling the bank. A blind hopeless black American is saying something very different. He is telling you about the extraordinary order of the world. But he is not telling you about his "fate." Fate is a luxury available only to those fortunate citizens with alternatives.[105]

The unique mode is not just the mark of a social condition, but also the kernel of a politics, of a strategy of cultural resistance that refuses incorporation into the "mainstream," into the transparency of standard usage. "Being told to 'speak proper,' meaning that you become fluent with the jargon of power," Baraka argues, "is also a part of not 'speaking proper.' That is, the culture which desperately understands that it does not 'speak proper,' or is not fluent with the terms of social strength, also understands somewhere that its desire to gain such fluency is done at a terrifying risk."[106] *Come Out* underlines a similar precision and political understanding in the singular syntax of Hamm's sentence, "I had to like open the bruise up and let some of the bruise blood come out to show them I was bleeding."[107]

Is it possible to hear in the piece's focus on the minutiae of the single phrase, on what Reich calls the "details of a sound,"[108] a parallel in a different medium to the linguistic work in serial poetry? "If you can get a focus on the individual part enough," Jack Spicer says, "you have a better chance of dictation. You have a better chance of being an empty vessel, of being filled up by whatever's Outside."[109] One of Ed Roberson's untitled early poems conjectures that "it must be that in the midst / of any tonal language / there is a constant huddle / of all substances' matters // where any accident of sound / could speak and / the sound of people's walk / talk." The poem imagines the condition of inhabiting a tonal language, where Reich's "speech melody" is explicitly bound to signification, where any sentence has a music and any music has a sentence. In the middle of the poem, there is an extraordinary series of lines:

> if i must think i must think
> i must think well
>
> this is to demonstrate
> i must think
> my meanings are tonal
>
> the bell ringing
> from the well
>
> in the line i must think
> it is tonal
> i must think well
>
> it is tonal   too / much
> as this is rhythm[110]

The sentence "I must think well" seems to shimmer and remake itself, shifting from a self-imposition to something else. When you read "the bell ringing / from the well // in the line," you are forced to hear the qualifier "well" of "I must think well" as also, simultaneously, a noun: a "well." The word resonates, a deep, fresh source discovered. You must believe these lines are tonal, that sound is all bound up with meaning, much as the knotted serial recurrence of the same phrase, rethought, reheard, "is rhythm." As Reich points out, there are moments when speech is "for various emotional reasons, almost song—when people speak, they sometimes sing."[111] In Roberson's book, there is a poem called "jacket" that takes up the mode of the book cover blurb, finding the music in that mode, offering an aesthetic statement in a satire, which on first glance seems all too simple:

> Many of these poems attempt to make happen to words that which happens to lines in an optical illusion. Many of these poems have that kind of architecture of things which live in the sea. . . . Yet they are not illusions. They are real: because the poetic of all our languages has the more potential for concretion.[112]

Discussing one of his later compositions, Steve Reich told an interviewer that the music's fabric was constructed of "different degrees of periodicity—say the difference between a metronome, a perfectly good drummer, a heart-beat and the waves on the shore."[113] To hear *Come Out* as serial is to hear it in its surroundings, as varying rates of repetition stuck side by side, in sound and outside it: the same beating, coming back. The title, then, is both a call and a revelation, a "concretion" that might be called poetic: seriality is not simply unbounded linearity (1, 2, 3 . . .), but moreover the overlaid accumulation of different patterns of recurrence.

Call it *Come Out.* Play it to show them. Over and over. Peel it until the indicative is haunted by the imperative. Squeeze it until the demand hidden in lament forces its way into the pulse.

afterword
Hearing across Media

Especially by Chapter 8, on musical influences in the serial poetics of Ed Roberson, it is hopefully apparent that throughout this book I have been attempting to do something more than provide nuanced interpretations of the formal interrelations between jazz and literature. As I begin to suggest in Chapter 5 on Mary Lou Williams and Cecil Taylor, my aim throughout has equally been to begin to think about the forms of jazz criticism itself. Shouldn't a criticism so deeply engaged with the art of innovation itself be innovative? If part of what literature learns from music, and vice versa, is to push the native medium beyond itself, to find new expressive possibilities by exceeding or distending the seeming limits of expression, why should critical scholarship be immune from or alien to such self-questioning, such self-extension, in the shadow of the examples it strives to explain? These questions culminate (but do not resolve) with Chapter 8, which is not just a reading of Roberson's poetry, but equally an attempt to figure out what it would mean to write criticism, too, in serial form, and to attend to the particular insights that emerge out of that mode (a paratactic shuttle among poetry, the periodical, political history, and music)—insights that could not have emerged otherwise.

The point is not that any criticism somehow *needs* to look like what it interprets. It does not. But it does seem to me that a criticism that would be adequate to the interface between music and literature should not proceed like just any criticism. And if a major element of what I have been tracking throughout this book is experimentation in pseudomorphosis—new possibilities found by hearing across media—then jazz criticism would have to hear across media, as well, and find itself transformed in the process.

I close by returning where I began, with the preeminent musician-writer in the history of jazz, Louis Armstrong, and with another example of "imaginative error"—this time not in oral history or in the written history erected around it, but instead in an instance of that other species of "jazz literature": an autobiographical text written by a musician. In September 1968, complaining of trouble breathing and swelling in his legs, Armstrong went at the behest of his regular physician to see the specialist Gary Zucker at Beth Israel Hospital in New York. Armstrong ended up being admitted at Beth Israel for treatment of heart problems from February to April 1969.[1] On March 31 he began writing what may be the most unusual and moving of his many autobiographical efforts, a seventy-seven-page handwritten manuscript he titled "Louis Armstrong+the Jewish Family in New Orleans, LA, the Year of 1907."[2] Every aspect of the document—from its fitful, sometimes confusing organization, to the wavering hand of Armstrong's pen, to the impassioned tone of numerous passages—seems to intensify its emotional charge. As critic and biographer Gary Giddins has written, the document is an "obsessive *cri du coeur*."[3]

"Louis Armstrong+the Jewish Family" (Figure A.1) is peculiar in part because of its generic shifting or instability. At times it takes on an almost third-person documentary flavor: "A Real life story and Experiences/At the age of Seven years old/With the KORNORFSKY FAMILY (Jewish family)/the year of 1907.//All Scenes happened in New Orleans La./Where Armstrong was Born./The year 1900" (6). There are unexpected if entertaining digressions, as when Armstrong explains the origins of the nickname "Satchmo" in 1932 (20–21). And there are many pages devoted to capsule biographical portraits of other New Orleans musicians: "Here is a short rundown of my idea of the choice musicians in my young days in New Orleans. Also, the Cream of the Crop at that time," Armstrong writes (26), offering comments on players including Honore Dutrey and Jelly Roll Morton (24); Freddie Keppard (25); Kid Ory, Mutt Carey, and Erskine Tate (28); Paul Barbarin, Alphone Picou, John Robichaux, and Buddy Petit (30). But the document is above all a heartfelt declaration of what Armstrong calls his "long time admiration for the Jewish People" (8).

When he discovered to his shock and dismay that his manager Joe Glaser had also been admitted to Beth Israel after a stroke and was in a coma, Armstrong insisted on visiting his old friend; after Glaser died on

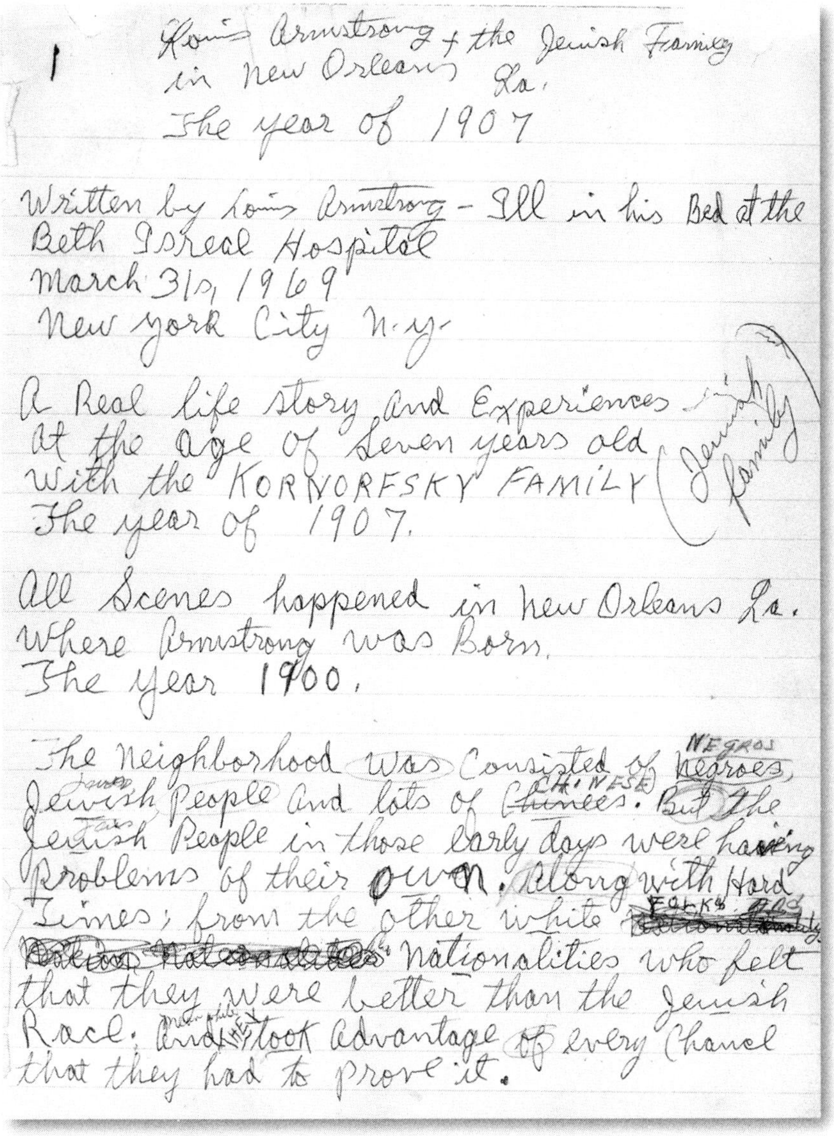
1
Louis Armstrong + the Jewish Family
in New Orleans La.
The year of 1907

Written by Louis Armstrong – Ill in his Bed at the
Beth Isreal Hospital
March 31, 1969
New York City N.Y.

A Real life story and Experiences
At the age of Seven years old
With the KORNORFSKY FAMILY
The year of 1907.

(Jewish family)

All Scenes happened in New Orleans La.
Where Armstrong was Born.
The Year 1900.

The Neighborhood was Consisted of ~~Negroes~~ NEGROS,
Jewish People and lots of ~~Chinees~~ CHINESE. But the
Jewish People in those early days were having
Problems of their own. Along with Hard
Times; from the other white FOLKS
nationalities who felt
that they were better than the Jewish
Race. And they took advantage of every Chance
that they had to prove it.

Figure A.1 Page 1 of "Louis Armstrong + the Jewish Family in New Orleans, LA, the Year of 1907." Louis Armstrong House and Archives at Queens College, City University of New York.

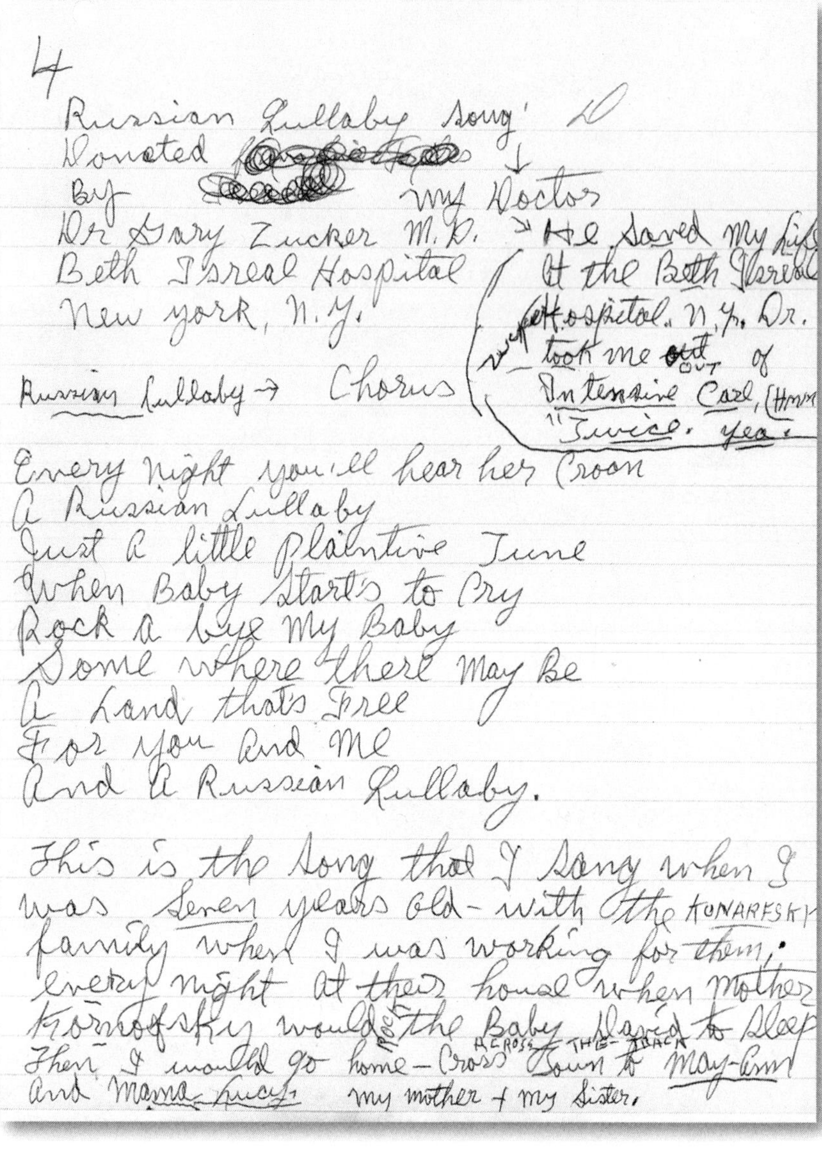

4

Russian Lullaby Song
Donated
By my Doctor
Dr Gary Zucker M.D.
Beth Isreal Hospital
New york, N.Y.

→ He saved my life
At the Beth Isreal
Hospital. N.Y. Dr.
took me out of
Intensive Care, (Hmm
"Twice. yea.

Russian Lullaby → Chorus

Every night you'll hear her Croon
A Russian Lullaby
Just a little plaintive Tune
When Baby Start's to Cry
Rock a bye My Baby
Some where there may be
A Land thats Free
For you and Me
And a Russian Lullaby.

This is the Song that I Sang when I was Seven years old—with the KONARESKY family when I was working for them, every night at their house when Mother Kornofsky would rock the Baby David to Sleep. Then I would go home—Cross Town ACROSS THE TRACK to May-Ann and Mama Lucy, my mother + my Sister.

Figure A.2 Page 4 of "Louis Armstrong + the Jewish Family in New Orleans, LA, the Year of 1907." Louis Armstrong House and Archives at Queens College, City University of New York.

June 4, Armstrong added (in a different pen) an inscription at the beginning of the memoir:

> I Dedicate this book
> to my Manager and pal
> Mr. Joe Glaser
> The best Friend
> That I've ever had
> May the Lord Bless Him
> Watch over him Always
> His boy + disciple who loved him
> dearly. Louis
> Satchmo
> Armstrong (8)[4]

Editor Thomas Brothers, in his prefatory note to the transcription of this document published in the collection *Louis Armstrong, in His Own Words,* explains that Armstrong was "inspired, apparently, by his doctor Gary Zucker, who had just sung a Russian lullaby from a Jewish family for whom he worked" (3). Armstrong alludes to this inspiration in the text itself with an idiosyncratic sort of annotation or heading on the fourth page (Figure A.2), followed directly by the lyrics of the song itself:

> Russian Lullaby Song'
> Donated
> By
> Dr. Gary Zucker M.D.
> Beth Israel Hospital
> New York, N.Y.
>
> My Doctor
> –> He Saved my Life
> at the Beth Israel
> Hospital, N.Y. Dr.
> Zucker took me out of
> Intensive care (HMM?
> "Twice. Yea.
>
> Russian Lullaby—> Chorus
>
> Every night you'll hear her Croon
> A Russian Lullaby

Just a little Plaintive Tune
When Baby Starts to Cry
Rock a bye My Baby
Some where there May Be
A Land that's Free
For you and Me
And A Russian Lullaby. (6)

Even confined to his sickbed, Armstrong seems to have retained his jocular sense of language (the interjection "HMM?" suggests mock-bewilderment at the notion of a "care" that would somehow be "intensive"; and the words "My Doctor," inserted interlineally using a different color ink, seem to be meant as a playful faux-deciphering of the abbreviation "M.D."). Armstrong goes on to explain, "This is the Song that I Sang when I was Seven years old—with the *KONARFSKY* family when I was working for them, every night at their house when Mother Kornofsky would rock the Baby David to Sleep" (7).

The Karnofskys were a family of Russian immigrants in New Orleans who hired Armstrong when he was a boy to work with their sons, collecting rags and junk and selling coal to residents in the city's "Red Light District." As he recounts, the Karnofskys, while struggling themselves, were generous with Armstrong, even helping him to purchase his first cornet. Thomas Brothers notes that there are a number of discrepancies between this narrative and Armstrong's earlier descriptions of his time working the Karnofskys, and some of the events seem more likely to have taken place around 1915 than in 1907 as the document implies.[5] But the empirical inaccuracies of the text seem outweighed by the warmth of Armstrong's feelings of gratitude and reminiscence, which seems encapsulated above all in the song, with its plaintive melancholy and stark aspiration for a "land that's free."

Brothers writes that the song seems to "catalyze" Armstrong's memory (3). Indeed, it does not appear only once in the opening pages of the text; the lyrics are reiterated in their entirety no fewer than four times over the course of the narrative (see 6–7, 17–18, 30, 33). There are slight variations in capitalization, punctuation, and language each time: thus in the first iteration the lyrics read "Every Night you'll hear her Croon," but a few pages later when they are repeated, the line is given as "Every night you'll hear me Croon" (Figure A.3). The lines "A Land—that's free / for you And Me" (30) (Figure A.4) are transformed, slightly, too, into "A land that's free for you—And Me" (33) (Figure A.5), with the shift in the positioning of the dash implying multiple renditions of the words, performed each time with different intonation and emphasis.[6] This is to say that Armstrong's writing practice again seems to display what Lawrence Gushee has termed the persistent "ethic of variation" in Armstrong's approach to musical improvisation: "no note is played automatically" and "even the most inconsequential motif is shaped, and any repetition is varied."[7] At the same time, one might say that in "Louis Armstrong + the Jewish Family" the song lyrics function less as an epigraph and more as a peculiar sort of *refrain:* the repeated chorus of a nostalgic lament for vanished youth that here somehow can only be framed as an expression of Armstrong's "long time admiration for the Jewish People" (8).

Even if the lyrics might be said to suggest the "sad slanting Slavic sound, all cheekbones and distance" that Federico García Lorca once described as characteristic of all Russian cradle songs, there is something peculiar about the specific lullaby that Armstrong is using here.[8] It is not simply a matter of the irony that the catalyst for memory is a form of music that is by definition soporific (after all, as García Lorca reminds us, the "fundamental object of the lullaby is to put the child that is not sleepy to sleep").[9] The lyrics themselves are striking because the song is a lullaby *about* a lullaby: it invokes a lullaby elsewhere that, even in its inconsequentiality and utilitarian function ("just a little plaintive tune / when baby starts to cry"), seems to encapsulate a longed-for "freedom" in a much broader civic sense that doesn't seem to have much to do with putting infants to sleep. Oddly, this "Russian" lullaby seems less a remnant of the old country than the characteristic aspirational longing of the *immigrant* for "a land that's free / for you and me."

A perusal of the Armstrong discography adds another wrinkle of complexity: around 1950, one of the staples of Armstrong's concert repertoire with his All-Stars was a song called "Russian Lullaby."[10] According to Dan Morgenstern, the song was bassist Arvell Shaw's feature number with the Armstrong All Stars from late 1949 to mid-1953, although Armstrong himself does not ever seem to have recorded a vocal version of the

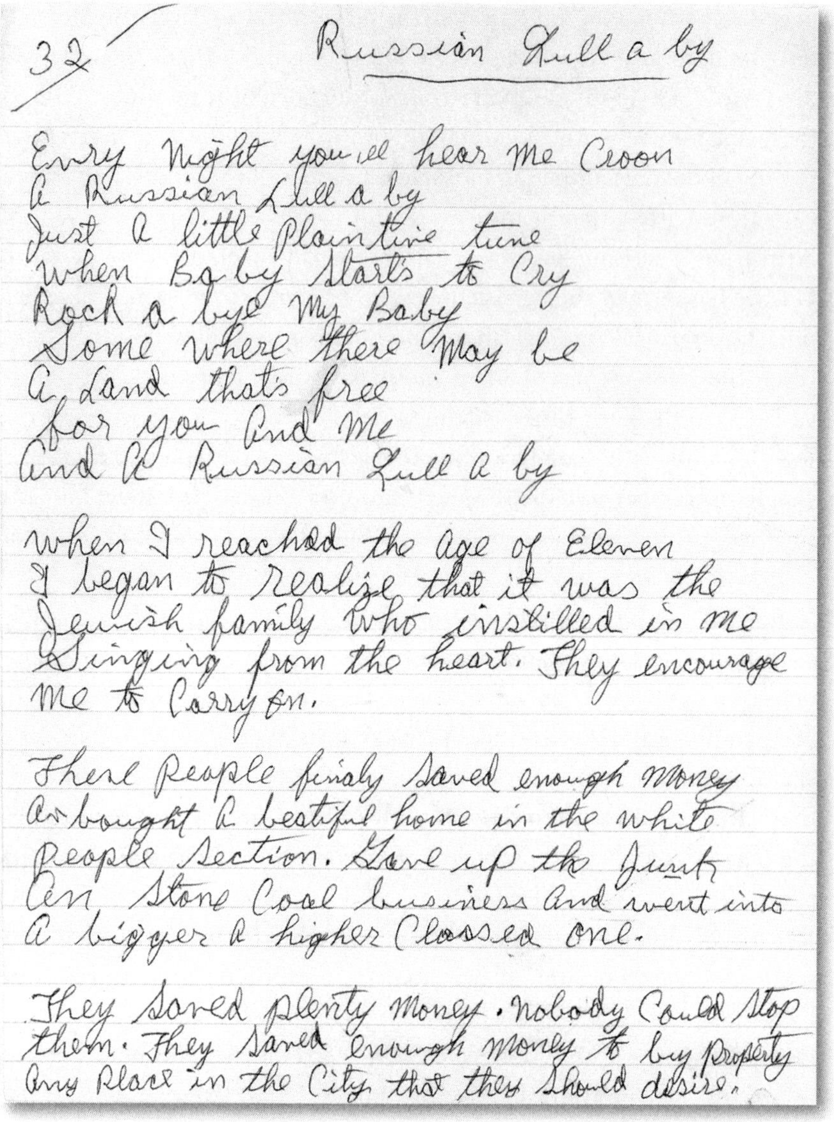

32

Russian Lull a by

Evry Night you'll hear me Croon
A Russian Lull a by
Just a little Plaintive tune
when Baby Starts to Cry
Rock a bye My Baby
Some where there May be
A Land that's free
for you And Me
And A Russian Lull a by

when I reached the age of Eleven
I began to realize that it was the
Jewish family who instilled in me
Singing from the heart. They encourage
me to Carry on.

There People finaly saved enough money
and bought a beatiful home in the white
people Section. Gave up the Junk
an Stone Coal business and went into
a bigger + higher Classed one.

They saved plenty money. nobody Could Stop
them. They saved enough money to buy property
any Place in the City that they should desire.

Figure A.3 From Page 32 of "Louis Armstrong + the Jewish Family in New Orleans, LA, the Year of 1907." Louis Armstrong House and Archives at Queens College, City University of New York.

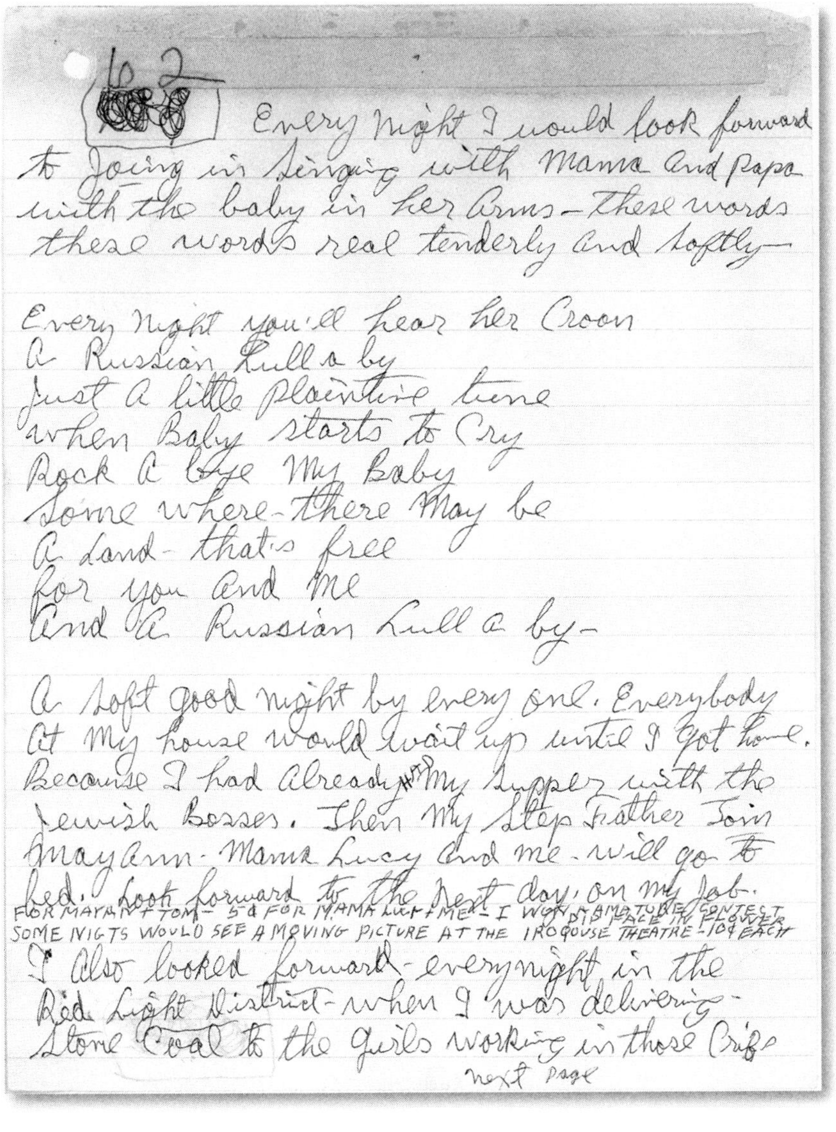

62

Every Night I would look forward
to Joing in Singing with Mama and Papa
with the baby in her Arms — these words
these words real tenderly and softly —

Every Night you'll hear her Croon
A Russian Lull a by
Just a little plaintive tune
when Baby starts to Cry
Rock A bye My Baby
Some where — there May be
A land — that's free
for you and Me
And A Russian Lull a by —

A soft good night by every one. Everybody
At My house would wait up until I Got home.
Because I had already ate My supper with the
Jewish Bosses. Then My Step Father Tom
May Ann — Mama Lucy and me — will go to
bed. Look forward to the next day, on my Job.
FOR MAYANN + TOM — 5¢ FOR MAMA LUCY + ME — I WON A AMATURE CONTEST DID PLACE IN FLOWER
SOME NIGTS WOULD SEE A MOVING PICTURE AT THE IROQOUSE THEATRE — 10¢ EACH
I also looked forward — everynight in the
Red Light District — when I was delivering —
Stone Coal to the Girls working in those Cribs
next page

Figure A.4 From Page 62 of "Louis Armstrong + the Jewish Family in New Orleans, LA, the Year of 1907." Louis Armstrong House and Archives at Queens College, City University of New York.

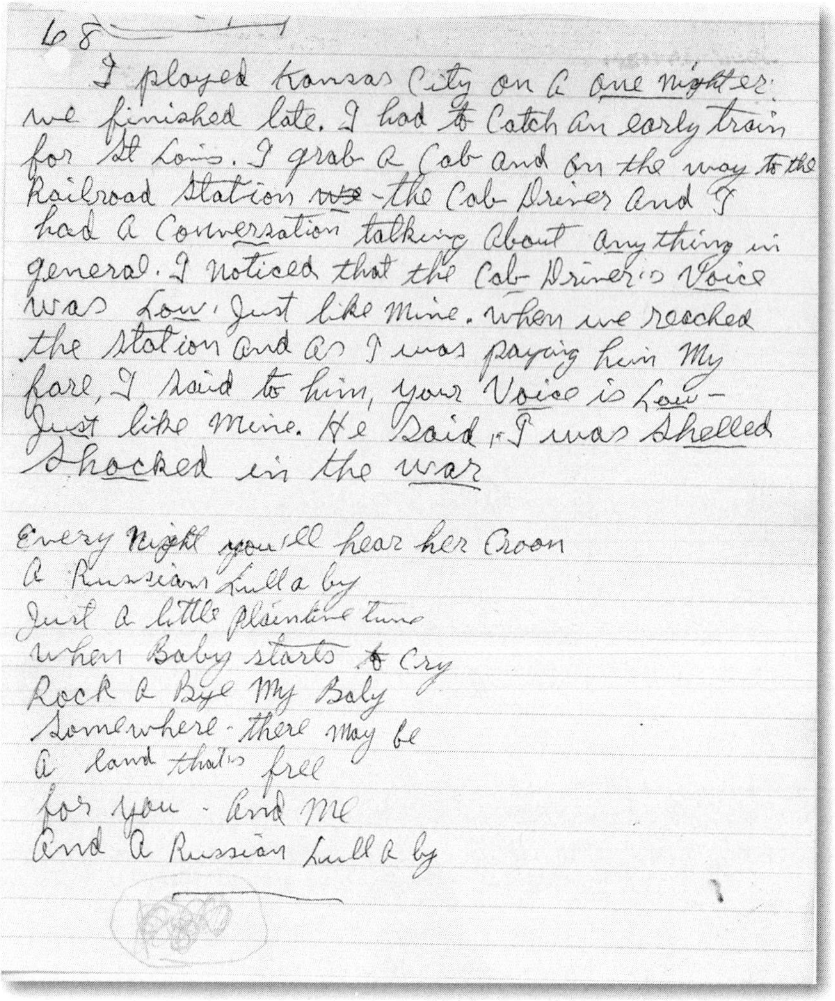

68

I played Kansas City on a one nighter. we finished late. I had to Catch an early train for St Louis. I grab a Cab and on the way to the Railroad Station ~~we~~ - the Cab Driver and I had a Conversation talking about anything in general. I noticed that the Cab-Driver's Voice was Low. Just like mine. when we reached the station and as I was paying him My fare, I said to him, your Voice is Low - Just like mine. He said, "I was Shelled Shocked in the war

Every night you'll hear her Croon
a Russian Lull a by
Just a little plaintive tune
when Baby starts to cry
Rock a Bye My Baby
Somewhere - there may be
a land that's free
for you - and me
And a Russian Lull a by

Figure A.5 From Page 68 of "Louis Armstrong + the Jewish Family in New Orleans, LA, the Year of 1907." Louis Armstrong House and Archives at Queens College, City University of New York.

tune.[11] Nevertheless the lyrics that Armstrong intersperses throughout "Louis Armstrong + the Jewish Family" in the spring of 1969 come *not* from the lullaby Mrs. Karnofsky sang in New Orleans in the early years of the twentieth century, but instead from the "Russian Lullaby" Armstrong had performed decades later with his own group. The song has nothing to do with Louisiana, but is instead an artifact of Tin Pan Alley in New York. In fact, "Russian Lullaby" was composed in the spring of 1927 by none other than Irving Berlin.[12]

In a 1996 oral history, Armstrong's doctor Gary Zucker is asked about this episode and about the lullaby he had "donated" by singing it to Armstrong while the musician was bedridden. Zucker recalls that Armstrong told him that "he wants to write down his life experiences, about all the Jews in his life. And he considered that the Jews had helped him more than anybody else. And that his experience with other people was wanting to take advantage of him." As he composed this memoir, Zucker adds, Armstrong was reminiscing in particular about his time as a child in New Orleans working for the Karnofskys. Armstrong told Zucker that he "loved listening to Mrs. Karnofsky sing this Russian lullaby," and was struggling to remember it until Zucker refreshed his memory by singing it to him. But when asked if he recalls the song in question, Zucker does not mention Irvin Berlin. He explains: "And this Russian lullaby, there's a thing called 'Oyfn Pripetshik.' " Zucker then begins to sing the song itself, performing the beginning of the first verse:

> Oyfn pripetchik brent a fayerl,
> Un in shtub iz heys,
> Un der rebe lernt kleyne kinderlekh,
> Dem alef-beys.

Then he resumes his narrative: "The English translation is that 'On the hearth there is a fire, warming the room, and the rabbi is teaching little children the ABCs.' That was one of them. And then there was another one he used to sing. Um, I don't remember it after so long."[13]

"Oyfn Pripetshik" (which can be translated as "At the Fireplace," "At the Hearth," or "On the Cooking Stove") is a well-known Yiddish song composed by M. M. Warshawsky around the turn of the twentieth century.[14] The intimate scene of instruction depicted in the song unfurls into a far-reaching argument about the value of Hebrew language-learning and religious instruction (which of course are intrinsically linked in the Judaic tradition) as a resource of "strength" in the midst of the "tears" and "sorrow" of the Exile (*Golus* in Yiddish, or *Galut* in Hebrew) of the Jewish people. The song continues:

Lernt, kinder, hot nit moyre,
Yeder onheyb iz shver;
Gliklekh der vos hot gelernt toyre,
Tsi darf der mentsh nokh mer?
Ir vet, kinder, elter vern,
Vet ir aleyn farshteyn,
Vifl in di oysyes lign trern,
Un vi fil geveyn.
Az ir vet, kinder, dem goles shlepn,
Oysgemutshet zayn,
Zolt ir fun di oysyes koyekh shepn,
Kukt in zey arayn!

Learn children, do not be afraid,
Every beginning is hard;
Lucky is the one has learned Torah,
What more does a person need?
When you grow older, children,
You will understand yourselves
How many tears lie in these letters,
And how much sorrow.
When you, children, will bear the Exile,
And will be exhausted,
May you derive strength from these letters,
Look in at them!

It seems unlikely that Armstrong would have known the meaning of the Yiddish lyrics when he was a child working with the Karnofskys, although Zucker says in his oral history that in 1969 he translated the song for Armstrong when he sang it at the musician's bedside in Beth Israel Hospital.[15] Yet there is something deeply moving in the parallel between Armstrong's compulsion to write this memoir—a compulsion tangible even in the tenuousness of his laborious scrawl—and a song about the promise that one can draw the fortitude to withstand the exhaustion of spiritual exile from the wellspring of alphabetic instruction.

There is no similarity between the lyrics and melody of "Oyfn Pripetshik" and Irvin Berlin's "Russian Lullaby."[16] And yet one might also argue that if "Louis Armstrong + the Jewish Family" seems to hover around this "imaginative error," something extraordinary happens in the memoir precisely *because* of this transposition, when one song replaces another as the kernel of evocative nostalgia. If Armstrong is longing for the intimacy of a hearth that wasn't exactly his own, a hearth that he had the chance to observe as a sort of privileged outsider, then it seems right, somehow, that the song associated with the memory would be a song *about* a song—that is, an evocation of intimacy witnessed or overheard ("Every night you'll hear her croon"). Despite the anachronism of "Russian Lullaby" (a popular song composed more than a decade after Armstrong was working for the Karnofskys), it also seems to interject the particularly New World and, one might add, African American flavor of Armstrong's longing—the way that the soporific security of the domestic hearth seems yoked to the prospect of a "world that's free / for you and me" in the most abstract political sense—into what would otherwise have been a more specific Jewish American immigrant scene of memory. Another way to put this would be to say that the transposition replaces a lyric about the state of Exile (that is, a sundering from the shelter of the Covenant, in which redemption is only imaginable in the realm of eschatology) with another lyric about the condition of diaspora (that is, the forcible scattering of a community which nonetheless maintains an aspirational, forward-looking quality: "Somewhere there may be . . .").

The most striking element of "Louis Armstrong + the Jewish Family" is not the lullaby, however. It is the many passages throughout the document in which Armstrong complains in bitter language of the lack of solidarity among African Americans, which he compares unfavorably with the example of the Jewish people he has known. As Ricky Riccardi summarizes it, "Armstrong used this document, which he referred to as a 'book,' to air out some grievances, especially when it came to issues of race."[17] According to scholar Daniel Stein, the text "reverses [Armstrong's] preference for black audiences" and goes against almost all of Armstrong's previous public statements, which were consistently imbued with racial pride. "Louis Armstrong + the Jewish Family," for Stein, is a "disillusioned narrative, which must be read in the context of the backlash against Armstrong's public image that followed his appearance as the King of the Zulus in the Mardi Gras parade of 1949 and as a reaction against the criticism leveled at him by civil rights activists."[18]

The raw hurt of these passages is redoubled by their repetitiveness, giving them almost a compulsive quality, like a wound being fingered again and again (to return to the metaphor I discussed in Chapter 2). "We were lazy and still are. We never did try to get together," Armstrong writes near the beginning of the memoir (8). Then on the following page:

> Negroes never did stick together and they never will. They hold too much malice—Jealousy deep down in their heart for the few Negroes who tries. But the odds were (are) against them. Of course, we are all well aware of the Congo Square—Slavery—Lynchings and all of that stuff. Maybe the Jewish people did not go through' All of those things, but they went through just as much. Still they stuck together." (9)

And then, over and over, almost the same point in almost the same language: "Boy—if the Negroes could stick together half that much. Hmm look where we would be today. But I doubt that it would ever happen. Too Much Malice and Hate Among us. And for no reason at all. Honest—these Jewish people accepted hard times far more better than my own people did" (30).

In other words, if as I suggested earlier "Russian Lullaby" (transposed by imaginative error in the place of "Oyfn Pripetshik") functions as a sort of refrain running through "Louis Armstrong + the Jewish Family," in fact there are *two* refrains structuring the memoir: the comforting memory of the lullaby, representing the hearth as a sort of diasporic harbor, on the one hand, and the bedeviling memory of racial disillusionment, on the other. The entire seventy-seven-page document is constructed as a strange double helix of memory, oscillating between agonized betrayal and adoptive warmth.

This is also the document I quoted in Chapter 1, the document in which Armstrong writes repeatedly about the importance of "purging" for maintaining one's health in conditions of poverty. In fact, the text ends with the extended and unforgettable description of the first time Armstrong used the laxative Swiss Kriss ("My wife Lucille started me to taking Swiss Kriss . . ."). Considered from this angle, one might even say that, rather than some sort of discomfiting revelation of the unseemly prejudices and bitterness of an old man, the memoir serves as a sort of "purge" itself: a way for Armstrong to expel and rid himself of the negativity built up during a lifetime as a public figure who received more than his share of mean-spirited backlash from black audiences, especially later in his life. From this perspective, it is not a coincidence that he begins composing this text in his hospital bed: for Armstrong, writing the memoir is an issue of *health,* as much as posterity.

Rather than condemn Armstrong's tone, or to explain it away as the excesses of a great man in his worst days, this is to begin to read "Louis Armstrong + the Jewish Family" as a powerful piece of writing that can only be described as innovative. It is a new brand of memoir, intuited in the exigencies of a brutal experience. And given that innovation here has everything to do with the way Armstrong's writing discovers a formal possibility in a musical refrain—even if, in the blush of memory, that music is a different music—to read this way is already to start to hear across media.

notes

Introduction

1. "The Cricket" [Editorial], *The Cricket: Black Music in Evolution* 1 (1968): a. On the history of *The Cricket,* see Christopher Funkhouser, "LeRoi Jones, Larry Neal, and 'The Cricket': Jazz and Poets' Black Fire," *African American Review* 37, nos. 2–3 (Summer–Autumn 2003): 237–244.
2. "The Cricket," b.
3. William Russell and Stephen W. Smith, "New Orleans Music," in *Jazzmen,* ed. Charles Edward Smith and Frederic Ramsey Jr. (New York: Harcourt, Brace and Co., 1939), 13.
4. Vic Hobson, *Creating Jazz Counterpoint: New Orleans, Barbershop Harmony, and the Blues* (Jackson: University Press of Mississippi, 2014), 3.
5. Russell and Smith, "New Orleans Music," in *Jazzman,* 10–11.
6. Donald M. Marquis, *In Search of Buddy Bolden: First Man of Jazz* (1978; repr., New York: Da Capo, 1980), 8.
7. One was the Belgian critic Robert Goffin's *La Nouvelle-Orléans, capitale du jazz* (New York: Editions de la Maison Française, 1946), which was not widely read in the United States because it was never translated. Goffin spoke to New Orleans elders such as Big Eye Louis Nelson, Alphonse Picou, Bob Lyons, and Louis Jones, who were unable to confirm either that Bolden was a barber or that he edited a newspaper.
8. Jelly Roll Morton recorded this song three times in the late 1930s: Jelly Roll Morton, "Buddy Bolden's Blues," rec. 1938, Library of Congress Archive of Folk Song 1658A (Rounder 1092); Jelly Roll Morton's New Orleans Jazzmen, "I Thought I Heard Buddy Bolden Say," rec. 14 September 1939 (Bluebird B-10434-B); Jelly Roll Morton, "Buddy Bolden's Blues," rec. 16 December 1939 (General 4003-A).
9. The last four titles are drawn from one of the vivid set lists in Danny Barker, *Buddy Bolden and the Last Days of Storyville,* ed. Alyn Shipton (London: Cassell, 1998), 20. The great banjo player and historian Barker admitted to Alyn Shipton that when he was preparing one of the articles collected in this book, the well-known "A Memory of King Bolden," which appeared in the *Evergreen Review* (September 1965), he had added "a little monkeyshine" to the oral histories he had conducted with New Orleans figures such as Dude Bottley (see ibid., viii).
10. Marquis, *In Search of Buddy Bolden,* 7. The quotation from William Russell comes from Marquis's conversation with him at Preservation Hall on September 12, 1970.
11. *The Cricket* 1, no. 1 (March 21, 1896), New Orleans Special Collections, Tulane University, quoted in Hobson, *Creating Jazz Counterpoint,* 11. Hobson also discusses another issue, vol. 1, no. 8 (July 24, 1897), which he located at Xavier University. The mistaken information that Bolden edited *The Cricket* seems to have originated with Bunk Johnson, the trumpeter who was one of the musicians interviewed for *Jazzmen;* Johnson later explained to Robert Goffin that "in reality, it was a friend of Buddy's who edited *The Cricket:* Otis Watts" (*La Nouvelle-Orléans,* 99). According to Hobson, Watts was not the editor of the periodical, but may have contributed to it.
12. Hobson, *Creating Jazz Counterpoint,* 3.
13. As Studs Terkel once put it: "You can't be too prepared for an interview, because you don't know what the person you're talking to's going to say. But you've got to be ready for anything. . . . In a way it's like jazz, you've got to improvise. Have a skeletal framework, but be ready to improvise within that"; see Studs Terkel, with Tony Parker, "Interviewing an

Interviewer," from *Studs Terkel: A Life in Words* (1997) 163–170, collected in Robert Perks and Alistair Thomson, eds., *The Oral History Reader* (London: Routledge, 1998), 127. One of the few works on jazz oral history in particular is Burton W. Peretti, "Oral Histories of Jazz Musicians: The NEA Transcripts as Texts in Context," in *Jazz among the Discourses,* ed. Krin Gabbard (Durham, NC: Duke University Press, 1995), 117–133, although Peretti explicitly limits his discussion to transcripts rather than the original recordings, thus arguably making it difficult to attend to the sonic and improvisational nature of the form (119).

14. Alessandro Portelli, "What Makes Oral History Different (1979)," in *The Death of Luigi Trastulli and Other Stories: Form and Meaning in Oral History* (Albany: State University of New York Press, 1991), 52.
15. Portelli, "Introduction," in *The Death of Luigi Trastulli and Other Stories*, ix.
16. Portelli, "What Makes Oral History Different," 51.
17. Portelli, "The Death of Luigi Trastulli: Memory and the Event" (1981), in *The Death of Luigi Trastulli and Other Stories*, 26.
18. "The Cricket," b–c.
19. "Gossip," *The Cricket* 3 (1969): 31.
20. "Inquiry," *The Cricket* 3 (1969): 28.
21. Michael Ondaatje, *Coming through Slaughter* (New York: Vintage, 1976), 24. Subsequent references will be indicated parenthetically in the text.
22. James Baldwin, "Many Thousands Gone" (1951), in James Baldwin, *Collected Essays,* ed. Toni Morrison (New York: Library of America, 1998), 19.
23. Frederick Douglass, *Narrative of the Life of Frederick Douglass,* ed. William L. Andrews and William S. McFeely (New York: Norton, 1997), 18; W. E. B. Du Bois, *The Souls of Black Folk,* ed. Brent Hayes Edwards (New York: Oxford University Press, 2007), 171. The phrase *the character of cognition* is adopted from Theodor Adorno's 1932 essay "On the Social Situation of Music." Despite the fact that Adorno invokes what he calls "jazz" as the preeminent instance of a music indelibly shaped by its "commodity character" (430), one might argue on the contrary that jazz is the very sort of music Adorno is otherwise calling for: a music that "is able to express—in the antinomies of its own formal language—the exigency of the social condition and to call for change through the coded language of suffering." Jazz fulfills, as much as any other twentieth-century music one might name, Adorno's dictum that "the *character of cognition* is to be demanded of any music which today wishes to preserve its right to existence. Through its material, music must give clear form to the problems assigned it by this material which is itself never purely natural material, but rather a social and historical product; solutions offered by music in this process stand equal to theories." See Theodor Adorno, "On the Social Situation of Music," in *Essays on Music,* ed. Richard Leppert, trans. Susan H. Gillespie (Berkeley: University of California Press, 2002), 393. This is not the place to rehash the heated debates around Adorno's castigation of "jazz," but it is worth noting (as many other scholars have) that it is not at all clear what music Adorno is referring to with the term. It is difficult to recognize the music of Armstrong and Ellington in Adorno's sneering remark that "the apparent improvisations of *hot* music are totally the expression of set norms which can be traced back to a very few basic types" (430).
24. Amiri Baraka (LeRoi Jones), *Blues People: Negro Music in White America* (1963; repr., New York: Harper Perennial, 2002), 152–153. Here is the entire passage, which can also be read as the kernel of what a couple of years later will become Baraka's theory of black culture as a "changing same": "Music, as paradoxical as it might seem, is the result of thought. It is the result of thought perfected at its most empirical, *i.e.,* as *attitude,* or *stance.* Thought is largely conditioned by references; it is the result of consideration of speculation against reference, which is largely arbitrary. There is no *one* way of thinking, since reference (hence value) is as scattered and dissimilar as men themselves. If Negro music can be seen to be the result of certain attitudes, certain specific ways of thinking about the world (and only ultimately about the *ways* in which music can be made), then the basic hypothesis of this book is understood. The Negro's music changed as he changed, reflecting shifting attitudes or (and this is equally important) *consistent attitudes within changed contexts.*"

25. Sidney Bechet, *Treat It Gentle* (New York: Da Capo, 1960), 204.
26. Baraka, *Blues People,* viii–ix.
27. Portelli, "Introduction," *The Death of Luigi Trastulli and Other Stories,* ix.
28. Bechet, *Treat It Gentle,* 48.
29. Ralph Ellison, "The Golden Age, Time Past" (1959), collected in Robert G. O'Meally, ed., *Living with Music: Ralph Ellison's Jazz Writings* (New York: Modern Library Classics, 2002), 51.
30. Ronald Radano, *Lying Up a Nation: Race and Black Music* (Chicago: University of Chicago Press, 2003), xiv. There are obvious parallels between my argument and Radano's important monograph, but my ultimate aims here are quite different. Radano's book analyzes the ways black music might be said to "lie up a nation," in the sense that it is taken as the irrefutable confirmation of a complex network of U.S. racial "myths," defined not as falsities or deceptions, but instead as "lying" in a sense Radano derives from the work of Zora Neale Hurston and Roland Barthes: "the stories we tell in giving texture and meaning in the making of our worlds" (3). Radano's project is unabashedly polemic: it is an attempt to "challenge . . . those strategies of containment that uphold the racial binaries informing the interpretation of black music" (ibid.). Specifically, Radano argues, the only way to attend to the "magical, miraculous quality of black performance" is to critique "black music's pervasive essentialism" (13). As he writes, "the true miracle of black sound derives neither from a simple African origin nor from an inherently 'spiritual nature' that seemingly 'jes grew.' It emerges instead from the alchemy of modern racial logic and the ironic differences that logic produces" (13). Thus Radano concludes that "continuing to uphold uncritically the myth of black music as a stable form or even as a 'changing same,' as Amiri Baraka calls it, forestalls consideration of the interracial background from which ideologies of black music developed in the first place" (3). The chapters in *Lying Up a Nation* are less concerned with twentieth-century black theorists of black music like Baraka; instead Radano provides a rich and incisive reading of primary texts mainly by white American folklorists, historians, and cultural commentators in the nineteenth century to demonstrate that the very notion of "black music" is a phenomenon that "grow[s] from the white racial imagination" (xiv). My aim here, however, is not to provide a more accurate critical genealogy (a better picture of that "interracial background"), but instead to consider the ramifications of certain figures of black music in the work of a host of black artists in the twentieth century, especially in the ways they thought about innovation and experimentation. In other words, I want to trace the ways twentieth-century black literature and music were both shaped by what Radano describes as a "conception of a discursively constituted black music standing between as it embodies the textual and musical, as resonance" (11).
31. Ibid., 15.
32. Daniel Stein, *Music Is My Life: Louis Armstrong, Autobiography, and American Jazz* (Ann Arbor: University of Michigan Press, 2012), 8.
33. Michael Cogswell, *Louis Armstrong: The Offstage Story of Satchmo* (Portland, OR: Collectors Press, 2003), 39, 82.
34. Armstrong's many autobiographical efforts include the partially ghostwritten 1936 book *Swing That Music;* the extensive "notebooks" he prepared for Robert Goffin in the mid-1940s; a second, classic book in 1954, *Satchmo: My Life in New Orleans;* the overlapping but not identical text "The Armstrong Story" of the same period; the continuations of and sequels to *Satchmo,* which include the 1959 manuscript "gauging" the joys of marijuana, titled "The Satchmo Story, 2nd Edition"; and the rambling, provocative, and moving document he wrote while ill near the end of his life, "Louis Armstrong + the Jewish Family in New Orleans, LA, the Year of 1907," *Swing That Music* (New York: Longmans, Green and Co., 1936) and *Satchmo: My Life in New Orleans* (New York: New American Library, 1954) are available in book form; the other documents are now collected in *Louis Armstrong, in His Own Words,* ed. Thomas Brothers (New York: Oxford University Press, 1999).
35. Tom Piazza, "Introduction," in *Setting the Tempo: Fifty Years of Great Jazz Liner Notes,* ed. Tom Piazza (New York: Anchor Doubleday, 1996), 1. Piazza's introduction to this anthology

is still the best short history of the jazz liner note as a genre. Piazza situates its emergence in the 1930s during the first wave of interest in the *history* of the still-young music, in which repackaged compilations of recordings from the previous decade (referred to using a term adopted from photography: *albums*) were issued with notes providing historical, biographical, and discographical information, often framing the compilation as representative of a geographical area *(Chicago Jazz),* or a performance location that gave rise to a particular style *(Riverboat Jazz).* Although its generic contours were more or less set by the advent of the LP (which imposed a strict length-limit—the limited space on the back cover of a record album—as well as certain norms and expectations in format), the liner note shifted again in the late 1950s when musicians (and some writers linked to the "New Music") began to write liner notes themselves; prominent examples included in *Setting the Tempo* include Bill Evans's famous notes for Miles Davis's *Kind of Blue* (Columbia CS 8163, 1959), Charles Mingus's notes to *The Black Saint and the Sinner Lady* (Impulse! Records A35, 1963), and Amiri Baraka's notes to John Coltrane's *Live at Birdland* (Impulse! Records AS-50, 1964).

36. Piazza, "Introduction," in *Setting the Tempo,* 2.
37. As Martin Williams pointed out many years ago, the limitations of the ten-inch record (which allowed only about three minutes to a side) imposed a structural constraint on the blues that did not exist in live performance; in the recorded form, however, this limitation compelled the greatest singers to achieve an economy of statement approaching the density and complexity of the sonnet form. For Williams, singers like Ida Cox and Sara Martin "give each blues a specifically poetic development which takes subtle advantage of the four-stanza limitation and creates a kind of classic form within it." See Martin Williams, "Recording Limits and Blues Form," in *The Art of Jazz: Essays on the Nature and Development of Jazz,* ed. Martin Williams (New York: Grove, 1959), 92. I have discussed the impact of this constraint on the blues poems in Hughes's second book, *Fine Clothes to the Jew;* see Brent Hayes Edwards, *The Practice of Diaspora: Literature, Translation, and the Rise of Black Internationalism* (Cambridge, MA: Harvard University Press, 2003), 60.
38. See Sascha Feinstein, *Jazz Poetry: From the 1920s to the Present* (Westport, CT: Greenwood Press, 1997); T. J. Anderson III, *Notes to Make the Sound Come Right: Four Innovators of Jazz Poetry* (Fayetteville: University of Arkansas Press, 2004); Aldon Lynn Nielsen, *Integral Music: Languages of African American Innovation* (Tuscaloosa: University of Alabama Press, 2004); and Meta DuEwa Jones, *The Muse Is Music: Jazz Poetry from the Harlem Renaissance to Spoken Word* (Urbana: University of Illinois Press, 2011). This is only a sampling, of course; there is likewise a wealth of impressive scholarship on jazz fiction.
39. See http://www.satchmo.net/thearchives/louis.shtml; Stephen Brower, ed., *Satchmo: The Wonderful World and Art of Louis Armstrong* (New York: Abrams, 2009).
40. Antoinette Burton, *Dwelling in the Archive: Women Writing House, Home, and History in Late Colonial India* (New York: Oxford University Press, 2003), 20.
41. Bechet, *Treat It Gentle,* 46.
42. Gayl Jones, *Corregidora* (1975; repr., Boston: Beacon, 1986), 96, 54.
43. Bechet, *Treat It Gentle,* 91.
44. Raymond Williams, *Marxism and Literature* (Oxford: Oxford University Press, 1977), 134.
45. Fred Moten, *In the Break: The Aesthetics of the Black Radical Tradition* (Minneapolis: University of Minnesota Press, 2003), 26.
46. Albert Murray, *Stomping the Blues* (New York: Da Capo, 1976), 108, 114.
47. For a brief overview of these extended techniques in the history of jazz trumpet, see Todd Bryant Weeks, *Luck's in My Corner: The Life and Music of Hot Lips Page* (New York: Routledge, 2008), 42.
48. Daniel Albright, *Panaesthetics: On the Unity and Diversity of the Arts* (New Haven, CT: Yale University Press, 2014). Subsequent page references will be given parenthetically in the text.
49. Albright summarizes the argument of Lessing's *Laokoon* (1766) that "artworks in a sequential medium pertain to action and should be loud, vigorous, expressive," while "artworks in a spatial medium pertain to stasis and should be decorous, calm, poised" (*Panaesthetics,* 3).

The Clement Greenberg quotation comes from John O'Brien, ed., *The Collected Essays and Criticism* (Chicago: University of Chicago Press, 1986), 1:25–34 (quoted in *Panaesthetics,* 215).

50. Nathaniel Mackey, "Expanding the Repertoire," *Tripwire* 5 (Fall 2001): 7.
51. Roland Barthes, "The Grain of the Voice," in *The Responsibility of Forms: Critical Essays on Music, Art, and Representation,* trans. Richard Howard (Berkeley: University of California Press, 1985), 267. Subsequent page references will be given parenthetically in the text. The French original was first published in the journal *Musique en jeu* in November 1972, and it is collected in Roland Barthes, *Oeuvres completes, tome II: 1966–1973,* ed. Eric Marty (Paris: Seil, 1993), 1436–1442.
52. Zora Neale Hurston, "Sprituals and Neo-Spirituals (1934)," in *Folklore, Memoirs, & Other Writings*, ed. Cheryl A. Wall (New York: Library of America, 1995), 871.
53. Murray, *Stomping the Blues,* 79.
54. I am not going to use the term *intermediality* to describe this interface among media, although it has come to be employed by a number of scholars over the past two decades. Note that Albright uses the term *intermedial* to describe a subjective and ultimately hallucinated element of the audience response to a work like an opera employing more than one medium (it is his name for the "imaginary artwork generated by the spectator through the interplay of two or more media"). In contrast, the scholarship on *intermediality* tends to employ the term in a normative fashion in a manner than could be accused of technological determinism (taking for granted the "independent properties of the medium" rather than understanding any medium to be not only a given "channel of communication" or the "specific material with which a particular kind of artist worked," but also—and unavoidably—a "form of social organization"). See Williams, *Marxism and Literature,* 159; John Guillory, "Genesis of the Media Concept," *Critical Inquiry* 36, no. 2 (Winter 2010): 347–348. For an introduction to the scholarship on intermediality, see, for example, Jürgen E. Müller, "Intermediality: A Plea and Some Theses for a New Approach in Media Studies," in *Interart Poetics: Essays on the Inter-Relations of the Arts and Media,* ed. Ulla-Britta Lagerroth, Hans Lund, and Erik Hedlin (Amsterdam: Rodopi, 1997), 295–304; Walter Bernhart, Steven Paul Scher, and Werner Wolf, eds., *Word and Music Studies: Defining the Field* (Amsterdam: Rodopi, 1999); and Werner Wolf, *The Musicalization of Fiction: A Study in the Theory and History of Intermediality* (Amsterdam: Rodopi, 1999). One jazz studies scholar who uses the term is Daniel Stein in his well-researched *Music Is My Life.*
55. See *The New Cab Calloway's Hepster's Dictionary: Language of Jive* (1944), collected in Cab Calloway and Bryant Rollins, *Of Minnie the Moocher & Me* (New York: Thomas Y. Crowell Company, 1976), 251–261; Babs Gonzales, *I Paid My Dues: Good Times—No Bread* (Newark, NJ: Expubidience, 1967); Charles Mingus, *Beneath the Underdog: His World as Composed by Mingus* (New York: Knopf, 1971); Leo Smith, *Notes (8 Pieces) Source: A New World Music: Creative Music* (n.p.: Leo Smith, 1973); Joseph Jarman, *Black Case, vol. I & II: Return from Exile* (Chicago: Art Ensemble of Chicago, 1977); Marion Brown, *Afternoon of a Georgia Faun: Views and Reviews* (n.p.: Nia Music, 1973); Marion Brown, "Faces and Places: The Music and Travels of a Contemporary Jazz Musician" (MA thesis, Wesleyan University, 1976); Marion Brown, *Recollections: Essays, Drawings, Miscellanea* (Frankfurt: Juergen A. Schmitt Publikationen, 1984); Anthony Braxton, *Tri-Axium Writings* (n.p.: Synthesis Music, 1985); Art Taylor, *Notes and Tones: Musician-to-Musician Interviews* (New York: Da Capo Press, 1993); William Parker, *Conversations* (Paris: RogueArt, 2011).
56. Robin D. G. Kelley, *Thelonious Monk: The Life and Times of an American Original* (New York: Free Press, 2009), 69.
57. Ibid., 69–70.
58. James Snead, "Repetition as a Figure of Black Culture," in *Black Literature and Literary Theory,* ed. Henry Louis Gates Jr. (New York: Methuen, 1984), 70.
59. Kelley, *Thelonious Monk,* 46.
60. Ibid., 46.

61. LeRoi Jones (Amiri Baraka), "Epistrophe," in *New Negro Poets U.S.A.*, ed. Langston Hughes (Bloomington: Indiana University Press, 1964), 73. This poem was originally published in Elias Wilentz, ed., *The Beat Scene* (New York: Corinth, 1960).
62. Amiri Baraka, "AM/TRAK," in *Poetry for the Advanced* (1979), collected in Amiri Baraka, *The LeRoi Jones/Amiri Baraka Reader,* ed. William J. Harris (1991; repr., New York: Thunder's Mouth Press, 1999), 267–272. Subsequent references will be indicated parenthetically in the text. I thank Amina Baraka for permission to quote Amiri Baraka's work.
63. Bechet, *Treat It Gentle,* 203.
64. "The Cricket," a, c.

1. Louis Armstrong and the Syntax of Scat

1. Boyd Atkins, "Heebie Jeebies" (Chicago: Consolidated Music Publishing House, 1926), 3–4. Sheet Music Collection, Music Division, New York Public Library for the Performing Arts. The sheet music was published after Armstrong's single, apparently in response to the record's popularity: it goes so far as to include a transcription of Armstrong's improvisation as a "'Skat' Chorus" (5), in which the piano accompaniment mirrors the melody and rhythm of Armstrong's scatting ("Skeep! Skipe! Skoop! Brip Ber Breep bar la bah"). At the same time the sheet music signals the inadequacy of its notation, glossing the transcription with the instruction that "Note: for correct interpretation of 'SKAT'CHORUS HEAR OKEH RECORD No. 8300." The discographical information for the recording is Louis Armstrong and His Hot Five, "Heebie Jeebies" (OKeh 8300, mx. 9534-A).
2. Louis Armstrong, "Jazz on a High Note," *Esquire,* December 1951, 85.
3. George Avakian, "Notes on Louis Armstrong and His Hot Five," *The Louis Armstrong Story,* vol. 1 (Columbia Records CL 851). Quoted in Stephen J. Casmier and Donald H. Matthews, "Why Scatting Is Like Speaking in Tongues: Post-Modern Reflections on Jazz, Pentecostalism and 'Africosmysticism,'" *Literature and Theology* 13, no. 2 (June 1999): 174. For other versions of this anecdote, see Hughes Panassié, *Louis Armstrong* (Paris: Les Nouvelles Editions Latines, 1969); Milton "Mezz" Mezzrow and Bernard Wolfe, *Really the Blues* (1946; repr., New York: Citadel Press, 1990), 119. The discographical information for the recording is Louis Armstrong and His Hot Five, "Heebie Jeebies," OKeh 8300, mx. 9534-A.
4. Richard Hadlock, *Jazz Masters of the Twenties* (New York: Collier, 1965), 26; Philippe Baudoin, "Introduction," *Anthology of Scat Singing,* vol. 1, *1924–1929* (Masters of Jazz MJCD 801, 1995), 19.
5. Other predecessors include a Chicago singer named Bo Diddly, as well as Gene Rodemich's June 1924 "Scissor Grinder Joe" and "Some of These Days," recorded by Coon and Sanders in November 1924. See also David Jasen, *Tin Pan Alley: The Composers, the Songs, the Performers and Their Times* (New York: Primus, Donald I. Fine, 1988), 6.
6. Will Friedwald, *Jazz Singing: America's Great Voices from Bessie Smith to Bebop and Beyond* (New York: Da Capo, 1996), 28, 16.
7. Alan Lomax, *Mister Jelly Roll* (1949; repr., New York: Pantheon, 1993), 156. Of course, even Morton's chronology is exaggerated, since Armstrong did not in fact enter the Colored Waif's Home for Boys in New Orleans until January 1913.
8. The *Oxford English Dictionary* defines the word *occasion* as meaning a "falling together or juncture of circumstances favourable or suitable to an end or purpose." Robert Creeley discusses poetics as occasion in this sense in his interview with William V. Spanos, "Talking with Robert Creeley," *Boundary 2* 6, no. 1 (Spring–Fall 1978): 19.
9. J. E. Lighter, ed., *Random House Historical Dictionary of American Slang* (New York: Random House Reference, 1994, 1997), 2:68.
10. I have located only a single issue of *Heebie-Jeebies: A Sign of Intelligence* still extant, in the Beinecke collection at Yale University (listed as volume 1, number 36, from August 1, 1925). The weekly, housed on Indiana Avenue in Chicago and edited by P. L. Prattis, actually predated Armstrong's recording; judging from the date, it commenced publication at the beginning of 1925. The magazine featured coverage of African American life both in

Chicago and elsewhere: political commentary; articles about prominent black figures of the day (Oscar de Priest, Nora Holt Ray, "Battling" Siki); listings for society dances, sports, sororities, and the events of black Chicago society. (The odd proposition of the title, reading "heebie-jeebies" as a [particularly African American?] "sign of intelligence," is not mentioned in the August 1925 issue.) It is unclear how long the journal was in publication, but at the end of 1926 A. Philip Randolph penned a lengthy rejoinder to an article in *Heebie-Jeebies* concerning the Pullman Porters. See Randolph, "Answering Heebie-Jeebies," *Messenger* 8, no. 2 (December 1926): 357–360.

11. Langston Hughes and Arna Bontemps, eds., *The Book of Negro Folklore* (New York: Dodd, Mead, 1958), 484. Mezzrow and Wolfe, *Really the Blues,* 374.
12. Mezzrow and Wolfe, *Really the Blues,* 212.
13. Gary Giddins defines scat as "improvised nonsense syllables" in *Visions of Jazz: The First Century* (New York: Oxford University Press, 1998), 86. The term is glossed as "singing in nonsense syllables" in Hughes and Bontemps, *Book of Negro Folklore,* 487. Similarly, Will Friedwald describes scatting as a "wordless performance, generally an improvised one," in *Jazz Singing,* xii. Charles O. Hartman explains it even more confusingly—"scat singing—the nonverbal imitation of jazz horn playing"—in *Jazz Text: Voice and Improvisation in Poetry, Jazz, and Song* (Princeton, NJ: Princeton University Press, 1991), 113. The *New Grove Dictionary of Jazz* speaks of "a technique of jazz singing in which onomatopoeic or nonsense syllables are sung to improvised melodies"; see Barry Kernfeld, ed., *New Grove Dictionary of Jazz* (New York: Macmillan, 1988), 2:425. And Clarence Major's *Juba to Jive: A Dictionary of African-American Slang* (New York: Viking Penguin, 1994) defines the word as "pure sounds without regard to their meaning" (399).
14. Roman Jakobson, "Language in Relation to Other Communication Systems," in *Linguaggi nella società e nella tecnica,* ed. Camillo Olivetti (Milan: Edizioni di Comunità, 1970), 12. The French is in the original.
15. On this recording, see Friedwald, *Jazz Singing,* 144. Paul Berliner also comments on quotation in jazz (both in scat singing and in instrumental performance) in his monumental *Thinking in Jazz: the Infinite Art of Improvisation* (Chicago: University of Chicago Press, 1994), 103–105.
16. Jean-Jacques Nattiez, *Music and Discourse: Toward a Semiology of Music,* trans. Carolyn Abbate (Princeton, NJ: Princeton University Press, 1990), 126, 127–128.
17. Ibid., 156.
18. Robert Walser, *Running with the Devil: Power, Gender, and Madness in Heavy Metal Music* (Hanover, CT: Wesleyan University Press, 1993), 28, 29. See also Susan McClary, *Conventional Wisdom: The Content of Musical Form* (Berkeley: University of California Press, 2000).
19. For an illustration of this point, chosen at random, compare the scat choruses of Betty Carter and Carmen McRae on their stunning recording of "Sometimes I'm Happy," *The Carmen McRae-Betty Carter Duets* (Great American Music Hall Records CD 2706–2, 1988). When the two singers exchange four-bar passages of scat, their "conversation" takes shape through a variety of phonemic choices and contrasts that gives the counterplay of their improvisations texture and rhetorical shape.
20. See Berliner, *Thinking in Jazz,* especially 201–205; Ingrid Monson, *Saying Something: Jazz Improvisation and Interaction* (Chicago: University of Chicago Press, 1996), especially 73–96; Brian Harker, "'Telling a Story': Louis Armstrong and Coherence in Early Jazz," *Current Musicology* 63 (1999): 46–83.
21. Billie Holiday with William Dufty, *Lady Sings the Blues* (1956; repr., New York: Penguin, 1984), 10. There is more to say about this passage. As my colleague Elin Diamond pointed out to me, it seems to link shifts in signification to reception ("the meaning used to change, depending on how I felt"), implying that scat's nonreferential syntax is channeled or recoded by a listener's affective disposition.
22. Nathaniel Mackey, *Bedouin Hornbook* (1986; repr., Los Angeles: Sun and Moon, 1993), 83.
23. N. comments that "inarticulacy spoke" (ibid., 182). Mackey's criticism takes up the notion of a "telling inarticulacy" in a number of instances; see, for example, Nathaniel Mackey,

"Sound and Sentiment, Sound and Symbol," in *Discrepant Engagement: Dissonance, Cross-Culturality, and Experimental Writing* (New York: Cambridge University Press, 1993), 253.

24. Mackey, "Sound and Sentiment," in *Discrepant Engagement,* 182–183.
25. Ibid., 63.
26. Ibid. Roland Barthes contends somewhat similarly that singing "rustles" a *utopia,* a no-place "of a music of meaning" where "language would be enlarged" and even "denatured" but without "meaning being brutally dismissed, dogmatically foreclosed." See Roland Barthes, "The Rustle of Language," in *The Rustle of Language,* trans. Richard Howard (New York: Hill and Wang, 1986), 77.
27. Albert Murray, *Stomping the Blues* (New York: Da Capo, 1976), 108, 114. Gunther Schuller makes a similar argument about music and speech in jazz (in relation to African drum languages) in his *Early Jazz: Its Roots and Musical Development* (New York: Oxford University Press, 1968), 5.
28. Clark Terry, "Mumbles," recorded in 1954, *Oscar Peterson Trio Plus One* (Mercury 60975); Clark Terry, "Trumpet Mouthpiece Blues," recorded July 1957, *Clark Terry Out on a Limb* (Argo LP 620).
29. Louis Armstrong, "The Armstrong Story" (ca. 1950s), Louis Armstrong House and Archives, Queens College/CUNY. See Louis Armstrong, "The Armstrong Story," in *Louis Armstrong, in His Own Words: Selected Writings,* ed. Thomas Brothers (Oxford: Oxford University Press, 1999), 52–53; Louis Armstrong, *Satchmo: My Life in New Orleans* (1955; repr., New York: Da Capo, 1986).
30. Mezzrow and Wolfe, *Really the Blues,* 220. On this subject, see also Neil Leonard, "The Jazzman's Verbal Usage," *Black American Literature Forum* 20, no. 12 (Spring–Summer 1986): 151–160.
31. Louis Armstrong and His Orchestra, "Sweet Sue (Just You)," recorded April 26, 1933 (Victor 24321).
32. See Slim Gaillard, Leo Watson, and Bam Brown, "The Avocado Seed Soup Symphony," AFRS "Jubilee" radio broadcast, December 1945, collected on *Leo Watson: The Original Scat Man* (Indigo Igo CD 2098, 1999).
33. Mezzrow and Wolfe, *Really the Blues,* 225.
34. Robert O'Meally, *The Jazz Singers* (Washington, DC: Smithsonian Collection of Recordings, 1998), 98.
35. Mezzrow and Wolfe, *Really the Blues,* 119.
36. Slim and Slam, "Chinatown, My Chinatown," recorded January 19, 1938 (mx. 22319.1); "Matzoh Balls," recorded October 4, 1939 (mx. w.26159-A); "African Jive," recorded July 24, 1941 (mx H.368–2), collected on *The Groove Juice Special* (Columbia CK 64898, 1996).
37. Calloway quoted in Dizzy Gillespie with Al Fraser, *To BE or Not . . . to BOP* (Garden City, NY: Doubleday, 1979), 111. Danny Barker also recounts this story in Nat Shapiro and Nat Hentoff, eds., *Hear Me Talkin' to Ya: The Story of Jazz as Told by the Men Who Made It* (New York: Dover Publications, 1955), 344.
38. Uncredited article, "Louis Armstrong Assails Bebop as Mere Technique," *Eve Leader,* July 13, 1949. Armstrong clippings file, Institute for Jazz Studies, Rutgers University. One anecdote claims that a different alterity was at the source of scat for Armstrong: his longtime friend Phoebe Jacobs heard him tell Cab Calloway that he got scat "from the Jews 'rockin,' he meant davening"—the stylized sway that accompanies prayer. Jacobs contends that "Louis never talked about this in public, because he feared people would assume he was making fun of Jews praying, which wasn't his intention at all." It is a fascinating connection (particularly given Armstrong's links to Jewish culture in his New Orleans childhood), even if it's more joking backstage banter than a discussion of performance technique, and even if it leaves open the rather complex question of Armstrong's "intention." See also Laurence Bergreen, *Louis Armstrong: An Extravagant Life* (New York: Broadway Books, 1997), 267–268.
39. Brian Harker has recently advanced the argument that most of these elements of scat singing actually coalesced in early jazz "novelty" and vaudeville *instrumental* performance. He of-

fers a reading of a 1923 book called *The Novelty Cornetist,* by a well-known musician named Louis Panico, who "gives detailed explanations and illustrations of such performance gimmicks as 'the laugh,' 'the sneeze,' 'the horse neigh,' 'the baby cry,' and the 'Chinese effect.'" In this light one might argue that the aesthetic continuum I have outlined is constitutive in the music; the key issue here would seem to be the music's negotiation of a politics of representation. One would have to consider a number of examples in this regard: Harker cites "naturalist" tunes like the Original Dixieland Jazz Band's "Livery Stable Blues" (1917) and "Bow Wow Blues" (1921), and Jelly Roll Morton's "Sidewalk Blues" (1926). Other sources on the period look elsewhere: trumpeter Rex Stewart describes his own fascination with Johnny Dunn, the "Ragtime King of the Trumpet," who would imitate a horse whinnying and a rooster crowing on his horn. See Harker, "Telling a Story," 48–49; Rex Stewart, *Boy Meets Horn,* ed. Claire P. Gordon (Ann Arbor: University of Michigan Press, 1991), 47.

40. Regarding the musical epigraphs, see Eric J. Sundquist, *To Wake the Nations: Race in the Making of American Literature* (Cambridge, MA: Harvard University Press, 1993), 492–493.
41. See, for example, W. E. B. Du Bois, *Dusk of Dawn: An Essay toward An Autobiography of a Race Concept* (1940), in *Writings*, ed. Nathan Huggins (New York: Library of America, 1986), 638; and W. E. B. Du Bois, *The Autobiography of W. E. B. Du Bois: A Soliloquy on Viewing My Life from the Last Decade of Its First Century* (New York: International Publishers, 1968), 62.
42. Du Bois, *The Souls of Black Folk*, in *Writings,* 538–539.
43. David Levering Lewis, *W. E. B. Du Bois: Biography of a Race, 1868–1919* (New York: Henry Holt, 1993), 15. Lewis notes that the lyric still defies the attempts of linguists to find sources or translations. He notes one possible source in Senegambian song of captivity (585n7).
44. Du Bois, *The Souls of Black Folk*, in *Writings,* 541.
45. Gary Giddins, "Louis Armstrong (The Once and Future King)," in *Visions of Jazz,* 86.
46. Zora Neale Hurston, "Spirituals and Neo-Spirituals," in *Folklore, Memoirs, & Other Writings*, ed. Cheryl Wall (New York: Library of America, 1995), 872. The musical examples include Armstrong, "Lazy River," recorded in Chicago on November 3, 1931 (OKeh 41541, mx. W 405058–4); "Stardust," recorded November 3, 1931 (OKeh 41530, mx. W 405061–1); "All of Me," recorded January 27, 1932 (OKeh 41552, mx. 405133-A).
47. On the meaning of obbligato in jazz, see Michael Jarrett, *Soundtracks: A Musical ABC Vols. 1–3* (Philadelphia: Temple University Press, 1998), 258.
48. See Nathaniel Mackey, "Cante Moro," in *Disembodied Poetics: Annals of the Jack Kerouac School,* ed. Anne Waldman and A. Schelling (Albuquerque: University of New Mexico Press, 1994), 78.
49. Wesley Brown, *Tragic Magic* (1978; repr., New York: Ecco Press, 1995), 5.
50. Gayelord Hauser, *Diet Does It* (New York: Coward-McCann, 1944); Hauser, *New Guide to Intelligent Reducing: How to Reduce and Stay Reduced for Life* (New York: Farrar, Straus and Young, 1955).
51. "Lose Weight the Satchmo Way," in Joshua Berrett, ed., *The Louis Armstrong Companion: Eight Decades of Commentary* (New York: Schirmer Books, 1999), 99–102. The Christmas card is reproduced in Gary Giddins, *Satchmo* (New York: Doubleday, 1988), 189.
52. Armstrong, *Satchmo,* 20.
53. Armstrong, "The Satchmo Story," in *Louis Armstrong, in His Own Words,* 114–115. The ellipses in brackets mark omissions; other ellipses are Armstrong's.
54. Martin Pops quotes Luther's narrative of achieving spiritual enlightenment while on the toilet; see Martin Pops, "The Metamorphosis of Shit," *Salmagundi* 56 (Spring 1982): 30. Sigmund Freud, "Character and Anal Eroticism," in *Character and Culture,* ed. Philip Rieff (New York: Macmillan, 1963), 29.
55. See Pops, "The Metamorphosis of Shit," 36. The anecdote concerning this title is recounted in Richard Ellman, *James Joyce,* rev. ed. (New York: Oxford University Press, 1983), 154.
56. Armstrong, letter to Joe Glaser (September 8, 1955), Music Division, Library of Congress.
57. Armstrong, "Lose Weight the Satchmo Way," in *The Louis Armstrong Companion,* 102.

58. Armstrong, "Louis Armstrong+the Jewish Family in New Orleans, LA., the Year of 1907" (1969–1970), Louis Armstrong Archives, Queens College/CUNY, in Brothers, *Louis Armstrong in His Own Words,* 35–36.
59. Quoted in Albert Murray, "Jazz Lips," *New Republic* 221, no. 21 (November 1999): 34.
60. In a more serious mood, he told another interviewer: "Got to get all those impurities out every day. That's my success. I mean, I don't try to be more than anybody, no better than anybody. I just want to stay among them, make that gig." See Richard Meryman, interview with Armstrong, *Life* (April 15, 1966), collected as Armstrong, *Louis Armstrong—a Self-Portrait* (New York: Eakins Press, 1971), 52.
61. Panassié, *Louis Armstrong,* 55.
62. Giddins, *Satchmo,* 14.
63. Dan Morgenstern, "Introduction," in Armstrong, *Satchmo,* ix.
64. Ibid., x. Some examples of writings published with careful attention to Armstrong's stylistic idiosyncrasies include Louis Armstrong, "Special Jive," *Harlem Tattler,* July 2, 1940, 7; Armstrong, "Special Jive," *Harlem Tattler,* July 19, 1940, 7, 19; "Louis and Letters," *Metronome,* April 1945, 48; "Chicago, Chicago, That Toddlin' Town: How King and Ol' Satch Dug It in the Twenties," *Esquire's Jazz Book* (1947): 40–43; Armstrong, "Europe—with Kicks," *Holiday* (June 1950): 11–13, 14, 16, 18, 20; "Ulceratedly Yours; Louis Armstrong," *Down Beat* 17, no. 4 (July 1950): 1, 19; "Jazz on a High Note," *Esquire,* December 1951, 85, 209–212. See the bibliography of Armstrong writings in Brothers, *Louis Armstrong, in His Own Words,* 221–224.
65. Brothers, "'Swing a Lot of Type Writing': An Introduction to Louis Armstrong," in *Louis Armstrong, in His Own Words,* xiii.
66. Armstrong, letter to Madeleine Berard (November 25, 1946), Louis Armstrong Archives, Letters-3, 1/6, Queens College. This letter is partially reprinted (with a number of unaccountable omissions and errors of transcription) in Berrett, *Louis Armstrong Companion,* 128–129.
67. Armstrong, letter to Mrs. Frances Church (March 10, 1946). Institute for Jazz Studies, Rutgers University.
68. Giddins, *Satchmo,* 23.
69. Armstrong, "The Armstrong Story" (ca. 1950s), Louis Armstrong House and Archives, Queens College/CUNY. Reprinted in Brothers, *Louis Armstrong, in His Own Words,* 49.
70. Armstrong, Letter to Joe Glaser (August 2, 1955), Library of Congress, collected in Brothers, *Louis Armstrong, in His Own Words,* 158–163.
71. Consider Friedrich A. Kittler's comment: "As a doubled spatialization of writing—first on the keyboard, then on the white paper—[the typewriter] imparts to texts an optimal optical appearance"; see Friedrich A. Kittler, *Gramophone, Film, Typewriter,* trans. Geoffrey Winthrop-Young and Michael Wutz (Stanford, CA: Stanford University Press, 1999), 228.
72. Baraka writes: "I'd have magnetically recorded . . . & translated into word—or perhaps even the final thought/feeling wd not be merely word or sheet, but *itself,* the xpression, three dimensional—able to be touched, or tasted or felt, or entered, or heard or carried like a speaking singing constantly communicating charm. *A typewriter is corny!*" See LeRoi Jones (Amiri Baraka), "Technology & Ethos," in *Raise Race Rays Raze* (New York: Vintage, 1971), 156.
73. See Kamau Brathwaite, *Conversations with Nathaniel Mackey* (Staten Island, NY: We Press/Xcp:Cross-Cultural Poetics, 1999); Stewart Brown, "Interview with Edward Kamau Brathwaite," *Kyk-Over-Al* 38 (June 1988): 84–93; Kamau Brathwaite, "Newstead to Neustadt," *World Literature Today* 68, no. 4 (Autumn 1994): 656–658.
74. Brothers, "Introduction," in *Louis Armstrong, in His Own Words,* xiv.
75. Ibid., xv, xiii. See also ibid., xiv; Brothers is right to depart from Kenney in reading all unconventional punctuation as indication of "irony," a "distance from the meanings of words."
76. Ibid., xiv, xv.
77. Armstrong, letter to Joe Glaser (August 2, 1955), Music Division, Library of Congress, collected in Brothers, *Louis Armstrong, in His Own Words,* 159. Armstrong tells the same story

elsewhere (not always attributing the advice to Black Benny), in ways that might help explain some of what seems to be an odd racial subservience in the letter to Glaser. In one interview in the late 1960s, he recalls that a group of black musicians playing one-nighters in Mississippi had been chased after a show and beaten with chains and knives by a group of white men, who hours earlier had been in the club dancing. Armstrong is disgusted by this practice of "nigger knocking" ("No reason—except they was so goddamn miserable they had to mess everybody else up, ya dig? *Peckerwoods!* Oh, this world's mothered some mean sons!"). But he contends that the militancy of the younger generation of African American men was simply not an available response in the context of such ever-present racial violence in earlier years: "If you didn't have a white captain to back you in the old days—to put his hand on your shoulder—you was just a damn sad nigger. If a Negro had the proper white man to reach the law and say, 'What the hell you mean locking up MY nigger?' then—quite naturally—the law would walk him free. Get in that jail *without* your white boss, and yonder comes the chain gang! Oh, danger was dancing all around you back then." The perspective here is less obsequious than pragmatic. (He segues directly from this story to explain the utility of his relationship with his manager Joe Glaser.) See Larry L. King, "Everybody's Louie," *Harper's Magazine* (November 1967): 67.

78. Brothers, *Louis Armstrong, in His Own Words,* 163.
79. Jed Rasula, "Understanding the Sound of Not Understanding," in *Close Listening: Poetry and the Performed Word,* ed. Charles Bernstein (New York: Oxford University Press, 1998), 242.
80. Murray, "Jazz Lips," 32, 30.
81. Giddins, *Satchmo,* 14.
82. Giddins, *Visions of Jazz,* 87.
83. Giddins, *Satchmo,* 111.
84. Ibid., 36. I have elided part of this quote because Giddins misreads one of the Armstrong manuscripts, arguing that Louis writes of Bill "Bojangles" Robinson as "comedian and danger in my race," and then extrapolating on the importance of a "threatening" physicality in Armstrong's aesthetic. In fact, as Thomas Brothers points out, it is much more likely that the portrait of Bojangles refers to him as a "comedian and *dancer.*" See Brothers, *Louis Armstrong, in His Own Words,* 193.
85. Giddins, *Satchmo,* 26.
86. Krin Gabbard, *Jammin' at the Margins: Jazz and the American Cinema* (Chicago: University of Chicago Press, 1996), 211.
87. Giddins, *Satchmo,* 26.
88. Nathaniel Mackey, *Dbjot Baghostus's Run* (Los Angeles: Sun and Moon, 1993), 154. This book is the second volume in his series entitled *From a Broken Bottle Traces of Perfume Still Emanate,* of which *Bedouin Hornbook* is the first.
89. Ibid., 155.
90. Quoted in Linda Prince, "Betty Carter: Bebopper Breathes Fire," *Down Beat,* May 1979, 13.
91. The phrase "accompaniments of the utterance" is taken from J. L. Austin, *Lecture VI, How to Do Things with Words* (1955; repr., Cambridge, MA: Harvard University Press, 1975), 76. I thank Fred Moten for directing me to this source. If scat mobilizes the index in particular, one would have to discuss scat as "improvisation" by taking into account the way that the index is temporally contingent: since a deictic gesture is registered in time, the index has what Rosalind Krauss calls "an existential connection to meaning, with the result that it can only take place on the spot"; see Rosalind Krauss, "Michel, Bataille et moi," *October* 68 (Spring 1994): 13. In writing, however, indexicality carries a temporal connotation but is not temporally contingent. The "on the spot" indicator can be added *after the fact*—thus Armstrong's predilection for inserting handwritten apostrophes and underlining to his letters in revising them.
92. Ralph Ellison, *Invisible Man* (1952; repr., New York: Harper and Row, 1989), 7. One can approach a reading of the famous reference to Armstrong in the prologue to *Invisible Man* only by taking up issues of indexicality. The unnamed narrator says that he plans to have

not just one but *five* phonographs in his basement "hole," playing Armstrong's version of "What Did I Do to Be So Black and Blue" "all at the same time" (6). This desire both calls for a certain intensification of listening ("when I have music I want to *feel* its vibration, not only with my ear but with my whole body") and parallels the room's excessive illumination (it is wired with 1,369 lightbulbs), thus extending a playful critique of the optical figures of Enlightenment metaphysics. But the call for amplification may be less about simply increasing the sonic volume and more about stressing a simultaneity and potential multiplicity of signification in the music—the "slightly different sense of time" it articulates, in which the listener can "slip into the breaks and look around" (7).

2. Toward a Poetics of Transcription

1. Ralph Ellison, "Richard Wright's Blues," in *Shadow and Act* (New York: Vintage, 1964), 78.
2. See Arnold Rampersad, *Ralph Ellison: A Biography* (New York: Knopf, 2007), 25–29, 47–80; and generally Ralph Ellison, *Living with Music: Ralph Ellison's Jazz Writings,* ed. Robert G. O'Meally (New York: Modern Library, 2002), especially the 1976 interview "Ralph Ellison's Territorial Vantage" (15–33).
3. James Baldwin, "The Uses of the Blues," in *The Cross of Redemption: Uncollected Writings,* ed. Randall Kenan (New York: Vintage, 2010), 70, 73.
4. Ellison, "Richard Wright's Blues," in *Shadow and Act,* 79.
5. See, for instance, the entry on *lyric* in the *Princeton Encyclopedia of Poetry and Poetics,* where James William Johnson writes that lyric poetry "may be said to retain most pronouncedly the elements of poetry which evidence its origins in musical expression . . . the musical element is intrinsic to the work intellectually as well as aesthetically." See James William Johnson, "Lyric," in *The New Princeton Encyclopedia of Poetry and Poetics,* ed. Alex Preminger and T. V. F. Brogan (Princeton, NJ: Princeton University Press, 1993), 713.
6. Craig Dworkin usefully points out that "music of course encompasses a range of works more expansive than the classical and Romantic imagination of the pleasant, mellifluous, or affecting" in "The Poetry of Sound," *PMLA* 123, no. 3 (May 2008): 759. See also the special section on "The New Lyric Studies," ed. Virginia Jackson, *PMLA* 123, no. 1 (January 2008): 181–234. Lytle Shaw points out the dearth of scholarship on African diasporic poetics in his review essay "Framing the Lyric," *American Literary History* 28, no. 2 (2016): 405, in which he considers some of the most influential current contributors to these debates: Virginia Jackson and Yopie Prins, eds., *The Lyric Theory Reader: A Critical Anthology* (Baltimore, MD: Johns Hopkins University Press, 2014); Gillian White, *Lyric Shame: The "Lyric" Subject of American Poetry* (Cambridge, MA: Harvard University Press, 2014); and Jonathan D. Culler, *Theory of the Lyric* (Cambridge, MA: Harvard University Press, 2015).
7. Sterling Brown, "The Blues as Folk Poetry," in *Folk-Say: A Regional Miscellany,* ed. B. A. Botkin (Norman: University of Oklahoma Press, 1930), 335.
8. Indirection is not coincidentally one of the key qualities of the lyric identified by Jonathan Culler (see *Theory of the Lyric*).
9. One study that approaches the history of modernist American literature (including but not limited to Harlem Renaissance poetry and prose) from such a perspective is T. Austin Graham's fine *The Great American Songbooks: Modernism, Musical Texts, and the Value of Popular Culture* (New York: Oxford University Press, 2012).
10. James Weldon Johnson, "Preface to the First Edition" (1922), in *The Book of American Negro Poetry,* ed. James Weldon Johnson (New York: Harcourt Brace Jovanovich, 1959), 19; James Weldon Johnson, "Preface to the Revised Edition" (1931), in *The Book of American Negro Poetry* (New York: Harcourt Brace Jovanovich, 1959), 6.
11. Langston Hughes, "The Negro Artist and the Racial Mountain," *Nation* 122, no. 3131 (June 1926): 692, 694.
12. Louis Zukofsky, "A Statement for Poetry," in *Prepositions: The Collected Critical Essays of Louis Zukofsky* (Berkeley: University of California Press, 1981), 19.
13. Zukofsky, "An Objective," in *Prepositions,* 16.

14. Kimberly Benston, "Performing Blackness: Re/Placing Afro-American Poetry," in *Afro-American Literary Study in the 1990s,* ed. Houston A. Baker Jr. (Chicago: University of Chicago Press, 1989), 165.
15. Caroline Levine, *Forms: Whole, Rhythm, Hierarchy, Network* (Princeton, NJ: Princeton University Press, 2015), 3.
16. See Slavoj Žižek, *Tarrying with the Negative: Kant, Hegel, and the Critique of Ideology* (Durham, NC: Duke University Press, 1993), 135; Henri Focillon, *The Life of Forms in Art (1934),* trans. Charles B. Hogan and George Kubler (New York: Zone Books, 1989), 34–35.
17. Christopher Funkhouser, "Being Matter Ignited: An Interview with Cecil Taylor," *Hambone* 12 (Fall 1995): 29.
18. Nat Hentoff, "The Persistent Challenge of Cecil Taylor," *Down Beat,* February 25, 1965, 17.
19. Eric Sundquist, *To Wake the Nations: Race in the Making of American Literature* (Cambridge, MA: Harvard University Press, 1993), 309–311.
20. Sherley Anne Williams, "The Blues Roots of Contemporary Afro-American Poetry," in *Afro-American Literature: The Reconstruction of Instruction,* ed. Dexter Fisher and Robert Stepto (New York: MLA, 1979), 72.
21. Ibid., 73.
22. Henry Louis Gates Jr., "Literary Theory and the Black Tradition," in *Figures in Black: Words, Signs, and the "Racial" Self* (New York: Oxford University Press, 1987), 34.
23. Stephen Henderson, *Understanding the New Black Poetry: Black Speech and Black Music as Poetic References* (New York: William Morrow, 1973), 61.
24. James Weldon Johnson, "Preface," in *The Book of American Negro Poetry*, 41.
25. Ibid.
26. Ibid., 6.
27. James Weldon Johnson and J. Rosamond Johnson, eds., *The Books of American Negro Spirituals* (New York: Viking, 1940), 2:19. This edition is a single-volume reprint of two anthologies originally published separately: *The Book of American Negro Spirituals* in 1925 and *The Second Book of Negro Spirituals* in 1926. The reprint edition retains the separate pagination of the two volumes. Subsequent references to these texts will be given parenthetically in the text as BANS I and BANS II, followed by the page number.
28. It should be apparent that this chapter takes up and extends the argument I make in Chapter 1 ("Variations on a Preface") in my book *The Practice of Diaspora: Literature, Translation, and the Rise of Black Internationalism* (Cambridge, MA: Harvard University Press, 2003). There I suggest that the explosion of anthologies and prefaced works on "Negro" subjects in the 1920s marks an effort to define and frame black culture, an effort that becomes central to the formulation of Western modernity in general. On the one hand, the larger argument juxtaposes works like James Weldon Johnson's *The Autobiography of an Ex-Colored Man* and *The Book of American Negro Poetry,* Claude McKay's *Harlem Shadows,* Blaise Cendrars's *Anthologie Nègre,* and René Maran's *Batouala* to point out that such a struggle is transatlantic, and that even when seemingly limited to a particular nation-space, such prefaces consistently involve a vision of an African diaspora stretching beyond nation and language. On the other hand, it considers the politics of such framing gestures, and suggests that to a large degree they operate on the level of *form,* using the relationship between preface and text to represent and to situate black expressive culture to various ends.
29. Regarding the controversies provoked by Hughes's early poetry, especially his second book *Fine Clothes to the Jew* (1927), see Arnold Rampersad, *The Life of Langston Hughes,* vol. 1, *1902–1941: I, Too, Sing America* (New York: Oxford University Press, 1986), 140; Henry Louis Gates Jr. and K. A. Appiah, eds., *Langston Hughes: Critical Perspectives Past and Present* (New York: Amistad, 1993), 60ff.; and Langston Hughes, *The Big Sea* (New York: Hill and Wang, 1940), 264.
30. Hughes explains in his autobiography *The Big Sea* that the poem "included the first blues verse I'd ever heard way back in Lawrence, Kansas, when I was a kid" (215). A number of singers recorded songs called "The Weary Blues" (although with different lyrics); and Steven C. Tracy has noted the similarity between the song lyrics quoted in the poem and

certain recorded blues in the period, such as Henry Thomas's 1928 "Texas Worried Blues"; see Steven C. Tracy, *Langston Hughes and the Blues* (Urbana: University of Illinois Press, 1988). Ma Rainey did not actually record the "Backwater Blues" herself, although Bessie Smith's 1927 classic has been covered (and sometimes, revised) by any number of singers, including Lonnie Johnson, Lead Belly, Big Bill Broonzy, Dinah Washington, and Lighnin' Hopkins. Regarding the 1927 flood, see Richard M. Mizelle Jr., *Backwater Blues: The Mississippi Flood of 1927 in the African American Imagination* (Minneapolis: University of Minnesota Press, 2014); John Barry, *Rising Tide: The Great Mississippi Flood of 1927 and How It Changed America* (New York: Simon and Schuster, 1997).

31. Sterling A. Brown, "Ma Rainey," in *Southern Road* (1932), collected in Michael S. Harper, ed., *The Collected Poems of Sterling A. Brown* (New York: Harper and Row, 1980), 63.
32. Brown, "Ma Rainey," collected in *Collected Poems of Sterling A. Brown,* 62.
33. Henry Edward Krehbiel, *Afro-American Folksongs: A Study in Racial and National Music* (New York: G. Schirmer, 1913). Natalie Curtis-Burlin, *Hampton Series of Negro Folk-Songs* (New York: G. Schirmer, 1918). The other most important work on the spirituals from a musicological standpoint was published around the same time as Johnson's collection: Nicholas Ballanta-Taylor, *Saint Helena Island Spirituals* (New York: G. Schirmer, 1925). For criticism on the debates around the origins of the Negro spiritual, see D. K. Wilgus, "Appendix: The Negro-White Spiritual," in *Anglo-American Folksong Scholarship since 1898*, ed. D. K. Wilgus (New Brunswick, NJ: Rutgers University Press, 1959), 345–407; Jon Cruz, *Culture on the Margins: The Black Spiritual and the Rise of American Cultural Interpretation* (Princeton, NJ: Princeton University Press, 1999); and Ronald Radano, *Lying Up a Nation: Race and Black Music* (Chicago: University of Chicago Press, 2003).
34. Jay Wright, "Desire's Design, Vision's Resonance: Black Poetry's Ritual and Historical Voice," *Callaloo* 10, no. 1 (Winter 1987): 21.
35. See Leroi Jones (Amiri Baraka), "Swing—from Verb to Noun," in Baraka, *Blues People: Negro Music in White America* (New York: William Morrow, 1963), 142–165; Nathaniel Mackey, "Other: From Noun to Verb," in *Discrepant Engagement: Dissonance, Cross-Culturality, and Experimental Writing* (Cambridge: Cambridge University Press, 1993), 265–286.
36. Mackey, "Other," in *Discrepant Engagement,* 266.
37. Toni Morrison, *Sula* (1973; repr., New York: Vintage, 1982), 35, 18.
38. Zora Neale Hurston, "Spirituals and Neo-Spirituals" (1934), collected in Zora Neale Hurston, *Folklore, Memoirs, & Other Writings* (New York: Library of America, 1995), 871.
39. James Weldon Johnson, *Along This Way* (New York: Viking, 1933), 338. Subsequent references will be given parenthetically in the text with the indication AW, followed by the page number.
40. Hurston writes: "Negro spirituals are not solo or quartette material. The jagged harmony is what makes it, and it ceases to be what it was when this is absent. Neither can any group by trained to reproduce it. Its truth dies under training like flowers under hot water. The harmony of the true spiritual is not regular. The dissonances are important and not to be ironed out by the trained musician. The various parts break in at any old time" ("Spirituals and Neo-Spirituals," 870). Compare her comments with those of Johnson in the *Book of American Negro Spirituals:* "Negroes harmonize instinctively.... The voices of Negroes, when untrained, are often overloud, perhaps rather blatant, sometimes even a bit strident; but they are *never discordant.* In harmony they take on an orchestra-like timbre.... Pick up four colored boys or young men anywhere and the chances are ninety out of a hundred that you have a quartet" (BANS I 35–36).
41. Eric Sundquist, among others, reads such uncertainty as failure. For Sundquist, Johnson's rhetoric "unites populism and elitism," shuffling between the two. One moment, Johnson writes that "Whatever new thing the *people* like is pooh-pooed; whatever is *popular* is spoken of as not worth the while. The fact is, nothing great or enduring, especially in music, has ever sprung full-fledged and unprecedented from the brain of any master; the best that he gives to the world he gathers from the hearts of the people, and runs it through the alembic

of his genius"; see James Weldon Johnson, *Autobiography of an Ex-Colored Man* (1912; repr., New York: Penguin Classics, 1990), 73. And then he turns the other way, emphasizing the *individual* creators of the spirituals rather than the masses, like "Ma" White and "Singing" Johnson (BANS 21ff.). Sundquist characterizes this wavering as a "residual aesthetic distrust of the folk" in Johnson; see Eric Sundquist, *Hammers of Creation: Folk Culture in Modern African-American Fiction* (Athens: University of Georgia Press, 1992), 24. I am suggesting that there may be another, productive potential in such ambivalence.

42. Nathaniel Mackey, "Sound and Sentiment, Sound and Symbol," in *Discrepant Engagement,* 253.
43. Stephen Slemon, "Interview with Wilson Harris (April 28, 1986)," *Ariel* 19 (July 1988): 48.
44. Žižek, *Tarrying with the Negative,* 135.
45. James Weldon Johnson, *God's Trombones: Seven Negro Sermons in Verse* (New York: Vintage, 1927), 5.
46. Ibid., 6–7.
47. Since he is thinking in terms of musical form offering a figure of the black body, it also may be that Johnson is thinking of the trombone as an especially *physical* instrument. Consider jazz dancer and critic Roger Pryor Dodge's comments on trombone style in jazz: "The Negro trombone player has become a sort of dancer in the rhythmic play of his right arm. He makes this instrument live, by improvising solos as natural to a trombone as the simplest of folk tunes are to the voice. This cannot be said of the trombone in any other music save jazz"; see Roger Pryor Dodge, "Harpsichords and Jazz Trumpets," *Hound and Horn* (July–September 1934), collected in Roger Pryor Dodge, *Hot Jazz and Jazz Dance* (New York: Oxford University Press, 1995), 19.
48. Duke Ellington, *Music Is My Mistress* (New York: Da Capo, 1973), 108–109.
49. Edward Kamau Brathwaite, "The African Presence in Caribbean Literature" (1970–73), collected in Brathwaite, *Roots* (Ann Arbor: University of Michigan Press, 1993), 211–212.
50. See Johnson, "Preface," 39–40; I discuss Johnson's move "a little afield" in *Practice of Diaspora,* 47–49.
51. Henry Louis Gates Jr., *The Signifying Monkey: A Theory of Afro-American Literary Criticism* (New York: Oxford University Press, 1988), 251.
52. Johnson, *God's Trombones,* 10–11.
53. Langston Hughes, *Fine Clothes to the Jew* (New York: Alfred A. Knopf, 1927), 83.
54. Benston, "Performing Blackness," in *Afro-American Literary Study in the 1990s,* 167.
55. Ibid., 183.
56. Ibid., 184.
57. This doubleness or ambiguity between transcription and score is also apparent in some of Hughes's later works, most notably the 1961 book-length suite *Ask Your Mama: 12 Moods for Jazz,* which likewise includes elements of a *score,* anticipating realization in future performance (such as the "leitmotif" from the "Hesitation Blues" and the "figurine" riff "Shave and a Haircut," both given in musical notation for an instrumentalist to accompany the poet in recital; as well as the descriptive "gloss" indications in italicized language running down the right side of the pages of the poem, again framed as instructions to a musical accompanist), as well as a *recording,* the result of a prior performance (such as the "Liner Notes for the Poetically Unhep" that follow the body of the suite like liner notes to accompany a commercial LP). Langston Hughes, *The Collected Works of Langston Hughes,* vol. 3, *The Poems: 1951–1967,* ed. Arnold Rampersad (Columbia: University of Missouri Press, 2001), 79–125. Hughes did in fact perform the suite with musicians, and he told one interviewer that "the music should not only be a background to the poetry, but should comment on it. I tell the musicians—and I've worked with several different modern and traditional groups—to improvise as much as they care around what I read. Whatever they bring of themselves to the poetry is welcome to me. I merely suggest the mood of each piece as a general orientation. Then I listen to what they say in their playing, and that affects my own rhythms when I read. We listen to each other"; quoted in Steven C. Tracy, "Poetry, Blues, and Gospel," in *Langston Hughes: The Man, His Art, and His Continuing Influence,* ed. C. James Trotman (New York: Garland, 1995), 56–57.

58. Obviously I do not mean that a blues poem *cannot* be put to music; some of Hughes's blues poems were indeed recorded by singers. To reiterate: I am trying here to get at the effect of the blues poem *on the page* as a literary artifact that exists in inextricable relation to the music it seems to point to, yet does not deliver. Incidentally, there is captivating documentation of the musical potential of Hughes's blues poems in the correspondence between Hughes and Zora Neale Hurston. In the spring and summer of 1928, when Hurston was doing fieldwork among black labor communities (railroad camps, lumber yards, phosphate mines) in the rural South, she took copies of *Fine Clothes to the Jew* with her and found to her delight that her interlocutors enjoyed Hughes's poems "immensely." The workers called Hughes's volume "De Party Book," Hurston writes in one letter, and adds: "They sing the poems right off, and July 1, two men came over with guitars and sang the whole book. Everybody joined in. It was the strangest and most *thrilling* thing. They played it well too. You'd be surprised. One man was giving the words out—lining them out as the preacher does a hymn and the others would take it up and sing. It was glorious!" See Hurston, letter to Hughes, July 10, 1928, collected in Carla Kaplan, ed., *Zora Neale Hurston: A Life in Letters* (New York: Doubleday, 2002), 121.
59. George Kent, "Langston Hughes and the Afro-American Folk and Cultural Tradition," in *Langston Hughes: Black Genius,* ed. Therman B. O'Daniel (New York: William Morrow, 1971).
60. In Northrup Frye's words, this is a "sentimental" use of music as opposed to a "technical" use of the term. See Frye, *Anatomy of Criticism* (Princeton, NJ: Princeton University Press, 1957), 255–256).
61. William Carlos Williams, "On Measure—Statement for Cid Corman," in *Selected Essays* (New York: New Directions, 1954), 337.
62. Robert Duncan, "Notes on Poetics Regarding Olson's *Maximus,*" in *Fictive Certainties* (New York: Norton, 1985), 69; Edward Kamau Brathwaite, "History of the Voice," in *Roots* (Ann Arbor: University of Michigan Press, 1993), 264. Monchoachi, "Quelle langue parle le poete?" ("What language does the poet speak?"), postface to *Nuit Gagée* (*Wagered Night*) (Paris: L'Harmattan, 1992), 66.
63. Slemon, "Interview with Wilson Harris," 47.
64. Henri Focillon, *The Life of Forms in Art (1948),* trans. Charles B. Hogan and George Kubler (Cambridge: Zone Books, 1989), 62.
65. See, for example, Paul De Man, "Anthropomorphism and Trope in Lyric," in *The Rhetoric of Romanticism* (New York: Columbia University Press, 1984), 239–262; Jonathan Culler, "Apostrophe," *diacritics* 7, no. 4 (December 1977): 59–69.
66. Culler, "Apostrophe," 66.
67. Ibid., 67. This passage also appears in the expanded and revised version of the *diacritics* article included in Culler, *Theory of the Lyric,* 227.
68. De Man, "Anthropomorphism," 254.
69. Nathaniel Mackey, "Interview by Edward Foster" (1992), collected in *Paracritical Hinge: Essays, Talks, Notes, Interviews* (Madison: University of Wisconsin Press, 2005), 268.
70. Frye, *Anatomy of Criticism,* 272.
71. On Guillén's adoption of the popular musical form of the *son* (and his interactions with Hughes), see especially William Scott, "Motivos de Translation," *New Centennial Review* 5, no. 2 (2005): 35–71; and Vera M. Kutzinski, "Havana Vernaculars: The *Cuba Libre* Project," in *The Worlds of Langston Hughes: Modernism and Translation in the Americas* (Ithaca, NY: Cornell University Press, 2012), 132–183. One wide-ranging and insightful attempt to track the African American poetic tradition across such an expanse is Meta DuEwa Jones's *The Muse Is Music: Jazz Poetry from the Harlem Renaissance to Spoken Word* (Urbana: University of Illinois Press, 2011).
72. Jeanette Robinson Murphy, "The Survival of African Music in America," in *The Negro and His Folklore in Nineteenth-Century Periodicals,* ed. Bruce Jackson (Austin: University of Texas Press, 1967), 329.
73. Sundquist, *To Wake the Nations,* 473, 531.

74. See Nathaniel Mackey, *Bedouin Hornbook* (1986; repr., Los Angeles: Sun and Moon, 1997), 48.
75. Wilson Harris, "The Writer and Society," in *Tradition, the Writer and Society* (London: Beacon, 1967), 52.
76. Paul Gilroy, *The Black Atlantic: Modernity and Double Consciousness* (Cambridge, MA: Harvard University Press, 1993), 36.

3. The Literary Ellington

1. James Baldwin, "Many Thousands Gone," *Partisan Review,* November–December 1951, collected in James Baldwin, *Collected Essays,* ed. Toni Morrison (New York: Library of America, 1998), 19.
2. Leroi Jones (Amiri Baraka), "The Myth of a 'Negro Literature,'" in Baraka, *Home: Social Essays* (New York: William Morrow, 1966), 106–107.
3. Duke Ellington, "The Duke Steps Out," *Rhythm,* March 1931, 20–22, collected in Mark Tucker, ed., *The Duke Ellington Reader* (New York: Oxford University Press, 1993), 49.
4. Ibid.
5. Ibid.
6. Ibid. This is not the only such reference. In 1930 a Manhattan reporter wrote: "At present [Ellington] is at work on a tremendous task, the writing, in music, of 'The History of the Negro,' taking the Negro from Egypt, going with him to savage Africa, and from there to the sorrow and slavery of Dixie, and finally 'home to Harlem'"; see Florence Zunser, "'Opera Must Die,' Says Galli-Curci! Long Live the Blues!" *New York Evening Graphic Magazine,* December 27, 1930, collected in Tucker, *Duke Ellington Reader,* 45.
7. Ellington, "The Duke Steps Out," 49.
8. The works in question are Roi Ottley, *New World A-Comin': Inside Black America* (Boston: Houghton Mifflin, 1943); Peter Abrahams, *Mine Boy* (1946; repr. London: Heineman, 1989); John Steinbeck, *Sweet Thursday* (New York: Viking, 1954). See Ellington's own description of the impetus for *New World A-Comin'* in Duke Ellington, *Music Is My Mistress* (Garden City, NY: Doubleday, 1973), 183. Subsequent page citations from this work will be cited parenthetically in the text with the initials MM, followed by the page numbers.
9. A number of these texts are available: *The Golden Broom and the Green Apple* (MM 200); *The River* (MM 201–2); "Program Outline for the Sacred Concert" (MM 270–79); *My People* (1963), eight-page typescript, Subseries 4B: Scripts, Box 8, Folder 7, Duke Ellington Collection, Archives Center, National Museum of American History, Smithsonian Institution.
10. Barry Ulanov, "The Ellington Programme," in *This Is Jazz,* ed. Ken Williamson (London, Newnes, 1960), 168.
11. Barry Ulanov, "Thumps Down," in "Two Thumps on 'A Drum,'" *Down Beat,* June 27, 1957, 18.
12. Duke Ellington, "We, Too, Sing 'America,'" a talk delivered on Annual Lincoln Day Services, February 9, 1941, Scott Methodist Church, Los Angeles, CA, *California Eagle* (February 13, 1941), collected in Tucker, *Duke Ellington Reader,* 146.
13. Richard O. Boyer, "The Hot Bach," *New Yorker,* June 24–July 8, 1944, collected in Tucker, *Duke Ellington Reader,* 239.
14. Duke Ellington, "Into Each Life Some Rain Must Fall (Duke's Poetry)," concert at Columbia University, May 20, 1964, *The New York Concert* (MusicMasters CD 01612-65112-2, 1995).
15. Duke Ellington, "Moon Maiden" (recorded July 14, 1969), *The Intimate Ellington* (Pablo/Fantasy OJCCD-730-2, 1977). I am grateful to David Lionel Smith for alerting me to this rendition, and for helping me track it down at short notice. Ellington's manuscript for "Moon Maiden" is located in the Duke Ellington Collection Subseries 1A: Manuscripts, Box 229, Folder 8, Archives Center, National Museum of American History, Smithsonian Institution. George Avakian, who was present at the recording session, confirms that Ellington recites in an overdub (personal communication, November 2000).

16. Duke Ellington, "Spaceman," Duke Ellington Collection Series 5: Correspondence, Box 6: Notes, undated, Archives Center, National Museum of American History, Smithsonian Institution. See also Ellington's unpublished essay, "The Race for Space" (ca. 1957), in Tucker, *Duke Ellington Reader,* 293–296.
17. Liner notes, *The Intimate Ellington.* Duke's claim notwithstanding, "Moon Maiden" is in fact not the first Ellington recording to feature his abilities as a vocalist; that distinction belongs to the obscure and odd version of "The Saddest Tale" that the band recorded in 1934. Another song under this title would be recorded in 1935 (with Billie Holiday singing) for the film *Symphony in Black;* however, the 1934 studio "The Saddest Tale" features Ellington himself, speaking a short lyric ("Saddest Tale Told on Land and Sea/Was the Tale When They Told the Truth about Me") over an instrumental backdrop.
18. Ellington uses this phrase in recounting a "cutting contest" between Sidney Bechet and Bubber Miley: "Call was very important in that music. Today, the music has grown up and become quite scholastic, but this was au naturel, close to the primitive, where people send messages in what they play, calling somebody, or making facts and emotions known. Painting a picture, or having a story to go with what you were going to play, was of vital importance in those days. The audience didn't know anything about it, but the cats in the band did" (MM 47).
19. Ellington, "Swing Is My Beat!" *New Advance,* October 1944, 1, 14, collected in Tucker, *Duke Ellington Reader,* 249.
20. Boyer, "The Hot Bach," in Tucker, *Duke Ellington Reader,* 226.
21. Ulanov, "Ellington Programme," 169.
22. Gary Giddins, "Duke Ellington (Part 3: At the Pulpit)," in *Visions of Jazz: The First Century* (New York: Oxford University Press, 1999), 501. The phrase *Shakespearean universality* was used by a London critic reviewing Ellington's first appearance at the Palladium; it is quoted in Tucker, *Duke Ellington Reader,* 216.
23. Strayhorn interview with Sinclair Traill and Gerald Lascelles, *Just Jazz* 3 (London: Four Square Books, 1959), quoted in David Hajdu, *Lush Life: A Biography of Billy Strayhorn* (New York: Farrar Straus and Giroux, 1996), 156.
24. "Monologue (Pretty and the Wolf)" was originally recorded for Columbia Records on May 24, 1951. The live version appears on *Duke Ellington Live from the 1956 Stratford Festival* (Berkeley, CA: Music and Arts CD-616, 1989). Ellington performed this recitation frequently in concert. There is even a version in the telecast *Music '55,* broadcast that summer by CBS, where Ellington recites "Pretty and the Wolf" seated at the piano against the backdrop of a series of drawings by Andy Warhol (specially commissioned for the program), which scroll across a screen from left to right. See Klaus Stratemann, *Duke Ellington Day by Day and Film by Film* (Copenhagen, Denmark: JazzMedia APS, 1992), 358.
25. "Music Press Release # 6 (for Saturday Morning Release, April 13, 1957)," Stratford Shakespearean Festival, Ontario Canada (April 10, 1957). Ellington clippings file, Institute for Jazz Studies, Rutgers University.
26. Stanley Dance, *The World of Duke Ellington* (New York: Charles Scribner's Sons, 1970), 32.
27. Bob Smith interview with Strayhorn, Vancouver (November 1, 1962). I thank David Hajdu for making this interview available to me.
28. Beatrice Washburn, "The Duke—'I Hear Music All the Time,'" *Miami Herald,* January 12, 1958.
29. Langston Hughes, "Shakespeare in Harlem," in *Shakespeare in Harlem* (New York: Alfred A. Knopf, 1942), collected in Langston Hughes, *Collected Poems of Langston Hughes,* ed. Arnold Rampersad (New York: Alfred A. Knopf, 1994), 260.
30. Rebecca Walkowitz has argued convincingly that Hughes's poem offers "a contrast not between two different *traditions* but between differences *within* traditions—Shakespeare or Harlem—that are thought to be undifferentiated. As 'Shakespeare in Harlem' points to Shakespeare's bawdy songs, it represents not 'low' Shakespeare so much as Shakespeare's own conjunction of high and low cultures"; see Rebecca Walkowitz, "Shakespeare in

Harlem: *The Norton Anthology,* 'Propaganda,' Langston Hughes," *Modern Language Quarterly* 60, no. 4 (December 1999): 515.

31. Irving Townsend, liner notes to Duke Ellington and his Orchestra, *Such Sweet Thunder* (Columbia CL 1033, 1957).
32. Ulanov, "Ellington Programme," 171. The phrase is taken from Hippolyta's speech in act 4, scene 1 of the play: "I never heard / So musical a discord, such sweet thunder" (lines 120–21).
33. Hajdu, *Lush Life,* 161.
34. "Music Press Release # 6 (for Saturday Morning Release, April 13, 1957)," Stratford Shakespearean Festival.
35. Stratemann, *Duke Ellington,* 239.
36. Stanley Crouch, Program Notes, Classical Jazz Series Concert, Alice Tully Hall, Lincoln Center for the Performing Arts (August 10, 1988), collected in Tucker, *Duke Ellington Reader,* 441.
37. "Sonnet for Sister Kate," Duke Ellington Collection Series 1A: Music Manuscripts, Box 363, Folder 6, Archives Center, National Museum of American History, Smithsonian Institution.
38. Bob Smith interview with Strayhorn, Vancouver (November 1, 1962).
39. Nathaniel Mackey, "Other: From Noun to Verb," in *Discrepant Engagement: Dissonance, Cross-Culturality, and Experimental Writing* (New York: Cambridge University Press, 1993), 269–270. It would be a mistake to underestimate the role of humor in this fugitive mode—the way that *Such Sweet Thunder* is composed not just of "parallels in miniatures" but also *caricatures.* This is equally an element in Ellington's own writings. For example, *The Afro-Eurasian Eclipse,* recorded in 1971 in the wake of Ellington's travels on U.S. State Department tours in the 1960s, was apparently inspired by Marshall McLuhan's claim in the late 1960s that the world was "going oriental, and that nobody will be able to retain his or her identity—not even the orientals" (MM 4). But Ellington's spoken introduction to the suite's opener, "Chinoiserie" (which he repeated word for word at each performance) only glancingly takes up McLuhan's proposition, preferring to jaunt through a self-deprecating run of alliteration and association that matches its rhetoric of pseudogallantry with its tongue-in-cheek allusion to "the piano player": "In this particular segment, ladies and gentlemen, we have adjusted our perspective to that of the kangaroo and the dijiridoo, which automatically puts us Down Under or Out Back. From this viewpoint, it is most improbable that anyone can tell who is enjoying the shadow of whom. Harold Ashby has been inducted into the responsibility and obligation of scraping off a tiny chip of the charisma of his chinoiserie, almost immediately after the piano player completes his riki-tiki." It is crucial to read this as serious play, though: to suggest, in other words, that the fugitive poetics of Ellington's language (its slippage along what Roman Jakobson would call the axis of equivalence) actually *enacts* McLuhan's proposition that the contemporary world is characterized by cultural mixing without progenitor—a state in which "it is most improbable that anyone can tell who is enjoying the shadow of whom"; see *The Afro-Eurasian Eclipse: A Suite in Eight Parts* (Fantasy Records OJCCD-645–2, 1975).
40. Albert Murray has gone much further, arguing that this effect is not at all exceptional, but instead that the entire Ellington band must be heard as one orchestrated "extension of the human voice." He writes: "such was the vocal orientation of Duke Ellington's genius that in addition to achieving the most highly distinctive overall instrumental orchestral sound (made up of instrumental voice extensions), he not only played his orchestra as if it were a single instrument (to an extent that cannot be claimed for any other composer or conductor) but expressed himself on it as if the three-man rhythm section, three trombones, four to six trumpets, five woodwinds (plus occasional strings) were actually the dimensions of one miraculously endowed human voice"; see Albert Murray, *Stomping the Blues* (New York: Da Capo, 1976), 114.
41. Duke Ellington and His Orchestra, "Black, Brown and Beige," *The Duke Ellington Carnegie Hall Concerts, January 1943* (Prestige Records 2PCD-34004-2, 1977).

42. See also the summary of Ellington's verbal introductions in Barry Ulanov, *Duke Ellington* (New York: Da Capo, 1975), 254–255.
43. Quoted in Brian Priestly and Alan Cohen, "Black, Brown and Beige" (I), *Composer* 51 (Spring 1974): 33–37; "Black, Brown and Beige" (II), *Composer* 52 (Summer 1974): 29–52; "Black, Brown and Beige" (III), *Composer* 53 (Winter 1974–1975): 29–32; collected in Tucker, *Duke Ellington Reader,* 195–196.
44. Priestly and Cohen, while demurring about any easy links between music and narrative, do offer some examples of the ways the suite format of *Black, Brown and Beige* may have arisen "from the demands of the programmatic motivation itself. In other words . . . the fragmentation and development of short thematic motifs in 'Black' is intended to represent musically the fragmentation of African tradition on American soil; similarly, the conflict during 'Work Song' between motifs referring to the blues scale . . . and those affirming the major mode . . . may just be a metaphor for the clash between two cultures" (Tucker, *Duke Ellington Reader,* 188–189).
45. Graham Lock, *Blutopia: Visions of the Future and Revisions of the Past in the Work of Sun Ra, Duke Ellington, and Anthony Braxton* (Durham, NC: Duke University Press, 1999), 2–3. Further references will be indicated parenthetically in the text.
46. Mark Tucker, "The Genesis of *Black, Brown and Beige,*" *Black Music Research Journal* 13, no. 2 (Fall 1993): 67–86.
47. Mark Tucker, *Ellington: The Early Years* (Urbana: University of Illinois Press, 1991), 7–8.
48. David Levering Lewis, *W. E. B. Du Bois: Biography of a Race,* vol. 1, *1868–1919* (New York: Henry Holt, 1993), 460. See also W. E. B. Du Bois, "The Star of Ethiopia," *Crisis* 11 (December 1915): 91–93; W. E. B. Du Bois, "The Drama among Black Folk," *Crisis* 12 (August 1916): 169–173; W. E. B. Du Bois, *A Pageant* (a four-page leaflet issued in 1915), in Herbert Aptheker, ed., *Annotated Bibliography of the Published Writings of W. E. B. Du Bois* (Millwood, NY: Kraus-Thompson Organization Ltd., 1973), 543.
49. Krin Gabbard compares Ellington's dignified role as a bandleader in his debut film, *Black and Tan* (1929), with Bessie Smith's role as a victimized woman in the film *St. Louis Blues* (1929). See Krin Gabbard, *Jammin' at the Margins: Jazz and the America Cinema* (Chicago: University of Chicago Press, 1996), 161–162. Gabbard (ibid., 210–211) follows Gary Giddins in arguing that Armstrong was able to "transcend the racist trappings" of his early films, such as the infamous *Rhapsody in Black and Blue* (1932); see also Gary Giddins, *Satchmo* (New York: Doubleday, 1988), 36.
50. Stratemann, *Duke Ellington,* 121.
51. Ulanov, *Duke Ellington,* 258.
52. Robert Bagar, quoted in ibid., 257. Of course, this complaint had been common in reviews of Ellington as soon as he began to experiment with longer forms: Ulanov quotes Constant Lambert, who in 1934 wrote: "Ellington's best works are written in what may be called ten-inch record form. . . . Into this three and a half minutes he compresses the utmost, but beyond its limits he is inclined to fumble" (259). See also Mike Levin, "Duke Fuses Classical and Jazz!," *Down Beat,* February 15, 1943, 12–13, collected in Tucker, *Duke Ellington Reader,* 169. Paul Bowles, "Duke Ellington in Recital for Russian War Relief," *New York Herald-Tribune,* January 25, 1943, collected in ibid., 166. On the critical reception of *Black, Brown and Beige,* see more generally Scott DeVeaux, "*Black, Brown and Beige* and the Critics," *Black Music Research Journal* 13, no. 2 (Fall 1993): 125–146; Andrew Homzy, "*Black, Brown and Beige* in Duke Ellington's Repertoire, 1943–1973," *Black Music Research Journal* 13, no. 2 (Fall 1993): 87–110; Brian Priestly and Alan Cohen, "Black, Brown and Beige," in Tucker, *Duke Ellington Reader,* 185–204.
53. Ulanov, *Duke Ellington,* 260.
54. Ibid., 259.
55. Duke Ellington, "Black," in *Black, Brown, and Beige,* undated typescript, 8. Duke Ellington Collection Series 4: Scripts, Box 3, Archives Center, National Museum of American History, Smithsonian Institution. I should note that scholars are still uncertain about the dating of this document. The typescript (based on an earlier handwritten draft), with the character

Boola, would seem related to Ellington's plans to write an "opera" of the same name in the later 1930s. The question remains, of course, whether this script was written before or after the premiere of musical *Black, Brown, and Beige* in 1943.

56. Duke Ellington, "Beige," in *Black, Brown, and Beige* typescript, 1, 3.
57. "Duke's Book Will Explain His Carnegie Hall Symph," *Variety,* June 9, 1943, 2, quoted in Lock, *Blutopia,* 110.
58. Carter Harman, audiotape interview of Ellington, Las Vegas, NV (1956), Oral History Collection 422, Tape 1, Archives Center, National Museum of American History, Smithsonian Institution.
59. Janna Tull Steed has also suggested that Ellington approaches the literary through a spiritual focus in this period. See her reading of another untitled Ellington manuscript, written on stationery from a Zurich hotel (the poem opens "His Every Day Cracked Up/in Empty Day/With Promises of only the Blackest/Stormy Night . . ."), in Janna Tull Steed, *Duke Ellington: A Spiritual Biography* (New York: Crossroad Publishing Co., 1999), 152.
60. Mercer Ellington with Stanley Dance, *Duke Ellington in Person: An Intimate Memoir* (New York: Da Capo, 1978), 171.
61. On Ellington's turn to religion, see ibid., 110–111.
62. *Forward Day by Day* (February 1–April 30, 1973) (Cincinnati, OH: Forward Movement Publications, 1973), 48. Duke Ellington Collection, Series 14: Religious Materials, Box 2: Pamphlets, Archives Center, National Museum of American History, Smithsonian Institution. The Ellington itinerary is taken from Stratemann, *Duke Ellington,* 653.
63. Stratemann, *Duke Ellington,* 584.
64. *Forward Day by Day* (February 1–April 30, 1969) (Cincinnati, OH, 1969), 48. Duke Ellington Collection, Archives Center, National Museum of American History, Smithsonian Institution.
65. Ellington, *Duke Ellington in Person,* 172.

4. The Race for Space

1. William H. Honan, "Le Mot Juste for the Moon," *Esquire,* July 1969, 53–56, 138–139.
2. John Szwed, *Space Is the Place: The Lives and Times of Sun Ra* (New York: Pantheon Books, 1997).
3. Amiri Baraka, "Sun Ra (1993)," in *Eulogies* (New York: Marsilio Publications, 1996), 174.
4. Jay Wright, "Desire's Design, Vision's Resonance: Black Poetry's Ritual and Historical Voice," *Callaloo* 10, no. 1 (1986): 14.
5. Sun Ra, *The Immeasurable Equation* (Chicago: Ihnfinity Inc./Saturn Research, 1972), 50.
6. Duke Ellington, "The Race for Space" (ca. 1957), collected in Mark Tucker, ed., *The Duke Ellington Reader* (New York: Oxford University Press, 1993), 296.
7. James Baldwin, *The Fire Next Time* (New York: Dial Press, 1963), collected in James Baldwin, *The Price of the Ticket: Collected Nonfiction, 1948–1985* (New York: St. Martin's, 1985), 379.
8. David Toop, "If You Find Earth Boring . . . Travels in the Outer Imagination with Sun Ra," in *Ocean of Sound: Aether Talk, Ambient Sound and Imaginary Worlds* (London: Serpent's Tail, 1995), 29.
9. Szwed, *Space Is the Place,* 140.
10. Barbara Christian, "The Race for Theory," *Cultural Critique* 6 (Spring 1987): 51–64.
11. Bert Vuijsje, "Sun Ra Spreekt," *Jazz Wereld,* October 1968, 17, quoted in Szwed, *Space Is the Place,* 140.
12. See Sun Ra, "Your Only Hope Now Is a Lie," transcript of a talk given at Soundscape, New York, November 11, 1979, in *Hambone* 2 (Fall 1982): 113. The recording of this talk is available on CD, as well, under the title "The Possibility of an Altered Destiny" on Sun Ra Arkestra, *Live from Soundscape* (Disk Union DIW-388B).
13. Sun Ra, *Extensions Out: The Immeasurable Equation Vol. 2* (Chicago: Ihnfinity Inc./Saturn Research, 1972), 128.

14. Graham Lock, *Forces in Motion: The Music and Thoughts of Anthony Braxton* (New York: Da Capo, 1988), 15.
15. John Corbett, "Sun Ra: Gravity and Levity," in *Extended Play* (Durham: Duke University Press, 1994), 311.
16. Thomas Kuhn, *The Structure of Scientific Revolutions* (Chicago: University of Chicago Press, 1962).
17. Tam Fiofori, "Sun Ra's Space Odyssey," *Down Beat,* May 1970, 14.
18. Toop, "If You Find Earth Boring," in *Ocean of Sound,* 27.
19. Szwed, *Space Is the Place,* 304–305.
20. Fiofori, "Sun Ra's Space Odyssey," 15.
21. Lock, *Forces in Motion*, 16.
22. Sun Ra, *Extensions Out,* 27.
23. James G. Spady, "Indigené=Folkski Equations in the Black Arts," *Black Scholar,* November–December 1978, 26.
24. Baraka, *Eulogies,* 171.
25. Sun Ra, "The Disguised Aim," "The Gardened of the Eatened," "The Invented Memory," The Cosmic-Blueprints," "Primary Lesson: The Second Class Citizens," "The Myth of Me," "The Plane: Earth," "Precision Fate," in *Umbra Anthology 1967–1968,* ed. David Henderson (New York: Umbra, 1968), 3–7.
26. Aldon Nielsen, *Black Chant: Languages of African-American Postmodernism* (New York: Cambridge University Press, 1997), 114–115.
27. Michael Oren, "The Umbra Poets' Workshop, 1962–1965: Some Socio-Literary Puzzles," in *Studies in Black American Literature,* vol. 2, *Belief vs. Theory in Black American Literary Criticism,* ed. Joe Weixlmann and Chester J. Fontenot (Greenwood, FL: Penkevill, 1986), 184.
28. Lorenzo Thomas, "Ascension: Music and the Black Arts Movement," in *Jazz among the Discourses,* ed. Krin Gabbard (Durham: Duke University Press, 1995), 260.
29. Lorenzo Thomas, "The Shadow World: New York's Umbra Workshop & Origins of the Black Arts Movement," *Callaloo* 4, no. 1 (October 1978): 64–65.
30. Lorenzo Thomas, "'Classical Jazz' and the Black Arts Movement," *African American Review* 29, no. 2 (Summer 1995): 239.
31. Amiri Baraka, *The Autobiography of Leroi Jones/Amiri Baraka* (New York: Freundlich Books, 1984), 204.
32. Ibid., 205.
33. Amiri Baraka, "The Changing Same (R&B and the New Black Music)" (1966), in *Black Music* (New York: Quill, 1967), 180–211.
34. "Editorial," *The Cricket* 1 (1968): a.
35. Sun Ra, "My Music Is Words," *The Cricket* 1 (1968): 4.
36. Ibid., 5.
37. Sun Ra, "And Some Music Is Not Music," *The Cricket* 1 (1968): 18.
38. Sun Ra, "My Music Is Words," 6.
39. Ibid., 7.
40. Sun Ra, *The Immeasurable Equation* (Philadelphia: Le Sony'r Ra, 1980).
41. Larry Neal, "Afterword," in *Black Fire: An Anthology of Afro-American Writing,* ed. Leroi Jones and Larry Neal (New York: William Morrow, 1968), 655.
42. Sun Ra, "Of the Cosmic Blueprints," in Jones and Neal, *Black Fire,* 214.
43. Larry Neal, "Afterword," in Jones and Neal, *Black Fire,* 355.
44. See Szwed, *Space Is the Place,* 62–73, 294–299.
45. Ibid., 106.
46. Sun Ra, *Jazz by Sun Ra* (Transition Records trip 10, 1957), reissued as *Sun Song* (Delmark DS 411, 1967).
47. Hentoff, quoted in Szwed, *Space Is the Place,* 159.
48. See ibid., 250–251.
49. Sun Ra, *Immeasurable Equation* (1972); Sun Ra, *Extensions Out.* There are other subsequent, slightly different collections published under the same title, such as Sun Ra, *The Immeasur-*

able Equation (Philadelphia: Le Sony'r Ra, 1980); and Sun Ra, *The Immeasurable Equation* (Philadelphia: El Saturn, 1985). The most thorough collection of Sun Ra's writings available is James L. Wolf and Hartmut Geerken, eds., *The Immeasurable Equation: The Collected Poetry and Prose* (Wartaweil, Germany: Waitawhile Press, 2006).

50. I am grateful to John Szwed for sharing these recordings with me. In 2011 Norton Records also released three vinyl-only compilations of Sun Ra reading poetry: Sun Ra and His Arkestra, *Strange Worlds In My Mind (Space Poetry Volume One)* (Norton Records ED-365, 2011); *The Sub-Dwellers (Space Poetry Volume Two)* (Norton Records ED-366, 2011); *The Outer Darkness (Space Poetry Volume Three)* (Norton Records ED-367, 2011).
51. Lorenzo Thomas, "The Mathemagic of Sun Ra," *Ann Arbor Sun,* April 5–19, 1974, 16.
52. Bert Vuijsje, "Sun Ra Spreekt," *Jazz Wereld,* October 1968, 16, 19, quoted in Szwed, *Space Is the Place,* 236.
53. Sun Ra, *Immeasurable Equation* (1972), 25.
54. Sun Ra, *Immeasurable Equation* (1980), 60.
55. Sun Ra, *Immeasurable Equation* (1972), 30.
56. Ibid., 36.
57. Sun Ra, *Extensions Out,* 40; Sun Ra, "The Visitation," in Jones and Neal, *Black Fire,* 213.
58. Sun Ra, *Extensions Out,* 1.
59. Sun Ra, *Immeasurable Equation* (1972), 15.
60. Sun Ra, *Extensions Out,* 41.
61. Szwed, *Space Is the Place,* 76.
62. Ibid., 80.
63. Sun Ra, "Your Only Hope Now Is a Lie," *Hambone* 2 (Fall 1982): 110, quoted in Szwed, *Space Is the Place,* 78.
64. Quoted in John Corbett, "One of Everything: Blount Hermeneutics and the Wisdom of Ra," in *The Wisdom of Sun Ra: Sun Ra's Polemical Broadsheets and Streetcorner Leaflets,* ed. John Corbett (Chicago: WhiteWalls, 2006), 5.
65. Szwed, *Space Is the Place,* 78.
66. Corbett, *Wisdom of Sun Ra.* Subsequent page references to this collection will be indicated parenthetically in the text.
67. Corbett, "One of Everything," in *The Wisdom of Sun Ra,* 6.
68. Sun Ra and the Myth Science Arkestra, *Cosmic Tones for Mental Therapy,* recorded in New York, 1963 (Saturn Research SR 408, 1967). This LP has been reissued on CD in tandem with *Art Forms of Dimensions Tomorrow* (Saturn Research SR 9956, 404, 1965) as Evidence CD 22036, 1992.
69. Sun Ra, "To the Peoples of the Earth," in Jones and Neal, *Black Fire,* 217.
70. Spady, "Indigené=Folkski Equations," 26.
71. Szwed, *Space Is the Place,* 327.
72. Jean-Louis Noames, "Visite au Dieu-Soleil," *Jazz Magazine* 125 (December 1969): 75, quoted in Szwed, *Space Is the Place,* 319–320.
73. Moshe Idel, *Language, Torah and Hermeneutics in Abraham Abulafia* (Albany: SUNY Press, 1989), 12, 99.
74. Ira Steingroot, "Sun Ra's Magical Kingdom," *Reality Hackers* 6 (Winter 1988): 46.
75. Sun Ra, *Immeasurable Equation* (1972), 53.
76. Sun Ra, "Your Only Hope Now Is A Lie," 106.
77. Sidney Lanier, *The Science of English Verse,* ed. P. Baum (1880; repr., Baltimore, MD: Johns Hopkins University Press, 1945).
78. Ibid., 21.
79. Ibid., 22.
80. Ibid., 29.
81. Ibid., 31.
82. Ibid., 47.
83. Aldon Nielsen, *Black Chant: Languages of African-American Postmodernism* (New York: Cambridge University Press, 1997), 256.

84. Szwed, *Space Is the Place,* 104.
85. Nathaniel Mackey, "Wringing the Word," *World Literature Today* 68, no. 4 (Autumn 1994): 733–740.
86. Edward Kamau Brathwaite, "History, the Caribbean Writer and *X/Self,*" in *Crisis and Creativity in the New Literatures in English,* ed. Geoffrey Davis and Hena Maes-Jelinek (Amsterdam: Rodopi, 1990), 33–34.
87. Edward Kamau Brathwaite, *X/Self* (New York: Oxford University Press, 1987), 113.
88. Edward Kamau Brathwaite, "X/Self's Xth Letters from the Thirteen Provinces," in *X/Self,* 84.
89. Sun Ra, *Immeasurable Equation* (1980).
90. Zora Neale Hurston, "Characteristics of Negro Expression" (1934), collected in Zora Neale Hurston, *The Sanctified Church* (Berkeley, CA: Turtle Island Press, 1983), 49.
91. Wilson Harris, *The Eye of the Scarecrow* (London: Faber and Faber, 1965), 95.

5. Zoning Mary Lou Williams Zoning

1. Bob Blumenthal, Introduction, liner notes to Mary Lou Williams, *Zoning* (Smithsonian Folkways SF CD 40811, 1995).
2. Peter O'Brien, liner notes to Mary Lou Williams, *Zoning* (Mary Records M-103, 1974). The 1995 Smithsonian Folkways reissue does not include O'Brien's notes.
3. Howard Mandel, *Future Jazz* (New York: Oxford University Press, 1999), 35.
4. Ben Sidran, *Black Talk* (New York: Da Capo, 1971); Jack V. Buerkle and Danny Barker, *Bourbon Street Black: The New Orleans Black Jazzman* (New York: Oxford University Press, 1973); Danny Barker, *Buddy Bolden and the Last Days of Storyville,* ed. Alyn Shipton (London: Cassell, 1998); Anthony Braxton, *Tri-Axium Writings,* 3 vols. (n.p.: Synthesis Music, 1988); George Lewis, "Experimental Music in Black and White: The AACM in New York, 1970–1985," in *Uptown Conversation: The New Jazz Studies,* ed. Robert G. O'Meally, Brent Hayes Edwards, and Farah Jasmine Griffin (New York: Columbia University Press, 2004), 50–101; George Lewis, *Power Stronger Than Itself: The Association for the Advancement of Creative Musicians* (Chicago: University of Chicago Press, 2008).
5. Some recordings in this vein include the following: Baby Dodds, *Talking and Drum Solos: Footnotes to Jazz, Vol. 1* (recorded in 1951) (Folkways F-2290); Willie "the Lion" Smith, "Reminiscing the Piano Greats" (recorded in Paris, January 29, 1959), Vogue CD 74321115062, 1992; Jelly Roll Morton's extensive interviews with Alan Lomax in 1938 at the Library of Congress; Duke Ellington, *A Drum Is a Woman* (Columbia CL 951); *Escapade Reviews the Jazz Scene: A Symposium in Sound* (Liberty 9005); Jo Jones, *The Drums* (Jazz Odyssey 008); Louis Armstrong, *A Musical Autobiography* (recorded in 1957) (Decca); Julian "Cannonball" Adderley, *A Child's Introduction to Jazz* (Wonderland 435); Art Hodes, *Recollections from the Past* (Solo Arts Records 41/42); Bunk Johnson, *This Is Bunk Johnson Talking, Explaining to You the Early Days of New Orleans* (American Music 643); Lil Armstrong, *Satchmo and Me* (Riverside 12–120); Coleman Hawkins, *Coleman Hawkins: A Documentary* (Riverside 1956). I thank John Szwed and Robert O'Meally for helping me compile this list.
6. "About the Artist," liner notes to Mary Lou Williams and Cecil Taylor, *Embraced: A Concert of New Music for Two Pianos Exploring the History of Jazz with Love* (Pablo 2620 108, 1978).
7. Mary Lou Williams, *A Keyboard History* (Jazztone Society J-1206). On this recording, see Linda Dahl, *Morning Glory: A Biography of Mary Lou Williams* (Berkeley: University of California Press, 1999), 245; Tammy Kernodle, *Soul on Soul: The Life and Music of Mary Lou Williams* (Boston: Northeastern University Press, 2004), 175–176.
8. Kernodle, *Soul on Soul,* 201.
9. Mary Lou Williams, spoken narration, *The History of Jazz* (Folkways FJ 2860, 1978). I am thinking of Du Bois's 1940 autobiography *Dusk of Dawn: An Essay toward an Autobiography of the Race Concept,* in *Writings* (New York: Library of America, 1986).

10. Mary Lou Williams, "Then Came Zombie Music," *Melody Maker,* May 8, 1954, 11. This document has been reprinted in Len Lyons, *The Great Jazz Pianists Speaking of Their Lives and Music* (New York: Quill, 1983), 73; Nat Shapiro and Nat Hentoff, eds., *Hear Me Talkin' To Ya: The Story of Jazz as Told by the Men Who Made It* (New York: Dover, 1955), 311.
11. Mary Lou Williams, "Music and Progress," *Jazz Record* 60 (November 1947): 23.
12. Barry Ulanov, "Mary Lou Williams," *Metronome,* July 1949, 12, 24.
13. John S. Wilson, interview with Williams for the National Endowment of the Arts/Institute of Jazz Studies Jazz Oral History Project, "Smithsonian Institution Interviews with Jazz Musicians," June 26, 1973, 103, 104.
14. See Kernodle, *Soul on Soul,* 112–116.
15. Max Jones, interview with Williams in Jones, ed., *Talking Jazz* (New York: Norton, 1988), 194.
16. Gerrard Pochonet, liner notes to *Mary Lou Williams* (Folkways FJ 2843, 1964). This 1964 solo piano performance of "A Fungus Amungus" has been reissued on *Mary Lou Williams Presents Black Christ of the Andes* (Smithsonian Folkways SFW CD 40816, 2004). Williams's papers even include a typescript draft of lyrics to "A Fungus Amungus," penned by one of her friends, the priest Anthony Woods: "There's a fungus among us,/Among us a fungus,/An itchin' type fungus among us.//The sextet is surely swinging'/'Cept the clarinet's really sick/Like there's a mushroom growin'/In his licorish stick." (Given the irregularity and dissonance of the tune as recorded, it is not at all clear whether these lyrics were meant to be sung with the composition as performed by Williams on piano.) Typescript, "There's a Fungus among Us," Music by Mary Lou Williams, Words by Anthony S. Woods S. J. Mary Lou Williams Papers, Institute of Jazz Studies, Rutgers University.
17. As it is put in another verse of Woods lyrics: "The horn man's moanin' woe!/When he should be squealin' whee!/I don't know if it's you,/But I'm sure it ain't me." Intriguingly, another stanza figures the misfit of "fungus" as a female presence in particular: "Like a lyric gal-soprano/In an all male jail./Like the thirteenth tone/In a twelve-tone scale."
18. James Weldon Johnson, *God's Trombones: Seven Negro Sermons in Verse* (1927; repr., New York: Penguin, 1976), 4–5.
19. William Melvin Kelley, *Dunfords Travels Everywheres* (Garden City, NY: Doubleday, 1970), 49.
20. Pochonet, liner notes to *Mary Lou Williams.*
21. Dahl, *Morning Glory,* 278.
22. See Raymond Williams, *Marxism and Literature* (New York: Oxford University Press, 1977), 124–126.
23. LeRoi Jones (Amiri Baraka), *The System of Dante's Hell* (New York: Grove, 1965).
24. Kimberly W. Benston, "Amiri Baraka: An Interview," *Boundary 2* 6, no. 2 (Winter 1978): 304. See *System of Dante's Hell,* 12, 64.
25. Jones, *System of Dante's Hell,* 99.
26. Quoted in Werner Sollors, *Amiri Baraka/LeRoi Jones: The Quest for a "Populist Modernism"* (New York: Columbia University Press, 1978), 140.
27. Jones, *System of Dante's Hell,* 64.
28. O'Brien, quoted in Dahl, *Morning Glory,* 302–303.
29. Jones, *System of Dante's Hell,* 119.
30. Kalamu ya Salaam, "Amiri Baraka Analyzes How He Writes," *African American Review* 37, nos. 2–3 (2003): 217. The phrase "Break out" repeats (in the form of a compulsion or imperative charge) through the sections of *System of Dante's Hell* (see, for example, 29, 36).
31. Jones, *System of Dante's Hell,* 15.
32. Williams, *History of Jazz.*
33. O'Brien, liner notes, *Zoning.* Again, as with "A Fungus Amungus," the composition "Zoning Fungus II" can be heard as an *example* of the avant-garde rather than a critique or a "zoning" of it. Indeed, a year later, this tune was selected (along with work by Gil Evans, Milford Graves, Sam Rivers, and Sunny Murray) to represent the "New York Section" on a Folkways Records sampler of experimental contemporary compositions; see *New American Music: Composers of the 1970s* (Folkways Records FTS 33901, 1975).

34. Press release, Donald Smith Promotions, "Jazz Greats Mary Lou Williams and Cecil Taylor Schedule March 8th Press Conference to Announce First Join Concert at Carnegie Hall," Mary Lou Williams clippings file, Institute of Jazz Studies, Rutgers University.
35. Taylor recounts first hearing Williams in his interview with Howard Mandel, "My Dinner with Cecil," *Down Beat* 67, no. 9 (September 2000): 36.
36. "Composer's Showcase to Present Religious Music of Mary Lou Williams and Cecil Taylor at the Whitney on January 10" (1975), Whitney Museum, undated press release, Mary Lou Williams Collection, Series 6, Box 14, MLW and Cecil Taylor "Embraced" Concert, 1977. The first half of the concert was composed of some of Williams's religious works for piano, trio, and vocal chorus (with the soloist Carline Ray): the pieces included "Gloria," "Lazarus," "Medi I," "Holy Ghost," "Solo for St. Cecilia," "Lamb of God," and the "Lord's Prayer." Taylor's section of the concert was a single new piece, "Ila Ila Tado: Voices in All Sounds," performed by Taylor on piano with Jimmy Lyons on alto saxophone and Andrew Cyrille on drums. See Williams's scrapbook of clippings from the event: Scrapbook, Mary Lou Williams Collection, Series 7, Box 15, Scrapbook 12 (1957–1958, 1960, 1974–1975). Also see Gary Giddins, "Mary Lou and That Mannish Thing," *Village Voice,* January 20, 1975, 109; John S. Wilson, "Two Jazz Pianists Share Religious-Music Concert," *New York Times,* January 12, 1975.
37. Gary Giddins, "The Avant-Gardist Who Came In from the Cold," in *Riding on a Blue Note: Jazz and American Pop* (New York: Da Capo, 1981), 285; see also Dahl, *Morning Glory,* 330.
38. Mary Lou Williams, "How This Concert Came About," *Embraced: A Concert of New Music For Two Pianos Exploring the History of Jazz with Love* (Pablo 2620 108, 1978). In a later interview, she says: "I felt that a strange foreign sound would enter in to the strains of jazz and would destroy the heritage, would destroy jazz completely. . . . Now we've waited I don't know how many years for a new sound in jazz and it hasn't come forth as yet." John S. Wilson, interview with Williams for the National Endowment of the Arts/Institute of Jazz Studies Jazz Oral History Project, 142–143.
39. Dahl, *Morning Glory,* 333.
40. Williams, "How This Concert Came About."
41. Mary Lou Williams, "Don't Destroy the Roots," undated typescript, Mary Lou Williams Collection, Series 5, Box 2.
42. Williams, "How This Concert Came About."
43. Giddins, "The Avant-Gardist Who Came In from the Cold," in *Riding on a Blue Note,* 286. The original review was titled "Mary Lou and Cecil Shake Hands," *Village Voice,* April 25, 1977.
44. Ibid., 286–287.
45. John S. Wilson, "Jazz: Strange Double Piano Bill," *New York Times,* April 19, 1977.
46. Phyl Garland, "The Lady Lives Jazz: Mary Lou Williams Remains as a Leading Interpreter of the Art," *Ebony,* October 1979, 57–58.
47. Giddins, "The Avant-Gardist Who Came In from the Cold," in *Riding on a Blue Note,* 286.
48. Nica de Koenigswarter, letter to Williams, April 18, 1977, Mary Lou Williams Collection, Series 2, Subseries 2B, Box 4. This letter is quoted in Dahl, *Morning Glory,* 335.
49. D. Antoinette Handy, "Conversation with Mary Lou Williams: First Lady of the Jazz Keyboard," *Black Perspective in Music* 8, no. 2 (Fall 1980): 202.
50. Len Lyons, "Mary Lou Williams," in *The Great Jazz Pianists Speaking of Their Lives and Music* (New York: Quill, 1983), 72. Soon after the concert, she reportedly said to a friend, Brother Mario Hancock, that Taylor "couldn't beat me. He tried. He tried [but] I gave him a hard way to go. He wanted to really make a fool of me, but I told him who I was" (Peter O'Brien, interview, January 2000, quoted in Kernodle, *Soul on Soul,* 262).
51. Dahl, *Morning Glory,* 255.
52. "Cecil Taylor," in Robert D. Rusch, ed., *Jazztalk: The Cadence Interviews* (Secaucus, NJ: Lyle Stuart, 1984), 52.
53. Ibid., 53.
54. Ibid., 53, 57.

55. Ibid., 57.
56. See Kernodle, *Soul on Soul,* 262; "Doggin' Around: A Noble Failure," unsigned review, *Jazz Journal International* 30 (August 1977): 15.
57. Williams, "Music and Progress," *Jazz Record* 60 (November 1947): 23.
58. Meinrad Buholzer, "Cecil Taylor: Interview," *Cadence* 10, no. 2 (December 1984): 6.
59. Ralph Ellison, "The Little Man at Chehaw Station: The American Artist and His Audience," in *Going to the Territory* (New York: Vintage, 1986), 26.
60. John S. Wilson, "Tradition and Innovation in Jazz Meet at the Williams-Taylor Concert," *New York Times,* April 15, 1977.
61. Williams, letter to Hallie, May 26, 1977, 4, Mary Lou Williams Collection, Series 5, Box 4.
62. Williams, letter to Cecil Taylor, May 13, 1977, 2. Mary Lou Williams Collection, Series 5, Box 4. In the folder there is also one undated draft, and others dated May 23 and July 29 (all four rework much of the same material).
63. Ibid., 5.
64. Ibid., 3.
65. Williams, "How This Concert Came About," liner notes to *Embraced.*
66. "About the Artist . . . ," liner notes to *Embraced.* In her book *Morning Glory,* Linda Dahl mentions an unpublished autobiographical manuscript titled *Zoning* (see 302–303), although I have not yet found a manuscript under this title in the Williams papers held at Rutgers.
67. Rusch, *Jazztalk,* 53.
68. Ferdinand de Saussure, *Course in General Linguistics,* ed. Charles Bally and Albert Sechehaye, trans. Wade Baskin (New York: McGraw-Hill, 1966), 9.
69. Friedrich Nietzsche, "On the Uses and Disadvantages of History for Life," in *Untimely Meditations,* ed. Daniel Breazeale, trans. R. J. Hollingdale (New York: Cambridge University Press, 1997), 63. The German original is Friedrich Nietzsche, *Vom Nutzen und Nachteil der Historie für das Leben* (Stuttgart: Philipp Reclam, 1970), 11. Page numbers will subsequently be given both for the English edition and the German original, in that order.
70. Ibid., 64/12.
71. Ibid., 64–65/14.
72. Ibid., 120/107.
73. He writes: "With the word 'the unhistorical' I designate the art [*Kunst*] and power of *forgetting* and of enclosing oneself within a bounded *horizon;* I call 'suprahistorical' the powers which lead the eye away from becoming towards that which bestows upon existence the character of the eternal and stable, towards *art* [*Kunst*] and *religion*" (ibid., 120/107).
74. Mary Lou Williams, "Music and Progress," *Jazz Record* 60 (November 1947): 23.
75. Nietzsche, "On the Uses and Disadvantages," in Breazeale, *Untimely Meditations,* 95–96/65.
76. Gary Giddins, "Search for a Common Language," *New York,* April 18, 1977, 110.
77. Cecil Taylor, "–Aquoueh R–Oyo" (1973), liner notes to *Air above Mountains (Buildings Within)* (Enja 3005, 1976).
78. Peter O'Brien, liner notes to Mary Lou Williams, *Zoning.*
79. There is a lovely phrase in Williams's liner notes to *Embraced* that may or may not be an instance of just the fugitivity I am after. She writes, "My effort on this concert was to show the full seep and history of this music called Jazz together with some of the musical struggles it has been up against in the last twenty years." Typographical error or not, it is difficult not to be charmed by an insinuation of unstable boundaries ("seep") just where one might expect to see a pronouncement of breadth, mastery, and grandeur ("sweep") (Williams, "How This Concert Came About").
80. In the Mary Lou Williams papers at the Institute of Jazz Studies, the expense notebooks are collected in Series 5, Boxes 8–9.
81. For a useful overview of *oikonomia,* see Otto Brunner, Werner Conze, and Reinhart Koselleck, eds., *Geschichtliche Grundbegriffe: historisches Lexikon zur politisch-sozialen Sprache in Deutschland* (Stuttgart: E. Klett, 1992), vol. 7.
82. In turning to the example of Williams's expense notebooks, I do not mean to suggest that the zoning (in the sense of *oikonomia*) they display is somehow the equivalent of the zoning

at stake in her concerts sketching *The History of Jazz.* Whereas the expense notebooks involve a daily practice of recording that is serial (day after day after day) but not cumulative, the jazz history concerts are structured as a didactic and suprahistorical chronology of the "peaks" of a progressive tradition. Instead my point is that it is possible to read an archive of zoning (whether the concerts or the notebooks) against the grain, attending to the unavoidable seepage or blur between supposedly airtight categories of what is recorded. I thank Susan Fraiman for asking me a question that pushed me to clarify this point.

83. Larry Neal, "Uncle Rufus Raps on the Squared Circle," collected in Larry Neal, *Visions of a Liberated Future: Black Arts Movement Writings,* ed. Michael Schwartz (New York: Thunder's Mouth, 1989), 104, 102.
84. Ibid., 104.
85. Ibid., 102.
86. Ibid., 103.
87. Ibid., 103, 105.
88. Ibid., 106. Even after this proclamation, however, we remain within the logic of economic accounting (perhaps not surprisingly, given that Uncle Rufus's entire speech is motivated by his interest in compelling the narrator to buy him drinks). Although Uncle Rufus says he was "pulling for both" Ali and Frazier, he admits slyly (in the last line of the piece): "But this time, your old uncle put his money on slow blues."

6. Let's Call This

1. Some of the key sources on the function of titles in literature and art are Gérard Genette, "Titles," in *Paratexts: Thresholds of Interpretation,* trans. Jane E. Lewin (Cambridge: Cambridge University Press, 1997), 55–103; Harry Levin, "The Title as a Literary Genre," *Modern Language Review* 72, no. 4 (October 1977): xxiii–xxxvi; Jerrold Levinson, "Titles," *Journal of Aesthetics and Art Criticism* 44, no. 1 (Autumn 1985): 29–39; Leo H. Hoek, *La marque du titre: dispositifs sémiotiques d'une pratique textuelle* (The Hague: Mouton, 1981); Theodor Adorno, "Titles: Paraphrases on Lessing," in *Notes to Literature,* trans. Shierry Weber Nicholsen (New York: Columbia University Press, 1992), 2:3–11; Laurence Brogniez, Marianne Jakobi and Cédric Loire, eds., *Ceci n'est pas un titre: les artistes et l'intitulation* (Lyon: Fage, 2014). The small and scattered bibliography of work on song and album titles in jazz includes Philippe Carrard, "Titling Jazz: On the Front Cover of Blue Note Records," *Genre* 37, no. 1 (Spring 2004): 151–172; Winston Smith, "Let's Call This: Race, Writing, and Difference in Jazz," *Public* 4–5 (1990–1991): 70–83; and John Szwed, "The Local and the Express: Anthony Braxton's Title Drawings," in *Crossovers: Essays on Race, Music, and American Culture* (Philadelphia: University of Pennsylvania Press, 2006), 215–219.
2. Levin, "Title as a Literary Genre," xxiii.
3. John Fisher, "Entitling," *Critical Inquiry* 11, no. 2 (December 1984): 288.
4. Umberto Eco, *Apostille au nom de la rose* (*Postscript to The Name of the Rose*) (Paris: Livre de Poche, 1987), 510, quoted in Gérard Genette, "Structure and Functions of the Title in Literature," trans. Bernard Crampé, *Critical Inquiry* 14, no. 4 (Summer 1988): 719.
5. John Ashbery, *The Poet's Craft,* ed. William Packard (New York: Paragon House, 1987), 79, quoted in Anne Ferry, *The Title to the Poem* (Stanford: Stanford University Press, 1996), 6.
6. See Robin D. G. Kelley, *Thelonious Monk: The Life and Times of an American Original* (New York: Free Press, 2009), 112. In the case of "Worry Later," the title was initially imposed by Orrin Keepnews, the producer on the April 1960 recording session for Riverside Records, and later changed by Monk himself. Keepnews recalls: "There is an explanation for the dual titling of the new tune he had written for this date, first issued as 'Worry Later' but subsequently known as 'San Francisco Holiday.' During rehearsal earlier in the week, I had asked the composer if he wanted to name his new tune now, or worry about it later. 'Worry later' was the response—and that, I decided, was an ideal title. But when Monk did worry about it some time later, he chose to rename the piece to commemorate the fact that Nellie and their two children had been with him on this trip, and it became 'San Francisco Holiday' ";

see Orrin Keepnews, "Three Separated Views of Thelonious," in *The View from Within: Jazz Writings, 1948–1987* (New York: Oxford University Press, 1988), 144.

7. Richard O. Boyer, "The Hot Bach," *New Yorker,* July 1, 1944, cited in Mark Tucker, ed., *The Duke Ellington Reader* (New York: Oxford University Press, 1993), 235.
8. There has been a persistent rumor, repeated in some Ellington scholarship and liner notes, that "Harlem Air Shaft" was originally titled "Rumpus in Richmond" (another tune recorded at the same session). But Edward Green has shown definitively that this is an error; see Green, "'Harlem Air Shaft': A True Programmatic Composition?" *Journal of Jazz Studies* 7, no. 1 (Spring 2011): 30, 36.
9. Green, "'Harlem Air Shaft': A True Programmatic Composition?" 36.
10. Ibid., 36–37.
11. Marion Brown, *Afternoon of a Georgia Faun* (ECM 1004 2310 444, 1970).
12. Marion Brown, "Faces and Places: The Music and Travels of a Contemporary Jazz Musician" (unpublished MA thesis, Wesleyan University, 1976), 1.
13. The recitation of "Karintha" is a track on Brown, *Geechee Recollections* (ABC Records, AS-9252, 1973). The third album in the "Georgia Trilogy" is *Sweet Earth Flying* (Impulse! AS-9275, 1974), the title of which is also derived from a phrase in Toomer's poem "Storm Ending," also published in *Cane.* Brown mentions Tutuola in his most extended description of the piece, an essay titled "Notes to *Afternoon of a Georgia Faun.*" He describes *Afternoon of a Georgia Faun* as "an extended structural improvisation based on structured sections that flow uninterruptedly into one another like links in a chain. It is divided into two sections, each of which develops within its own contextural possibilities. The first part represents nature—raindrops, water, feelings of loneliness in an imaginary forest of the mind (like Tutuola's *My Life in the Bush of Ghosts*), animals heard and seen, in worship or celebration, voices from afar, the sounds of wind breathing life through trees. It sounds more 'primitive' than the second part which begins with Chick's piano interlude—the contemporary world of electricity and electro-magnetic energy, stop and go, interruptions, earth and moon"; see Marion Brown, "Notes to *Afternoon of a Georgia Faun,*" in Marion Brown, *Afternoon of a Georgia Faun: Views and Reviews* (n.p.: Nia Music, 1973), 1.
14. Eric Porter, *What Is This Thing Called Jazz? African American Musicians as Artists, Critics, and Activists* (Berkeley: University of California Press, 2002), 246.
15. John Turner, "Marion Brown's *Afternoon of a Georgia Faun,*" in Brown, *Afternoon of a Georgia Faun,* 14.
16. Ibid., 19.
17. Ibid., 20.
18. Mort Maizlish, "Marion Brown," *Jazz & Pop* 6, no. 10 (October 1967): 13.
19. "The New Jazz, a Panel Discussion with Marion Brown, John Norris, Ted O'Reilly and John Sinclair," *Coda* 7, no. 7 (April–May 1966): 4.
20. Porter, *What Is This Thing Called Jazz?,* 248.
21. Aldon Lynn Nielsen, *Black Chant: Languages of African-American Postmodernism* (Tuscaloosa: University of Alabama Press, 1997), 215.
22. Turner, "Marion Brown's *Afternoon of a Georgia Faun,*" in Brown, *Afternoon of a Georgia Faun,*16.
23. "In Conversation Part II: On the Other Side of Everybody's River" (1983 interview with Terence Beedle and Juergen Abi Schmitt), in Marion Brown, *Recollections: Essays, Drawings, Miscellanea* (Frankfurt: JAS Publications, 1984), 181. Brown's exquisite compositions for piano are available on Amina Claudine Myers, *Poems for Piano: The Piano Music of Marion Brown* (Sweet Earth Records SER 1005, 1979).
24. Ed Roberson, "The Sculpture of Thaddeus Mosley: Four Pieces," *Hambone* 15 (Fall 2000): 96. The exhibition catalogue is David Lewis, *Thaddeus Mosley: African American Sculptor* (Pittsburgh: University of Pittsburgh Press, 1997).
25. The term *anchorage* comes from Roland Barthes's well-known work on the function of the caption in press photography. According to Barthes, "in every society various techniques are developed intended to *fix* the floating chain of signifieds in such a way as to counter the

terror of uncertain signs; the linguistic message is one of these techniques. . . . The denominative function corresponds exactly to an *anchorage* of all the possible (denoted) meanings of the object by recourse to a nomenclature"; see Roland Barthes, "The Rhetoric of the Image," in *Image—Music—Text,* trans. Stephen Heath (New York: Hill and Wang, 1977), 39.

26. Graham Lock, "Riddles of a Chicago Alchemist," *Wire* 62 (August 1989): 27.
27. George E. Lewis, "Singing Omar's Song: A (Re)construction of Great Black Music," *Lenox Avenue* 4 (1998): 77. On Braxton's titles, see especially Szwed, "Local and the Express" in *Crossovers.*
28. Lewis, "Singing Omar's Song," 77.
29. John Hollander, "'Haddocks' Eyes': A Note on the Theory of Titles," in *Vision and Resonance: Two Senses of Poetic Form* (Oxford: Oxford University Press, 1975), 214.
30. It should be immediately apparent that some of Threadgill's imperative titles repurpose recognizable idioms, some simply appropriated as found objects ("Calm Down") and some reworked or "tilted" in canny ways. "Do the Needful," for instance, is not a new formulation (the first instance cited in the *Oxford English Dictionary* goes back to a 1709 article by Richard Steele in *The Tatler*); more recently, it has been associated with certain variants of postcolonial English, especially in South Asia. I thank Vijay Iyer for reminding me that it is a relatively familiar idiom in the Indian diaspora.
31. Lock, "Riddles of a Chicago Alchemist," 27.
32. Francis Davis, "Positively Charged," in *Outcats: Jazz Composers, Instrumentalists, and Singers* (New York: Oxford, 1990), 62.
33. Henry Threadgill Oral History, Session 3, conducted by Brent Hayes Edwards, December 23, 2009, Cortlandt Manor, New York. I am grateful to Hiie Saumaa for transcribing these recordings.
34. Ted Panken, "Henry Threadgill: Influences" (1996 interview), http://www.jazzhouse.org/library/index.php3?read=panken3, 7.
35. Davis, "Positively Charged," in *Outcats,* 61; Henry Threadgill, as told to Steven Buchanan, *Be-Bop and Beyond* 4, no. 2 (April 1986): 22.
36. Howard Mandel, "Henry Threadgill: Music to Make the Sun Come Up," *Down Beat* 52, no. 7 (July 1985): 26.
37. Henry Threadgill, *Song out of My Trees* (Black Saint 120154–2, 1994).
38. Larry Birnbaum, "Outside Moves In: Henry Threadgill Inks a Major-Label Deal," *Down Beat* 62, no. 3 (March 1995): 19.
39. Henry Threadgill Oral History, Session 3, conducted by Brent Hayes Edwards, December 23, 2009.
40. Jim Macnie, "Henry Threadgill: Global Jelly Roll with the Bismark of Jazz," *Musician* 197 (April 1995): 42. Macnie adds, "A prayer here, a party there, and you've got a complex opus by a guy who holds dear all things kaleidoscopic" (42).
41. Tony Scherman, "Music Like Nobody Else's, Not for Everyone," *New York Times,* January 7, 1996, 32.
42. Henry Threadgill Oral History, Session 3, December 23, 2009.
43. Ibid.
44. "The Other's Language: Jacques Derrida Interviews Ornette Coleman, 23 June 1997," trans. Timothy S. Murphy, *Genre* 37, no. 2 (Summer 2004): 327.
45. "Henry Threadgill," undated promotional brochure, Island Records.
46. Birnbaum, "Outside Moves In," 17.
47. Henry Threadgill Oral History, Session 3, December 23, 2009.
48. Threadgill himself calls his use of language above all "poetic." See Lock, "Riddles of a Chicago Alchemist," 27: "I use terms that seem appropriate for the music, and sometimes that takes on kind of a *poetic* nature."
49. Jakobson writes: "What is the empirical linguistic criterion of the poetic function? In particular, what is the indispensable feature inherent in any piece of poetry? To answer this question we must recall the two basic modes of arrangement used in verbal behavior, *se-*

lection and *combination*. . . . The selection is produced on the basis of equivalence, synonymy and antinomy, while the combination, the build-up of the sequence, is based on contiguity. *The poetic function projects the principle of equivalence from the axis of selection into the axis of combination.* Equivalence is promoted to the constitutive device of the sequence"; see Roman Jakobson, "Linguistics and Poetics," in *Language in Literature,* ed. Krystyna Pomorska and Stephen Rudy (Cambridge, MA: Harvard University Press, 1987), 71.

50. Lock, "Riddles of a Chicago Alchemist," 27.

7. Notes on Poetics Regarding Mackey's *Song*

1. Louis Zukofsky, "A Statement for Poetry," in *Prepositions* (Berkeley: University of California Press, 1981), 19. The phrase "research at the interstice" is Ed Roberson's; see Ed Roberson, *The Aerialist Narratives,* collected in *Voices Cast Out to Talk Us In* (Iowa City: University of Iowa Press, 1995), 89.
2. Mackey discusses "telling inarticulacy" in the extraordinary essay, "Sound and Sentiment, Sound and Symbol," collected in Nathaniel Mackey, *Discrepant Engagement: Dissonance, Cross-Culturality, and Experimental Writing* (New York: Cambridge University Press, 1993), 252–253. For music as an "alternate vocality," see his "Cante Moro," in Nathaniel Mackey, *Paracritical Hinge: Essays, Talks, Notes, Interview* (Madison: University of Wisconsin Press, 2005), 203.
3. Mackey, "Cante Moro," in *Paracritical Hinge,* 206.
4. Mackey, "Wringing the Word," *World Literature Today* 68, no. 4 (Autumn 1994): 734.
5. N.'s letter on falsetto is found in *Bedouin Hornbook, Book One of From a Broken Bottle Traces of Perfume Still Emanate* (1986; repr., Los Angeles: Sun and Moon, 1998), 62–64. Subsequent references will be indicated parenthetically in the text with page numbers preceded by the initials BH. "Cante Moro" is Mackey's extended take on flamenco and on Garcia Lorca's influential essay on *duende;* Federico Garcia Lorca, "The Theory and Function of the *Duende,*" trans. J. L. Gili, in *The Poetics of the New American Poetry,* ed. Donald Allen and Warren Tallman (New York: Grove Press, 1973), 91–103. For Mackey's comments on the Song of the Andoumboulou, see his interview with Peter O'Leary, *Chicago Review* 43, no. 1 (Winter 1997), collected in *Paracritical Hinge,* 297–298. The main ethnological source on the Dogon is the work of Marcel Griaule and Germaine Dieterlen: for the Andoumboulou, see especially Marcel Griaule, *Masques Dogons* (1938; repr., Paris: Insitut d'Ethnologie, Musée de l'Homme, 1994), 55ff., 153ff.; and Marcel Griaule and Germaine Dieterlen, *Le Renard Pâle* (Paris: Institut d'Ethnologie, 1965), trans. Stephen C. Infantino as *The Pale Fox* (Chino Valley, AZ: Continuum Foundation, 1986), 209ff.
6. In enumerating these connotations, I am indebted in part to Charles O. Hartman's work on voice and poetics; see the introduction to *Jazz Text: Voice and Improvisation in Poetry, Jazz, and Song* (Princeton, NJ: Princeton University Press, 1991), 3–4.
7. The phrase the "limits of the sayable" comes from the preface to the anthology *Moment's Notice,* coedited by Mackey and Art Lange: "it is particularly unsurprising that a music which so frequently and characteristically aspires to the condition of speech, reflecting critically, it seems, upon the limits of the sayable, should have provoked and proved of enormous interest to practitioners of the art of the word—writers." See "Editors' Note," in Nathaniel Mackey and Art Lange, eds., *Moment's Notice: Jazz and Poetry and Prose* (Minneapolis: Coffee House Press, 1993).
8. Mackey writes of language as orphaned from an inaccessible prior "wholeness" that putatively gave it birth in "Sound and Sentiment, Sound and Symbol" (*Discrepant Engagement,* 233). The phrase "methodologic fissures" comes from Cecil Taylor's "–Aqoueh R–Oyo," liner note to the 1973 *Air Above Mountains (buildings within)* (Enja 3005). On black culture's strategy of accepting and even anticipating "cuts" and slips in expression, also see James Snead, "Repetition as a Figure of Black Culture," in *Black Literature and Literary Theory,* ed. Henry Louis Gates Jr. (New York: Methuen, 1984), 67.

9. Mackey, "Cante Moro," 186.
10. Ibid., 193.
11. Mackey, *Paracritical Hinge,* 257–258.
12. Mingus, *The Black Saint and the Sinner Lady* (Impulse MCAD-5649). It seems appropriate to offer Mingus as gloss to Mackey's serial poetics, in part to signal the ways Mingus's music itself can be heard as a revisioning of the "serial" form, in its own medium. In an essay on Edward Kamau Brathwaite titled "New Series 1 (Folk Series)," Mackey comments: "I have borrowed the title of this essay from Charles Mingus. Fishing for a title for a composition during a recording session, Mingus answered his own question 'What could replace *Opus?*' (what could replace the Eurocentric, elite connotations the word carries) with the tentative 'New Series 1 . . . *Folk* Series'" (*Discrepant Engagement,* 155). The allusion is to Mingus's 1960 *Charles Mingus Presents Charles Mingus* (Candid 9005).
13. Nathaniel Mackey, *Eroding Witness* (Urbana: University of Illinois Press, 1985); Nathaniel Mackey, *School of Udhra* (San Francisco: City Lights, 1993); Nathaniel Mackey, *Whatsaid Serif* (San Francisco: City Lights, 1998); Nathaniel Mackey, *Splay Anthem* (New York: New Directions, 2006); Nathaniel Mackey, *Nod House* (New York: New Directions, 2011); Nathaniel Mackey, *Blue Fasa* (New York: New Directions, 2015).
14. Robert Duncan, "Notes on Poetics Regarding Olson's *Maximus,*" in *Fictive Certainties* (New York: New Directions, 1985), 68–75.
15. Duncan adopts these terms from Ezra Pound, *How to Read* (1931), collected in *Literary Essays of Ezra Pound*, ed. T. S. Eliot (1935; repr. New York: New Directions, 1968), 15–40. Pound further elaborates this model in *ABC of Reading* (London: Faber & Faber, 1934), 37, 63, 102.
16. Robert Duncan, *Passages* 1-29, collected in Duncan, *Bending the Bow* (New York: New Directions, 1968); Charles Olson, *The Maximus Poems* (Berkeley, CA: University of California Press, 1983); Jack Spicer, *The Heads of the Town up to the Aether* (1961), in *The Collected Books of Jack Spicer*, ed. Robin Blaser (Santa Rosa, CA: Black Sparrow, 1989), 115–183.
17. Mackey, *Paracritical Hinge,* 276.
18. Mackey, *Eroding Witness,* 50.
19. Robin Blaser, "The Practice of Outside," in *The Collected Books of Jack Spicer,* ed. Blaser (Santa Rosa, CA: Black Sparrow Press, 1989), 278. Jack Spicer's own comments on the serial form can be found in "Excerpts from the Vancouver Lectures," in Allen and Tallman, *Poetics of the New American Poetry,* 227–234. These talks are available in their entirety in Peter Gizzi, ed., *The House That Jack Built: The Collected Lectures of Jack Spicer* (Hanover, NH: University Press of New England, 1998).
20. Of course, it is not at all clear from this explication that Blaser understands serial ("twelve tone") composition—which manipulates tone rows, but doesn't rely on anything like a sequence of "rooms" or spaces (either harmonic or melodic). In fact, Spicer himself made no such claim for the term: in one lecture, he declared unequivocally that the serial poem is "a lousy name. It simply means that you go from one point to another to another, not really knowing where you are from point A to point B" (Gizzi, *House That Jack Built,* 73).
21. Mackey has written about the representations of black music in Williams's "Ol' Bunk's Band" and *Man Orchid;* see Mackey, *Discrepant Engagement,* 240–253.
22. Denise Levertov, "Williams and the *Duende,*" in *New and Selected Essays* (New York: New Directions, 1992), 33–43. Williams's "The Sound of Waves" appears in Charles Tomlinson, ed., *The Collected Poems* (New York: New Directions, 1985), 182–183.
23. Mackey, *Discrepant Engagement,* 176.
24. Mackey, "Song of the Andoumboulou: 10," *School of Udhra,* 5–6. Subsequent references will be indicated parenthetically in the text with page numbers preceded by the initials SU.
25. Mackey, *Paracritical Hinge,* 296.
26. Marjorie Garber, "Out of Joint," in *The Body in Parts: Fantasies of Corporeality in Early Modern Europe,* ed. David Hillman and Carla Mazzio (New York: Routledge, 1997), 35.
27. Marcel Griaule, *Conversations with Ogotemmêli: An Introduction to Dogon Religious Ideas,* trans. R. Butler et al. (New York: Oxford University Press, 1965), 43–44. The French orig-

inal is Marcel Griaule, *Dieu d'eau: entretiens avec Ogotemmêli* (1948; repr., Paris: Fayard, 1966), 52.

28. The phrase *vatic scat* comes from the poem "Slipped Quadrant," *School of Udhra,* 86. One might moreover suggest that this joint-work on the syntax of subjectivity is rooted in Mackey's critique of what he has described as a "predicament of subjectivity in the lyric that we inherit within a Western tradition which has legacies of domination and conquest and moral complication that make those claims to subjectivity and sublimity hard to countenance." In response, his work makes recourse to "African traditional wisdoms and neo-African and Caribbean sources of access to a kind of subjectivity—or just the whole realm of subjectivity that is called into question as one of the repercussions of that oppressive legacy in the West" (Mackey, *Paracritical Hinge,* 268).
29. There is not space here to extend this argument, but for me, it is these factors—and particularly their ambivalent formal function—that distinguish Mackey's "under-the-line" poems from some potential precursors, such as Jack Spicer's *Hommage to Creeley* in *The Heads of the Town Up to the Aether* and William Carlos Williams's *Kora in Hell,* both of which feature this formal splitting, with passages at the bottom of the page graphically set off from the "main" serial form. Furthermore, in Spicer and Williams, the paradigm is much more explicitly one of *footnotes*—both refer to the bottom-half sections as "explanatory notes" to the main poem. On the contrary, *School of Udhra* never valorizes its spatialization, and leaves ambiguous (discrepant, as Mackey would have it) the relationship between voices above and under the line.
30. Mackey, *Discrepant Engagement,* 123–124. Interestingly, Mackey's next publication of a section of *Song of the Andoumboulou* seemed to have been designed in part to counter the graphic emphasis—what Wilson Harris would call the "eye-based bias"—of *School of Udhra.* Although many sections of the series were published individually in small journals, and numbers 18–20 were printed in a limited-edition letter-press edition by Moving Parts Press in 1994, the first substantial collection after *School of Udhra* was a compact disc recording of Mackey reading. Mackey, with Royal Hartigan on drums and percussion and Hafez Modirzadeh on reeds and flutes, *Strick: Song of the Andoumboulou 16–25* (Memphis, TN: Spoken Engine Co., 1995). Only subsequently were these poems collected in print, making legible the "graphic impulse" of the "under-the-line" poems. *Song of the Andoumboulou: 16–35* are found in Mackey, *Whatsaid Serif.* The "under-the-line" poems have continued to be a feature of the series in the books that have followed (*Splay Anthem, Nod House,* and *Blue Fasa*).
31. Mackey, *Whatsaid Serif,* 82.
32. Roberson, *Voices Cast Out,* 64.
33. Mackey, *Whatsaid Serif,* 9.
34. Mackey, *Paracritical Hinge,* 297.
35. See Willi Apel, *Harvard Dictionary of Music,* 2nd ed. (Cambridge, MA: Harvard University Press, 1974), 725. It should be noted that there is some discrepancy even in this standard usage: originally, *reprise* referred to "the repetition of the exposition *before* the development, usually indicated by the repeat sign" (ibid., emphasis added). So we find again that problematic of going beyond: the uncertainty as to whether repetition precedes development (sets it off) or closes it (sums it up).
36. Nathaniel Mackey, *Djbot Baghostus's Run* (Los Angeles: Sun and Moon, 1993), 59–69. The allusion appears in an addition to one of the letters, one of the dreamlike prose pieces N. comes to call "The Creaking of the Word: After-the-Fact Lecture/Libretti." The text invokes Monk's version of the tune (on the 1957 *Thelonious Himself*) only by name, but one might hear the Basie-Davis arrangement, too, as what Mackey might term a "Namesake Epigraph" to this citation (BH 227). There is not space to pursue this here, but I would argue that the "After-the-Fact Lecture/Libretti" in the prose do much the same formal work as the "under-the-line" poems in *School of Udhra*—in the epistolary work, then, they are a simultaneous challenge to and extension of the serial form of the letters. Mackey has almost said as much: "It's possible that these things that are called 'after-the-fact lecture/libretti'

are pushing a possibility that now resides in those letters, that are enclosures or attachments to those letters" (*Paracritical Hinge,* 300).

37. Stanley Dance, liner notes to *Basie, Getz and Vaughan Live at Birdland,* a live recording from December 1954 (Roulette RE-126, 1975). I would like to thank Robert O'Meally for drawing my attention to this record, and in engaging me in a number of useful discussions around the idea of reprise.
38. Chris Albertson, liner notes to Count Basie and His Orchestra, *April in Paris* (1956; reissue Verve MGV-8102, 1997). The arrangement is also discussed in Albert Murray, *Good Morning Blues: The Autobiography of Count Basie* (New York: Donald I. Fine, 1985), 318. Basie's phrase "one more once" also has enjoyed some resonance in the anecdotes of jazz culture. Duke Ellington even picked it up as the title of one of the pieces he composed—without a reprise, though—for the session that brought the two great orchestras together ("One More Once," on *Duke 56/62* Vol. 2 [CBS 88654 (French printing), 1984]; this is an outtake from the sessions on July 6, 1961, which was not included in the original Basie/Ellington release, *First Time! The Count Meets the Duke* [Columbia CS8515]).
39. Mackey, *Whatsaid Serif,* 107.
40. Mackey, "Cante Moro," 191.
41. I am indebted to Peter X. Feng for this insight. On uses of the vamp, see generally Albert Murray, *Stomping the Blues* (New York: Da Capo, 1976), 93ff.
42. Albertson, liner notes to Count Basie, *April in Paris.* Of course, as Peter X. Feng pointed out to me, it is appropriate that this anecdote would involve a *telethon*—a mediatized event that attempts to elicit response, to provoke other voices to call in, providing witness and (economic) support.
43. James Snead, "Repetition as a Figure of Black Culture," in *Black Literature and Literary Theory,* ed. Henry Louis Gates Jr. (New York: Methuen, 1984), 64, 67.
44. In fact, though, the figure of weaving could be said to introduce both versions of this metaphysics in Mackey's work alone. His writing emphasizes weaving as what the Dogon call "the creaking of the word" (the phrase they use to name the base of their looms): "It is the noise upon which the word is based, the discrepant foundation of all coherence and articulation, of the purchase upon the world fabrication affords" (Mackey, *Discrepant Engagement,* 19). But Mackey also turns to weaving as a figure for inherent "intervals" of absence (in Roberson's sense), as in this passage from *Bedouin Hornbook:* "One afternoon six years ago I sat at the end of a thread. At the other end of that thread was the eye of a needle. The needle's tip rested some distance below me in a space between two threads of cloth—two wefts and two warps crossed so as to make it a square. With the square as its pivot (or inverse pivot) the needle spun as I swung the thread but could not be disengaged. What this was was the Veil I've since come to know. Seeing it so, I intuit a 'space' we're all immigrants from" (BH 13–14).
45. Roberson, *Voices Cast Out,* 17.
46. Mackey, *Paracritical Hinge,* 292–293.
47. Mackey, *Eroding Witness,* 50.
48. Wilson Harris, *The Eye of the Scarecrow* (London: Faber and Faber, 1965), 102.
49. Mackey, *Discrepant Engagement,* 161.
50. Mackey, *Whatsaid Serif,* 108.
51. Later in the "Manifesto of the Unborn State of Exile," there is the following passage: "Language is one's medium of the vision of consciousness. . . . Whatever sympathy one may feel for a concrete poetry—where physical objects are used and adopted—the fact remains (in my estimation) that the original grain or grains of language cannot be trapped or proven. It is the sheer mystery—the impossibility of trapping its own grain—on which poetry lives and thrives. And this is this stuff of one's essential understanding of the reality of the original Word, the Well of Silence. Which is concerned with a genuine sourcelessness, a fluid logic of image" (Harris, *Eye of the Scarecrow,* 95).
52. Geneviève Calame-Griaule, *Serrures Dogon: analyse ethno-morphologique* (Paris: Musée de l'Homme, 1976). The translation is my own. See also Germaine Dieterlen, "La Serrure et sa

clef (Dogon, Mali)," in *Echanges et communications: Mélanges offerts à Claude Levi-Strauss,* ed. J. Pouillon and P. Maranda (The Hague: Mouton, 1970), 1:7–28.

53. Billie Holiday recorded Louis McKay's "Fine and Mellow" both early and late in her career: there is an initial studio session for Commodore Records in 1939 and the better-known Verve version in 1956, live at Carnegie Hall in New York.

8. Come Out

1. Ed Roberson, *Lucid Interval as Integral Music* (Pittsburgh: Harmattan, 1984), collected in Ed Roberson, *Voices Cast Out to Talk Us In* (Iowa City: University of Iowa Press, 1995). Subsequent references to the 1995 edition will be indicated parenthetically in the text.
2. Phone conversation with Ed Roberson, February 21, 1998. Jack Spicer, "Homage to Creeley," in *The Heads of the Town Up to the Aether (1960–1961),* in *The Collected Books of Jack Spicer,* ed. Robin Blaser (Santa Barbara: Black Sparrow, 1989), 115–148.
3. Kathleen Crown, "'Down Break Drum': An Interview with Ed Roberson (Part 1)," *Callaloo* 33, no. 3 (Summer 2010): 675.
4. Ibid.
5. Ibid., 653.
6. See Amitai F. Avi-ram, "*Apo Koinou* in Audre Lorde and the Moderns: Defining the Differences," *Callaloo* 26 (Winter 1986): 193–208.
7. William Empson, *Seven Types of Ambiguity,* rev. ed. (New York: New Directions, 1947), 75, 50.
8. Crown, "Down Break Drum," 661.
9. Ed Roberson, "Ask for 'How High the Moon,'" in *The Aerialist Narratives,* collected in Roberson, *Voices Cast Out,* 143.
10. Ibid., 62.
11. Michel Foucault, "The Father's 'No,'" collected in *Language, Counter-Memory, Practice: Selected Essays and Interviews,* ed. Donald F. Bouchard, trans. Bouchard and Sherry Simon (Ithaca, NY: Cornell University Press, 1977), 75.
12. Michel Foucault, *Histoire de la folie à l'âge classique* (Paris: Gallimard, 1972), 579. The translation is my own. In this connection, see also George MacLennan, *Lucid Interval: Subjective Writing and Madness in History* (Leicester: Leicester University Press, 1992).
13. Foucault, *Histoire,* 578.
14. Ibid., 580–581.
15. Crown, "Down Break Drum," 676.
16. Joseph Conte, *Unending Design: The Forms of Postmodern Poetry* (Ithaca, NY: Cornell University Press, 1991), 18–19; Umberto Eco, *The Open Work,* trans. Anna Cancogni (Cambridge, MA: Harvard University Press, 1989).
17. Conte, *Unending Design,* 15.
18. Pierre Boulez, "Series," collected in *Notes of an Apprenticeship,* trans. Herbert Weinstock (New York: Alfred A. Knopf, 1968), 303–304.
19. Conte, *Unending Design,* 24.
20. Paul Griffiths, "Serialism," in *The New Grove Dictionary of Music and Musicians,* ed. Stanley Sadie (London: Macmillan 2001), 23:116. Eco makes the same point, noting that the literary works he discusses (Mallarmé, Kafka, Joyce) are "substantially different from the post-Webernian musical composers" he considers (Eco, *Open Work,* 11). He later quotes Poullion to the effect that "a relation is *structurelle* when it plays a determining role within a given organization," and notes: "serial thought produced open-structured *(structurelles)* realities (even when those realities appear unstructured)" (218).
21. Jack Spicer, "Vancouver Lecture Two: The Serial Poem and *The Holy Grail,*" in *The House That Jack Built: The Collected Lectures of Jack Spicer,* ed. Peter Gizzi (Middletown, CT: Wesleyan/New England, 1998), 73.
22. Ibid., 52.
23. Robert Duncan, *Bending the Bow* (New York: New Directions, 1968), iv.

24. See, for example, Spicer, *House That Jack Built,* 81, 140, 141; Robert Creeley, "Writing," in *The Collected Essays of Robert Creeley* (Berkeley: University of California Press, 1989), 528, 531; Creeley, interview with John Sinclair and Robin Eichelle, in Donald Allen, ed., *Contexts of Poetry: Interviews* (Bolinas, CA: Four Seasons Foundation, 1973), 48–49; Robert Creeley, "Notes Apropos 'Free Verse,'" in *Naked Poetry: Recent American Poetry in Open Forms,* ed. Stephen Berg and Robert Mtzey (Indianapolis: Bobbs-Merrill, 1969), 186–187. Conte discusses the influence of Charlie Parker on Creeley's poetics (202–203). With Charles Olson, the matter is trickier; Conte quotes a 1952 letter from Olson to Cid Corman in which he declares that "form must be carefully extricated" from technique, just as carefully as Boulez is after form in serial structure"; see Charles Olson, *Letters for Origin: 1950–1956,* ed. Albert Glover (New York: Paragon House, 1988), 103–104, quoted in Conte, *Unending Design,* 38. This isn't exactly evidence that Olson was directly influenced by serial music in his composition of the Maximus poems. One could just as easily cite moments in Olson such as the interview where he says that in the 1950s, "there was no poetic. It was Charlie Parker. Literally, it was Charlie Parker"; see Charles Olson, *Muthologos: The Collected Lectures and Interviews,* ed. George Butternick (Bolinas: Four Seasons, 1979), 2:71.
25. Jack Spicer, "The Poet and Poetry—a Symposium," *Occident Magazine,* Fall 1949, collected in Spicer, *House That Jack Built,* 230. George M. Cohan (1878–1942) was a composer, lyricist, playwright, actor, and vaudeville song-and-dance man, best known as the creator of hit Broadway tunes such as "I'm a Yankee Doodle Dandy" (1904), "Give My Regards to Broadway" (1904), and "Over There" (1917). Sophie Tucker (1884–1966), the "Last of the Red Hot Mamas," was a Russian-born immigrant who became a famous vaudeville entertainer and singer.
26. Nathaniel Mackey, "Introduction: And All the Birds Sing Bass," in Nathaniel Mackey, *Discrepant Engagement: Dissonance, Cross-Culturality, and Experimental Writing* (New York: Cambridge University Press, 1993), 3.
27. See also Roberson's "The skipping stone stays out of the water" in *The Aerialist Narratives,* collected in Roberson, *Voices Cast Out,* 107–108.
28. See Ed Roberson, *Etai-Eken* (Pittsburgh: University of Pittsburgh Press, 1975), 31; "Taking the Print," in *The Aerialist Narratives,* collected in Roberson, *Voices Cast Out,* 78. A similar approach can be seen in Michael Warner's recent attempt to highlight periodicity rather than disciplinary categorization in analyzing what he terms the "temporality of circulation"; see Michael Warner, "*Publics and Counterpublics* (New York: Zone Books, 2002), 94–95.
29. Crown, "Down Break Drum," 681.
30. "75 in Harlem Throw Fruit at Policemen," *New York Times,* April 18, 1964, 27.
31. "Lawyer for 5 Tells Court Police Roughed Up Clients," *New York Times,* April 19, 1964, 47.
32. "Woman Is Killed in Harlem Store," *New York Times,* April 30, 1964, 71.
33. Junius Griffin, "Whites Are Target of Harlem Gang," *New York Times,* May 3, 1964, 43.
34. Junius Griffin, "Anti-White Harlem Gang Reported to Number 400," *New York Times,* May 6, 1964, 1, 36.
35. Junius Griffin, "Grand Jury Investigation Urged into Anti-White Gang in Harlem," *New York Times,* May 10, 1964, 61.
36. "The Harlem 'Blood Brothers,'" *New York Times,* May 8, 1964, 32; Carl J. Pelleck, "Harlem's Hate Gang: What It Is," *New York Post,* May 10, 1964, 3; "Police Find No Hate Links to Rifle Club," *New York Post,* May 13, 1964, 2; Anthony Scaduto, "A Look at the Rifle Clubs: Can Hate Groups Masquerade as Legitimate Sportsmen?" *New York Post,* May 17, 1964, 29; Junius Griffin, "N.A.A.C.P. Assails Reports of Gang," *New York Times,* May 11, 1964, 27; Clark, quoted in Les Matthews and George Barner, "They Still Can't Prove That 'Blood Gang' Lie!" *Amsterdam News,* May 23, 1964, 1, 55.
37. Nat Hentoff, "The Bloodless 400," *Village Voice,* May 28, 1964, 8. Also see Nat Hentoff, "On the Trail of the Blood Brothers," *Village Voice,* June 11, 1964, 6.
38. Susan Goodman, "Whites Cheer Malcolm X for Blasts at Whites," *Village Voice,* June 4, 1964, 3.

39. Junius Griffin, "Harlem: The Tension Underneath," *New York Times,* May 29, 1964, 1, 13.
40. Cy Egan and Richard Barr, "Behind the Riots: The Trigger, the Sequence," *New York Journal American,* July 20, 1964, 3.
41. Sue Reinert, "A Week Ago, It Started Like This," *New York Herald Tribune,* July 26, 1964, 8.
42. Paul L. Montgomery and Francis X. Clines, "Thousands Riot in Harlem Area; Scores Are Hurt," *New York Times,* July 19, 1964, 1. The statistics are drawn from Fred Ferretti and Martin G. Berck, "Tinderbox Harlem: New Outbreaks Snap Uneasy Truce," *New York Herald Tribune,* May 20, 1964, 1, 6; Joe R. Feagin and Paul B. Sheatsley, "Ghetto Appraisals of a Riot," *Public Opinion Quarterly* 32, no. 3 (Autumn 1968): 353; and F. C. Shapiro and J. W. Sullivan, *Race Riots: New York 1964* (New York: Crowell, 1964).
43. The *Herald Tribune* covers Kenneth Clark's press conference to refute the "Blood Brotherhood" story, but uses it as an opportunity to consider the data gathered by his organization's research on conditions in Harlem, rather than to relay the *Times* story. "Harlem Anger and 'Instant Reality,'" *New York Herald Tribune,* May 8, 1964, 19.
44. See, for example, Peter Kihss, "Harlem Riots Spread over 3 Decades," *New York Times,* July 20, 1964, 17.; John G. Rogers, "In 1943, It Was Like This in Harlem," *New York Herald Tribune,* July 26, 1964, 8; Joseph Endler and James W. Sullivan, "Harlem Explodes: Negroes Battle Police," *New York Herald Tribune,* July 19, 1964, 3; Ferretti and Berck, "Tinderbox Harlem," 1, 6.
45. Kenneth Clark, "Behind the Harlem Riots—Two Views," *New York Herald Tribune,* July 20, 1964, 1, 7.
46. Young, quoted in "Harlem Anger and 'Instant Reality,'" *New York Herald Tribune,* May 8, 1964, 19.
47. See Arnold Rampersad, *The Life of Langston Hughes,* vol. 2, *1941–1967: I Dream a World* (New York: Oxford University Press, 1988), 62–66; Donna Akiba Sullivan Harper, *Not So Simple: The "Simple" Stories by Langston Hughes* (Columbia: University of Missouri Press, 1996), 39.
48. Harper, *Not So Simple,* 100, 101.
49. In the first stories, the narrator was identified as Hughes himself; later on he became a different character, usually nameless but occasionally identified as Ananias Boyd. See Donna Akiba Sullivan Harper, ed., *The Collected Works of Langston Hughes,* vol. 8, *The Later Simple Stories* (Columbia: University of Missouri Press, 2002), 1; Harper, *Not So Simple,* 78.
50. Langston Hughes, "Simple's Birth," *New York Post,* October 29, 1965, 52.
51. Langston Hughes, "Refugees," *New York Post,* October 22, 1965, 44.
52. Langston Hughes, "Concernment," in *Simple's Uncle Sam* (New York: Hill and Wang, 1965), 152.
53. In one early column, "Let's Laugh a Little," *Chicago Defender* (November 6, 1943), reprinted as the foreword to the collection *Simple Stakes a Claim* (1957), Hughes writes that "Humor is a weapon, too, of no mean value against one's foes. In the Latin American countries, it is used socially." Harper, ed., *Collected Works,* 20.
54. Langston Hughes, "Police Dilemma," *New York Post,* May 29, 1964, 22.
55. Langston Hughes, "Pose-Outs," *New York Post,* May 22, 1964, 36.
56. "Shakespeare," *New York Post,* May 8, 1964, 40.
57. This is a point Ralph Ellison makes, as well, for instance, in "Roscoe Runjee and the American Language" (Black Perspective Conference, May 14, 1972), collected in John F. Callahan, ed., *The Collected Essays of Ralph Ellison* (New York: Modern Library, 1995), 458. Of course, as I discussed in Chapter 3, Hughes himself had published a collection of poetry called *Shakespeare in Harlem* (New York: Knopf, 1942).
58. Langston Hughes, "Wigs for Freedom," in *Simple's Uncle Sam,* 140.
59. Ibid., 139.
60. Ibid., 140.
61. Ibid., 143.

62. Langston Hughes, "The Teachers," *New York Post,* June 26, 1964, 40.
63. The special columns are Langston Hughes, "The Harlem Story," *New York Post,* July 21, 1964, 47; "Harlem—II," *New York Post,* July 22, 1964, 3; "Harlem—III," *New York Post,* July 23, 1964, 29.
64. Hughes, "Harlem Story," 47. In a poem published that fall, Hughes seems to extend this lament. The poem is a fanciful catalogue (its capital letters seeming to emphasize the urgency) of political activists and saviors of various stripes: "SEND FOR THE PIED PIPER AND LET HIM PIPE THE RATS AWAY./SEND FOR ROBIN HOOD TO CLINCH THE ANIT-POVERTY CAMPAIGN./ . . . SEND FOR DEAD BLIND LEMON TO SING THE B FLAT BLUES./SEND FOR ROBESPIERRE TO SCREAM, *'ÇA IRA! ÇA IRA! ÇA IRA!'/SEND (GOD FORBID—HE'S NOT DEAD LONG ENOUGH!)/FOR LUMUMBA TO CRY 'FREEDOM NOW!'"* After having listed names from Old Man Moses to Lenin, Harriet Tubman to W. E. B. Du Bois, the poem concludes with a parenthetical, literary last resort: "(And if nobody comes, send for me.)" See Langston Hughes, "Harlem Call: After the 1964 Riots," *American Dialog,* October–November 1964, 37. He later changed the title to "Final Call." See Arnold Rampersad, ed., *The Collected Poems of Langston Hughes* (New York: Knopf, 1994), 545.
65. Langston Hughes, "Harlem: The Down Boys," *New York Post,* July 26, 1964, 27.
66. Langston Hughes, "Clean-Up Squads," *New York Post,* July 31, 1964, 30.
67. Langston Hughes, "For New York," *New York Post,* August 7, 1964, 35.
68. Jimmy Breslin, "Fear and Hate—Sputtering Fuse," *New York Herald Tribune,* July 20, 1964, 1, 17.
69. Jimmy Breslin, "The Lull," *New York Herald Tribune,* July 29, 1964, 17. This is a continual theme in his articles: "And the streets were frightening. Not because of what was going on. They were frightening because of the emptiness." Jimmy Breslin, "North of 110th St.," *New York Herald Tribune,* Tuesday, July 21, 1964, 1, 19. See also Jimmy Breslin, "More to Come?" *New York Herald Tribune,* July 23, 1964, 13; Jimmy Breslin, "Our Town's Nightmare of Racial Violence," *New York Herald Tribune,* July 24, 1964, 1; Jimmy Breslin, "How It Was and May Be in New York," *New York Herald Tribune,* July 26, 1964, 1.
70. Walter Winchell, "Interviews," *New York Journal American,* May 10, 1964, 17.
71. Hughes, "Harlem," 27.
72. "A Voice on Lawyer is Urged for Poor," *New York Times,* November 12, 1966, 30; "Convictions of 6 in 1964 Harlem Slaying Reversed," *New York Times,* November 30, 1968, 78; "Judge Accused of Racial Slur against 'Harlem 6,'" *New York Times,* February 22, 1969, 16 (during the retrial, State Supreme Court Justice Gerald Culkin remarked, "These boys wouldn't know a good attorney from a good watermelon"); "State Court Justice Is Cleared by Panel on Racism Charge," *New York Times,* April 24, 1968, 31.

    One defendant, Robert Rice, was retried and found guilty in 1970, in a verdict that was thrown out again in 1973. Arnold H. Lubasch, "Judge Throws Out Murder Conviction of One Defendant in Harlem Six Case," *New York Times,* July 18, 1973. Meanwhile, Daniel Hamm pled guilty to manslaughter and was paroled in March 1973 (though the parole was revoked immediately). The others eventually pled guilty and received suspended sentence in order to avoid the ordeal of another court case. Lacey Fosburgh, "'Harlem 4' to Stand Trial Fourth Time on Murder Charge," *New York Times,* June 29, 1972, 1, 35; "Harlem Four: 'Hardest Day of Our Lives,'" *New York Times,* April 8, 1973, 23.
73. See advertisement, "Harlem's Condemned 6: A Public Hearing," *Village Voice,* April 14, 1966; "Benefit Aids Appeal of 6 Convicted of Harlem Killing," *New York Times,* April 18, 1966, 21; "'The Harlem Six'—Benefit to Appeal Conviction in Store Owner's Murder," *New York Herald Tribune,* April 17, 1966, 27.
74. Town Hall program, April 17, 1966, Town Hall Archives, Music Division, New York Public Library for the Performing Arts.
75. The interviews were recorded by Willie Jones, the same employee of Harlem Youth Opportunities Unlimited who had been cited as corroborating the "Blood Brothers" story by the

New York Times; see Truman Nelson, *The Torture of Mothers* (1965; repr., Boston: Beacon Press, 1968), 55–57.

76. Ibid., 3.
77. Ibid., 34.
78. Ibid., 13–15.
79. Jean-Paul Sartre, "Preface" to Frantz Fanon, *The Wretched of the Earth,* trans. Constance Farrington (New York: Grove, 1963), 14.
80. Nelson, *Torture of Mothers,* 95.
81. Charles Reznikoff, "Prolegomena," unpublished ms., San Diego, quoted in Linda Simon, "Reznikoff: The Poet as Witness," in *Charles Reznikoff: Man and Poet,* ed. Martin Hindus (Orono, Maine: National Poetry Foundation/University of Maine), 241.
82. Charles Reznikoff, "Early History of a Writer," quoted in Milton Hindus, *Charles Reznikoff: A Critical Essay* (Santa Barbara: Black Sparrow, 1977), 8.
83. See Janet Sutherland, "Reznikoff and His Sources," in Hindus, *Charles Reznikoff: Man and Poet,* 304–305.
84. L. S. Dembo, *The Contemporary Writer* (Madison: University of Washington Press, 1972), 207.
85. Charles Reznikoff, *Testimony,* vol. 1, *The United States (1885–1915) Recitative* (Santa Barbara: Black Sparrow Press, 1978), 22–23.
86. Hayden Carruth, "A Failure of Contempt," *Poetry* (1966), quoted in Sutherland, "Reznikoff and His Sources," 297.
87. Simon, "Reznikoff," 244–245.
88. "Steve Reich," in William Duckworth, *Talking Music: Conversations with John Cage, Philip Glass, Laurie Anderson, and Five Generations of American Experimental Composers* (1995; repr., New York: Da Capo, 1999), 297. Additional information was provided by Reich in a phone conversation, August 16, 2004.
89. Steve Reich, liner notes to *Steve Reich: Early Works* (Elektra Nonesuch 9 79169–2, 1987).
90. Duckworth, *Talking Music,* 297.
91. "First Interview with Michael Nyman," *The Musical Times* vol. 112 (1971), collected in Steve Reich, *Writings on Music, 1965–2000,* ed. Paul Hiller (New York: Oxford University Press, 2002), 53.
92. For example, "Steve Reich," *New Grove Dictionary of Music and Musicians,* ed. Stanley Sadie (New York: Grove, 2001), 21:128. The first time Reich played the piece in a concert of his own music was a month and a half later; see Carman Moore, "Park Place Electronics," *Village Voice,* June 9, 1966, 17.
93. Phone conversation with Steve Reich, August 16, 2004.
94. Abbey Lincoln has said that she was not comfortable with the screams in the middle section of "Triptych," but that (her then husband) Roach insisted. See Fred Moten's suggestive reading of this moment in relation to Frederick Douglass's memorable discussion (in his 1845 *Narrative*) of the screams of his aunt Hester as she is being beaten: in Moten's words, Lincoln's screams are "not the reduction of but the reduction to phonic materiality where re-engendering prefaces and works itself. No originary configuration of attributes but an ongoing shiftiness, a living labor of engendering to be organize din its relation to a politico-aesthesis"; see Fred Moten, *In the Break: The Aesthetics of the Black Radical Tradition* (Minneapolis: University of Minnesota Press, 2003), 24.
95. "Steve Reich," in Duckworth, *Talking Music,* 313. On the subject of canons, also see Steve Reich, liner notes to *Steve Reich: Early Works* (Elektra Nonesuch 9 79169–2, 1987); Rebecca Y. Kim, "From New York to Vermont: Conversation with Steve Reich," *Current Musicology* 67–68 (2002): 351–352.
96. As David Schwartz observes, "The repetition of 'come out' sounds like a direct address to the listener, an imperative"; see David Schwartz, "Listening Subjects: Semiotics, Psychoanalysis, and the Music of John Adams and Steve Reich," in *Keeping Score: Music, Disciplinarity, Culture,* ed. David Schwarz, Anahid Kassabian, and Lawrence Seigel (Charlottesville: University of Virginia Press, 1997), 291.

97. On the history and complexities of this metaphor (from the Supreme Court decision in *Brown v. Board of Education*), see especially Charles Ogletree Jr., *All Deliberate Speed: Reflections on the First Half Century of Brown v. Board of Education* (New York: W. W. Norton, 2004), 9–11.
98. Emily Wasserman, "An Interview with Composer Steve Reich," *Artforum* 10, no. 9 (1972): 45.
99. Steve Reich, "Music as a Gradual Process," collected in Steve Reich, *Writings on Music, 1965–2000,* ed. Paul Hiller (New York: Oxford University Press, 2002), 34.
100. Ibid., 35.
101. Jason Gross, "Steve Reich: Early Tape Pieces," http://www.furious.com/perfect/ohm/reich2.html.
102. "Music and Language," interview with Barbara Basting, *du* [Zurich] vol. 5 (May 1996), collected in Reich, *Writings on Music,* 198–199.
103. Ibid., 199–200. See also "Answers to Questions about *Different Trains*" (1994), in Wolfgang Gratzner, *Nähe und Distanz—Nachgedachte Musik der Gegenwart* (1995), collected in Reich, *Writings on Music,* 181; Gross, "Steve Reich"; Kim, "From New York to Vermont," 362.
104. Leroi Jones (Amiri Baraka), "Expressive Language," in Baraka, *Home: Social Essays* (New York: William Morrow, 1966), 171.
105. Ibid., 171.
106. Ibid., 171.
107. One indication that Reich was fully aware of the political implications of his composition—specifically, in the way it draws attention to the syntactical precision of Hamm's sentence—can be found in his admiring commentary on the devastatingly austere dance Anne Teresa De Keersmaeker made to *Come Out* in 1982. Describing her dance suite *Fase,* set to four key examples of Reich's "phase music" (*Piano Phase; Come Out; Clapping Music;* and *Violin Phase*), Reich writes: "The second section, *Come Out,* is done on a darkened stage with two small hanging lamps directly over the dancers' heads while they sit on stools. It suggests a police station. The movements, all done while sitting, serve to intensify the feelings of interrogation, brutality, anger, and sexuality that are all implicit in the tape: implicit but never understood or mentioned by music critics, until de Keersmaeker captured both the technique and the audible theater in *Come Out*" (Reich, "De Keermaeker, Kylian, and European Dance" (2000), collected in *Writings on Music,* 214). On the genesis and conception of the dance, see "Fase, Four Movements to the Music of Steve Reich," in Anne Teresa De Keersmaeker and Bojana Cvejic, *A Choreographer's Score: Fase, Rosas danst Rosas, Elena's Aria, Bartók* (Brussels: Mercatorfonds/Rosas, 2012), especially 37–46.
108. "Repeating Phases: Steve Reich," *Parabola* 13 (Summer 1988): 52.
109. Spicer, "Vancouver Lecture 2," in *House That Jack Built,* 55.
110. Ed Roberson, *Etai-Eken* (Pittsburgh: University of Pittsburgh Press, 1975), 27.
111. K. Robert Schwarz, "Steve Reich: Back on Track," *Ear Magazine* 14, no. 2 (April 1989): 32.
112. Ed Roberson, *When Thy King Is a Boy* (Pittsburgh: University of Pittsburgh Press, 1970), 60.
113. Michael Nyman, "Steve Reich," *Music and Musicians* 25 (January 1977): 19. Reich makes this observation in relation to his *Music for 18 Musicians.*

Afterword

1. Ricky Riccardi, *What a Wonderful World: The Magic of Louis Armstrong's Later Years* (New York: Pantheon Books, 2011), 268.
2. Louis Armstrong, "Louis Armstrong+the Jewish Family in New Orleans, LA, the Year of 1907" (March 31, 1969–1970), collected in Thomas Brothers, ed., *Louis Armstrong, in His Own Words: Selected Writings* (New York: Oxford University Press, 1999), 3. Subsequent page references to this published version will be indicated parenthetically. The original holograph manuscript is located in the Louis Armstrong Archives at Queens College/CUNY.
3. Gary Giddins, *Satchmo* (New York: Doubleday, 1988), 20.

4. See Riccardi, *What a Wonderful World,* 269.
5. Brothers, *Louis Armstrong, in His Own Words,* 192–193.
6. In quoting the slight variations in the song lyrics, I am citing page references to *Louis Armstrong, in His Own Words* because it is the most easily available published version of this text. But I have slightly revised Brothers's transcriptions in that book in an attempt to capture with as much precision as possible the details of Armstrong's handwriting. (Any such precision is inherently limited however by the persistent idiosyncrasy of Armstrong's holograph manuscripts: the differences between upper case and lower case, or between a dash and a dot, are often ambiguous, to an extent that defies any attempt to "normalize" his writing practice into standard print conventions.)
7. Lawrence Gushee, "The Improvisation of Louis Armstrong," in *In the Course of Performance: Studies in the World of Musical Improvisation,* ed. Bruno Nettl and Melinda Russell (Chicago: University of Chicago Press, 1998), 292, quoted in Daniel Stein, *Music Is My Life: Louis Armstrong, Autobiography, and American Jazz* (Ann Arbor: University of Michigan Press, 2012), 103. In his own discussion of "Louis Armstrong+the Jewish Family," Stein reads these variations as evidence of the "performative ethos that suffuses all of Armstrong's expressions" and the "obvious intermedial interface between his writings and his music" (103).
8. Federico García Lorca, "On Lullabies (Las nanas infantiles) (1928)," trans. A. S. Kline (2008), http://www.poetryintranslation.com/klineaslullabies.htm, accessed July 15, 2016.
9. Ibid. In a similar vein, Rivka Galchen has observed that lullabies can be defined "functionally" as "a song used to lull a child to sleep. In this sense, the distinctive burden of a lullaby is to be interesting enough to capture a child's attention, but not interesting enough to keep the child awake"; see Rivka Galchen, "The Melancholy Mystery of Lullabies," *New York Times Magazine,* October 14, 2015, 53.
10. There are a number of recordings of Armstrong playing "Russian Lullaby" in concert, including a live recording from New York in April 1950 included on the LP *Satchmo on Stage* (Decca DL 8330, 1957), which is also available in CD form as part of the box set *The Complete Decca Studio Recordings of Louis Armstrong And the All Stars* (Mosaic Records MQ8–146, 1993).
11. Email from Dan Morgenstern, March 1, 2007.
12. It seems that Berlin composed "Russian Lullaby" in the spring of 1927 while on vacation with family in Palm Beach, Florida. See Edward Jablonski, *Irving Berlin: American Troubadour* (New York: Henry Holt, 1999), 132. The best-known jazz recording of the song is probably Ella Fitzgerald's version, recorded March 17, 1958, and released on the LP album *Ella Fitzgerald Sings the Irving Berlin Song Book* (Verve MG VS-6005-2, 1958).
13. "Yes, he used to sing the melody. And maybe she was also . . . I was using Yiddish, and so he didn't know the words, but I translated the words for him. Then there was one other, I don't remember, I gave him the words for it, maybe I'll remember it another time" (Gary Zucker Oral History, conducted by Michael Cogswell, January 26, 1996, Louis Armstrong Collection, Queens College-CUNY, accession number 1996.51.1). The transcription of the recording is my own. The catalog information about this recording comes from an e-mail from Ricky Riccardi of the Armstrong Collection staff, March 25, 2014. I thank Riccardi for his generous assistance.
14. On this song and M. M. Warshawsky (1848–1907), see Emanuel Rubin, *Music in Jewish History and Culture* (Sterling Heights, MI: Harmonie Park Press, 2006), 186.
15. According to Zucker: I was using Yiddish, and so he didn't know the words, but I translated the words for him. Then there was one other, I don't remember, I gave him the words for it, maybe I'll remember it another time" (Gary Zucker Oral History). I have adapted the translation of the lyrics from Alex Aroeste, "Oyfn Pripetshik—Yiddish Song," USC Digital Folklore Archives, http://folklore.usc.edu/?p=31584.
16. Without knowing that the song was in fact "Oyfn Pripetshik," Dan Morgenstern conjectured that given the "generic Russian nature of the Berlin tune," perhaps the Karnofsky

lullaby "had become conflated in [Armstrong's] mind with the tune he had so frequently been exposed to much more recently, but that the similarity was for real." But a comparison of the two songs reveals little in the way of musical similarity. E-mail from Dan Morgenstern, March 1, 2007.

17. Riccardi, *What a Wonderful World,* 272.
18. Stein, *Music Is My Life,* 102.

acknowledgments

Written gradually over many years and in many archives, this book could not have taken shape without the unique hothouse atmosphere of the Jazz Study Group at Columbia University, founded nearly two decades ago by Robert G. O'Meally. The Jazz Study Group has held twice- or thrice-yearly seminars on wide-ranging topics such as "Women in Jazz"; "Thelonious Monk and Jazz Biography"; "Jazz and the Avant-Garde"; "The Politics of Swing"; "Jazz and Dance"; "Jazz and Africa"; "Jazz and the Art of Photography"; "Musicians' Collectives"; "The Recording Studio as Jazz Scene"; "Jazz in South Africa"; and "Jazz and Desire." A convivial, lively, and astonishingly fertile arena for discussion, the group has gathered a sundry collective of musicians, writers, visual artists, journalists, and scholars in fields including literature, history, art history, anthropology, and music, to read one another's works-in-progress, to hear concerts and lecture-demonstrations, and to interact with a stellar pantheon of visitors (who have included Amiri Baraka, Albert Murray, Randy Weston, Abbey Lincoln, Nathaniel Mackey, Branford Marsalis, George Avakian, Jimmy Slyde, William Parker, Robert Farris Thompson, Bill Dixon, and Gary Giddins).

I presented early versions of a few sections of this book at Jazz Study Group events, and was aided immensely in other respects by informal interactions and ongoing correspondence with a number of group members, many of whom have become some of my closest colleagues and collaborators. Indeed, given that the Jazz Study Group—and subsequently, the larger Center for Jazz Studies at Columbia—was founded while I was a graduate student, my own participation in the group has shadowed my own trajectory as a scholar, and provided at once a welcoming port, the promise of endless provocation, and a loose-knit ongoing conversation that has been a central through-line in my own life. I am grateful to all the colleagues who have participated in the Jazz Study Group over the years, including Daphne Brooks, Danny Dawson, Kevin

Fellezs, Krin Gabbard, Kevin Gaines, John Gennari, Maxine Gordon, Farah Jasmine Griffin, William J. Harris, Diedre Harris-Kelley, Vijay Iyer, Travis Jackson, Robin Kelley, George Lewis, Bill Lowe, Jacqui Malone, Tim Mangin, Ingrid Monson, Jason Moran, Fred Moten, Dawn Norfleet, Damon Phillips, Richard Powell, David Lionel Smith, John Szwed, Mark Tucker, Sherrie Tucker, Michael Veal, Penny Von Eschen, Chris Washburne, and Salim Washington. I also want to thank the staff of the Center for Jazz Studies—including Nicole Stahlmann, Donia Allen, Dan Beaudoin, Tad Schull, Claire Ittner, and especially the center's indispensable program coordinator, Yulanda McKenzie-Grant—for making the center such a welcoming space for interdisciplinary work in jazz studies.

I have presented material from a number of sections in this book at various institutions and events around the United States and in Europe, including the North Carolina Jazz Festival, the Newport Jazz Festival, the Duke Ellington Society, the University of Chicago, the University of Delaware, Haverford College, Harvard University, Hunter College-CUNY, Johns Hopkins University, New York University, Pennsylvania State University, the University of Pittsburgh, Rutgers University, SUNY-Buffalo, SUNY-Stonybrook, the University of Virginia, and Yale University. I thank the colleagues who invited me to speak on these occasions, including Tayna Agathocleous, Cathy Cohen, Elin Diamond, Peter X. Feng, Henry Louis Gates Jr., Michael Gomez, Jang Wook Huh, Pericles Lewis, Meredith McGill, Michael Moon, Aldon Nielsen, Robert O'Meally, Imani Owens, Mark Tucker, and Carolyn Williams. When participants at various events gave me particularly helpful feedback or suggestions, I have tried to thank them in the endnotes—at the site of their interventions, as it were. More generally I am grateful for comments I have received on various sections of this book from Kimberly Benston, Suzanne Preston Blier, Jeremy Braddock, Martin Harries, Randy Matory, Elaine Scarry, Gus Stadler, and Tina Zwarg.

This is a book that has also "grown up" slowly and sometimes fitfully in the best incubator of all: the classroom. I thank the undergraduate and graduate students at Rutgers, NYU, and Columbia who have taken my classes in music and poetics, serial poetics, black literature and music, and especially the lecture course Jazz and the Literary Imagination that I have been teaching at Columbia for the past nine years. The book is by no means a transcript of the lecture, which increasingly has elements of a multimedia performance to it. If anything, to me it is a reminder that while they can certainly overlap and shape one another in various ways, the book and the lecture are distinct arenas, each providing different sorts of resonance, circulation, feedback, dissent, and dialogue. If the book offers the opportunity to elaborate an argument in well-wrought language and to amplify it with a full range of citation, the lecture provides a space of open-ended experimentation, even improvisation, within the rich back-and-forth of pedagogy, pointing to other avenues of inquiry and investigating other examples (Sidney Bechet, James Baldwin, Julio Cortázar, Emmanuel Dongala, Henry Dumas, Michael Harper, Gayl Jones, Michael Ondaatje, Jackie Kay) that are taken up only glancingly, if at all, in these pages. Nevertheless the coincidence between the subtitle of this book and the title of my lecture class is due to their shared concern with a small but challenging set of questions that they both are driven to answer.

I am grateful for the generous assistance provided by a number of archivists and librarians at various institutions including Michael Cogswell and Ricky Riccardi at the Armstrong Archives at Queens College-CUNY; Annie Kuebler, Reuben Jackson, and Jeff Tate at the Archives Center in the National Museum of American History; Annie Kuebler, Dan Morgenstern, Tad Hershorn, Adriana Cuervo, Vincent Pelote, and Elizabeth Surles at the Institute of Jazz Studies at Rutgers University in Newark; and Larry Appelbaum in the Music Division at the Library of Congress. Materials from the Louis Armstrong collections at the Library of Congress and at Queens College-CUNY are reproduced with the permission of the Louis Armstrong Foundation. Materials from the Mary Lou Williams collection at Rutgers-Newark are reproduced with the permission of the Mary Lou Williams Foundation. I have also repeatedly drawn on the personal archives of friends and colleagues for a number of hard-to-find sources: I especially want to thank David Hajdu, Fred Moten, Robert O'Meally, Ben Young, and John Szwed for sharing resources with me. Fred and Bob, along with a few other friends (Adam Shatz, Damien Bonelli, Ntone Edjabe, Stephen Casmier), have also been consistent listening companions—both at concerts and in each other's living rooms—and our conversations about the meanings of the music have informed the writing of this book at every turn.

Some themes in this book have been explored in different form in *Callaloo, Critical Inquiry, Hambone, Journal of the Society for American Music,* and *Representations,* as well as in the Columbia University Press anthologies *The Jazz Cadence of American Culture* and *Uptown Conversation: The New Jazz Studies.* I thank Ginger Thornton, Katy Karasek, and especially the irreplaceable Charles Rowell at *Callaloo,* Nathaniel Mackey at *Hambone,* Jennifer Crewe and Philip Leventhal at Columbia University Press, Lauren Berlant and Jay Williams of *Critical Inquiry,* and Katherine Bergeron of *Representations* for those opportunities, as well as the blind peer reviewers at the latter two journals.

Lindsay Waters, my editor at Harvard University Press, possesses not only an incisive intelligence, a puckish sense of humor, and a keen editorial eye, but also a bottomless reservoir of patience. I am eternally grateful to him for sticking with me, supporting me, and—in unexpected cell phone calls out of the blue!—hectoring me into pulling this book together, even as other projects keep threatening to distract my attention. I am also thankful to the staff at Harvard UP, including the editorial assistant Joy Deng and the designer Tim Jones, as well as Melody Negron and the copyediting team at Westchester Publishing Services. I was thrilled to be able to collaborate on the cover art with Peter Mendelsund, one of my oldest friends and the most extraordinary polymath I know, who (as he puts it) almost accidentally happened into an acclaimed career as a designer at Knopf.

I was fortunate that the book manuscript was reviewed by an all-star lineup of peer readers: Krin Gabbard, Bernard Gendron, and Fred Moten all provided invaluable feedback at precisely the right moment as I was revising the introduction and rethinking the way the pieces fit together. I thank them for their time and advice. A special word of thanks goes to Amanda Peery at Harvard UP, who not only shepherded the manuscript through the review and approval process but also offered to read the entire manuscript herself and gave me a wealth of feedback from the vantage of a nonspecialist reader, which helped me figure out how to handle some important revisions and late additions toward the end of the writing process.

A couple of those other "projects" that have pulled me away from writing have been my children, Balthazar and Ella: my wee magi and budding Messi; my sweet *vaquita de San Antonio* and resident dreamweaver. *Je ne sais pas trop comment les remercier—ni toi, Nora—pour les routines journalières et chaque jour extraordinaires d'une vie partagée. Donc je ne peux que signaler la singularité de ce que je retrouve chaque matin, chaque soir, avec la langue de la rue de Turenne, la langue des calanques—la langue qui n'est ni la tienne ni la mienne mais le terrain où l'on s'est retrouvé.*

I have dedicated this book to Robert O'Meally, Robert Stepto, and Cheryl Wall, the three scholars in the field of African American literature who, in different ways and at different stages of my life, from my undergraduate studies through my current position at Columbia, have been pivotal for me: as teachers, role models, mentors, colleagues, and friends. If T. S. Eliot dedicated *The Waste Land* to Ezra Pound with an Italian phrase describing him as "the better craftsman" (*il miglior fabbro*), it seems to me that the dedication is not only a tribute to Pound's erudition and skill as a maker of verse himself but also an oblique admission of Pound's pivotal role in editing and shaping Eliot's poem—and in this sense a recognition of the degree to which even individual acts of creation are always, and often crucially, products of a social setting and thus the result of collaboration on any number of levels, whether avowed or not. Teaching and advising nearly a generation of students of my own, I have come to appreciate more and more the value of this too-often-unsung labor, which often spins its aftereffects in ways that can be hard to notice or take years to germinate. I dedicate this book to them, then, not only to recognize the inspiration that their scholarship, teaching, and collegiality has provided for my own work, but also to point out that broader collaborative backdrop that makes possible everything we do as students, teachers, and scholars.

index